球类项目运动规则与裁判法

（中英文对照）

石丽菊　张立伟　编著

U0808472

中国石化出版社

内 容 提 要

球类运动是大众体育中开展得最普遍、也是大家最喜闻乐见的运动项目。本书涵盖足球、篮球、排球、乒乓球、羽毛球、网球等常见球类运动以及台球、壁球、保龄球等休闲球类项目。通过中英文对照的方式、图文并茂地介绍了与上述球类运动相关的竞赛规则、基本技能战术、最新裁判法等内容，旨在打开球类运动的英文知识之窗，力求将更多、更新颖、更国际化的球类运动和裁判员知识介绍给读者。本书具有科学性、知识性、时代性、针对性和可读性，语言通俗易懂。

本书可供体育竞赛工作者（赛事组织者、裁判员、教练员、运动员）、体育院校学生、体育英语爱好者、国际赛事的体育记者以及广大体育爱好者阅读和参考。

图书在版编目(CIP)数据

球类项目运动规则与裁判法 / 石丽菊,张立伟编著.
—北京:中国石化出版社,2012.5(2024.8 重印)
ISBN 978-7-5114-1560-8

Ⅰ.①球… Ⅱ.①石… ②张… Ⅲ.①球类运动-竞赛规则-汉、英②球类运动-裁判法-汉、英 Ⅳ.①G840.4

中国版本图书馆 CIP 数据核字(2012)第 080325 号

中国石化出版社出版发行
地址:北京市东城区安定门外大街 58 号
邮编:100011 电话:(010)57512500
发行部电话:(010)57512575
http://www.sinopec-press.com
E-mail:press@sinopec.com
北京科信印刷有限公司印刷
全国各地新华书店经销
*
787×1092 毫米 16 开本 22 印张 546 千字
2012年5月第1版 2024年8月第6次印刷
定价:48.00 元

前　言

生命在于运动，越来越多的人关注体育，热爱体育和参与体育，体育在现代人心中的地位越来越重要。而球类运动是大众体育中开展得最普遍、也是大家最喜闻乐见的运动项目。本书包含足球、篮球、排球、乒乓球、羽毛球、网球等常见球类运动和台球、壁球、保龄球等休闲球类项目内容，通过中英文对照、图文并茂的方式，对运动概述、最新规则简介、最新裁判法等板块进行论述，打开球类运动的英文知识之窗，力求将更多、更新颖、更现代、更国际化的球类运动和裁判员知识介绍给大家，使大家能看着学、跟着练。本书在传授球类运动锻炼技能的同时，力求使读者感受到球类运动的魅力，进而提高对体育和英语的兴趣。本书具有科学性、知识性、时代性、针对性和可读性，语言通俗易懂。本书的读者对象可以是体育竞赛工作者(赛事组织者、裁判员、教练员、运动员)、体育院校学生(综合性大学体育院系、专业体育院校)、体育英语爱好者、国际赛事的体育记者以及广大体育爱好者等，对象较为广泛。

本书编著者搜集了大量国内外已出版的同类书籍并进行比较，发现如下不同之处：首先，现已出版的同类书籍很少是完全中英文对照的，如国内的一些著作中，大部分都是中文裁判规则，而本书却加大了英文写作的比重，搜集国际上通用的比赛和裁判英文规则及术语，网罗最新英文用语，真正做到中英文对照；其次，大多数同类书籍的改版时间相对滞后，许多球类国际裁判规则在近一两年已经发生了巨大变化，而本书做到了尽量完全更新目前国际上最新球类项目比赛及裁判规则。

因此，经过编者精心剪辑和设计，以完全中英文对照、图文并茂的方式展现了当今世界上各种各样的球类运动项目比赛和裁判规则，希望为广大裁判员、教练员、运动员提供较全面的规则阐述，无论是在国际比赛中还是在训练时都可以顺畅地与外国裁判员、教练员、运动员、赛事组织者进行沟通、交流，甚至申诉、抗议；而对于体育教师或是英语教师则提供了较翔实权威的教学科研教材，在教授一个运动项目之前，能够针对他们也许以往不太了解的一些基本知识和方法进行快速阅读。尤其对于体育英语专业的学生或是国际赛事的双语记者更是提供了较便捷的学习指导；对于广大球类运动爱好者来说，这本书为他们提供了一份精神食粮，一个学习英语的补充读物。大家在轻松阅读之时，不但可以学习到专业英语，还能从中感受到体育运动之美。

本书由辽宁石油化工大学石丽菊(硕士，研究方向英语教学)、张立伟(硕士，研究方向体育教育训练学)老师共同编写。同时，本书的编写获得各方面的鼓励与支持，得到了多名专家的指导，为此我们一并表示衷心的感谢。真诚地希望广大读者对本书提出宝贵意见，以便我们今后对该系列书籍进行修订，使之逐步完善。

目　　录

第一篇 足 球

第一章　足球竞赛规则与裁判法

1　比赛场地

1.1　尺寸

比赛场地必须是长方形，边线的长度必须长于球门线的长度。

长度：最短 90 米(100 码)，最长 120 米(130 码)

宽度：最短 45 米(50 码)，最长 90 米(100 码)

1.2　国际比赛

长度：最短 100 米(110 码)，最长 110 米(120 码)

宽度：最短 64 米(70 码)，最长 75 米(80 码)

1.3　场地标记

比赛场地是用线来标明的，这些线作为场内各个区域的边界线应包含在各个区域之内。

两条较长的边界线叫边线，两条较短的线叫球门线。

所有线的宽度不超过 12 厘米(5 英寸)。

比赛场地被中线划分为两个半场。

在场地中线的中点处做一个中心标记，以距中心标记 9.15 米(10 码)为半径画一个圆圈。

1.4　球门区

球门区在场地的两端，规定如下：

从距每个球门柱内侧 5.5 米(6 码)处，画两条垂直于球门线的线。这些线伸向比赛场地内 5.5 米(6 码)，与一条平行于球门线的线相连接。由这些线和球门线组成的区域范围是球门区。

1.5　罚球区

罚球区在场地的两端，规定如下：

从距每个球门柱内侧 16.5 米(18 码)处，画两条垂直于球门线的线。这些线伸向比赛场地内 16.5 米(18 码)，与一条平行于球门线的线相连接。由这些线和球门线组成的区域范围是罚球区。

在每个罚球区内距球门柱之间等距离的中点 11 米(12 码)处设置一个罚球点。

在罚球区外，以距每个罚球点 9.15 米(10 码)为半径画一段弧。

1.6　旗杆

在场地每个角上各竖一根不低于 1.5 米(5 英尺)的平顶旗杆，上系小旗一面。

在中线的两端、边线以外不少于 1 米(1 码)处，也可以放置旗杆。

1.7　角球弧

在比赛场地内，以距每个角旗杆 1 米(1 码)为半径画一个四分之一圆。

1.8 球门

球门必须放置在每条球门线的中央。

它们由两根距角旗杆等距离的垂直的柱子和连接其顶部的水平的横梁组成。两根柱子之间的距离是 7.32 米(8 码),从横梁的下沿至地面的距离是 2.44 米(8 英尺)(如图 1-1 所示)。

两根球门柱和横梁具有不超过 12 厘米(5 英寸)的相同的宽度与厚度。球门线与球门柱和横梁的宽度是相同的。球门网可以系在球门及球门后面的地上,并要适当地撑起以不影响守门员。球门柱和横梁必须是白色的。

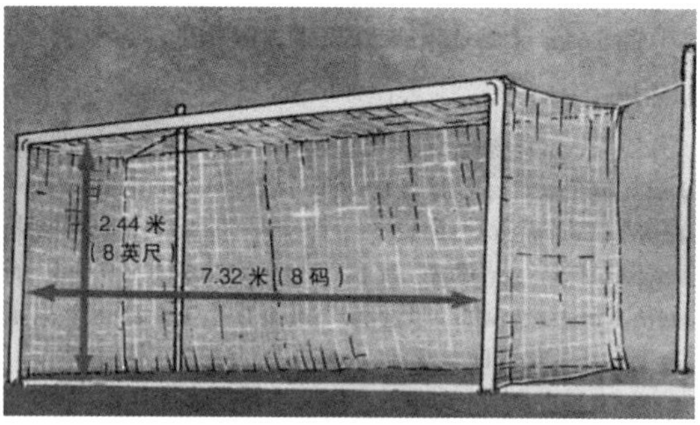

图 1-1 球门示意图

1.9 安全性

球门必须牢固地固定在地上,如果符合这个要求才可使用移动球门。

2 球

2.1 球的要求

- 圆形;
- 用皮革或其他适当的材料制成;
- 圆周不长于 70 厘米(28 英寸)、不短于 68 厘米(27 英寸);
- 重量在比赛开始时不多于 450 克(16 英两)、不小于 410 克(14 英两);
- 压力在海平面上等于 0.6~1.1 个大气压力(600~1100 克/平方厘米、8.5~15.6 磅/平方英寸)。

2.2 坏球的更换

如果球在比赛过程中破裂或损坏:

- 停止比赛;
- 用更换的球在原球破漏时所在地点以坠球方式重新开始比赛。

如果球在开球、球门球、角球、任意球、罚球点球或掷界外球等成死球时破裂或损坏:

- 按照相应的规定重新开始比赛。
- 在比赛中未经裁判员许可不得更换球。

3 队员

3.1 队员人数

一场比赛应有两队参加,每队上场队员不得多于 11 名,其中必须有一名守门员。如果任何一队少于 7 人则比赛不能开始。

3.2　正式比赛

在由国际足联、洲际联合会或国家协会主办的正式比赛中，每场比赛最多可以使用 3 名替补队员。

竞赛规程应说明可以有几名替补队员被提名，从 3 名到最多不超过 7 名。

3.3　其他比赛

在其他比赛中，可依据下列规定使用替补队员：

- 有关参赛队在最多替换人数上达成协议；
- 在比赛前通知裁判员。

如果比赛开始前未通知裁判员或各参赛队未达成任何协议，则可以使用的替补队员人数不得超过 3 名。

3.4　所有的比赛

在所有的比赛中，替补队员名单必须在比赛开始前交给裁判员。未被提名的替补队员不得参加比赛。

3.5　替补程序

替补队员时必须遵守以下规定：

- 替补前应先通知裁判员；
- 替补队员在被替补队员离场、并得到裁判员信号后，方可进入比赛场地；
- 替补队员只能在比赛停止时从中线处进场；
- 当替补队员进入比赛场地，即完成了替补程序；
- 从那时起，替补队员成为场上队员，而被替补队员终止为场上队员；
- 被替补下场的队员不得再次参加本场比赛；
- 所有替补队员无论上场与否，裁判员均有权对其行使职权。

3.6　更换守门员

任何场上队员都可与守门员互换位置，并规定：

- 互换位置前通知裁判员；
- 在比赛停止时互换位置。

3.7　违规/判罚

3.7.1　如替补队员未经裁判员许可擅自进入比赛场地：

- 停止比赛；
- 对该替补队员予以警告并出示黄牌令其离开比赛场地；
- 在比赛停止时球所在地点以坠球方式重新开始比赛。

3.7.2　如果队员与守门员互换位置前未得到裁判员许可：

- 继续比赛；
- 有关队员将在比赛成死球时被警告并被出示黄牌。

3.7.3　对于任何其他违反此规则的：

- 有关队员将被警告并被出示黄牌。

3.8　重新开始比赛

如果裁判员停止比赛执行警告：

- 由对方队员在比赛停止时球所在地点踢间接任意球重新开始比赛。

3.9 队员和替补队员被罚令出场

队员在开球前被罚令出场，只可从被提名的替补队员中选一人替换。

凡被提名的替补队员被罚令出场，无论是在开球前或在比赛开始后，均不得替换。

4 队员装备

4.1 安全性

队员不得使用或佩戴可能危及自己及其他队员的装备或任何物件(包括各种珠宝饰物)。

4.2 基本装备

4.2.1 队员必需的基本装备

- 运动上衣；
- 短裤——如穿紧身内裤，必须与短裤的主色同一颜色；
- 护袜；
- 护腿板；
- 足球鞋。

4.2.2 护腿板

- 必须由护袜全部包住；
- 由适当的材料制成(橡胶、塑料或其他类似材料)；
- 提供适当程度的保护。

4.2.3 守门员

- 每名守门员的服装颜色必须有别于其他队员、裁判员和助理裁判员。

4.3 违规/判罚

4.3.1 对于任何违反规则的：

- 比赛不需要停止；
- 裁判员指出上场队员的装备有问题后，该队员应离开此赛场去调整装备；
- 除非该队员已经调整好装备，否则应在比赛停止成死球时离开比赛场地；
- 离开比赛场地调整装备的队员在未得到裁判员许可前不得重新进场；
- 裁判员在允许队员回场前需检查队员装备；
- 队员只有在比赛成死球时方可重新进入比赛场地。

队员因违反以上规则而离开比赛场地，在未得到裁判员同意即进入(或重新进入)比赛场地时，将被警告并被出示黄牌。

4.3.2 如果裁判员停止比赛执行警告：

- 由对方队员在比赛停止时球所在地点踢间接任意球重新开始比赛。

5 裁判员

5.1 裁判员的权力

每场比赛由一名裁判员控制，他具有全部权力去执行与比赛有关的竞赛规则。

5.2 权限和职责

- 执行竞赛规则；
- 与助理裁判员及当有第四官员时，和他们一起控制比赛；
- 确保任何比赛用球符合规则第二章的要求；

- 记录比赛时间和比赛成绩；
- 因违反规则停止、推迟或终止比赛；
- 因外界干扰停止、推迟或终止比赛；
- 如果他认为队员受伤严重，则停止比赛，并确保将其移出比赛场地(受伤的队员只有在比赛重新开始后才能重返比赛场地)。
- 如果他认为队员只受轻伤，则允许比赛继续进行直到成死球；
- 确保队员因受伤流血时离开比赛场地。该队员经护理后流血停止，在得到裁判员许可后方可重回场地；
- 当一个队被犯规而根据“有利”条款能获利时，则允许比赛继续进行。如果预期的“有利”在那一时刻没有接着发生，则判罚最初的犯规；
- 当队员同时出现一种以上的犯规时，则对较严重的犯规进行处罚；
- 裁判员不必立即向可以被警告和罚令出场的队员进行处罚，但当比赛成死球时必须这样做；
- 向对自己行为不负责任的球队官员进行处罚，并可酌情将其驱逐出比赛场地及周围地区；
- 对于自己未看到的情况，可根据助理裁判员的意见进行判罚；
- 确保未经批准的人员不得进入比赛场地；
- 比赛停止后重新开始比赛；
- 将在赛前、赛中或赛后向队员和球队官员进行的纪律处分，及其他事件的情况用比赛报告提交有关部门。

5.3 裁判员的决定

裁判员根据与比赛相关的事实所做出的决定是最终的决定。

只有在比赛未重新开始前，裁判员可以根据自己的判断或助理裁判员的意见而改变确实不正确的决定。

6 助理裁判员

6.1 职责

每场比赛应委派两名助理裁判员，他的职责(由裁判员决定)应为示意：

- 当球的整体越出比赛场地时；
- 应由哪一队踢角球、球门球或掷界外球；
- 可以判罚处于越位位置的队员时；
- 当要求替换队员时；
- 当发生裁判员视线外的不正当行为或任何其他事件时；
- 无论何时，当犯规发生时助理裁判员比裁判员更接近于犯规地点(特别是这种犯规情况发生在罚球区内)；
- 当踢球点球时，在球被踢之前守门员是否向前移动，以及球踢出后是否进门。

6.2 协助

助理裁判员还应依据竞赛规则协助裁判员控制比赛。在特殊情况下，助理裁判员可以进入场内协助裁判员控制好 9.15 米的距离。

助理裁判员如有过分干预或不合适的表现时，裁判员可解除其职责并将报告提交有关部门。

7　比赛规定的时间

7.1　比赛时间

比赛分为两个半场，每半场45分钟。特殊情况经裁判员和双方同意另定除外。

任何改变比赛时间的协议(如因光线不足每半场减少到40分钟)必须在比赛开始之前制定，并要符合竞赛规程。

7.2　中场休息

队员有中场休息的权利，中场休息不得超过15分钟。竞赛规程必须注明中场休息的时间，只有经裁判员同意方可改变中场休息时间。

7.3　允许补充的时间

在每半场比赛中损失的所有时间应予补足：

- 替换队员(秒)；
- 对队员伤势的估计；
- 将受伤队员移出比赛场地进行治疗；
- 拖延时间；
- 任何其他原因。

根据裁判员的判断补足损失的时间。

7.4　罚球点球

如果执行罚球点球或重新执行罚球点球，每半场结束时间可延长至罚球点球结束。

7.5　决胜期

竞赛规程可以规定再进行两个半场相等时间的比赛。规则第八章的规定也能适用。

7.6　中止的比赛

除竞赛规程另有规定外，中止的比赛应重新进行。

8　比赛开始和重新开始

8.1　预备

通过掷币，猜中的队决定上半场比赛的进攻方向。

另一队开球开始比赛。

猜中的队在下半场开球开始比赛。

下半场比赛两队交换比赛场地。

8.2　开球

开球是比赛开始和重新开始的一种方式：

- 在比赛开始时；
- 在进球得分后；
- 在下半场比赛开始时；
- 在决胜期两个半场开始时。

开球可以直接射门得分。

8.2.1　程序

- 所有队员在本方半场内；

- 开球队的对方队员，应距球至少 9.15 米(10 码)，直到比赛进行；
- 球应放定在中心标记上；
- 裁判员发出信号；
- 当球被踢并向前移动时比赛即为进行；
- 开球队员在球未经其队员触及前不得再次触球。

某队进球得分后，由另一队开球。

8.2.2　违规/判罚

如果开球队员在其他队员触球前再次触球：

- 由对方队在犯规发生地点踢间接任意球。

在开球程序上的其他犯规：

- 重新开球。

8.3　坠球

坠球是在比赛进行中因竞赛规则未提到的原因而需要暂停比赛之后，重新开始比赛的一种方法(如图 1-2 所示)。

8.3.1　程序

裁判员在比赛停止时球所在的地点坠球。

当球触地比赛即为重新开始。

8.3.2　违规/判罚

8.3.2.1　重新坠球：

- 如果球接触地面前被队员触及；
- 如果球在接触地面前未经队员触及而离开比赛场地。

图 1-2　坠球示意图

8.3.2.2　特殊情况：

- 判给守方在其球门区内的任意球，可从球门区内的任何地点踢出。
- 判给攻方在其对方球门区内的间接任意球，从距犯规发生地点最近的、与球门线平行的球门区线上踢出。
- 比赛暂停之后，在距比赛停止时球所在的球门区内的地点最近的、与球门线平行的球门区线上坠球，重新开始比赛。

9　比赛进行及死球

9.1　比赛成死球

下列情况比赛成死球：

- 当球不论从地面或空中全部越过球门线或边线时；
- 当比赛已被裁判员停止时。

9.2　比赛进行

其他所有时间均为比赛进行中，包括(如图 1-3)：

- 球从球门柱、横梁或角旗杆弹回场内；
- 球从比赛场地上的裁判员或助理裁判员身上弹回场内。

图 1-3　球的界定

10　计胜方法

10.1　进球得分

当球的整体从球门柱间及横梁下越过球门线，而此前未违反竞赛规则，即为进球得分（如图 1-4 所示）。

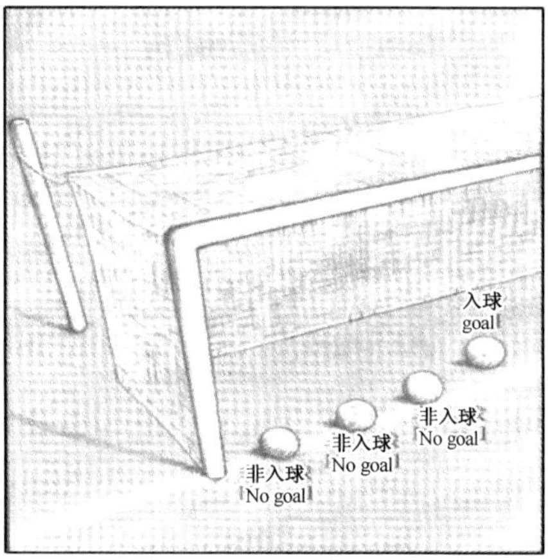

图 1-4　入球得分示意图

10.2　获胜的队

在比赛中进球数较多的队为胜者。如两队进球数相等或均未进球，则比赛为平局。

10.3　竞赛规程

竞赛规程应说明，若比赛结束为平局，是否采用决胜期或国际足球理事会同意的其他步骤以决定比赛的胜者。

11　越位

11.1　越位位置

队员处于越位位置本身并不是犯规。

队员处于越位位置：

- 队员距球和最后第二名对方队员更接近于对方球门线。

队员不处于越位位置：

- 他在本方半场内；
- 他齐平于最后第二名对方队员；
- 他齐平于最后两名对方队员。

11.2　犯规

处于越位位置的队员，在同队队员踢或触及球的一瞬间，裁判员认为其就下列情况而言“卷入”了现实比赛中时才被判为越位犯规：

- 干扰比赛；
- 干扰对方队员；

- 利用越位位置获得利益。

11.3　没有犯规

如果队员直接从下列情况接到球，则没有越位犯规：

- 球门球；
- 掷界外球；
- 角球。

11.4　违规/判罚

对于任何越位犯规，裁判员应判给对方在犯规发生地点踢间接任意球。

12　犯规与不正当行为

下列情况将被判罚犯规或不正当行为：

12.1　直接任意球

12.1.1　裁判员认为，如果队员草率地、鲁莽地或使用过分的力量违反下列六种犯规中的任何一种，将判给对方踢直接任意球：

- 踢或企图踢对方队员；
- 绊摔或企图绊摔对方队员；
- 跳向对方队员；
- 冲撞对方队员；
- 打或企图打对方队员；
- 推对方队员。

12.1.2　如果队员违反下列四种犯规中的任何一种，也判给对方踢直接任意球：

- 为了得到对球的控制而抢截对方队员时，于触球前触及对方队员；
- 拉扯对方队员；
- 向对方队员吐唾沫；
- 故意手球（不包括守门员在本方罚球区内）。

在犯规发生地点踢直接任意球。

12.2　罚球点球

在比赛进行中无论球在什么位置，如果队员在本方罚球区内违反了上述十种犯规中的任何一种，应被判罚球点球。

12.3　间接任意球

12.3.1　如果守门员在本方罚球区内违反下列四种犯规中的任何一种，将判给对方踢间接任意球：

- 用手控制球后在发出球之前持球超过6秒；
- 在发出球之后未经其他队员触及，再次用手触球；
- 用手触及同队队员故意踢给他的球；
- 用手触及同队队员直接掷入的界外球。

12.3.2　裁判员认为，队员在出现下列情况时，也将判给对方踢间接任意球：

- 动作具有危险性；
- 阻挡对方队员；
- 阻挡对方守门员从其手中发球；

• 因规则第十二条以前未提及的任何其他犯规，而停止比赛被警告或罚令出场。

在犯规发生地点踢间接任意球。

12.4　纪律制裁

只允许对场上队员、替补队员或替补下场的队员出示红牌或黄牌。

12.5　可警告的犯规

如果队员违反下列七种犯规中的任何一种，将被警告并被出示黄牌：

• 犯有非体育行为；
• 以语言或行动表示异议；
• 持续违反规则；
• 延误比赛重新开始；
• 当以角球或任意球重新开始比赛时，不退出规定的距离；
• 未得到裁判员许可进入或重新进入比赛场；
• 未得到裁判员许可故意离开比赛场地。

12.6　罚令出场的犯规

如果队员违反下列七种犯规中的任何一种，将被罚令出场并被出示红牌：

• 严重犯规；
• 暴力行为；
• 向对方或其他任何人吐唾沫；
• 用故意手球破坏对方的进球或明显的进球得分机会（不包括守门员在本方罚球区内）；
• 用可判为任意球或罚球点球的犯规，破坏对方向本方球门移动着的明显的进球得分机会；
• 使用无礼的、侮辱的或辱骂性的语言及动作；
• 在同一场比赛中得到第二次警告。

被罚令出场的队员必须立即离开比赛场地附近及技术区域。

13　任意球

13.1　任意球的种类

任意球分为直接任意球和间接任意球两种。

无论是直接任意球还是间接任意球，踢球时必须将球放定。踢球队员在球未经其他队员触及前不得再次触球。

13.1.1　直接任意球

• 如果直接任意球直接踢入对方球门，判为得分。
• 如果直接任意球直接踢入本方球门，判给对方踢角球。

13.1.2　间接任意球

当裁判员判间接任意球时，应单臂上举过头，并保持这种姿势直到球踢出后被其他队员触及或成死球时为止。

只有当球进门前触及到另一名队员才可得分。

• 如果间接任意球直接踢入对方球门，判为球门球；
• 如果间接任意球直接踢入本方球门，判给对方踢角球。

13.2 任意球的位置

13.2.1 在罚球区内的任意球

属于守方的直接或间接任意球：

- 所有对方队员距球至少 9.15 米(10 码)；
- 所有对方队员应站在罚球区外直到比赛进行；
- 当球被直接踢出罚球区比赛即为进行；
- 可以在球门区内任何一点踢任意球。

属于攻方的间接任意球：

- 所有对方队员距球至少 9.15 米(10 码)直到比赛进行，除非他们已站在本方球门柱之间的球门线上；
- 当球被踢并移动时比赛即为进行；
- 在对方球门区内踢间接任意球时，应在距犯规发生地点最近的、与球门线平行的球门区线上执行。

13.2.2 在罚球区外的任意球

- 所有对方队员距球至少 9.15 米(10 码)直到比赛进行；
- 当球被踢并移动时比赛即为进行；
- 在犯规发生地点踢任意球。

13.3 违规/判罚

13.3.1 当踢任意球时，对方队员比规定距离更接近于球：

- 应重踢。

13.3.2 当守方在本方罚球区内踢任意球时，球未被直接踢出罚球区：

- 应重踢。

13.3.3 由除守门员外的队员踢任意球。

如果比赛进行后，踢球队员在其他队员触球前再次触球(用于除外)：

- 由对方在犯规发生地点踢间接任意球。

如果比赛进行后，踢球队员在其他队员触球前故意用手触球：

- 由对方在犯规发生地点踢直接任意球；
- 如果犯规发生地点在踢球队员本方罚球区内，将判罚球点球。

13.3.4 由守门员踢任意球。

如果比赛进行后，守门员在其他队员触球前再次触球(用手除外)：

- 由对方在犯规发生地点踢间接任意球。

如果比赛进行后，守门员在其他队员触球前故意用手触球：

- 如果犯规发生地点在守门员本方罚球区外，由对方在犯规发生地点踢直接任意球；
- 如果犯规发生地点在守门员本方罚球区内，由对方在犯规发生地点踢间接任意球。

14 罚球点球

当比赛进行中，一个队在本方罚球区内由于违反了可判为直接任意球的十种犯规之一而被判罚的任意球，应执行罚球点球。

罚球点球可以直接进球得分。

在每半场比赛或决胜期上下半场结束时，应允许延长时间执行完罚球点球。

14.1 球

- 放定在罚球点上。

14.2 主罚球点球的队员:

- 确认由谁主罚。

14.3 防守方守门员

- 停留在本方球门柱间的球门线上，面对主罚队员，直至球被踢出。

除主罚队员外的队员应处于:

- 比赛场地内;
- 罚球区外;
- 罚球点后;
- 距罚球至少9.15米(10码)。

14.4 裁判员

- 应在队员处于规则规定的位置后发出执行罚球点球的信号;
- 做出罚球点球完成后的决定。

14.5 程序

- 主罚队员向前踢出罚球点球;
- 在其他队员触球前主罚队员不得再次触球;
- 当球被踢并向前移动时比赛即为进行。

在比赛进行当中，以及在上半场或全部比赛结束而延长时间执行或重新执行罚球点球时，如果球在越过球门柱间和横梁下之前遇到下列情况，应判定得分:

- 该球触及任何一个或连续触及两个球门柱、横梁、守门员。

14.6 违规/判罚

14.6.1 如果裁判员发出执行罚球点球信号后，球进入比赛之前发生下列情况:

(1) 主罚队员在踢球点球时违反竞赛规则:

- 裁判员允许踢出该点球;
- 如果球进入球门，应重踢;
- 如果球未进入球门，不应重踢。

(2) 守门员违反竞赛规则:

- 裁判员允许踢出该球点球;
- 如果球进入球门，得分有效;
- 如果球未进入球门，应重踢。

(3) 主罚队员的同队队员进入罚球区，或在罚球点前，或距罚球点少于9.15米(10码):

- 裁判员允许踢出该球点球;
- 如果球进入球门，应重踢;
- 如果球未进入球门，不应重踢;
- 如果该队员触及了从守门员、横梁或门柱弹回的球，裁判员将停止比赛，由防守方踢间接任意球重新开始比赛。

(4) 守门员的同队队员进入罚球区，或在罚球点前，或距罚球点少于9.15米(10码):

- 裁判员允许踢出该球点球;
- 如果球进入球门，得分有效;

- 如果球未进入球门，应重踢。

（5）攻守双方队员都违反竞赛规则：

- 应重踢。

14.6.2 如果球点球踢出之后：

（1）主罚队员在其他队员触球前再次触球（用手除外）：

- 由对方在犯规发生地点踢间接任意球。

（2）主罚队员在其他队员触球前故意用手触球：

- 由对方在犯规发生地点踢直接任意球。

（3）球被外来因素触及而影响了其向前移动：

- 应重踢。

（4）球从守门员、横梁或球门柱弹回比赛场地内，接着被外来因素触及：

- 裁判员停止比赛；
- 在被外来因素触及的地点坠球重新开始比赛。

15 掷界外球

掷界外球是重新开始比赛的一种方法。

掷界外球不能直接进球得分。

15.1 判为掷界外球

- 当球的整体不论从地点或空中越过边线时；
- 从球越出边线外掷界外球；
- 判给最后触球队员的对方。

15.2 程序

在掷出球的一瞬间，掷球者应：

- 面向比赛场地；
- 任何一只脚的部分站在边线上或站在边线外的地上；
- 使用双手；
- 将球从头后经头顶掷出。

掷球队员在其他队员触球前不得再次触球。

球一进入比赛场地，比赛即为进行。

15.3 违规/判罚

15.3.1 由除守门员外的队员掷界外球

如果比赛进行后，掷球队员在其他队员触球前再次触球（用手除外）：

- 由对方在犯规发生地点踢间接任意球。

如果比赛进行后，掷球队员在其他队员触球前故意用手触球：

- 由对方在犯规发生地点踢直接任意球；
- 如果犯规发生地点在掷球队员本方罚球区内，则判罚球点球。

15.3.2 由守门员掷界外球

如果比赛进行后，守门员在其他队员触球前再次触球（用手除外）：

- 由对方在犯规发生地点踢间接任意球。

如果比赛进行后，守门员在其他队员触球前故意用手触球：

- 如果犯规发生地点在守门员本方罚球区外，由对方在犯规发生地点踢直接任意球；
- 如果犯规发生地点在守门员本方罚球区内，由对方在犯规发生地点踢间接任意球。

如果对方队员不正当地阻碍掷球队员或分散其注意力：

- 他将因非体育行为被警告并被出示黄牌。

对于任何其他违反此规则的：

- 由对方掷界外球。

16　球门球

球门球是重新开始比赛的一种方法。

球门球可以直接射入对方球门而得分。

16.1　判为球门球

- 当球的整体不论从地面或空中越过球门线，而最后触球者为攻方队员，且根据规则第十节不是进球得分时。

16.2　程序

- 由防守方从球门区内的任何一点踢球；
- 对方应在罚球区外直至比赛进行；
- 踢球队员在其他队员触球前不得再次触球；
- 当球被直接踢出罚球区，比赛即为进行。

16.3　违规/判罚

如果球未被直接踢出罚球区进入比赛：

- 应重踢。

16.3.1　由除守门员外的队员踢球门球

如果比赛进行后，踢球队员在其他队员触球前再次触球(用手除外)：

- 由对方在犯规发生地点踢间接任意球。

如果比赛进行后，踢球队员在其他队员触球前故意用手触球：

- 由对方在犯规发生地点踢直接任意球；
- 如果犯规发生地点在踢球队员本方罚球区内，则判罚球点球。

16.3.2　由守门员踢球门球

如果比赛进行后，守门员在其他队员触球前再次触球(用手除外)：

- 由对方在犯规发生地点踢间接任意球。

如果比赛进行后，守门员在其他队员触球前故意用手触球：

- 如果犯规发生地点在守门员本方罚球区外，由对方在犯规发生地点踢直接任意球。
- 如果犯规发生地点在守门员本方罚球区内，由对方在犯规发生地点踢间接任意球。

对于任何其他违反此规则的：

- 应重踢。

17　角球

角球是重新开始比赛的一种方法。

角球可以直接射入对方球门而得分。

17.1 判为角球

当球的整体不论从地面或空中越过球门线，而最后触球者为守队员，且根据规则第十节不是进球得分时。

17.1.1 程序

- 将球放在离球出界处最近的角旗杆的角球弧内；
- 不得移动角旗杆；
- 对方应在距球至少9.15米(10码)以外，直至比赛进行；
- 当球被踢并移动比赛即为进行；
- 踢球队员在其他队员触球前不得再次触球。

17.1.2 违规/判罚

17.1.2.1 由除守门员外的队员踢角球

如果比赛进行后，踢球队员在其他队员触球前再次触球(用手除外)：

- 由对方在犯规发生地点踢间接任意球。

如果比赛进行后，踢球队员在其他队员触球前故意用手触球：

- 由对方在犯规发生地点踢直接任意球；
- 如果犯规发生地点在踢球队员本方罚球区内，则判罚球点球。

17.1.2.2 由守门员踢角球

如果比赛进行后，守门员在其他队员触球前就再次触球(用手除外)：

- 由对方在犯规发生地点踢间接任意球。

如果比赛进行后，守门员在其他队员触球前故意用手触球：

- 如果犯规发生地点在守门员本方罚球区外，由对方在犯规发生地点踢直接任意球；
- 如果犯规发生地点在守门员本方罚球区内，由对方在犯规发生地点踢间接任意球。

对于任何其他犯规：

- 应重踢。

17.2 决定比赛胜负的程序

金球制和踢球点球决胜是根据竞赛规程的要求，当比赛打成平局需要决出胜队时采用的办法。

17.2.1 金球制

金球制的程序

- 在规定比赛时间结束后进行的加时赛中，先进球的一方即为胜方。
- 在加时赛中，双方均无进球则互踢球点球决出胜方。

17.2.2 踢球点球决胜

踢球点球决胜的程序

- 裁判员选定用于踢球点球的球门。
- 采用投币方式，猜中的一方先踢。
- 裁判员对踢球点球做记录。
- 按照下列解释，两队应各踢5次。
- 双方轮流踢。
- 如果两队在踢满5次前，一队的进球数已多于另一队踢满5次时可能射中的球数，则不需再踢。

• 如果两队均已踢满5次，双方进球数相同或均未进球，则按同样轮流的顺序踢球点球，直至双方踢球次数相同(无需踢5次球)，而一队较另一队多进一球时为止。

• 在踢球点球过程中，场上守门员受伤不能继续比赛时，可由竞赛规程规定的最大限额内，被提名而尚未使用过的替补队员进行替换。

• 除上一条所述的情况，只有比赛结束时，包括在规定的延长期比赛结束时在场上的队员方可参加踢球点球。

• 每次应由不同的队员踢球点球，直至双方符合资格的队员均踢过一次后，方可踢第二次。

• 在踢球点球的过程中，符合资格的队员可以与守门员互换位置。

• 除踢球点球的队员和两名守门员外，其他所有队员必须在中圈内。

• 踢球点球队员一方的守门员，必须在罚球区以外的球门线与罚球区线交汇处的比赛场地内。

• 除非另有所述，有关足球竞赛规则和国际足球理事会的决议应在踢球点球决胜时实施。

• 比赛结束，踢球点球决胜之前，如果双方人数不等，人数多的一方应减去多出的人数与对方人数一致，并通知裁判员出场队员的名字和号码。球队队长负责此事。

• 在开始踢球点球决胜之前，裁判员应确定留在中圈里的双方队员人数一致后再执行踢球点球。

17.3 技术区域

在规则第三条国际中球理事会议二中解释了技术区域的概念，它是联系比赛与替补席的特殊区域(如图1-5所示)。

技术区域的大小和位置可以根据体育场的情况做适当改变，以下提供的是一般性指导：

• 技术区域的范围是指，从替补席两侧向外1米及向延伸至距边线1米的区域。

• 建议用标记线明确该区域。

图1-5 技术区域

• 技术区域内的人数由竞赛规程决定。

• 根据竞赛规程，在比赛前确认替补席内的具体人员。

• 只允许1人在技术区域内进行战术指挥，指挥后必须返回替补席。

• 教练员和其他官员须在替补席上，除非诸如场上队员受伤，裁判员允许教练员或医生进场察看伤情时。

• 教练员或其他在技术区域内的人员要对自己的行为负责。

17.4 第四官员

- 第四官员由竞赛规程指派。同时，在其他三名比赛裁判员中的任何一名不能担任执法工作时上场替补。
- 比赛开始前，组委会一定要明确在裁判员不能继续担任临场工作的情况下，应由第四官员担任比赛的裁判员，还是由第一助理裁判员担任裁判员，而第四官员担任助理裁判员。
- 根据裁判员的要求，负责赛前、赛中和赛后的赛场管理。
- 负责比赛中的换人。
- 负责比赛换球。如果比赛中需要更换比赛球，则必须征得裁判员的同意并由第四官员提供，方可使用备用球，从而使比赛停顿时间减至最少。
- 负责检查替补队员入场前的装备，如发现上场的替补队员装备不符合竞赛规则的要求，应告知裁判员。
- 第四官员应在整场比赛中协助裁判员进行工作。他必须向裁判员指正被误给警告的队员，或已经被警告了第二次的队员而并未将其罚令出场，以及发生在裁判员和助理裁判员视野以外的暴力行为。不过，裁判员持有对比赛相关事实做出决定的权力。
- 比赛结束后，第四官员应向有关负责机构提交有关裁判员和助理裁判员没有看到的任何不正当行为，或其他事故报告。第四官员必须将所写报告内容通报裁判员和助理裁判员。
- 他有权将技术区域内任何人的不负责任的行为通知裁判员。

18 图解

进攻队员接到同队9号队员的传球，为越位。因为他较球和最后第二名防守队员更接近于对方球门线，并利用越位位置获得了利益。

进攻队员接到同队 8 号队员的传球，不越位。因为当球被踢时，他齐平于最后第二名防守队员。

进攻队员 9 号不越位。因为当同队 7 号队员将球传给他时，他齐平于最后第二名防守队员。

队员直接接得界外掷球，不越位。

进攻队员 9 号越位。因为他对守门员构成了干扰而“卷入”现实比赛中。

进攻队员 9 号越位。因为他处于越位位置，且对守门员构成了干扰。

躺在球门区地上的队员不越位。因为他对守门员不构成干扰而未“卷入”现实比赛中。

当同队 10 号队员射门时，虽然一名进攻队员处于越位位置，但他不应被判罚越位，因为他没有利用越位位置获得利益，而未“卷入”现实比赛中。

6 号队员踢出的球从门柱弹向一名处于越位位置的同队队员，他要被判罚。因为当球被踢时，他处于越位位置，并利用此越位位置获得了利益而“卷入”现实比赛中。

同队队员踢出的球从守门员身上弹向处于越位位置的 8 号队员，他要被判罚。因为当球被踢时，他利用越位位置获得了利益而“卷入”现实比赛中。

球被同队队员踢向守门员，一名进攻队员跑向他去争抢。

守门员将球踢向场地远处，进攻队员 7 号转身到场内的一个位置上。

球被进攻队员的一名同队队员截住后，踢给右边上的另一名同队队员，处于越位位置的进攻队员 9 号不被判罚。因为他没有利用越位位置获得利益而未“卷入”现实比赛中。

进攻方将球踢向球门，当进攻队员跑向该球时，一名防守队员跳起用手触球。这名防守队员因破坏了对方明显的进球得分机会而被罚令出场。

球被向前踢给一名进攻队员，守门员在罚球区外用手触球。守门员因破坏了对方明显的进球得分机会而被罚令出场。

进攻队员 10 号踢出的球接近了球门，当球将要越过球门线进入球门时，一名防守队员用手将球击出横梁。这要判罚球点球，并因破坏对方的进球而将这名防守队员罚令出场。

一名防守队员在本方罚球区内故意用手触球，裁判员判罚球点球。因为没有明显的进球得分机会被破坏，所以他不被罚令出场。如果这个球是意外地碰到防守队员的手，则没有犯规。

守门员在本方罚球区内扑倒了一名进攻队员而被判罚球点球。因为进攻队员的进攻方向正在偏离球门，而没有明显的进球得分机会，所以守门员不被罚令出场。

当进攻队员 10 号在边线附近向前跑动时，被一名防守队员绊倒。10 号队员没有明显的进球得分机会，所以防守队员不被罚令出场。

当一名进攻队员正向球门移动并有明显的进球得分机会时，他被防守队员绊倒。防守队员因破坏了对方明显的进球得分机会而被罚令出场。

当进攻队员运球向球门移动时被防守队员绊倒。因他没有明显的进球得分机会，所以防守队员不被罚令出场。

一名进攻队员被防守队员绊倒在罚球区内，应判罚球点球。因为进攻队员的进攻方向正在偏离球门而没有明显的进球得分机会，所以防守队员不被罚令出场。

当一名进攻队员试图运球晃过对方守门员时，被守门员扑倒。守门员因破坏了对方明显的进球得分机会而被罚令出场。

第二章　足球裁判员法定手势

1　裁判员手势的信号

Indirect Free Kick
间接任意球

Advantage
有利

Direct Free Kick
直接任意球

Caution
警告

Sending off
罚令出场

2 助理裁判员的信号

Substitution
替换

Offside
越位

Throw-in
掷界外球

Offside on the near side of the field
近端越位

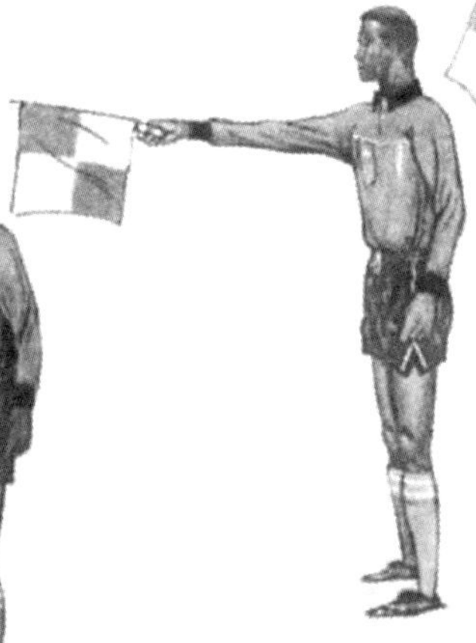

Offside in the centre of the field
中间越位

Offside on the far side of the field
远端越位

第三章 足球英文规则

THE LAWS OF FOOTBALL

LAW 1–The Field of Play

Field surface

Matches may be played on natural or artificial surfaces, according to the rules of the competition.

The color of artificial surfaces must be green.

Where artificial surfaces are used in either competition matches between representative teams of member associations affiliated to FIFA or international club competition matches, the surface must meet the requirements of the FIFA Quality Concept for Football Turf or the International Artificial Turf Standard, unless special dispensation is given by FIFA.

Field markings

The field of play must be rectangular and marked with lines. These lines belong to the areas of which they are boundaries.

The two longer boundary lines are called touch lines. The two shorter lines are called goal lines.

The field of play is divided into two halves by a halfway line, which joins the midpoints of the two touch lines.

The centre mark is indicated at the midpoint of the halfway line. A circle with a radius of 9.15m (10yds) is marked around it.

Marks may be made off the field of play, 9.15m (10yds) from the corner arc and at right angles to the goal lines and the touch lines, to ensure that defending players retreat this distance when a corner kick is being taken.

Dimensions

The length of the touch line must be greater than the length of the goal line.

Length (touch line):	minimum	90m	(100yds)
	Maximum	120m	(130yds)
Width (goal line):	minimum	45m	(50yds)
	Maximum	90m	(100yds)

All lines must be of the same width, which must be not more than 12cm (5ins).

International matches

Length:	minimum	100m	(110yds)
	maximum	110m	(120yds)
Width:	minimum	64m	(70yds)
	maximum	75m	(80yds)

The goal area

Two lines are drawn at right angles to the goal line, 5. 5m (6yds) from the inside of each goalpost. These lines extend into the field of play for a distance of 5. 5m (6yds) and are joined by a line drawn parallel with the goal line. The area bounded by these lines and the goal line is the goal area.

The penalty area

Two lines are drawn at right angles to the goal line, 16. 5m (18yds) from the inside of each goalpost. These lines extend into the field of play for a distance of 16. 5m (18yds) and are joined by a line drawn parallel with the goal line.

The area bounded by these lines and the goal line is the penalty area.

Within each penalty area, a penalty mark is made 11m (12yds) from the midpoint between the goalposts and equidistant to them.

An arc of a circle with a radius of 9. 15m (10yds) from the centre of each penalty mark is drawn outside the penalty area.

Flag posts

A flag post, not less than 1. 5m (5ft) high, with a non-pointed top and a flag must be placed at each corner.

Flag posts may also be placed at each end of the halfway line, not less than 1m (1yd) outside the touch line.

The corner arc

A quarter circle with a radius of 1m (1yd) from each corner flag post is drawn inside the field of play.

Goals

A goal must be placed on the centre of each goal line.

A goal consists of two upright posts equidistant from the corner flag posts and joined at the top by a horizontal crossbar. The goalposts and crossbar must be made of wood, metal or other approved material. They must be square, rectangular, round or elliptical in shape and must not be dangerous to players.

The distance between the posts is 7. 32m (8yds) and the distance from the lower edge of the crossbar to the ground is 2. 44m(8ft).

The position of the goalposts in relation to the goal line must be according to the graphics below.

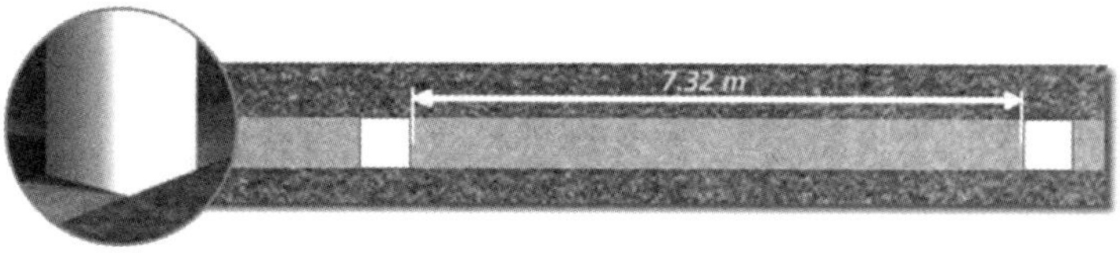

If the shape of the goalposts is square (viewed from above), the sides must be parallel or perpendicular to the goal line. The sides of the crossbar must be parallel or perpendicular to the field plane.

If the shape of the goalposts is elliptical (viewed from above), the longest axis must be perpendicular to the goal line. The longest axis of the crossbar must be parallel to the field plane.

If the shape of the goalposts is rectangular (viewed from above), the longest side must be perpendicular to the goal line. The longest side of the crossbar must be parallel to the field plane.

Both goalposts and the crossbar have the same width and depth, which do not exceed 12cm (5ins). The goal lines must be of the same width as the goalposts and the crossbar. Nets may be attached to the goals and the ground behind the goal, provided that they are properly supported and do not interfere with the goalkeeper.

The goalposts and crossbars must be white.

Safety

Goals must be anchored securely to the ground. Portable goals may only be used if they satisfy this requirement.

LAW 2–THE BALL

Qualities and measurements

The ball is:

- spherical
- made of leather or other suitable material
- of a circumference of not more than 70cm (28ins) and not less than 68cm (27ins)
- not more than 450g (16oz) and not less than 410g (14oz) in weight at the start of the match
- of a pressure equal to 0.6~1.1 atmosphere (600~1100g/cm^2) at sea level (8.5lbs/sq in~15.6lbs/sq in)

Replacement of a defective ball

If the ball bursts or becomes defective during the course of a match:

- the match is stopped
- the match is restarted by dropping the replacement ball at the place where the original ball

became defective, unless play was stopped inside the goal area, in which case the referee drops the replacement ball on the goal area line parallel to the goal line at the point nearest to where the original ball was located when play was stopped.

If the ball bursts or becomes defective during a penalty kick or during kicks from the penalty mark as it moves forward and before it touches any player or the crossbar or goalposts:

- the penalty kick is retaken

If the ball bursts or becomes defective whilst not in play at a kick-off, goal kick, corner kick, free kick, penalty kick or throw-in:

- the match is restarted accordingly

The ball may not be changed during the match without the authority of the referee.

Decisions of the International F.A. Board

Decision 1

In addition to the requirements of Law 2, acceptance of a ball for use in matches played in an official competition organized under the auspices of FIFA or the confederations is conditional upon the ball bearing one of the following:

- *the official "FIFA APPROVED" logo*
- *the official "FIFA INSPECTED" logo*
- *the "INTERNATIONAL MATCHBALL STANDARD" logo*

Such a logo on a ball indicates that it has been tested officially and found to be in compliance with specific technical requirements, different for each logo and additional to the minimum specifications stipulated in Law 2. The list of the additional requirements specific to each of the respective logos must be approved by the International F. A. Board. The institutes conducting the tests are subject to the approval of FIFA.

Member association competitions may also require the use of balls bearing any one of these three logos.

Decision 2

In matches played in an official competition organized under the auspices of FIFA, the confederations or the member associations, no form of commercial advertising on the ball is permitted, except for the emblem of the competition, the competition organizer and the authorized trademark of the manufacturer.

The competition regulations may restrict the size and number of such markings.

LAW 3–THE PLAYERS

Number of Players

A match is played by two teams, each consisting of not more than eleven players, one of whom is the goalkeeper. A match may not start if either team consists of fewer than seven players.

Number of substitutions

Official competitions

Up to a maximum of three substitutes may be used in any match played in an official competition organized under the auspices of FIFA, the confederations or the member associations.

The rules of the competition must state how many substitutes may be nominated, from three up to a maximum of seven.

Other matches

In national "A" teammatches, up to a maximum of six substitutes may be used.

In all other matches, a greater number of substitutes may be used provided that:

- the teams concerned reach agreement on a maximum number
- the referee is informed before the match

If the referee is not informed, or if no agreement is reached before the match, no more than six substitutes are allowed.

Substitution procedure

In all matches, the names of the substitutes must be given to the referee prior to the start of the match. Any substitute whose name is not given to the referee at this time may not take part in the match.

To replace a player with a substitute, the following conditions must be observed:

- the referee must be informed before any proposed substitution is made
- the substitute only enters the field of play after the player being replaced has left and after receiving a signal from the referee
- the substitute only enters the field of play at the halfway line and during a stoppage in the match
- the substitution is completed when a substitute enters the field of play
- from that moment, the substitute becomes a player and the player he has replaced becomes a substituted player
- the substituted player takes no further part in the match
- all substitutes are subject to the authority and jurisdiction of the referee, whether called upon to play or not

Changing the goalkeeper

Any of the other players may change places with the goalkeeper, provided that:

- the referee is informed before the change is made
- the change is made during a stoppagein the match

Infringements and sanctions

If a substitute or substituted player enters the field of play without the referee's permission:

- the referee stops play (although not immediately if the substitute or substituted player does not interfere with play)
- the referee cautions him for unsporting behavior and orders him to leave the field of play
- if the referee has stopped play, it is restarted with an indirect free kick for the opposing team from the position of the ball at the time of the stoppage (see Law 13-Position of free kick)

If a player changes places with the goalkeeper without the referee's permission before the change is made:

- the referee allows play to continue
- the referee cautions the players concerned when the ball is next out of play

In the event of any other infringements of this Law:

- the players concerned are cautioned

• the match is restarted with an indirect free kick, to be taken by a player of the opposing team from the position of the ball at the time of the stoppage (see Law 13–Position of free kick)

Players and substitutes sent off

A player who has been sent off before the kick-off may be replaced only by one of the named substitutes.

A named substitute who has been sent off, either before the kick-off or after play has started, may not be replaced.

LAW 4–THE PLAYERS' EQUIPMENT

Safety

A player must not use equipment or wear anything that is dangerous to himself or another player (including any kind of jewellery).

Basic equipment

The basic compulsory equipment of a player comprises the following separate items:

• a jersey or shirt with sleeves–if undergarments are worn, the color of the sleeve must be the same main color as the sleeve of the jersey or shirt

• shorts–if undershorts or tights are worn, they must be of the same main color as the shorts

• stockings

• shin guards

• footwear

Shin guards

• are covered entirely by the stockings

• are made of rubber, plastic or a similar suitable material

• provide a reasonable degree of protection

Colors

• The two teams must wear colors that distinguish them from each other and also the referee and the assistant referees

• Each goalkeeper must wear colors that distinguish him from the other players, the referee and the assistant referees

Infringements and sanctions

In the event of any infringement of this Law:

• play need not be stopped

• the player at fault is instructed by the referee to leave the field of play to correct his equipment

• the player leaves the field of play when the ball next ceases to be in play, unless he has already corrected his equipment

• any player required to leave the field of play to correct his equipment must not re-enter without the referee's permission

• the referee checks that the player's equipment is correct before allowing him to re-enter the field of play

• the player is only allowed to re-enter the field of play when the ball is out of play

A player who has been required to leave the field of play because of an infringement of this Law and who re-enters the field of play without the referee' s permission must be cautioned.

Restart of play

If play is stopped by the referee to administer a caution:

- the match is restarted by an indirect free kick taken by a player of the opposing team from the place where the ball was located when the referee stopped the match (see Law 13-Position of free kick)

LAW 5-THE REFEREE

The authority of the referee

Each match is controlled by a referee who has full authority to enforce the Laws of the Game in connection with the match to which he has been appointed.

Powers and duties

The Referee:

- enforces the Laws of the Game
- controls the match in cooperation with the assistant referees and, where applicable, with the fourth official
- ensures that any ball used meets the requirements of Law 2
- ensures that the players' equipment meets the requirements of Law 4
- acts as timekeeper and keeps a record of the match
- stops, suspends or abandons the match, at his discretion, for any infringements of the Laws
- stops, suspends or abandons the match because of outside interference of any kind
- stops the match if, in his opinion, a player is seriously injured and ensures that he is removed from the field of play. An injured player may only return to the field of play after the match has restarted
- allows play to continue until the ball is out of play if a player is, in his opinion, only slightly injured
- ensures that any player bleeding from a wound leaves the field of play. The player may only return on receiving a signal from the referee, who must be satisfied that the bleeding has stopped
- allows play to continue when the team against which an offence has been committed will benefit from such an advantage and penalizes the original offence if the anticipated advantage does not ensue at that time
- punishes the more serious offence when a player commits more than one offence at the same time
- takes disciplinary action against players guilty of cautionable and sending-off offences. He is not obliged to take this action immediately but must do so when the ball next goes out of play
- takes action against team officials who fail to conduct themselves in a responsible manner and may, at his discretion, expel them from the field of play and its immediate surrounds
- acts on the advice of the assistant referees regarding incidents that he has not seen

- ensures that no unauthorized persons enter the field of play
- indicates the restart of the match after it has been stopped
- provides the appropriate authorities with a match report, which includes information on any disciplinary action taken against players and/or team officials and any other incidents that occurred before, during or after the match.

Decisions of the referee

The decisions of the referee regarding facts connected with play, including whether or not a goal is scored and the result of the match, are final. The referee may only change a decision on realizing that it is incorrect or, at his discretion, on the advice of an assistant referee or the fourth official, provided that he has not restarted play or terminated the match.

LAW 6-THE ASSISTANT REFEREES

Duties

Two assistant referees may be appointed whose duties, subject to the decision of the referee, are to indicate:

- when the whole of the ball leaves the field of play
- which team is entitled to a corner kick, goal kick or throw-in
- when a player may be penalized for being in an offside position
- when a substitution is requested
- when misconduct or any other incident occurs out of the view of the referee
- when offences have been committed whenever the assistant referees have a better view than the referee (this includes, in certain circumstances, offences committed in the penalty area)
- whether, at penalty kicks, the goalkeeper moves off the goal line before the ball is kicked and if the ball crosses the line.

Assistance

The assistant referees also assist the referee in controlling the match in accordance with the Laws of the Game. In particular, they may enter the field of play to help control the 9.15m (10yds) distance. In the event of undue interference or improper conduct, the referee will relieve an assistant referee of his duties and make a report to the appropriate authorities.

LAW 7-THE DURATION OF THE MATCH

Periods of play

The match lasts two equal periods of 45 minutes, unless otherwise mutually agreed between the referee and the two teams. Any agreement to alter the duration of the periods of play (e.g. to reduce each half to 40 minutes because of insufficient light) must be made before the start of play and must comply with competition rules.

Half-time interval

Players are entitled to an interval at half-time.

The half-time interval must not exceed 15 minutes.

Competition rules must state the duration of the half-time interval.

The duration of the half-time interval may be altered only with the consent of the referee.

Allowance for time lost

Allowance is made in either period for all time lost through:

- substitutions
- assessment of injury to players
- removal of injured players from the field of play for treatment
- wasting time
- any other cause

The allowance for time lost is at the discretion of the referee.

Penalty kick

If a penalty kick has to be taken or retaken, the duration of either half is extended until the penalty kick is completed.

Abandoned match

An abandoned match is replayed unless the competition rules provide otherwise.

LAW 8–THE START AND RESTART OF PLAY

Definition of kick-off

A kick-off is a way of starting or restarting play:

- at the start of the match
- after a goal has been scored
- at the start of the second half of the match
- at the start of each period of extra time, where applicable

A goal may be scored directly from the kick-off.

Procedure

Before a kick-off at the start of the match or extra time

- a coin is tossed and the team that wins the toss decides which goal it will attack in the first half of the match.
- the other team takes the kick-off to start the match.
- the team that wins the toss takes the kick-off to start the second half of the match.
- in the second half of the match, the teams change ends and attack the opposite goals.

Kick-off

- after a team scores a goal, the kick-off is taken by the other team.
- all players must be in their own half of the field of play
- the opponents of the team taking the kick-off are at least 9.15 m (10 yds) from the ball until it is in play
- the ball must be stationary on the centre mark
- the referee gives a signal
- the ball is in play when it is kicked and moves forward
- the kicker must not touch the ball again until it has touched another player

Infringements and sanctions

If the player taking the kick-off touches the ball again before it has touched another player:

- an indirect free kick is awarded to the opposing team to be taken from the position of the ball when the infringement occurred (see Law 13-Position of free kick). In the event of any other infringement of the kick-off procedure:

- the kick-off is retaken

Definition of dropped ball

A dropped ball is a method of restarting play when, while the ball is still in play, the referee is required to stop play temporarily for any reason not mentioned elsewhere in the Laws of the Game.

Procedure

The referee drops the ball at the place where it was located when play was stopped, unless play was stopped inside the goal area, in which case the referee drops the ball on the goal area line parallel to the goal line at the point nearest to where the ball was located when play was stopped.

Play restarts when the ball touches the ground.

Infringements and sanctions

The ball is dropped again:

- if it is touched by a player before it makes contact with the ground
- if the ball leaves the field of play after it makes contact with the ground, without a player touching it

LAW 9-THE BALL IN AND OUT OF PLAY

The ball is out of play when:

- it has wholly crossed the goal line or touch line whether on the ground or in the air
- play has been stopped by the referee

Ball in play

The ball is in play at all other times, including when:

- it rebounds off a goalpost, crossbar or corner flag post and remains in the field of play
- it rebounds off either the referee or an assistant referee when they are on the field of play

LAW 10-THE METHOD OF SCORING

Goal scored

A goal is scored when the whole of the ball passes over the goal line, between the goalposts and under the crossbar, provided that no infringement of the Laws of the Game has been committed previously by the team scoring the goal.

Winning team

The team scoring the greater number of goals during a match is the winner. If both teams score an equal number of goals, or if no goals are scored, the match is drawn.

Competition rules

When competition rules require there to be a winning team after a match or home-and-away tie, the only permitted procedures for determining the winning team are those approved by the International F. A. Board, namely:

- away goals rule

- extra time
- kicks from the penalty mark

LAW 11-OFFSIDE

Offside position

It is not an offence in itself to be in an offside position.

A player is in an offside position if:

- he is nearer to his opponents' goal line than both the ball and the second-last opponent

A player is not in an offside position if:

- he is in his own half of the field of play or
- he is level with the second-last opponent or
- he is level with the last two opponents

Offence

A player in an offside position is only penalized if, at the moment the ball touches or is played by one of his team, he is, in the opinion of the referee, involved in active play by:

- interfering with play or
- interfering with an opponent or
- gaining an advantage by being in that position

No offence

There is no offside offence if a player receives the ball directly from:

- a goal kick
- a throw-in
- a corner kick

Infringements and sanctions

In the event of an offside offence, the referee awards an indirect free kick to the opposing team to be taken from the place where the infringement occurred (see Law 13-Position of free kick).

LAW 12-FOULS AND MISCONDUCT

Fouls and misconduct are penalized as follows:

Direct free kick

A direct free kick is awarded to the opposing team if a player commits any of the following seven offences in a manner considered by the referee to be careless, reckless or using excessive force:

- kicks or attempts to kick an opponent
- trips or attempts to trip an opponent
- jumps at an opponent
- charges an opponent
- strikes or attempts to strike an opponent
- pushes an opponent
- tackles an opponent

A direct free kick is also awarded to the opposing team if a player commits any of the following three offences:

- holds an opponent
- spits at an opponent
- handles the ball deliberately (except for the goalkeeper within his own penalty area)

A direct free kick is taken from the place where the offence occurred (see Law 13-Position of free kick).

Penalty kick

A penalty kick is awarded if any of the above ten offences is committed by a player inside his own penalty area, irrespective of the position of the ball, provided it is in play.

Indirect free kick

An indirect free kick is awarded to the opposing team if a goalkeeper, inside his own penalty area, commits any of the following four offences:

- controls the ball with his hands for more than six seconds before releasing it from his possession
- touches the ball again with his hands after he has released it from his possession and before it has touched another player
- touches the ball with his hands after it has been deliberately kicked to him by a team-mate
- touches the ball with his hands after he has received it directly from a throw-in taken by a team-mate

An indirect free kick is also awarded to the opposing team if, in the opinion of the referee, a player:

- plays in a dangerous manner
- impedes the progress of an opponent
- prevents the goalkeeper from releasing the ball from his hands
- commits any other offence, not previously mentioned in Law 12, for which play is stopped to caution or send off a player

The indirect free kick is taken from the place where the offence occurred (see Law 13-Position of free kick).

Disciplinary sanctions

The yellow card is used to communicate that a player, substitute or substituted player has been cautioned. The red card is used to communicate that a player, substitute or substituted player has been sent off. Only a player, substitute or substituted player may be shown the red or yellow card. The referee has the authority to take disciplinary sanctions from the moment he enters the field of play until he leaves the field of play after the final whistle. A player who commits a cautionable or sending-off offence, either on or off the field of play, whether directed towards an opponent, a team-mate, the referee, an assistant referee or any other person, is disciplined according to the nature of the offence committed.

Cautionable offences

A player is cautioned and shown the yellow card if he commits any of the following seven offences:

- unsporting behavior
- dissent by word or action
- persistent infringement of the Laws of the Game
- delaying the restart of play
- failure to respect the required distance when play is restarted with a corner kick, free kick or throw-in
- entering or re-entering the field of play without the referee's permission
- deliberately leaving the field of play without the referee's permission

A substitute or substituted player is cautioned if he commits any of the following three offences:

- unsporting behavior
- dissent by word or action
- delaying the restart of play

Sending-off offences

A player, substitute or substituted player is sent off if he commits any of the following seven offences:

- serious foul play
- violent conduct
- spitting at an opponent or any other person
- denying the opposing team a goal or an obvious goal scoring opportunity by deliberately handling the ball (this does not apply to a goalkeeper within his own penalty area)
- denying an obvious goal scoring opportunity to an opponent moving towards the player's goal by an offence punishable by a free kick or a penalty kick
- using offensive, insulting or abusive language and/or gestures
- receiving a second caution in the same match

A player, substitute or substituted player who has been sent off must leave the vicinity of the field of play and the technical area.

LAW 13–FREE KICKS

Types of free kick

Free kicks are either direct or indirect.

The direct free kick

Ball enters the goal

- if a direct free kick is kicked directly into the opponents' goal, a goal is awarded
- if a direct free kick is kicked directly into the team's own goal, acorner kick is awarded to the opposing team

The indirect free kick

Signal

The referee indicates an indirect free kick by raising his arm above his head. He maintains his arm in that position until the kick has been taken and the ball has touched another player or goes out of play.

Ball enters the goal

A goal can be scored only if the ball subsequently touches another player before it enters the goal:

- if an indirect free kick is kicked directly into the opponents' goal, a goal kick is awarded
- if an indirect free kick is kicked directly into the team's own goal, a corner kick is awarded to the opposing team

Procedure

For both direct and indirect free kicks, the ball must be stationary when the kick is taken and the kicker must not touch the ball again until it has touched another player.

Position of free kick

Free kick inside the penalty area

Direct or indirect free kick to the defending team:

- all opponents must be at least 9.15m (10yds) from the ball
- all opponents must remain outside the penalty area until the ball is in play
- the ball is in play when it is kicked directly out of the penalty area
- a free kick awarded in the goal area may be taken from any point inside that area

Indirect free kick to the attacking team:

- all opponents must be at least 9.15 m (10yds) from the ball until it is in play, unless they are on their own goal line between the goalposts
- the ball is in play when it is kicked and moves
- an indirect free kick awarded inside the goal area must be taken on the goal area line parallel to the goal line at the point nearest to where the infringement occurred

Free kick outside the penalty area

- all opponents must be at least 9.15m (10yds) from the ball until it is in play
- the ball is in play when it is kicked and moves
- the free kick is taken from the place where the infringement occurred or from the position of the ball when the infringement occurred (according to the infringement)

Infringements and sanctions

If, when a free kick is taken, an opponent is closer to the ball than the required distance:

- the kick is retaken if, when a free kick is taken by the defending team from inside its own penalty area, the ball is not kicked directly out of the penalty area:
- the kick is retaken

Free kick taken by a player other than the goalkeeper

If, after the ball is in play, the kicker touches the ball again (except with his hands) before it has touched another player:

- an indirect free kick is awarded to the opposing team, to be taken from the place where the infringement occurred (see Law 13-Position of free kick)

If, after the ball is in play, the kicker deliberately handles the ball before it has touched another player:

- a direct free kick is awarded to the opposing team, to be taken from the place where the infringement occurred (see Law 13-Position of free kick)

• a penalty kick is awarded if the infringement occurred inside the kicker's penalty area

Free kick taken by the goalkeeper

If, after the ball is in play, the goalkeeper touches the ball again (except with his hands), before it has touched another player:

• an indirect free kick is awarded to the opposing team, to be taken from the place where the infringement occurred (see Law 13–Position of free kick)

If, after the ball is in play, the goalkeeper deliberately handles the ball before it has touched another player:

• a direct free kick is awarded to the opposing team if the infringement occurred outside the goalkeeper's penalty area, to be taken from the place where the infringement occurred (see Law 13–Position of free kick)

• an indirect free kick is awarded to the opposing team if the infringement occurred inside the goalkeeper's penalty area, to be taken from the place where the infringement occurred (see Law 13–Position of free kick)

LAW 14–THE PENALTY KICK

A penalty kick is awarded against a team that commits one of the ten offences for which a direct free kick is awarded, inside its own penalty area and while the ball is in play.

A goal may be scored directly from a penalty kick.

Additional time is allowed for a penalty kick to be taken at the end of each half or at the end of periods of extra time.

Position of the ball and the players

The ball:

• must be placed on the penalty mark the player taking the penalty kick:

• must be properly identified

The defending goalkeeper:

• must remain on his goal line, facing the kicker, between the goalposts until the ball has been kicked

The players other than the kicker must be located:

• inside the field of play

• outside the penalty area

• behind the penalty mark

• at least 9.15m (10yds) from the penalty mark

Procedure

• After the players have taken positions in accordance with this law, the referee signals for the penalty kick to be taken

• The player taking the penalty kick must kick the ball forward

• He must not play the ball again until it has touched another player

• The ball is in play when it is kicked and moves forward

When a penalty kick is taken during the normal course of play, or time has been extended at half-time or full time to allow a penalty kick to be taken or retaken, a goal is awarded if, before passing between the goalposts and under the crossbar:

- the ball touches either or both of the goalposts and/or the crossbar and/or the goalkeeper

The referee decides when a penalty kick has been completed.

Infringements and sanctions

If the referee gives the signal for a penalty kick to be taken and, before the ball is in play, one of the following occurs:

the player taking the penalty kick infringes the Laws of the Game:

- the referee allows the kick to be taken
- if the ball enters the goal, the kick is retaken
- if the ball does not enter the goal, the referee stops play and the match is restarted with an indirect free kick to the defending team from the place where the infringement occurred the goalkeeper infringes the Laws of the Game:
- the referee allows the kick to be taken
- if the ball enters the goal, a goal is awarded
- if the ball does not enter the goal, the kick is retaken

a team-mate of the player taking the kick infringes the Laws of the Game:

- the referee allows the kick to be taken
- if the ball enters the goal, the kick is retaken
- if the ball does not enter the goal, the referee stops play and the match is restarted with an indirect free kick to the defending team from the place where the infringement occurred

a team-mate of the goalkeeper infringes the Laws of the Game:

- the referee allows the kick to be taken
- if the ball enters the goal, a goal is awarded
- if the ball does not enter the goal, the kick is retaken

a player of both the defending team and the attacking team infringe the Laws of the Game:

- the kick is retaken

If, after the penalty kick has been taken:

the kicker touches the ball again (except with his hands) before it has touched another player:

- an indirect free kick is awarded to the opposing team, the kick to be taken from the place where the infringement occurred (see Law 13–Position of Free Kick)

the kicker deliberately handles the ball before it has touched another player:

- a direct free kick is awarded to the opposing team, to be taken from the place where the infringement occurred (see Law 13–Position of free kick) the ball is touched by an outside agent as it moves forward:
- the kick is retaken

the ball rebounds into the field of play from the goalkeeper, the crossbar or the goalposts and is then touched by an outside agent:

- the referee stops play
- play is restarted with a dropped ball at the place where it touched the outside agent, unless it touched the outside agent inside the goal area, in which case the referee drops the ball on the goal area line parallel to the goal line at the point nearest to where the ball was located

when play was stopped

LAW 15–THE THROW-IN

A throw-in is a method of restarting play.

A throw-in is awarded to the opponents of the player who last touched the ball when the whole of the ball crosses the touch line, either on the ground or in the air.

A goal cannot be scored directly from a throw-in.

Procedure

At the moment of delivering the ball, the thrower:

- faces the field of play
- has part of each foot either on the touch line or on the ground outside the touch line
- holds the ball with both hands
- delivers the ball from behind and over his head
- delivers the ball from the point where it left the field of play

All opponents must stand no less than 2 m (2 yds) from the point at which the throw-in is taken.

The ball is in play when it enters the field of play.

After delivering the ball, the thrower must not touch the ball again until it has touched another player.

Infringementsand sanctions

Throw-in taken by a player other than the goalkeeper

If, after the ball is in play, the thrower touches the ball again (except with his hands) before it has touched another player:

- an indirect free kick is awarded to the opposing team, to be taken from the place where the infringement occurred (see Law 13–Position of free kick)

If, after the ball is in play, the thrower deliberately handles the ball before it has touched another player:

- a direct free kick is awarded to the opposing team, to be taken from the place where the infringement occurred (see Law 13–Position of free kick)
- a penalty kick is awarded if the infringement occurred inside the thrower's penalty area

Throw-in taken by the goalkeeper

If, after the ball is in play, the goalkeeper touches the ball again (except with his hands), before it has touched another player:

- an indirect free kick is awarded to the opposing team, to be taken from the place where the infringement occurred (see Law 13–Position of free kick)

If, after the ball is in play, the goalkeeper deliberately handles the ball before it has touched another player:

- a direct free kick is awarded to the opposing team if the infringement occurred outside the goalkeeper's penalty area, to be taken from the place where the infringement occurred (see Law 13–Position of free kick)

● an indirect free kick is awarded to the opposing team if the infringement occurred inside the goalkeeper's penalty area, to be taken from the place where the infringement occurred (see Law 13-Position of free kick)

If an opponent unfairly distracts or impedes the thrower:

● he is cautioned for unsporting behavior

For any other infringement of this Law:

● the throw-in is taken by a player of the opposing team

LAW 16-THE GOAL KICK

A goal kick is a method of restarting play.

A goal kick is awarded when the whole of the ball passes over the goal line, either on the ground or in the air, having last touched a player of the attacking team, and a goal is not scored in accordance with Law 10.

A goal may be scored directly from a goal kick, but only against the opposing team.

Procedure

● The ball is kicked from any point within the goal area by a player of the defending team

● Opponents remain outside the penalty area until the ball is in play

● The kicker must not play the ball again until it has touched another player

● The ball is in play when it is kicked directly out of the penalty area

Infringements and sanctions

If the ball is not kicked directly out of the penalty area from a goal kick:

● the kick is retaken

Goal kick taken by a player other than the goalkeeper

If, after the ball is in play, the kicker touches the ball again (except with his hands) before it has touched another player:

● an indirect free kick is awarded to the opposing team, to be taken from the place where the infringement occurred (see Law 13-Position of free kick)

If, after the ball is in play, the kicker deliberately handles the ball before it has touched another player:

● a direct free kick is awarded to the opposing team, to be taken from the place where the infringement occurred (see Law 13-Position of free kick)

● a penalty kick is awarded if the infringement occurred inside the kicker's penalty area

Goal kick taken by the goalkeeper

If, after the ball is in play, the goalkeeper touches the ball again (except with his hands) before it has touched another player:

● an indirect free kick is awarded to the opposing team, to be taken from the place where the infringement occurred (see Law 13-Position of free kick)

If, after the ball is in play, the goalkeeper deliberately handles the ball before it has touched another player:

● a direct free kick is awarded to the opposing team if the infringement occurred outside the goalkeeper's penalty area, to be taken from the place where the infringement occurred (see Law

13-Position of free kick)

- an indirect free kick is awarded to the opposing team if the infringement occurred inside the goalkeeper's penalty area, to be taken from the place where the infringement occurred (see Law 13-Position of free kick)

In the event of any other infringement of this Law:

- the kick is retaken

LAW 17-THE CORNER KICK

A corner kick is a method of restarting play.

A corner kick is awarded when the whole of the ball passes over the goal line, either on the ground or in the air, having last touched a player of the defending team, and a goal is not scored in accordance with Law 10.

A goal may be scored directly from a corner kick, but only against the opposing team.

Procedure

- The ball must be placed inside the corner arc nearest to the point where the ball crossed the goal line
- The corner flag post must not be moved
- Opponents must remain at least 9.15 m (10 yds) from the corner arc until the ball is in play
- The ball must be kicked by a player of the attacking team
- The ball is in play when it is kicked and moves
- The kicker must not play the ball again until it has touched another player

Infringements and sanctions

Corner kick taken by a player other than the goalkeeper

If, after the ball is in play, the kicker touches the ball again (except with his hands) before it has touched another player:

- an indirect free kick is awarded to the opposing team, to be taken from the place where the infringement occurred (see Law 13-Position of free kick)

If, after the ball is in play, the kicker deliberately handles the ball before it has touched another player:

- a direct free kick is awarded to the opposing team, to be taken from the place where the infringement occurred (see Law 13-Position of free kick)
- a penalty kick is awarded if the infringement occurred inside the kicker's penalty area

Corner kick taken by the goalkeeper

If, after the ball is in play, the goalkeeper touches the ball again (except with his hands) before it has touched another player:

- an indirect free kick is awarded to the opposing team, to be taken from the place where the infringement occurred (see Law 13-Position of free kick)

If, after the ball is in play, the goalkeeper deliberately handles the ball before it has touched another player:

- a direct free kick is awarded to the opposing team if the infringement occurred outside the goalkeeper's penalty area, to be taken from the place where the infringement occurred (see Law 13-Position of free kick)

- an indirect free kick is awarded to the opposing team if the infringement occurred inside the goalkeeper's penalty area, to be taken from the place where the infringement occurred (see Law 13-Position of free kick)

In the event of any other infringement:

- the kick is retaken

第二篇 篮 球

第一章　篮球竞赛规则及裁判法

1　定义

1.1　篮球比赛

篮球比赛由两个队参加，每队出场 5 名队员。每队的目标是在对方球篮得分，并阻止对方队得分。

比赛由裁判员、记录台人员和技术代表(如到场)管理。

1.2　球篮：对方/本方

被某队进攻的球篮是对方的球篮，由某队防守的球篮是本方的球篮。

1.3　比赛的胜者

在比赛时间结束时得分较多的队，将是比赛的胜者。

2　球场

2.1　比赛场地

比赛场地应是一块平坦、且无障碍物的硬质地面(图 2-1)。其尺寸是：长 28 米、宽 15 米，从界线的内沿丈量。

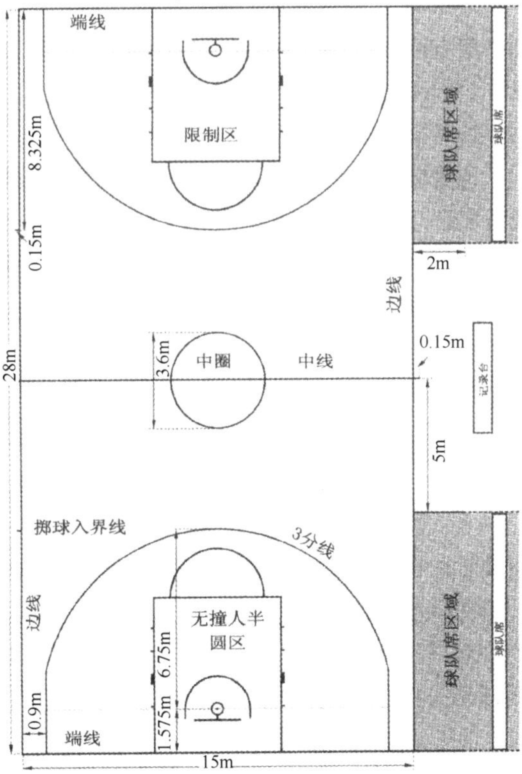

图 2-1　比赛场地的全部尺寸

2.2　后场

某队的后场由该队本方的球篮、篮板的界内部分以及由该队本方球篮后面的端线、两条边线和中线所限定的比赛场地部分组成。

2.3　前场

某队的前场由对方的球篮、篮板的界内部分以及对方球篮后面的端线、两条边线和距对方球篮最近的中线内沿所限定的比赛场地部分组成。

2.4　线

所有的线应用白色画出，宽5厘米并清晰可见。

2.4.1　界线

比赛场地是由两条端线和两条边线组成的界线所限定。这些线不是比赛场地的部分。

任何障碍物包括在球队席就座的人员距比赛场地应至少2米。

2.4.2　中线、中圈和罚球半圆

中线应从两边线的中点画出并平行于两端线。它向每条边线外延伸0.15米。

中圈应画在比赛场地的中央，半径是1.80米（从圆周的外沿丈量）。如果中圈里面着色，它必须与限制区内的颜色相同。

两个罚球半圆应画在比赛场地上，半径是1.80米（从圆周的外沿丈量），它的圆心在两条罚球线的中点上（图2-2）。

2.4.3　罚球线、限制区和抢篮板球分位区

罚球线应画成与每条端线平行。从端线内沿到它的最外沿应是5.80米，其长度是3.60米。它的中点应落在连接两条端线中点的假想线上。

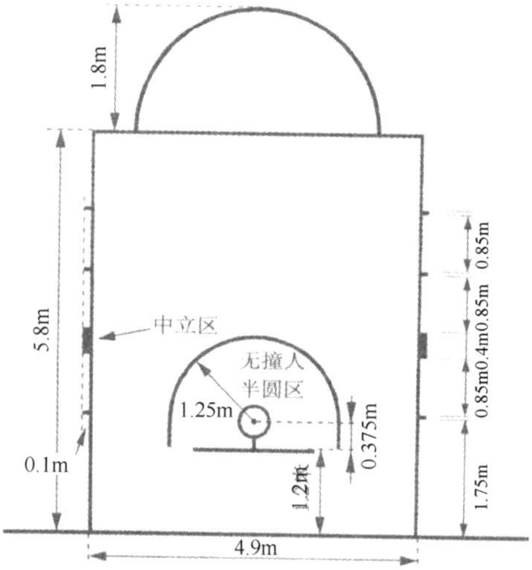

图2-2　限制区

限制区应是画在比赛场地上的一个长方形区域，它由端线、延长的罚球线和起自端线（外沿距离端线的中点2.45米），终于延长的罚球线外沿的线所限定。除了端线外，这些线都是限制区的一部分。限制区内必须着色。

罚球时留给队员们的沿限制区两侧的抢篮板球分位区，应按图2-2画出。

2.4.4　3分投篮区

某队的3分投篮区（图2-2和图2-3）是除对方球篮附近被下述条件限定的区域之外的整个比赛场地的地面区域。这些条件包括：

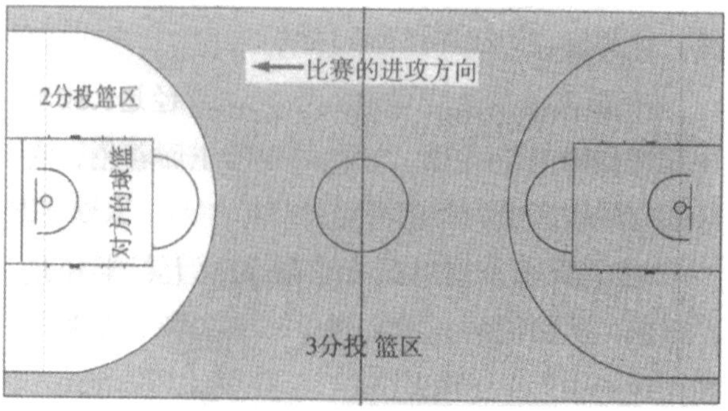

图2-3　2分和3分投篮区

• 两条从端线引出的两条垂直于端线的平行线，其外沿距离边线的内沿 0.90 米。

• 以对方球篮中心正下方场地上的点为原点，画一个半径(圆弧外沿)是 6.75 米的圆弧。此原点距离端线中点的内沿是 1.575 米，且该圆弧与两平行线相交。3 分线不是 3 分投篮区的一部分。

2.4.5 球队席区域

球队席区域应由两条线在场外画出(图 2-1)。

球队席区域内必须有 14 个座位供教练员、助理教练员、替补队员和随队人员使用。任何其他人员应在球队席后面至少 2 米处。

2.4.6 掷球入界线

两条 0.15 米长的掷球入界线应画在记录台对侧、比赛场地外的边线上，其外沿距离最近端线内沿是 8.325 米。

2.4.7 无撞人半圆区

无撞人半圆应在场地上画出，其界线是：

• 以球篮中心正下方的场地上的点为原点，以半径(半圆内沿)为 1.25 米的半圆；

• 与端线垂直的两条平行线，内沿距球篮中心正下方的场地上的点距离是 1.25 米，其长度是 0.375 米并距离端线内沿 1.2 米。

无撞人半圆区由与篮板前沿平行的假想线和上述平行线末端连接封闭构成。

无撞人半圆区的界线不是无撞人半圆区的一部分。

2.5 记录台和替换椅子的位置(图 2-4)

3 器材

需要下列器材：

• 挡件，包括：

——篮板。

——含有抗压篮圈和篮网的球篮。

——篮板支撑构架(包括包扎物)。

• 篮球。

• 比赛计时钟。

• 记录板。

• 24 秒计时钟。

• 记录表。

• 队员犯规标志牌。

• 交替拥有指示器。

• 比赛地板。

• 比赛场地。

• 足够的照明。

篮球器材更详细的描述见“附录：篮球器材”。

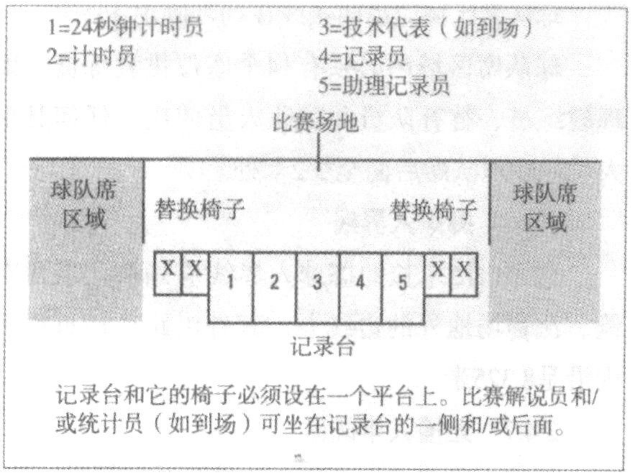

图 2-4 记录台和替换椅子

3.1 篮板和篮板支撑

3.1.1 篮板要用整块适宜的透明材料(最好具有适当韧度的安全玻璃)建造。

3.1.2 篮板的尺寸应是横宽 1.80 米，竖高 1.05 米。

3.1.3 篮板上的所有线条应按下述要求画出：

- 如果篮板是透明的，用白色。
- 在所有其他的情况中用黑色。

3.1.4　篮板的前面须平整且按图 2-5 所示标出：

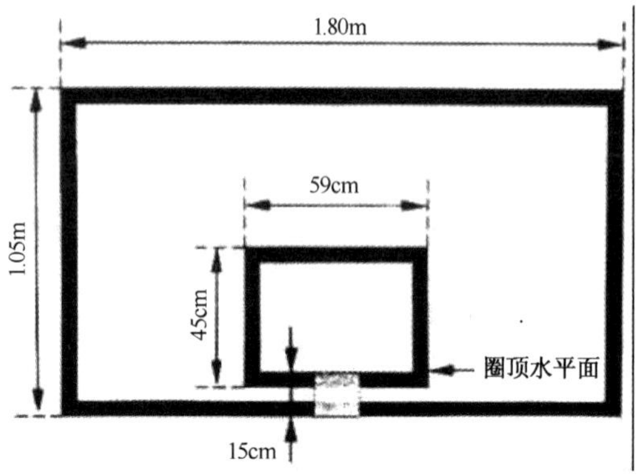

图 2-5　正规的篮板标志

3.1.5　篮板要按下述要求牢固地安置：

- 在球场两端，与地面成直角，平行于端线；
- 篮板前面的中央垂直线延伸至地面，与地面的接触点落在与端线成直角的假想线上，此点距离端线内沿中点 1.2 米。

3.1.6　篮板上的包扎物应按图 2-6 所示：

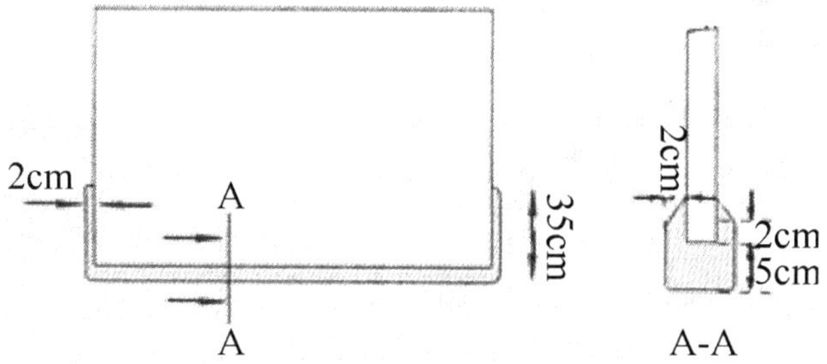

图 2-6　篮板包扎

3.1.7　篮板支撑应按下述要求(图 2-7)：

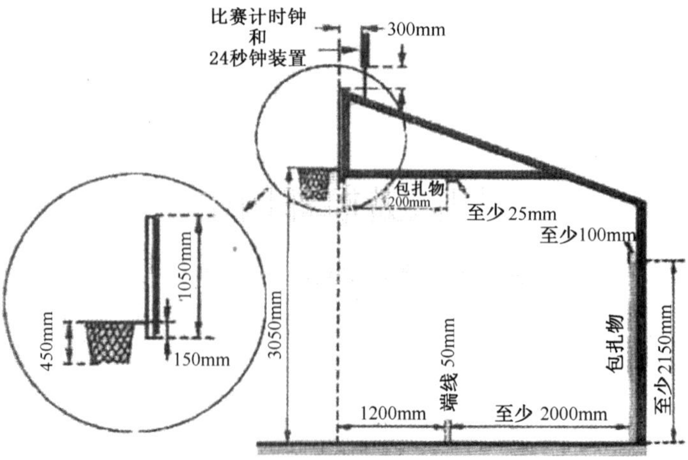

图 2-7　正规的篮板支撑

• 篮板支撑构架(包括包扎物)的前面应距端线外沿至少 2 米。构架与背景相比应颜色鲜明，以便它对队员是清晰可见的。

• 篮板支撑应与地板固定致使它不能移动。

• 篮板后的任何篮板支撑应在其下表面给予包扎，从板面起包扎距离为 1.2 米。包扎物的最小厚度应为 5 厘米，并且密度应和在篮板上包扎物的相同。

• 所有篮板支撑构架必须有一个在面向球场的表面上被完全包扎的基座，其包扎高度从地面起最少 2.15 米。包扎物的最小厚度应为 10 厘米。

3.1.8　包扎物应被制造成可防止肢体部位被夹住。

3.2　球篮

球篮(图 2-8)应由篮圈和篮网组成。

3.2.1　篮圈应按下列要求制造：

• 材料应是实心钢材，内径 45 厘米，漆成橙色。

• 圈材直径最小是 1.6 厘米，最大为 2.0 厘米，在其下沿设有为系篮网的附加系统，以防止手指被夹住。

• 篮网应系在每一篮圈的 12 个(围绕篮圈)等距离的位置上。连接篮网的器件不应有任何尖棱或容得手指进入的空隙。

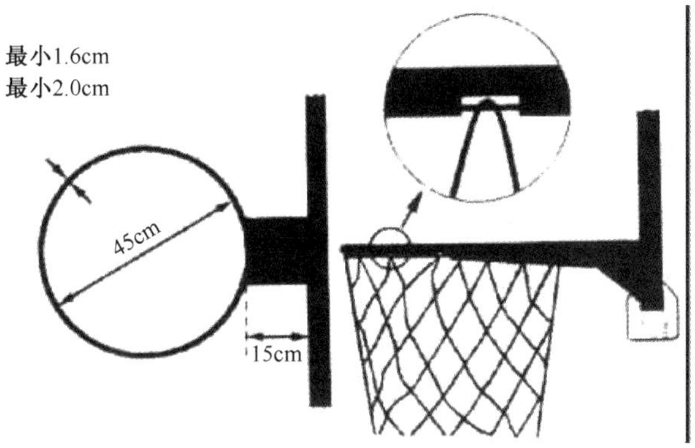

图 2-8　正规的篮圈

• 篮圈应固定在支撑篮板的构架上，这样，任何作用在篮圈上的力不能被传递到篮板上。因此，在篮圈、固结件和篮板(玻璃或其他透明材料)之间不应有直接的接触。然而，空隙要足够的小，以防止手指进入。

• 每一篮圈的顶沿应位于水平，距地面 3.05 米，与篮板的两条竖边等距离。

• 从篮板面到篮圈内沿的最近点是 15 厘米。

3.2.2　可以使用抗压篮圈。

3.2.3　篮网应符合下列要求：

• 篮网应是白色的细绳悬挂在篮圈上，并制作成当球穿过球篮时有短暂的停留。网长不短于 40 厘米，不长于 45 厘米。

• 为系在篮圈上，每一篮网要有 12 个小环。

• 篮网的上半部应是半硬的，以防止：

——篮网反弹上去穿过篮圈可能形成障碍物。

——球被篮网托在或回弹出篮网。

3.3 篮球

3.3.1 球应是圆形的，为认可的单纯的橙色并带有8瓣按惯例成型的镶片和黑色的接缝。

3.3.2 外壳应是皮革、合成皮革、橡胶或合成物质制成。

3.3.3 充气后使球从大约1.8米的高度（从球的底部量起）落到球场的地面上，反弹起来的高度在1.2米至1.4米之间（从球的顶部量起）。

3.3.4 球的接缝的宽度不得超过0.635厘米。

3.3.5 球的圆周不得小于74.9厘米，不得大于78厘米（7号）。重量不得少于567克，不得多于650克。

3.3.6 主队应提供至少两个按照上述规格的并使用过的球。主裁判员是确定球是否合乎标准的唯一鉴定人。如果经鉴定，两球均不适宜作为比赛用球，主裁判员可以选择客队提供的球或从两队做赛前准备活动的用球中选择一个。

3.4 专用器材

主队应提供下列专用器材供裁判员及记录台人员使用：

3.4.1 比赛计时钟和计秒表

3.4.1.1 比赛计时钟为比赛的各节计时和在比赛各节间的休息时使用，并且放置在让与比赛有关的包括观众在内的每一个人都能清楚地看到的地方。

3.4.1.2 应使用一个适宜的可见装置（不是比赛计时钟）或计秒表作为暂停计时。

3.4.1.3 如果主比赛计时钟放置在比赛场地中央的上方，那么在比赛场地两端足够高的地方各设一个同步的副比赛计时钟，要让与比赛有关的包括观众在内的每一个人都能看到。每一个副比赛计时钟应指示剩余的比赛时间。

3.4.2 24秒钟装置

3.4.2.1 24秒钟装置要有一个控制单元去操纵该装置以及符合下述规格的显示单元：

- 数字倒计数型，用秒指示时间。
- 两队都不控制球时，装置上不显示。
- 具有能停止并在重新开始时能继续倒计时的能力。

3.4.2.2 显示单元应按以下方式设置（图2-9）：

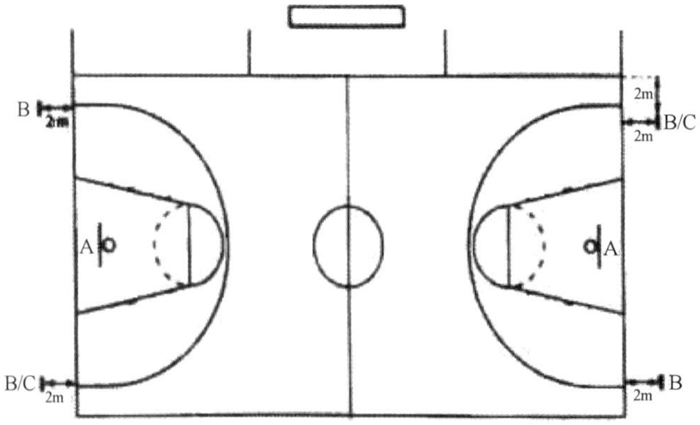

图2-9 24秒钟装置显示单元的设置

- 两个显示单元应分别架设在每块篮板的上方且位于篮板后面，距离在30至50厘

米之间或

- 4 个显示单元应分别设置在球场 4 个角落的地面上，在每条端线的后面 2 米处，或
- 两个显示单元设置在地面上，处于斜对角位置。记录台在左侧的显示单元应设置在到那里最近的角落。两个单元均应在每条端线后 2 米并距边线延长部分 2 米。

3. 4. 2. 3　显示单元应让与比赛有关的包括观众在内的每一个人清楚地看到。

3. 4. 3　信号

至少要有两种独立的声响信号，能发出显然不同的和非常响亮的声响：

- 一种是为计时员和记录员所用。对于计时员，该信号在指示一节或决胜期比赛时间终了时应自动地发出声响。对于记录员和计时员，当已请求了暂停、替换等，暂停开始后过去了 50 秒钟或有可纠正的失误的情况要引起裁判员的注意，在适当时候要手动操纵信号发出声响。
- 一种是为 24 秒钟计时员所用，在指示 24 秒钟周期结束时应自动地发出声响。

两种信号要足够强，在最不利或嘈杂的情况下也容易被听到。

3. 4. 4　记录板

记录板应让与比赛有关的包括观众在内的每一个人清楚地看到。

记录板至少应显示：

- 比赛时间。
- 比分。
- 现时的节数。
- 要登记的暂停次数。

3. 4. 5　记录表

国际篮联所有主要的正式比赛，应使用经国际篮联世界技术委员会批准的正式记录表。

3. 4. 6　队员犯规标志牌

为记录员提供队员犯规标志牌。标志牌应是白色的，上面分别标有数字 1 至 5(从 1 至 4 的数字为黑色，5 为红色)，数字的最小尺寸为：长 20 厘米，宽 10 厘米。

3. 4. 7　全队犯规标志

为记录员提供两个全队犯规标志。全队犯规标志应是红色的，最小尺寸为：宽 20 厘米，长 35 厘米，当放在记录台上时要让与比赛有关的包括观众在内的每一个人清楚地看到。也可以使用电的或电子装置，只要装置的颜色和尺寸与上述指定的相同。

3. 4. 8　全队犯规指示器

应有一个指明犯规到 5 次的适宜装置，指明某队已达到了全队犯规处罚状态。

3. 5　国际篮联的主要正式比赛所需的设施和器材

以下提及的设施和器材是国际篮联下述主要正式比赛所需的：奥林匹克比赛；世界男子、女子，青年男子、女子，青少年男子、女子锦标赛；洲际男子、女子，青年男子、女子锦标赛。这些设施和器材也推荐给所有其他的比赛。

3. 5. 1　所有的观众必须坐在距离比赛场地界线外沿至少 5 米处。

3. 5. 2　比赛场地(图 2-10)应是：

- 木制。
- 用 2 厘米宽的界线标定。

• 用鲜明反差的颜色画出一条至少 2 米宽的外侧界线。

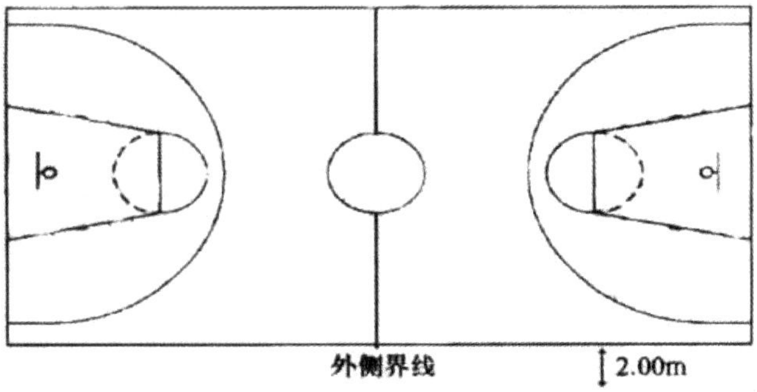

图 2-10　国际篮联的主要正式比赛所用的比赛场地

外侧界线的颜色应与中圈和限制区的颜色相同。

3.5.3　应准备 4 名擦地人员，每半块比赛场地 2 人。

3.5.4　篮板应由适当韧度的安全玻璃制成。

3.5.5　球的表面应由皮革制成。为进行训练和赛前的准备活动，竞赛的组织者要提供至少 12 个制作和规格相同的球。

3.5.6　比赛场地上的照明不得少于 1500 勒克斯。这个标准应在比赛场地上方 1.5 米处测量。该照明应符合电视传播的要求。

3.5.7　比赛场地应配备下述电子器材，从记录台、比赛场地、球队席以及与比赛有关的包括观众在内的每一个人都能清楚地看到。

3.5.7.1　两块大记录板，球场每端各一块（图 2-11）。

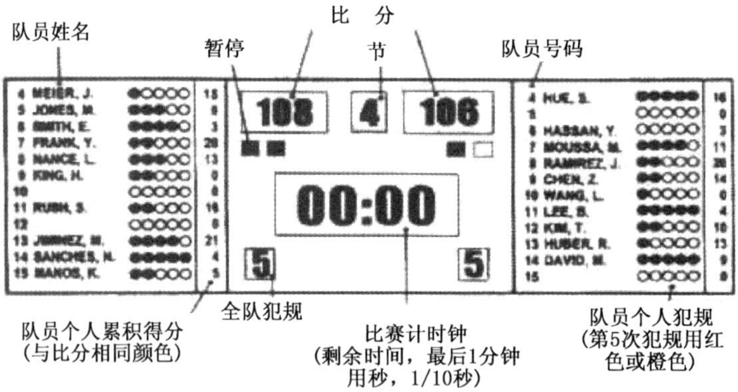

图 2-11　国际篮联的主要正式比赛所用的记录板

• 放置在比赛场地中央上方的记录板（呈立方体）不排斥使用两块记录板的必要性。

• 应给计时员提供一个操纵比赛计时钟的控制台，并应给助理记录员提供一个单独的控制台。

• 记录板应包含一个清晰可见的数字倒计数型的钟，在一节或决胜期的比赛时间结束时能自动地发出非常响亮的信号。

• 记录板上的比赛计时钟和比赛得分显示的高度最低是 30 厘米。

• 所有的计时钟都应同步且始终显示比赛剩余时间的总数。

• 在每一节或决胜期的最后 60 秒钟期间，应用秒和 1/10 秒为单位来指明剩余时间的总数。

- 主裁判员应指定其中一个计时钟为比赛计时钟。
- 记录板还应指明：

—每位队员的号码，有队员的姓更好。

—每队的得分数，有每位队员个人的得分数更好。

—球队中每位队员发生犯规的次数(这不排除需要由记录员指明犯规次数的标志牌)。

—全队犯规次数从 1 到 5(具有停在最大值 5 的功能)。

—节数从 1 到 4 并且用( )表示决胜期。

—暂停次数从 0 到 2。

3.5.7.2 带有一个副比赛计时钟和一个发光的红色电灯的 24 秒钟装置(图 2-12)应安装在每块篮板后面，距离在 30 至 50 厘米之间。

图 2-12 国际篮联主要正式比赛用的比赛计时钟和 24 秒钟装置

- 24 秒钟装置应是自动的数字倒计数型装置，以秒来指明时间，并能自动发出非常响亮的信号来指示 24 秒钟周期的结束。
- 24 秒钟装置应与主要的比赛计时钟连接，以便：

—当主要的比赛计时钟停止时，该装置也应停止。

—当主要的比赛计时钟开始启动时，该装置必须能手动开始启动。

—当该装置发出声响时，主要的比赛计时钟应停止。

- 24 秒钟装置和副比赛计时钟上数字显示的颜色应不同。
- 所有的副比赛计时钟应符合上述的详细说明。
- 每块篮板上方并位于篮板后面的电灯应是：

—当一节或决胜期比赛时间结束的信号响时和主要的比赛计时钟同步发出红色亮光。

—当 24 秒钟周期结束的信号响时和 24 秒钟装置同步发出红色亮光。

4 球队

4.1 定义

4.1.1 当一名球队成员按照竞赛组织部门的规程规定(包括年龄限制)已被批准为某队参赛时，他是合格参赛的球队成员。

4.1.2 当一名球队成员的姓名在比赛开始前已被登记在记录表上，并且他既没有被取消比赛资格又没有发生 5 次犯规，是有资格参赛的球队成员。

4.1.3 在比赛时间内，一名球队成员：

- 当他在比赛场地上，并且有资格参赛时是一名队员。
- 当他未在比赛场地上，但他有资格参赛时是一名替补队员。
- 当他已发生 5 次犯规，并且不再有资格参赛时是一名出局的队员。

4.1.4　在比赛休息期间，所有有资格参赛的球队成员被认为是队员。

4.2　规定

4.2.1　每个队应按下列要求组成：

- 不超过12名有资格参赛的球队成员，包括一名队长。
- 一名教练员，如果球队需要可有一名助理教练员。
- 最多5名有专门职责的随队人员可坐在球队席上，如球队管理、医生、理疗师、统计员、翻译等。

4.2.2　在比赛时间内，每队应有5名队员在场上并可被替换。

4.2.3　一名替补队员成为队员和一名队员成为替补队员：

- 当裁判员招呼替补队员进入比赛场地时。
- 在暂停或比赛休息期间，一名替补队员向记录员请求替换时。

4.3　服装

4.3.1　球队成员的着装应符合下述要求：

- 背心前后的主色相同。
- 所有队员必须把他们的背心塞进他们的比赛短裤内。允许穿着连体的服装。
- 短裤前后的主色相同，但没必要与背心的颜色相同。
- 球队所有队员穿着主色相同的短袜。

4.3.2　每一球队成员应穿前后有号码的背心。其清楚的单色号码与背心的颜色有明显的区别。号码应清晰可见，并且：

- 后背的号码应至少高20厘米。
- 前胸的号码应至少高10厘米。
- 号码应至少宽2厘米。
- 球队应使用4至15的号码。国家联合会为举办竞赛，有权批准最多两位数字的任何其他号码。
- 同队队员不应佩戴相同的号码。
- 任何广告或标志离号码应至少5厘米。

4.3.3　球队必须至少有两套背心，并且：

- 秩序册中队名列前的队(主队/“A”队)应穿浅色背心(最好白色)。
- 秩序册中队名列后的队(客队/“B”队)应穿深色背心。
- 然而，如果两队同意，他们可以互换背心的颜色。

4.4　其他装备

4.4.1　队员使用的所有装备必须合乎比赛要求。任何被设计成增加队员高度的或延伸范围的，或用任何其他方法得到不正当利益的装备是不允许的。

4.4.2　队员不应佩戴可能使其他队员受伤的装备(物品)。

- 下列物品不允许：

—手指、手、手腕、肘或前臂部位的护具、模件或保护套，它们由皮革、塑料、软塑料、金属或任何其他坚硬的物质制造，即使表面有软的包扎。

—能割破或引起擦伤的物品(指甲必须剪短)。

—头饰、头发饰物和珠宝饰物。

- 下列物品是允许的：

—肩、上臂、大腿或小腿部位的保护装备，如果其包裹严实。

—与短裤主色相同的(长于短裤的)紧身内裤。

—与背心主色相同的弹力护肘。

—与短裤主色相同的弹力长筒袜。如用于护大腿，则要高于膝盖；如用于护小腿，则要低于膝盖。

—被适当包扎的膝部保护架。

—伤鼻保护器，即使用硬质材料制成。

—不会对其他队员造成危险的眼镜。

—无色透明的牙套。

—由不会发生擦伤的单色棉布、软塑料或橡胶制成的头带，最宽是5厘米。

—无色透明的手臂、肩膀及腿部的运动贴布。

4.4.3　比赛中，任何商业广告、促销产品或慈善团体的名称、标记、徽标或其他标识，包括上面提到的但不限于这些，都不允许显示在队员的肢体上、头发中或其他部位上。

4.4.4　本条款中没有明确提到的任何其他装备，必须被国际篮联技术委员会批准。

5　队员：受伤

5.1　如果队员受伤，裁判员可以停止比赛。

5.2　如果球是活球时发生了受伤情况，裁判员应等到控制球队投篮、失去控制球、持球停止进攻或球成死球时才能鸣哨。如果，当有必要去保护受伤队员时，裁判员可立即停止比赛。

5.3　如果受伤队员不能立即(大约15秒钟)继续比赛，或如果他接受治疗，他必须被替换，除非该队场上队员被减到少于5名。

5.4　教练员、助理教练员、替补队员、出局的队员和随队人员经裁判员允许可进入比赛场地，在受伤队员被替换前照料他。

5.5　如果医生判断受伤队员需要即时地治疗，医生不经裁判员允许可进入比赛场地。

5.6　比赛期间，任一正在流血或有伤口的队员必须被替换。该队员只有在流血已经停止并且受伤部位或伤口已被全面安全地包扎后才可返回比赛场地。如果在记录员发出替换信号之前，任一队获得了暂停，在此期间，该受伤队员或任一名正在流血或有伤口的队员恢复了，该队员可以继续比赛。

5.7　已经被教练员指定为比赛开始时上场的队员如果受伤了，他可以被替换。在这种情况下，如果对方也希望替换，他们有权替换相同数量的队员。

6　队长：职责和权力

6.1　队长(CAP)是一名由教练员指定的在比赛场地上代表他的球队的队员。在比赛期间，他可与裁判员联系以获得信息，做此举要有礼貌。但是，只能在球成死球和比赛计时钟停止时。

6.2　如果球队抗议比赛的结果并在记录表上标有“球队抗议队长签名”栏内签名，队长应在比赛结束时立即通知主裁判员。

7 教练员：职责和权力

7.1 至少在预定的比赛开始前 20 分钟，每位教练员或他的代表应将该场比赛中合格参赛的球队成员的姓名和相应的号码以及球队的队长、教练员和助理教练员的名单交给记录员。所有在记录表上填入姓名的球队成员有权参加比赛，即使他们在比赛开始后才到达。

7.2 至少在预定的比赛开始前 10 分钟，每位教练员应以在记录表上签字来确认已填入的他们球队成员的姓名、相应号码和教练员们的姓名。同时，他们应指明比赛开始上场的 5 名队员。“A”队教练员应首先提供这个资料。

7.3 只允许教练员、助理教练员、球队成员和随队人员坐在球队席和停留在他们的球队席区域内。

7.4 教练员或助理教练员可在比赛期间去记录台以获得统计资料，而且只能在球成死球和比赛计时钟停止时。

7.5 只允许教练员在比赛期间保持站立。在比赛期间，他可与队员们讲话，只要他停留在他们的球队席区域内。

7.6 如果有助理教练员，他的姓名必须在比赛开始前填入记录表内(不需要他签字)。如果教练员因任何原因不能继续工作，他应承担教练员的所有职责和权力。

7.7 当队长离开比赛场地时，教练员应通知裁判员担任场上队长的队员号码。

7.8 如果没有教练员，或如果教练员不能继续工作，并且记录表内没有填入助理教练员(或后者不能继续工作)，队长应担任教练员。如果队长必须离开比赛场地，他可以继续担任教练员。如果他在取消比赛资格的犯规后必须离开，或因为受伤不能担任教练员，替换他的队员替代他当教练员。

7.9 在规则没有限定罚球队员的所有情况中，教练员应指定本队的罚球队员。

8 比赛时间、比分相等和决胜期

8.1 比赛应由 4 节组成，每节 10 分钟。

8.2 在预定的比赛开始之前，应有 20 分钟的比赛休息期间。

8.3 在第一节和第二节(上半时)之间，第三节和第四节(下半时)之间以及每一决胜期之前应有 2 分钟的比赛休息期间。

8.4 两个半小时之间的比赛休息期间应是 15 分钟。

8.5 一次比赛休息期间开始于：

- 预定的比赛开始之前 20 分钟；
- 结束一节的比赛计时钟信号响时。

8.6 一次比赛休息期间结束于：

- 第一节开始，在跳球中，当球离开主裁判员的手时。
- 所有其他节开始，当掷球入界队员可处理球时。

8.7 如果第四节的比赛时间结束时比分相等，比赛有必要再继续一个或几个 5 分钟的决胜期来打破平局。

8.8 如果结束比赛时间的比赛计时钟信号响时，或恰好之前发生了犯规，在比赛时间结束之后应执行最后的罚球。

8.9　如果作为罚球的结果需要一个决胜期，那么，在比赛时间结束后发生的所有犯规，应被视为在比赛休息期间发生的，在决胜期开始之前应执行罚球。

9　比赛或节的开始和结束

9.1　在跳球中，当球离开主裁判员的手时第 1 节开始。

9.2　所有其他节开始时，当掷球入界队员可处理球时，该节开始。

9.3　如果某一队在比赛场地上准备比赛的队员不足 5 名，比赛不能开始。

9.4　对所有的比赛，在秩序册中队名列前的队(主队)应拥有记录台(面对比赛场地)左侧的球队席和本方球篮。

然而，如果两队同意，他们可互换球队席和/或球篮。

9.5　在第 1 节和第 3 节前，球队有权在对方的球篮所在的半场做赛前准备活动。

9.6　球队下半时应交换球篮。

9.7　在所有的决胜期中，球队应继续进攻与第四节比赛方向相同的球篮。

当结束比赛时间的比赛计时钟信号响时，一节、决胜期或比赛应结束。

10　球的状态

10.1　球可以是活球或死球。

10.2　球成活球，当：

- 跳球中，球离开裁判员抛球的手时。
- 罚球中，罚球队员可处理球时。
- 掷球入界中，掷球入界队员可处理球时。

球成活球。

10.3　球成死球，当：

- 任何投篮或罚球中篮时。
- 活球中，裁判员鸣哨时。
- 在一次罚球中球明显不会进入球篮，且该次罚球后接着有：

—另一(多次)罚球时。

—进一步的罚则(罚球和/或球权)时。

- 比赛计时钟信号响以结束每节时。
- 某队控制球 24 秒计时钟信号响时。
- 投篮中飞行的球在下述情况后被任一队的队员触及时：

—裁判员鸣哨。

—比赛计时钟信号响以结束每节。

—24 秒计时钟信号响。

球成死球。

10.4　不成死球情况，当：

- 投篮的球在飞行中。

—裁判员鸣哨时。

—比赛计时钟信号响以结束每节时。

—24 秒计时钟信号响时。

● 罚球的球在飞行中，裁判员除罚球队员之外的任何规则违犯而鸣哨时。

● 对方队员在做投篮动作并控制着球时，一名队员对任何对方队员犯规，并且他以连续动作完成犯规发生前已开始的投篮。

球不成死球，如中篮计得分。

如果：

—在裁判员鸣哨后做了一个全新的投篮动作。

—名队员在做连续的投篮动作中，结束一节的比赛计时钟信号响起或 24 秒计时钟信号响起。

此规定不适用，并且如中篮不计得分。

11 队员和裁判员的位置

11.1 一名队员的位置由他正接触着的地面所确定。

当队员跳起在空中时，他保持着他最后接触地面时所拥有的相同位置。这包括界线、中线、3 分线、罚球线、标定限制区的各线和标定无撞人半圆区的各线。

11.2 一名裁判员的位置的确定与一名队员的位置的确定相同。当球触及裁判员时，如同触及裁判员所位于的地面一样。

12 跳球和交替拥有

12.1 定义

12.1.1 在第 1 节开始时，一名裁判员在中圈、在任何两名互为对方的队员之间将球抛起，一次跳球发生。

12.1.2 当双方球队各有一名或多名队员有一手或两手紧握在球上，以至不采用粗野动作任一队员就不能获得控制球时，一次争球发生。

12.2 跳球程序

12.2.1 每一跳球队员的双脚应站立在靠近该队本方球篮的中圈半圆内，一脚靠近中线。

12.2.2 如果一名对方队员要求占据其中一个位置，同队队员不得围绕圆圈占据相邻的位置。

12.2.3 然后，裁判员应在两名互为对方的队员之间将球向上（垂直地）抛起，其高度超过任一队员跳起能达到的高度。

12.2.4 在球到达它的最高点后，球必须被至少一名或两名跳球队员用手拍击。

12.2.5 在球被合法地拍击前，任一跳球队员都不应离开他的位置。

12.2.6 在球触及非跳球队员或地面前，任一跳球队员都不得抓住球或拍击球超过两次。

12.2.7 如果球未被至少一名跳球队员拍击，则应重新跳球。

12.2.8 在球被拍击前，非跳球队员的身体部分不得在圆圈上或圆圈（圆柱体）上方。

违反第 12.2.1、12.2.4、12.2.5、12.2.6 和 12.2.8 是违例。

12.3 跳球情况

当：

● 宣判了一次争球时。

• 球出界，但是裁判员无法判定谁是最后触球的队员或意见不一致时。

• 在最后一次或仅有一次不成功的罚球中，双方队员发生违例时。

• 一个活球夹在篮圈和篮板之间时(罚球之间除外)。

• 任一队既没有控制球又没有球权球成死球时。

• 在抵消了双方球队的相等罚则后，没有留下其他要执行的犯规罚则以及在第一次犯规或违例之前任一队既没有控制球也没有球权时。

• 除第 1 节外，所有节将开始时。

一次跳球情况发生。

12.4 交替拥有的定义

12.4.1 交替拥有是以掷球入界而不是以跳球来使球成活球的一种方法。

12.4.2 交替拥有掷球入界：

• 开始于：

掷球入界队员可处理球时。

• 结束于：

—球触及场上队员或被场上队员合法触及时。

—掷球入界发生违例时。

—掷球入界中活球在篮圈和篮板之间时。

12.5 交替拥有的程序

12.5.1 在所有跳球情况中，双方球队将交替拥有在最靠近发生跳球情况的地点掷球入界权。

12.5.2 在跳球后未在场上获得控制活球的队应拥有第一次交替拥有球权。

12.5.3 在任一节结束时，对下一次交替拥有有权的队应在记录台对侧的中线延长线以掷球入界开始下一节，除非有进一步的罚球和球权罚则要执行。

12.5.4 应由指向对方球篮的交替拥有箭头来指明对交替拥有掷球入界有权的队。当交替拥有掷球入界结束时，交替拥有箭头的方向立即反转。

12.5.5 某队在交替拥有掷球入界中违例，使该队失掉交替拥有掷球入界。交替拥有箭头应立即反转，指明违例队的对方在下一次跳球情况中对交替拥有掷球入界有权。于是将球判给违例队的对方在最初的掷球入界地点掷球入界继续比赛。

12.5.6 在除第 1 节之外的其他每节开始前，或交替拥有掷球入界中，任一球队犯规不使掷球入界队失掉该交替拥有掷球入界。

13 如何打球

13.1 定义

在比赛中，球只能用手来打，并且球可向任何方向传、投、拍、滚或运，但受本规则的限制。

13.2 规定

队员不能带球跑，故意踢或用腿的任何部分阻挡球或用拳击球。

然而，球意外地接触到腿的任何部分，或腿的任何部分意外地触及球，不是违例。

违反第 13.2 是违例。

14　控制球

14.1　定义

14.1.1　当某队一名队员在控制活球中正拿着或运着一个活球，或可处理一个活球时，球队控制球开始。

14.1.2　当：

- 某队一名队员控制一个活球时
- 球在同队队员之间传递时

是球队继续控制球。

14.1.3　当：

- 一名对方队员获得控制球时
- 球成死球时
- 在投篮或者罚球中，球已经离开队员的手时

是球队控制球结束。

15　队员正在做投篮动作

15.1　定义

15.1.1　投(投篮或罚篮)：队员手中持球，然后朝对方球篮将球掷入空中。

拍：用手直接把球打向对方球篮。

扣：用一手或双手迫使球向下进入对方球篮。

拍和扣也被认为是投篮。

15.1.2　投篮动作：

● 开始于：队员通常在球离手前开始做投篮连续动作，根据裁判员的判断，他已经向对方的球篮投、拍或扣球，开始得分尝试时。

● 结束于：球已离开队员的手时，如果是跳起在空中的投篮队员，他还须双脚落回地面。虽然投篮队员被认为是在做得分尝试，但他的手臂可能被对方队员抓住，以此来阻碍他得分。在这种情况下球是否离开队员的手不是关键因素。

在跑动的合法步数和投篮动作之间没有联系。

15.1.3　投篮动作中的连续运动：

- 开始于：球已在队员手中停留，并开始投篮动作(通常是向上)时。
- 在投篮尝试中须包括队员的手臂和/或身体运动。
- 结束于：球已离开队员的手时，或者，做了一个全新的投篮动作时。

16　球中篮和它的得分值

16.1　定义

16.1.1　当活球从上方进入球篮并停留在球篮内或穿过球篮时，是球中篮。

16.1.2　当有极少部分的球体在篮圈中并在篮圈水平面以下时，就认为球在球篮中。

16.2　规定

16.2.1　球已进入对方的球篮，对投篮的队按如下方式计得分：

- 一次罚球中篮计 1 分。

- 从 2 分投篮区域中篮计 2 分。
- 从 3 分投篮区域中篮计 3 分。
- 在最后一次或者仅有一次的罚球中，球触及篮圈后，在球进入球篮之前被一名进攻队员或者防守队员合法地触及，中篮计分。

16.2.2 如果队员意外地将球投入本方球篮，中篮计 2 分，登记为对方队的场上队长名下。

16.2.3 如果队员故意地将球投入本方球篮，这是违例，中篮不计得分。

16.2.4 如果队员使球整体从下方穿过球篮，这是违例。

16.2.5 为了使队员在掷球入界获得球权时，或者最后 1 次，或者仅有 1 次罚球后抢篮板球时可以尝试投篮，比赛计时钟必须显示 0:00.3(3/10 秒)或者更多。如果计时钟显示 0:00.2 或者 0:00.1，唯一的投篮方式就是拍球或者直接扣篮得分。

17 掷球入界

17.1 定义

由界外掷球入界队员将球传入比赛场地内时，掷球入界发生。

17.2 程序

17.2.1 裁判员必须将球递交给执行掷球入界的队员或置于他可处理。只要：

- 裁判员距执行掷球入界的队员不超过 4 米。
- 执行掷球入界的队员是在裁判员指定的正确地点。

他也可将球抛或反弹给执行掷球入界的队员。

17.2.2 队员应在最靠近违犯或比赛被裁判员停止的地点执行掷球入界，正好在篮板后面的地点除外。

17.2.3 只有在下列的情况中，在记录台对侧的中线延长线执行掷球入界：

- 在非第 1 节的所有节的开始。
- 由技术犯规、违反体育道德的犯规或取消比赛资格的犯规引起的罚球之后。

掷球入界的队员应在记录台对侧，双脚分别跨立在中线延长线的两边，并有权将球传给比赛场地上任何地点的同队队员。

17.2.4 在第四节的最后 2 分钟和每一决胜期的最后 2 分钟期间，在后场拥有球权的队暂停之后，随后的掷球入界应在记录台对侧，该队前场的掷球入界线处执行。

17.2.5 控制活球队的队员或拥有球权队的队员发生侵人犯规后，随后的掷球入界应在最靠近违犯的地点执行。

17.2.6 每当球进入球篮，但该投篮或罚球无效，则随后的掷球入界应在罚球线延长线执行。

17.2.7 投篮成功或最后一次或仅有一次的罚球成功后：

非得分队的任一队员应在该队端线后的任一地点掷球入界。这也适用于成功的投篮或成功的最后一次或仅有一次的罚球后的一次暂停或任一比赛中断之后，在裁判员将球递交给执行掷球入界的队员或将球置于他可处理后。

执行掷球入界的队员可横向移动或后移，并且球可在端线后的同队队员之间传递，但是，当界外第一位队员可处理球时，5 秒钟计算开始。

17.3　规定

17.3.1　执行掷球入界的队员不应：

- 球离手超过 5 秒钟。
- 球在手中时步入比赛场地内。
- 掷球入界的球离手后，使球触及界外。
- 在球触及另一队员前，在场上触及球。
- 直接使球进入球篮。

在球离手前，从界线外指定的掷球入界地点(投篮成功或最后一次罚球成功后，从该队的端线后掷球入界除外)在一个或两个方向上横向移动总距离超过 1 米。然而，只要情况许可，他从界线后退多远都可以。

17.3.2　在掷球入界中其他队员不应：

- 在球被掷过界线前，将身体的任何部位越过界线。
- 当掷球入界地点的界线外任何障碍物和界线之间少于 2 米时，靠近执行掷球入界队员在 1 米以内。

违犯第 17.3 款是违例。

17.4　罚则

将球判给对方队员在原掷球入界的地点掷球入界。

18　暂停

18.1　定义

教练员或助理教练员请求中断比赛是暂停。

18.2　规定

18.2.1　每次暂停应持续 1 分钟。

18.2.2　在暂停机会期间可以准予暂停。

18.2.3　当：

- (对于双方队)球成死球，比赛计时钟停止以及当裁判员已结束了与记录台的联系时。
- (对于双方队)在最后一次或仅有一次的罚球成功后球成死球时。
- (对于非得分队)投篮得分时。

一次暂停机会开始。

18.2.4　当队员在掷球入界或第 1 次或仅有一次的处罚可处理球时，一次暂停机会结束。

18.2.5　在上半时的任何时间每队可准予 2 次暂停；在下半时的任何时间可准予 3 次暂停，以及每一决胜期的任何时间可准予 1 次暂停。

18.2.6　未用过的暂停不得遗留给下班时或决胜期。

18.2.7　除了对方队员投篮得分并且没有宣判违犯后准予的暂停外，应给首先提出暂停请求的教练员的队登记暂停。

18.2.8　在第四节的最后 2 分钟或每一决胜期的最后 2 分钟内，在一次成功的投篮后比赛计时钟停止时，不允许得分队暂停，除非裁判员已停止了比赛。

18.3　程序

18.3.1　只有教练员或助理教练员有权请求暂停。他应与记录员建立目光联系或亲自到记录员处清楚地要求暂停，并用手做出正确的常规手势。

18.3.2　一次暂停请求只可在记录员发出该次暂停请求的信号之前被取消。

18.3.3　暂停时段：

- 当裁判员鸣哨并给出暂停手势时开始。
- 当裁判员鸣哨并招呼球队回到比赛场地上时结束。

18.3.4　暂停机会一开始，记录员就应发出他的信号，通知裁判员已提出了暂停请求。

18.3.5　在暂停期间以及第二节、第四节或每一决胜期开始之前的比赛休息期间，队员们可以离开比赛场地并坐在球队席上，允许在球队席区域内的人员可以进入比赛场地，只要这些球队成员留在他们的球队席区域附近。

18.3.6　如果第1次或仅有一次的罚球，球置于罚球队员可处理之后，任一队请求了一次暂停。如果：

- 最后一次或仅有一次的罚球成功。
- 最后一次或仅有一次罚球随后还有在记录台对侧的中线延长线的掷球入界。
- 在多次罚球之间宣判了犯规。这种情况下，应完成多次罚球，在新的犯规罚则执行之前。
- 在最后一次或仅有一次的罚球后，在球成活球前宣判了一次犯规。在这种情况下，在执行新的犯规罚则之前。
- 在最后一次或仅有一次的罚球后，在球成活球前宣判了一次违例。在这种情况下，在执行掷球入界之前。

这次暂停应被准予。

如果一个以上的犯规罚则造成连续的罚球单元和/或球权，每个单元分别处理。

19　替换

19.1　定义

替补队员请求中断比赛成为队员是一次替换。

19.2　规定

19.2.1　在替换机会期间球队可以替换队员。

19.2.2　一次替换机会开始：

- (对于双方队)当球成死球，比赛计时钟停止，以及当裁判员已结束了与记录台的联系时。
- (对于双方队)在最后一次或仅有一次的罚球成功或球成死球。
- (对于非得分队)在第四节的最后2分钟或每一决胜期的最后2分钟期间，投篮得分时。

19.2.3　一次替换机会结束于掷球入界的队员可处理球时，或第1次或仅有一次的罚球可处理球时。

19.2.4　队员已成为替补队员和替补队员已成为队员，分别不能重新进入比赛或离开比赛，直到一个比赛的计时钟运行片段之后球再次成死球为止。除非：

- 某队场上队员已被减到少于 5 名。
- 作为纠正失误的结果，拥有罚球权的队员已被合法地替换后坐在球队席上。

19.2.5　在第四节的最后 2 分钟或每一决胜期的最后 2 分钟期间，在一次成功的投篮后比赛计时钟停止时，不允许得分队替换，除非裁判员已停止了比赛。

19.3　程序

19.3.1　只有替补队员有权请求替换。他（不是教练员或助理教练员）应到记录台清楚地要求替换或者坐在替换的椅子上。他必须立即做好比赛的准备。

19.3.2　一次替换请求可以被撤销，但只可在记录员发出该次替换请求的信号之前。

19.3.3　替换机会一开始，记录员就应发出他的信号通知裁判员替换请求已提出。

19.3.4　替补队员应停留在界线外，直到裁判员鸣哨、给出替换手势和招呼他进入比赛场地。

19.3.5　已被替换的队员不必向裁判员或记录员报告，允许他直接去他的球队席。

19.3.6　替换应尽可能快地完成。已发生第五次犯规或已被取消比赛资格的队员必须立即被替换（大约 30 秒钟内）。根据裁判员的判断，如果有不必要的延误，应给违犯的队登记一次暂停。如果该队没有剩余的暂停，可登记教练员一次技术犯规（“B”）。

19.3.7　如果在一次暂停或非半时的比赛休息期间中请求替换，该替换队员必须在比赛前向记录台报告。

19.3.8　如果罚球队员因为：

- 受伤了。
- 已发生第五次犯规
- 已被取消比赛资格。

他必须被替换。罚球必须由替换他的替补队员执行，并且该替补队员在比赛的下一个计时钟运行片段前不能再次被替换。

19.3.9　第 1 次或仅有一次的罚球，球置于罚球队员可处理之后，如果任一队请求替换，则在下列情况下替换应被准予：

- 最后一次或仅有一次的罚球成功。
- 最后一次或仅有一次罚球随后还有在记录台对侧的中线延长线掷球入界。
- 在多次罚球之间宣判了犯规。这种情况下，多次罚球应完成，在新的犯规罚则执行之前允许替换。
- 在最后一次或仅有一次的罚球后，在球成活球前宣判了一次犯规。这种情况下，在执行新的犯规罚则之前允许替换。
- 在最后一次或仅有一次的罚球后，在球成活球前宣判了一次违例。这种情况下，在执行掷球入界之前允许替换。

如果一个以上的犯规罚则造成连续的罚球单元，每个单元分别处理。

20　比赛因弃权告负

20.1　规定

如果球队：

- 在预定的开始时间后 15 分钟，球队不到场或不能使 5 名队员入场准备比赛。
- 其行为阻碍比赛继续进行。

- 在主裁判员通知比赛后拒绝比赛。

那么，该队由于弃权使比赛告负。

20.2　罚则

20.2.1　判给对方队获胜，且比分为20∶0。此外，弃权的队在名次排列中应得0分。

20.2.2　对于两场比赛（主和客）总分定胜负的一组比赛和季后赛（三战定胜负），在第一场、第二场或第三场比赛中弃权的队应使该组比赛或季后赛因“弃权”告负。这不适用于季后赛（五战定胜负）。

20.2.3　如果在一次联赛中，一个球队弃权两次，该队应被取消资格，并且该队在所有比赛的结果都视为无效。

21　比赛因缺少队员告负

21.1　规定

在比赛中，如果某队在比赛场地上准备比赛的队员少于2名，该队因缺少队员使比赛告负。

21.2　罚则

21.2.1　如判获胜的队领先，则在此赛停止时的比分应有效。如判获胜的队不领先，则比分应记录为2∶0，对该队有利。此外，缺少队员的队在名次排列中应得1分。

21.2.2　对于两场比赛（主和客）总分定胜负的一组比赛，在第一场或第二场比赛中缺少队员的队应使该组比赛因“缺少队员”告负。

22　违例

22.1　定义

违例是违犯规则。

22.2　罚则

将球判给对方队员在最靠近发生违例的地点掷球入界，正好在篮板后面的地点除外，除非本规则另有规定。

23　队员出界和球出界

23.1　定义

23.1.1　当队员身体的任何部分接触界线上、界线上方或界线外的除队员以外的地面或任何物体时，即是队员出界。

23.1.2　当球触及了：

- 界外的队员或任何其他人员时。
- 界线上、界线上方或界线外的地面或任何物体时。
- 篮板支撑架、篮板背面或比赛场地上方的任何物体时。

是球出界。

23.2　规定

23.2.1　在球出界、甚至球触及了除队员以外的其他物体而出界之前，最后触及球或被球触及的队员是使球出界的队员。

23.2.2　如果球出界是由于触及了界线上或界线外的队员或被他所触及，是该队员使球出界。

23.2.3　在争球期间，如果队员移动到界外或他的后场，一次跳球情况发生。

24 运球

24.1 定义

24.1.1 运球是指一名队员控制一个活球的一系列动作：掷、拍、在地面上滚动球或者故意将球掷向篮板。

24.1.2 当在场上已获得控制活球的队员将球掷、拍、滚、运在地面上，或故意将球掷向篮板并在球触及另一队员之前再次触及球时是运球开始。

当队员双手同时触及球或允许球在一手或双手中停留时是运球结束。

在运球的时候球可被掷向空中，只要掷球的队员用手再次触及球之前球触及地面或另一队员。

当球不与队员的手接触时，队员可行进的步数不受限制。

24.1.3 队员意外地失掉并随后在场上恢复控制活球，被认为是漏接球。

24.1.4 下列情况不是运球：

- 连续的投篮。
- 一次运球的开始或结束时的漏接球。
- 从其他队员的附近用拍击球来试图获得控制球。
- 拍击另一队员控制的球。
- 拦截传球并获得控制球。
- 只要不发生带球走违例，将球在两手之间抛接并在球触及地面前允许在一手或两手中停留。

24.2 规定

队员第一次运球结束后不得再次运球，除非在两次运球之间由于下述原因他在场上已失去了控制活球：

- 投篮。
- 球被对方队员触及。
- 传球或漏接，然后球触及了另二队员或被另一队员触及。

25 带球走

25.1 定义

25.1.1 当队员在场上持着一个活球，其一脚或双脚超出本规则所述的限制向任一方向非法移动是带球走。

25.1.2 在场上正持着一个活球的队员用同一脚向任一方向踏出一次或多次，而其另一脚(称为中枢脚)不离开与地面的接触点时是旋转(合法移动)。

25.2 规定

25.2.1 对在场上接住活球的队员确立中枢脚：

- 双脚站在地面上时：

——一脚抬起的瞬间，另一脚成为中枢脚。

- 移动时：

—如果一脚正触及地面，该脚成为中枢脚。

—如果双脚离地和队员双脚同时落地，一脚抬起的瞬间，则另一脚成为中枢脚。

—如果双脚离地和队员一脚落地，于是，该脚成为中枢脚。如果队员跳起那只脚并双脚同时落地停止，那么哪只脚都不是中枢脚。

25.2.2　在场上控制了活球并已确立中枢脚的队员的带球行进：

• 双脚站在地面时：

—开始运球，在球出手之前中枢脚不得抬起。

—传球或投篮，队员可跳起中枢脚，但在球出手之前任一脚不得落回地面。

• 移动时：

—传球或投篮，队员可跳起中枢脚并一脚或双脚同时落地。但一脚或双脚抬起后在球出手之前任一脚不得落回地面。

—开始运球，在球出手之前中枢脚不得抬起。

• 停止时哪只脚都不是中枢脚：

—开始运球，在球出手之前哪只脚都不得抬起。

—传球或投篮，一脚或双脚可抬起，但在球出手前不得落回地面。

25.2.3　队员跌倒、躺或坐在地面上：

• 当一名队员持球时跌倒和在地面上滑动，或躺、或坐在地面上获得控制球是合法的。

• 如果而后该队员持着球滚动或试图站起来是违例。

26　3 秒钟

26.1　规定

26.1.1　当某队在前场控制活球并且比赛计时钟正在运行时，该队的队员不得停留在对方队的限制区内超过持续的 3 秒钟。

26.1.2　队员在下列情况中应被默许：

• 他试图离开限制区。

• 他在限制区内，当他或他的同队队员正在做投篮动作并且球正离开或恰已离开投篮队员的手时。

• 他在限制区内已接近 3 秒钟时运球投篮。

26.1.3　为证实队员自身位于限制区外，他必须将双脚置于限制区外的地面上。

27　被严密防守的队员

27.1　定义

一名队员在场上正持着活球，这时对方队员处于积极的防守姿势，距离不超过 1 米，该队员是被严密防守。

27.2　规定

一名被严密防守的队员必须在 5 秒钟内传、投或运球。

28　8 秒钟

28.1　规定

28.1.1　当：

• 一名队员在他的后场获得控制活球时。

● 在掷球入界中，球触及后场的任何队员或者被后场的任何队员合法触及，掷球入界队员所在队仍拥有在后场的球权。

该队必须在8秒钟内使球进入该队的前场。

28.1.2 当：

● 没有被任何队员控制，球触及前场时。

● 球触及或者被双脚在他前场的进攻队员合法触及时。

● 球触及或者被有部分身体在他后场的防守队员合法触及时。

● 球触及有部分身体在控制球队前场的裁判员时。

● 运球队员在后场往前场运球的过程中，双脚和球都进入前场时。

就是球队使球进入该队的前场。

28.1.3 当先前已控制球的同一队由于下列情况的结果被判在后场掷球入界时，8秒钟应从剩余时间处连续计算：

● 球出界。

● 一名同队队员受伤。

● 一次跳球情况。

● 一次双方犯规。

● 双方球队的相等罚则抵消。

29 24秒钟

29.1 规定

29.1.1 当：

● 一名队员在场上控制一个活球时。

● 在一次掷球入界中，球触及任何一名场上队员或者被他合法触及，掷球入界队员所在的球队仍然控制着球时，该队必须在24秒钟内尝试投篮。

一次24秒钟内投篮的构成：

● 在24秒计时钟的信号发出前，球必须离开队员的手；

● 球离开了队员的手后，球必须触及篮圈或进入球篮。

29.1.2 在临近24秒钟结束时尝试了一次投篮，并且球在空中时24秒计时钟信号响：

● 如果球进入球篮，没有违例发生，信号应被忽略并且计中篮得分。

● 如果球触及篮圈但未进入球篮，没有违例发生，信号应被忽略并且比赛应继续。

● 如果球未碰篮圈，一次违例已发生。然而，如果对方队员即时和清楚地获得了控制球，信号应被忽略并且比赛应继续。

关系到干涉得分和干扰得分的所有限制应适用。

29.2 程序

29.2.1 如果裁判员停止了比赛：

● 因为不控制球的球队犯规或者违例（不是因为球出界）。

● 因为任何与不控制球的球队有关的正当原因。

● 因为任何与双方球队都无关的正当原因。

球权应判给先前控制球的球队。

如果掷球入界在其后场执行，24 秒计时钟应复位到 24 秒。

如果掷球入界在其前场执行，24 秒计时钟应按照下述原则复位：

- 当比赛被停止时，如果 24 秒计时钟显示为 14 秒或者更多，24 秒计时钟不应复位，而是从被停止的时间处连续计算。
- 当比赛被停止时，如果 24 秒计时钟显示为 13 秒或者更少，24 秒计时钟应复位到 14 秒。

然而，根据裁判员的判断，如果对方将被置于不利，24 秒计时钟应从停止的时间处连续计算。

29. 2. 2　如果某队已控制球或双方队都未控制球时，24 秒计时钟错误地发出信号，此信号应被忽略并且比赛应继续。

然而，根据裁判员的判断，如果控制球队已被置于不利，应停止比赛，24 秒计时钟应被纠正并且把球判给该队。

30　球回后场

30. 1　定义

30. 1. 1　当：

- 球触及后场时。
- 球触及或者被有部分身体接触后场的进攻队员合法触及时。
- 球触及有部分身体接触后场的裁判员时。

是球进入某队的后场。

30. 1. 2　当一个控制活球队的队员在他的前场最后触及进入前场的球，随后他或他的同队队员又首先触及进入后场的球，球已非法回到后场。

这个限制适用于在某队前场的所有情况，包括掷球入界。然而，它不适用于队员从他的前场跳起，仍在空中时建立新的球队控制球，然后落在该队的后场内。

30. 2　规定

控制活球队的队员不得使球非法地回到他的后场。

30. 3　罚则

球应判给对方在他们的前场最靠近违犯的地点掷球入界，正好在篮板后面的地点除外。

31　干涉得分和干扰得分

31. 1　定义

投篮或罚球：

- 开始于：球离开正在做投篮动作的队员的手时。
- 结束于：

—球从上方直接进入球篮并且停留其中或穿过球篮时。

—球不再有进入球篮的可能性时。

—球触及篮圈时。

—球触及地面时。

—球成为死球时。

31.2 规定

31.2.1 在一次投篮中，当一名队员触及完全在篮圈水平面之上的球时，并且：

- 球是下落飞向球篮中。
- 在球已碰击篮板后。

干涉得分发生。

31.2.2 在一次罚球中，当一名队员触及飞向球篮的、触及篮圈前的球时，干涉得分发生。

31.2.3 干涉得分的限制适用于：

- 球不再有进入球篮的可能性前。
- 球触及篮圈前。

31.2.4 当：

- 在一次投篮，最后一次或者仅有的一次罚球后，当球与篮圈接触时，队员触及球篮或篮板。
- 在一次罚球(随后还有进一步的罚球)后，球有进入球篮的可能性时，一名队员触及球、球篮或篮板时。
- 队员从下方伸手穿过球篮并触及球时。
- 当球在球篮中，防守队员触及球或者球篮从而阻止球穿过球篮时。
- 队员使篮板颤动或者抓球篮，根据裁判员的判定，这种手段已妨碍球进入球篮或者使球进入球篮时。
- 队员抓球篮打球时。

干扰得分发生。

31.2.5 当：

- 球在投篮队员的手中或者一次投篮的飞行中，裁判员鸣哨时。
- 投篮的球在飞行中，结束一节的比赛计时钟信号响时。

在球已触及篮圈之后仍有进入球篮的可能时，队员不得触及球。

涉及干涉得分和干扰得分的所有限制应适用。

31.3 罚则

31.3.1 如果一名进攻队员发生违例，不判给得分。将球判给对方队员在罚球线延长线掷球入界，除非本规则另有规定。

31.3.2 如果一名防守队员发生违例，应判给进攻队：

- 当球在罚球中出手时，得1分。
- 当球在2分投篮区域出手时，得2分。
- 当球在3分投篮区域出手时，得3分。

判给的得分就如同球进入球篮一样。

31.3.3 如果防守队员在最后一次或仅有一次的罚球中发生干涉得分违例，应判给进攻队得1分，随后执行防守队员技术犯规的罚则。

32 犯规

32.1 定义

32.1.1 犯规是对规则的违犯，含有与对方队员的非法身体接触和/或违反体育道德的举止。

32.1.2　一个队可被宣判任何数量的犯规，不考虑罚则，犯规者的每一犯规应被登记，记入记录表并相应地被处罚。

33　接触：一般原则

33.1　圆柱体原则

圆柱体原则定义为一名站在地面上的队员占据一个假想的圆柱体内的空间。它包括该队员上面的空间(如图 2-13)，并受下列限定：

- 前面由手的双掌。
- 后面由臀部。
- 两侧由双臂和双腿的外侧。

双手和双臂可以在躯干前面伸展，其肘部的双臂弯曲不超过双脚的位置，因此两前臂和双手举起的、他双脚间的距离应依据他的身高有所不同。

图 2-13　圆柱体原则

33.2　垂直原则

在比赛中，每一队员都有权占据未被对方队员已经占据的任何场上位置(圆柱体)。

这个原则保护队员所占据的地面空间和当他在此空间内垂直跳起时的上方空间。

队员一离开他的垂直位置(圆柱体)并与已经建立了他自己的垂直位置(圆柱体)的对方队员发生身体接触，离开他的垂直位置(圆柱体)的队员对此接触负责。

防守队员垂直地离开地面(在他的圆柱体内)或在他自己的圆柱体内把双手和双臂伸展在他的上方，则不必判罚。

无论是在地面上或在空中的进攻队员不应用下列方式与处于合法防守位置的防守队员发生接触。

- 用他的手臂为自己扩展更多的空间(清除障碍)。
- 在投篮中或紧接投篮后伸展他的双腿或双臂去造成接触。

33.3　合法防守位置

当一名防守队员：

- 面对对手，并且
- 双脚着地时。

他就占据了最初的合法防守位置.

合法防守位置从地面到天花板，垂直地伸展到他(圆柱体)的上方。他可将他的双臂和双手举过头或垂直跳起，但是他必须在假想的圆柱体内使双手和双臂保持垂直的姿势。

33.4　防守控制球的队员

当防守控制(正持着或运着)球的队员时，时间和距离的因素不适用。

每当对方队员在持球队员面前占据了一个最初的合法防守位置(甚至是一瞬间完成的)，持球队员必须预料到被防守并必须准备停步或改变他的方向。

防守队员占据一个最初的合法防守位置，必须在占据位置前没有造成接触。

一旦防守队员已占据了一个最初的合法防守位置，他可移动以便防守他的对手，但他不得伸展他的双臂、双肩、双髋或双腿，并通过这样做来造成接触以阻止从他身边通过的运球队员。

判断一起涉及持球队员的撞人/阻挡情况时，裁判员应运用下列原则：

- 防守队员必须以面对持球队员并双脚着地来占据一个最初的合法防守位置。
- 防守队员为保持最初的合法防守位置，可保持静立、垂直跳起、侧移或后移。
- 在保持最初合法防守位置的移动中，一脚或双脚可以瞬间离地，只要该移动是侧向或向后的，而不是朝向持球队员前移的。
- 接触必须发生在躯干上，在这样的情况下，防守队员被认为已经先在接触地点了。
- 已占据了合法防守位置的防守队员可以在他的圆柱体之内转身以避免受伤。

在上述任何情况中，应认为该接触是由持球队员造成的。

33.5　防守不控制球的队员

不控制球的队员有权在球场上自由地移动，并占据任何未被另一队员已经占据的位置。

当防守不控制球的队员时，时间和距离的因素应适用。防守队员不能如此靠近和/或如此快地在移动的对方队员的路径中占据一个位置，以致后者没有足够的时间或距离停步或改变他的方向。

此距离直接与对方队员的速度成正比，不要少于正常的 1 步，也不必要多于正常的 2 步。

如果一名防守队员在占据最初的合法防守位置中不顾及时间和距离的因素，并与对方队员发生接触，他对该接触负责。

一旦一名防守队员已经占据了一个最初的合法防守位置，为防守对方队员他可移动。他不得在对方队员的路径中伸展臂、肩、臀或腿去阻止该对方队员从他身边通过。他可以在他的圆柱体内转身以避免受伤。

33.6　腾空的队员

从场上某地点跳起在空中的队员有权再落回同一地点。

他有权落在场上的另一地点，只要在起跳时落地点以及起跳和落地点之间的直接路径上，在起跳的时间尚未被对方队员占据。

如果一名队员已跳起并落地，可是他的冲力使其接触了在落地点之外已占据了一个合法防守位置的对方队员，则该跳起队员对此接触负责。

在队员已跳起在空中后，对方队员不得移动到他的路径上。

移动到腾空队员的身下并造成接触，通常是违反体育道德的犯规，某些情况下可能是取消比赛资格的犯规。

33.7　掩护：合法的和非法的

掩护是试图延误或阻止一名不持球的对方队员到达他希望到达的场上位置。

当正在掩护对手的队员：

- 发生接触时是静止的(在他的圆柱体内)。
- 发生接触时双脚着地。

是合法的掩护。

当正在掩护对手的队员：

- 发生接触时正在移动。
- 在静止对手的视野之外做掩护，发生接触时，没有给出足够的距离。

- 发生了接触时，对移动中的对手没有顾及时间和距离的因素。

是非法的掩护。

如果在静止对手的视野之内做掩护(前面的或侧面的)，做掩护的队员可按自己的意愿靠近对手以建立掩护，只要没有接触。

如果在静止对手的视野之外做掩护，做掩护的队员必须允许对手向掩护迈出正常的一步而不发生接触。

如果对手在移动中，时间和距离的因素应适用。做掩护的队员必须留出足够的空间，以便被掩护的队员能通过停步或改变方向来避免掩护。

要求的距离是不要少于正常的 1 步，也不必要多于正常的 2 步。

与已经建立掩护的队员的任何接触，由被合法掩护的队员负责。

33.8 撞人

撞人是持球或不持球队员推开或移动对方队员躯干的非法身体接触。

33.9 阻挡

阻挡是阻碍持球或不持球对方队员行进的非法身体接触。

如果试图做掩护的队员在移动中与静止或后退的对方队员发生接触，则判罚掩护队员一起阻挡犯规。

如果队员不顾球，面对着对方队员并随着对方队员的移动而移动他的位置，除非包含其他因素。该队员对所发生的任何接触负主要责任。所谓“除非包含其他因素”是指被掩护的队员故意推人、撞人和拉人。

队员在场上占据位置时把他的手臂或肘伸在他的圆柱体之外是合法的，但当对方队员试图通过时，它们必须被移到他的圆柱体之内。如果手臂或肘是在他的圆柱体之外并发生接触，这是阻挡或拉人。

33.10 无撞人半圆区

球场上画出无撞人半圆区的目的是，指定一个特定的区域用于解释篮下的撞人/阻挡情况。向无撞人半圆区的任何突破情况中，当：

- 进攻队员腾空并控制球，并且
- 他试图投篮或者传球，并且
- 防守队员的双脚在无撞人半圆区内。

进攻队员与防守队员在无撞人半圆区内的身体接触不应被宣判为进攻犯规，除非进攻队员非法地使用他的手、手臂或者身体。

33.11 用手和/或手臂接触对方队员

用手触及对方队员，本身未必是犯规。

裁判员应判定引起接触的队员是否已经获得了不公正的利益。如果队员引起的接触在任何方面限制对方队员的移动自由，这样的接触是犯规。

当防守队员处于防守位置，并且他的手或手臂放置在持球或不持球的对方队员身上并保持接触以阻碍他行进，就发生了非法用手或非法伸展手臂。

反复地触及或“戳刺”持球或不持球的对方队员是犯规，因为这可导致粗野的比赛。

当持球进攻队员：

- 为了获得不公正的利益，用手臂或肘“勾住”或缠绕防守队员。
- 为了阻止防守队员的防守或试图抢球，或为了在他和防守队员之间扩展更大的空间而“推开”防守队员。

- 运球时，用伸展的前臂或手去阻止对方队员获得控制球。

这是持球进攻队员的犯规。

当不持球的进攻队员为了：

- 摆脱去接球；
- 阻止防守队员的防守或试图抢球；
- 扩展更大的个人空间。

而“推开”防守队员，这是不持球进攻队员的犯规。

33.12 居中策应

垂直原则(圆柱体原则)适用于居中策应。

位于中锋位置的进攻队员和防守队员必须尊重彼此的垂直位置(圆柱体)的权利。

位于中锋位置的进攻队员或防守队员用肩或髋将他的对方队员挤出位置，或用伸展的肘、臂、膝或身体的其他部位去干扰对方队员的活动自由，是犯规。

33.13 背后非法防守

背后非法防守是防守队员从对方队员的背后与其发生的身体接触。防守队员正试图去抢球的事实，不证明从背后与对方队员发生接触是正当的。

33.14 拉人

拉人是干扰对方队员移动自由的非法身体接触。这种接触(拉人)可能发生在身体的任何部位。

33.15 推人

推人是队员用身体的任何部位强行移动或试图移动控制或未控制球的对方队员时发生的非法身体接触。

34 侵人犯规

34.1 定义

侵人犯规是：无论在活球或死球的情况下，攻守双方队员发生的身体接触的犯规。

队员不应通过伸展他的手、臂、肘、肩、髋、膝、脚或将其身体弯曲成“不正常的姿势”(超出他的圆柱体)去拉、阻挡、推、撞、绊对方队员，或阻止对方队员进行；也不得放纵任何粗野或猛烈的动作去这样做。

34.2 罚则

应登记犯规队员一次侵人犯规。

34.2.1 如果对没有做投篮动作的队员发生犯规：

- 由非犯规的队在最靠近违犯的地点掷球入界重新开始比赛。
- 如果犯规的队处于全队犯规处罚状态，则应运用第41条(全队犯规：处罚)的规定。

34.2.2 如果对正在做投篮动作的队员发生犯规，应按下列所述判给投篮队员若干罚球：

- 如果投篮成功：应计得分并追加1次罚球。
- 如果从2分投篮区的投篮不成功：2次罚球。
- 如果从3分投篮区的投篮不成功：3次罚球。
- 在结束一节的比赛计时钟信号响时或恰好响之前，或当24秒计时钟信号响时或恰好响之前，投篮队员被犯规了，此时球仍在该队员的手中，并且随后投篮成功：中篮不应计得分，应判给 2 次或 3 次罚球。

35 双方犯规

35.1 定义

35.1.1 双方犯规是两名互为对方的队员大约同时相互发生侵人犯规的情况。

35.2 罚则

应给每一犯规队员登记一次侵人犯规。不判给罚球。比赛应按下列所述重新开始：

在发生双方犯规的大约同一时间，如果：

- 投篮得分，或最后一次或仅有一次的罚球得分，应将球判给非得分队从端线的任何地点掷球入界。
- 某队已控制球或拥有球权，应将球判给该队在最靠近违犯的地点掷球入界。
- 任一队都没有控制球也没有球权，发生一次跳球情况。

36 违反体育道德的犯规

36.1 定义

36.1.1 根据裁判员的判断，一名队员不是在规则的精神和意图的范围内合法地试图去直接抢球，发生的接触犯规是违反体育道德的犯观。

36.1.2 在整场的比赛中裁判员必须对违反体育道德犯规解释一致并只判定其所做所为。

36.1.3 判断犯规是否是违反体育道德的，裁判员应运用如下原则：

- 如果一名队员不努力去抢球并发生身体接触，这是一起违反体育道德的犯规。
- 如果一名队员在努力抢球中造成过分的身体接触(严重犯规)，这是一起违反体育道德的犯规。
- 如果防守队员试图阻止一次快攻，从对方队员身后或侧面与其发生身体接触，并且在进攻队员和对方球篮之间没有防守队员，这是一起违反体育道德的犯规。
- 如果一名队员正合法地努力去抢球(正常的争抢)发生了犯规，这不是违反体育道德的犯规。

36.2 罚则

36.2.1 应给犯规队员登记一次违反体育道德的犯规。

36.2.2 应判给被犯规的队员执行罚球，以及随后：

- 在记录台对面的中线延长线掷球入界。
- 在中圈跳球开始第一节。

应按下述原则判给若干罚球：

- 如果对没有做投篮动作的队员发生犯规：2 次罚球。
- 如果对正在做投篮动作的队员发生犯规：如果中篮应计得分并加 1 次罚球。
- 如果对正在做投篮动作的队员发生犯规，并且球未中篮：2 次或 3 次罚球。

36.2.3 当队员被登记 2 次违反体育道德的犯规时，他应被取消比赛资格。

36.2.4 如果队员在 36.2.3 情况下被取消比赛资格，应只处罚违反体育道德的犯规罚则，不追加取消比赛资格的罚则。

37 取消比赛资格的犯规

37.1 定义

37.1.1 队员、替补队员、出局的队员、教练员、助理教练员或随队人员的任何恶劣的违反体育道德的行为是取消比赛资格的犯规。

37.1.2 已被取消比赛资格的教练员应由登记在记录表上的助理教练员接替。如果记录表上没有登记助理教练员，应由队长(CAP)接替。

37.2 罚则

37.2.1 应给犯规者登记一次取消比赛资格的犯规。

37.2.2 每当犯规者依据这些规则的各个条款被取消比赛资格，他应去该队的休息室，并在比赛期间留在那里，或者他也可以选择离开体育馆。

37.2.3 罚球应判给：

- 如果是一起非身体接触犯规：由对方教练员指定的任一本队队员；
- 如果是一起身体接触犯规：被犯规的队员。

以及随后：

- 在记录台对面的中线延长线掷球入界。
- 在中圈跳球开始第一节。

37.2.4 罚球的次数应按如下规定：

- 如果对没有做投篮动作的队员犯规：2 次罚球。
- 如果对正在做投篮动作的队员犯规：如果中篮应计得分并加 1 次罚球。
- 如果对正在做投篮动作的队员犯规，并且球未中篮：2 次或 3 次罚球。

38 技术犯规

38.1 行为规定

38.1.1 比赛的正当行为要求双方球队的成员(队员、替补队员、教练员、助理教练员、出局的队员和随队人员)与裁判员、记录台人员以及技术代表(如到场)有完美和真诚的合作。

38.1.2 每支球队应尽最大的努力去获取胜利，但胜利的取得必须符合体育道德精神和公正竞赛的要求。

38.1.3 任何故意的或再三的不合作，或不遵守本规则的精神，应被认为是一次技术犯规。

38.1.4 裁判员可以通过警告或甚至宽容那些明显是无意的，并不直接影响比赛的、轻微的违犯来预防技术犯规的发生，除非在警告后又重复出现同样的违犯。

38.1.5 如果在球成活球后发现了一次违犯，比赛应停止并登记一次技术犯规。应将技术犯规视同发生在它被登记的时候一样来执行罚则。在违犯与比赛停止之间的间隔内无论发生了什么都应保持有效。

38.2 暴力行为

38.2.1 比赛中可能发生与体育道德精神和公正竞赛相违背的暴力行为。裁判员应立即制止，如有必要，通过负责维持公共秩序的保安人员来制止。

38.2.2 无论何时，在队员、替补队员、出局的队员、教练员、助理教练员或随队人员之间，在比赛场地上或其附近发生暴力行为，裁判员应采取必要的措施去制止他们。

38.2.3 任何上述人员公然地挑衅对方队员或裁判员，应被取消比赛资格。主裁判员必须将此事件报告给竞赛的组织部门。

38.2.4 保安人员可以进入比赛场地，只要裁判员要求这样做。然而，如果带有明显采用暴力行为意图的观众进入球场，保安人员必须立即干预以保护球队和裁判员。

38.2.5 所有其他区域，包括入口、出口、过道、休息室等，由竞赛组织部门和负责维持公共秩序的保安人员管辖。

38.2.6 裁判员绝不允许队员、替补队员、出局的队员、教练员、助理教练员和随队人员可能导致比赛器材损坏的粗野行为出现。

当裁判员观察到这类行为时，应立即给违犯队的教练员一次警告。

如果重复该行为，应立即宣判有关的违犯者一次技术犯规。

38.3 定义

38.3.1 技术犯规是没有身体接触的犯规，行为种类包括但不限于：

- 无视裁判员的警告。
- 无礼地触碰裁判员、技术代表、记录台人员或球队席人员。
- 与裁判员、技术代表、记录台人员或对方队员交流中没有礼貌。
- 使用很可能冒犯或煽动观众的粗话或手势。
- 戏弄对方队员或在他的眼睛附近摇手妨碍其视觉。
- 过分挥肘。
- 在球穿过球篮之后故意地触及球或阻碍迅速地执行掷球入界以延误比赛。
- 跌倒以伪造一次犯规。
- 悬吊在篮圈上，致使队员的重量由篮圈支撑，除非扣篮后，队员瞬间地抓住篮圈，或者，根据裁判员的判断，如果他正试图防止自己受伤或使另一名队员不受伤。
- 在最后一次或仅有一次的罚球中防守队员干涉得分，应判给进攻队得 1 分，随后执行登记在该防守队员名下的技术犯规罚则。

38.3.2 教练员、助理教练员、替补队员、出局的队员或随队人员的技术犯规是与裁判员、技术代表、记录台人员或对方队员交流中没有礼貌或无礼地触碰他们的犯规；或是一次程序上的或管理性质的违犯。

38.3.3 当出现下述情况时教练员应被取消：

- 由于自身违反体育道德行为的结果而被登记了 2 次技术犯规（“C”）时。
- 由于球队席人员（助理教练员、替补队员、出局的队员或随队人员）的违反体育道德的行为而被登记了 3 次技术犯规（三次全部登记为“B”或者其中一次是“C”）。

38.3.4 如果教练员在 38.3.3 情况下被取消比赛资格，应只处罚技术犯规的罚则，不追加取消比赛资格的罚则。

38.4 罚则

38.4.1 如果：

- 判罚队员技术犯规。应作为队员的犯规登记在该队员名下，并计入全队犯规中。
- 判罚教练员（“C”）、助理教练员（“B”）、替补队员（“B”）、出局的队员（“B”）或随队人员（“B”）。应登记在该教练员名下，并不计入全队犯规次数中。

38.4.2 应判给对方队员 2 次罚球，并随后：

- 在记录台对面的中线延长线掷球入界。
- 在中圈跳球开始第一节。

39 打架

39.1 定义

打架是两名或多名互为对方队的人员(队员、替补队员、出局的队员、教练员、助理教练员和随队人员)之间的肢体冲突。

本条款仅适用于在打架中或在可能导致打架的任何情况中离开球队席区域界限的教练员、助理教练员、替补队员、出局的队员和随队人员。

39.2 规定

39.2.1 在打架中或在可能导致打架的任何情况中离开球队席区域的替补队员、出局的队员或随队人员应被取消比赛资格。

39.2.2 在打架中或在可能导致打架的任何情况中，为了协助裁判员维持或恢复秩序，只允许教练员和/或助理教练员离开球队席区域，协助裁判员维持或恢复秩序。在这种情况中，他不应被取消比赛资格。

39.2.3 如果教练员和/或助理教练员离开球队席区域，并不协助或试图协助裁判员维持或恢复秩序，他应被取消比赛资格。

39.3 罚则

39.3.1 不论由于离开球队席区域而被取消比赛资格的教练员、助理教练员、替补队员、出局的队员或随队人员的数量有多少，应给教练员登记一次单一的技术犯规(“B”)。

39.3.2 如果双方球队的成员在本条规定下被取消比赛资格并且没有留下其他要执行的犯规罚则，比赛应按下面所述重新开始：

由于打架而停止比赛，大约在同一时间，如果：

- 投篮得分，应将球判给非得分队从端线的任何地点掷球入界。
- 某队已控制球或拥有球权，应将球判给该队在记录台对侧的中线延长线掷球入界。
- 任一队都没有控制球也没有球权，一次跳球情况发生。

39.3.3 所有的取消比赛资格的犯规应不计入全队犯规次数中。

39.3.4 所有涉及在场上打架的队员或在打架之前发生的任何情况的可能存在的犯规罚则，应按第 42 条(特殊情况)处理。

40 队员 5 次犯规

40.1 一名队员已发生了 5 次侵人犯规和/或技术犯规，裁判员应通知其本人，他必须立即离开比赛，并且必须在 30 秒钟内被替换。

40.2 先前已发生了第五次犯规的队员的犯规，被认为是一名出局的队员的犯规，并登记在教练员名下和在记录表上记入“B”。

41 全队犯规：处罚

41.1 定义

41.1.1 在一节中某队全队犯规已发生了 4 次时，该队处于全队犯规处罚状态。

41.1.2 在比赛休息期间发生的所有全队犯规应被认为是发生在随后一节或决胜期比赛中的犯规。

41.1.3 在决胜期内发生的所有全队犯规应被认为是发生在第四节比赛中的犯规。

41.2 规定

41.2.1 当某队处于全队犯规处罚状态时，所有随后发生的对未做投篮动作的队员的侵人犯规应被判2次罚球，代替掷球入界。

41.2.2 如果控制活球队的队员或拥有球权队的队员发生了一起侵人犯规，这样的犯规应判对方队员一次掷球入界。

42 特殊情况

42.1 定义

在一次犯规后的同一个停止比赛计时钟期间又发生了一次或多次犯规时，可能出现特殊情况。

42.2 程序

42.2.1 应登记所有的犯规，并确认所有的罚则。

42.2.2 应确定所有犯规发生的次序。

42.2.3 双方球队所有相等的罚则和所有双方犯规的罚则应按照它们宣判的顺序被抵消。一旦罚则已被抵消，就认为它们从未发生过。

42.2.4 作为最后罚则一部分的拥有球的权利，应当取消任何先前的拥有球的权利。

42.2.5 在第一次或仅有一次的罚球中，或在掷球入界中，一旦球已成为活球，那么该罚则就不再能用来抵消任何剩余罚则。

42.2.6 所有剩余的罚则应按它们被宣判的次序执行。

42.2.7 如果双方球队抵消了相等的罚则后，没有留下其他要执行的罚则，比赛应按下述原则重新开始比赛：

在第一次违犯发生的大约同一时间，如果：

- 投篮得分，应将球判给非得分队从端线的任何地点掷球入界。
- 某队已控制球或拥有球权，应将球判给该队在最靠近第1次违犯的地点掷球入界。
- 任一队都没有控制球也没有球权，发生一次跳球情况。

43 罚球

43.1 定义

43.1.1 一次罚球是给予一名队员从罚球线后的半圆内的位置上，在无争抢的情况下得1分的机会。

43.1.2 一次单一的犯规罚则带来的所有罚球和/或随后的球权被定义为一个罚球单元。

43.2 规定

43.2.1 当宣判了一次侵人犯规，应按下述原则判给罚球：

- 被犯规的队员应执行全部罚球。
- 如果他被请求替换，他必须在离开比赛前执行完该罚则的全部罚球。
- 如果他由于受伤、已发生他的第五次犯规或已被取消比赛资格必须离开比赛，替换他的替补队员应执行罚球。如果没有有效的替补队员，应由他的教练员指定任意一名同队队员执行罚球。

43.2.2　当宣判了一次技术犯规时，由对方队的教练员指定他球队中的任一队员执行罚球。

43.2.3　罚球队员：

- 应在罚球线后并在半圆内占据一个位置。
- 可用任何方式罚篮，并且以这样的方式使球从上方进入球篮或使球触及篮圈。
- 在裁判员将球置于他可处理后，在5秒钟内应将球出手。
- 不应触及罚球线或进入限制区，直到球已进入球篮或已触及篮圈。
- 不应做假动作罚球。

43.2.4　在分位区的队员们有权占据这些空间交错的分位区，这些分位区的深度应被看做是1米(图2-14)。

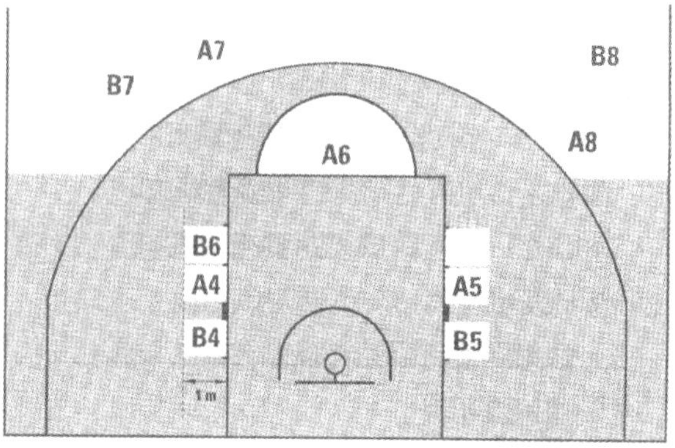

图2-14　在罚球中队员的位置

在罚球中，这些队员们不应该：

- 占据他们无权占据的分位区。
- 在球离开罚球队员的手前进入限制区、中立区或离开他的分位区。
- 用他的行为扰乱罚球队员。

43.2.5　不在分位区内的队员们应留在罚球线延长线和3分投篮线后面，直到罚球结束。

43.2.6　在罚球后接着有另一罚球单元或一次掷球入界，所有队员应留在罚球线延长线和3分投篮线后面。

违犯第43.2.3、43.2.4、43.2.5和43.2.6是违例。

43.3　罚则

43.3.1　如果罚球成功并且罚球队员违例，中篮应不计得分。

应将球判给对方队员在罚球线延长线掷球入界，除非还要执行后续的罚球或者球权。

43.3.2　如果罚球成功并且除罚球队员外的任一队员发生违例：

- 如果中篮，应计得分。
- 违例应不究。

如果是最后一次或仅有一次的罚球，应将球判给对方队员从端线的任何地点掷球入界。

43.3.3　如果罚球不成功并且发生违例：

• 罚球队员的同队队员在最后一次或仅有一次的罚球中违例，应将球判给对方队员在罚球线延长线掷球入界，除非该队有进一步的球权。

• 罚球队员的对方队员违例，应判给罚球队员再罚一次。

• 双方球队在最后一次或仅有一次的罚球中都违例，一次跳球情况发生。

44 可纠正的失误

44.1 定义

如果仅在下述情况中某条规则被无意地忽视了，裁判员可纠正其失误：

• 判给不应得的罚球。

• 没有判给应得的罚球。

• 不正确地判给得分或取消得分。

• 允许不该罚球的队员执行罚球。

44.2 一般程序

44.2.1 要纠正上述提到的失误，它们必须在失误后且开动了比赛计时钟之后的第一次死球后球成活球之前被裁判员、技术代表(如到场)或记录台人员发现。

44.2.2 发现了一起可纠正的失误时，裁判员可立即停止比赛，只要不把任一队置于不利。

44.2.3 在失误发生以后到失误被发现之前，可能发生的任何犯规、得分、用去的时间和附加的活动，应保持有效。

44.2.4 在失误纠正之后，除非规则另有规定，比赛应在因纠正失误时而被停止的地点重新开始，应将球判给在纠正失误停止比赛时拥有球权的队。

44.2.5 一旦一个可纠正的失误被发现：

• 如果涉及纠正失误的队员已被合法替换后坐在球队席上(不是第五次犯规或者被取消比赛资格)，他必须重新进入比赛场地(除非他受伤了)参加该失误的纠正(此时他成为一名队员)。在完成纠正失误后，他可以继续留在比赛中，除非已再次请求了一次合法的替换，在此情况下他才可以离开比赛场地。

• 如果该队员因为受伤、5 次犯规或者已被取消比赛资格而被替换，替换他的队员必须参加该失误的纠正。

44.2.6 主裁判员已在记录表上签字后，可纠正的失误不能被纠正。

44.2.7 主裁判员在记录表上签字前，记录员在记录中或计时员在计时中的任何失误，包括比分、犯规次数、暂停次数、消耗或遗漏的时间，裁判员可在任何时间纠正。

44.3 特殊程序

44.3.1 判给不应得的罚球：

由于失误而执行的罚球应被取消，并且比赛应按下述原则重新开始：

• 如果失误之后比赛计时钟没有开动，应将球判给罚球被取消的队从罚球线延长线掷球入界。

• 如果失误之后比赛计时钟已开动，并且在失误被发现时控制球(或拥有球权)的队与该失误发生时控制球的队是同一队；或在失误被发现时没有球队控制球，应将球判给在失误发生时拥有球权的队。

• 如果比赛计时钟已开动，并且在该失误被发现时控制球(或拥有球权)的队是在该失误发生时控制球队的对方球队，发生一次跳球情况。

- 如果比赛计时钟已开动，并且在该失误被发现时，判了一个包含罚球的犯规，应该执行罚球。然后，将球判给在该失误发生时控制球的队掷球入界。

44.3.2　没有判给应得的罚球：

- 如果在该失误发生后球权没有改变，在该失误纠正后应如同任何正常的罚球后一样地重新开始比赛。
- 如果在错误地判给了掷球入界的球权之后，该队得分了，则失误应不究。

44.3.3　允许错误的队员执行了罚球：

该执行的罚球应被取消，并将球判给对方在罚球线延长线掷球入界，除非还有另外的违犯罚则要执行。

45　裁判员、记录台人员和技术代表

45.1　裁判员应是一名主裁判员和一名或两名副裁判员．他们应由记录台人员和技术代表协助。

45.2　记录台人员应是一名记录员、一名助理记录员、一名计时员和一名 24 秒钟计时员。

45.3　一名技术代表应坐在记录员和计时员之间。比赛中他的主要职责是监督记录台人员的工作，并协助主裁判员和副裁判员使比赛顺利进行。

45.4　担任一场比赛的裁判员不应与场上任一队有任何方式的联系。

45.5　裁判员、记录台人员和技术代表应按照这些规则来指导比赛，并无权同意改变这些规则。

45.6　裁判员的服装应由裁判员汗衫、黑色长裤、黑色袜子和黑色篮球鞋组成。

45.7　裁判员和记录台人员应着装一致。

46　主裁判员：职责和权力

主裁判员应：

46.1　检查和批准在比赛过程中使用的所有器材。

46.2　指定正式的比赛计时钟、24 秒钟装置、计秒表，并确认记录台人员。

46.3　从主队提供的至少两个用过的球中挑选比赛球。如果两个球中没有一个适宜作为比赛球，他可挑选最好质量的合用的球。

46.4　不允许任何队员佩戴可能对其他队员造成伤害的物品。

46.5　执行跳球开始第一节和管理掷球入界开始所有其他节。

46.6　当情况需要时有权停止比赛。

46.7　有权判定某队弃权。

46.8　在比赛时间结束时或在任何他认为有必要的时候，仔细地审查记录表。

46.9　在比赛时间结束时，认可和在记录表上签字，终止裁判员对比赛的管理和联系。裁判员应在预定的比赛开始时间前 20 分钟到达球场，此时他们的权力应开始，当裁判员批准比赛时间结束时他们的权力应结束。

46.10　在早于预定的比赛开始前 20 分钟或在比赛时间结束和核查及在记录表上签字之间发生了任何弃权或队员、教练员、助理教练员或随队人员的违反体育道德的行为，主

裁判员必须在签字之前在记录表的反面记录该事件。在这种情况下，主裁判员(技术代表，如果到场)必须向竞赛的组织部门递交详细的报告。

46.11　每当有必要或裁判员的意见不一致时做出最终的决定。为做出最终的决定，他可与副裁判员、技术代表和/或记录台人员商量。

46.12　有权对本规则中未明确规定的任何事项做出决定。

47　裁判员：职责和权力

47.1　裁判员有权对不论发生在界线内或界线外包括记录台、球队席以及紧靠线后的区域所发生的对规则的违犯做出宣判。

47.2　当发生一起违犯规则、一节结束或裁判员发现有必要中断比赛时，裁判员应鸣哨；在一次成功的投篮、一次成功的罚球之后或当球成活球时，裁判员不应鸣哨。

47.3　当判定身体接触或违例时，裁判员应在每一个实例中注重和考虑下列基本原则：

- 规则的精神和意图以及坚持比赛完整的需要。
- 运用“有利/无利”概念中的一致性，裁判员不应企图靠不必要地打断比赛的流畅来处罚附带的身体接触，况且这样的接触没有给有责任的队员以利益，也未置他的对方队员于不利。
- 在每场比赛中运用常识的一致性，要记住有关队员的能力以及他们在比赛中的态度和行为。
- 在比赛控制和比赛流畅之间保持平衡的一致性，对于参与者们正想做什么以及宣判什么对比赛是正确的要有一种感觉。

47.4　如果其中一队提出抗议，主裁判员(技术代表，如果到场)应在比赛时间结束后的1小时内向竞赛的组织部门报告该抗议。

47.5　如果一位裁判员受伤或因任何其他原因，在事故发生的5分钟内还不能继续执行职责，比赛应继续。除有可能以有资格的替补裁判员更换受伤的裁判员外，另一位裁判员应单独执裁直到比赛结束。在与技术代表商议之后，另一裁判员将决定此可能的更换。

47.6　对所有的国际比赛，如果有必要用口语使宣判清楚，则应使用英语处理。

47.7　每一裁判员有权在他的职责范围内作出宣判，但无权不顾或质问另一裁判员作出的宣判。

48　记录员和助理记录员：职责

48.1　应给记录员提供记录表，他应：

- 登记比赛开始时上场的队员和所有参加比赛的替补队员的姓名和号码。当有关比赛开始时上场的5名队员、替换或队员的号码违反本规则时，他应尽快通知最靠近的裁判员。
- 记入投篮和罚球得分以及累积分。
- 记录登记在每个队员名下的犯规。当登记任一队员第五次犯规时，记录员必须立即通知裁判员。他应记录登记在每一位教练员名下的犯规。当教练员被取消比赛资格时，他必须立即通知裁判员。同样，他必须立即通知裁判员某队员已发生二次违反体育道德的犯规并应被取消比赛资格。

• 登记暂停。当某队已提出暂停请求，在下次暂停机会时通知裁判员。当教练员在该半时或决胜期中不再有剩余暂停时，他应通过裁判员通知该教练员。

• 操作交替拥有箭号来指明下一次交替拥有。在第一半时结束后，由于球队在第二半时将交换球篮，记录员应立即调整交替拥有箭号的方向。

48.2　记录员还应：

• 举牌指明每一队员发生犯规的次数，举到双方教练员看到的程度。标志牌上有该队员发生犯规的次数。

• 在一节中，某队第四次全队犯规后，当球成活球时将全队犯规标志放置在记录台上靠近该队球队席的一端。

• 实现替换。

• 仅当球成死球，并在球再次成活球之前发出他的信号。记录员的信号声响不停止比赛计时钟或比赛，也不使球成死球。

48.3　助理记录员应操纵记录板和协助记录员。至于记录板和记录表之间的任何差异不能被解决，记录表应居先，并且记录板应相应地被改正。

48.4　如果记录错误被发现：

• 在比赛中，记录员必须等到第一次死球时才发出他的信号。在比赛时间结束之后和在主裁判员签字之前，该错误应被改正，即使这个更正影响比赛的最终结果。

• 在主裁判员们已在记录表上签字之后，该错误不再可能被纠正。主裁判员必须向竞赛的组织部门送交详细的报告。

49　计时员：职责

49.1　应给计时员提供一块比赛计时钟和一块计秒表，并应：

• 计量比赛时间、暂停和比赛休息时间；

• 保证一节比赛时间结束时自动和非常洪亮地发出信号；

• 如果他的信号失灵或未被听到，他应立即使用任何可能的办法通知裁判员；

• 第三节开始前至少 3 分钟时，通知球队和裁判员。

49.2　计时员应按下列所述计量比赛时间：

• 开动比赛计时钟，当：

—跳球中，球被跳球队员合法地拍击时。

—在最后一次或仅有一次的罚球不成功，并且球继续是活球，球触及一名场上队员或被他触及时。

—掷球入界时，球触及场上队员或被他触及时。

• 停止比赛计时钟，当：

—在一节比赛时间的末尾时间终了时。

—球是活球，裁判员鸣哨时。

—某队已请求暂停，对方队投篮得分时。

—第四节的最后 2 分钟和任一决胜期的最后 2 分钟内投篮得分时。

—某队控制球时 24 秒钟装置响起信号时。

49.3　计时员应按下列所述计量要登记的暂停：

• 裁判员给出要登记的暂停手势，立即开动计时装置；

- 当要登记的暂停已走过 50 秒钟时发出他的信号；
- 当暂停已结束时发出他的信号。

49.4 计时员应按下列所述计量比赛休息期间：

- 先前的一节已结束，立即开动计时装置；
- 在第一节和第三节之前，距该节开始剩余 3 分钟、1 分钟和 30 秒钟时发出他的信号；
- 在第二节、第四节和每一决胜期之前，距该节开始剩余 30 秒钟时发出他的信号。

50 24 秒钟计时员：职责

应给 24 秒钟计时员提供一个 24 秒钟装置，并按下列要求操作该装置：

50.1 开动或重新开动，当：

- 某队在场上控制一个活球。
- 在掷球入界中，球触及或被任何一名场上队员合法触及。

如果对方队员仅仅触球，如果同一个队仍然控制球，则不开始一个新的 24 秒钟周期。

50.2 每当裁判鸣哨停止比赛，是因为：

- 宣判一起犯规或者违例(不是因为防守一方使球出界)。
- 因非控制球队的行为停止比赛。
- 因与双方球队无关的行为停止比赛，除控制球的一方被置于不利。

24 秒钟计时装置应操作如下：

(1) 停止并复位到 24 秒钟并不显示影像：

—投篮或传球的球合法中篮。

—投篮球触及对方篮圈(除非球停留在篮圈和篮板之间)。

—球队被给予一次从后场掷球入界或者罚球的权利。

—对规则的违犯是由控制球队造成的。

(2) 停止但不复位到 24 秒钟，当先前控制球的球队在他的前场被判给掷球入界的权利，这时 24 秒计时装置上显示的时间为 14 秒钟或更多。

(3) 停止并复位到 14 秒钟，当先前控制球的球队在他的前场被判给掷球入界的权利，这时 24 秒计时装置上显示的时间为 13 秒钟或更少。

50.3 停止但不复位到 24 秒钟，当原先已控制球的同一个队由于如下的结果被判给掷球入界时：

- 球出界。
- 一名同队队员受伤了。
- 一次跳球情况。
- 一起双方犯规。
- 双方球队的相等罚则抵消。

50.4 在任一节中，在球成死球并且比赛计时钟停止后，比赛计时钟的剩余时间少于 24 秒钟或 14 秒钟，则关闭 24 秒计时钟。

24 秒钟装置的信号不停止比赛计时钟或比赛，也不使球成死球，除非某队正在控制球。

第二章　篮球裁判员法定手势

在本章中阐明的手势是唯一正式的手势。它们必须被所有的裁判员在所有的比赛中使用。记录台人员也要通晓这些手势，这是很重要的。

1　得分

（1）1 分：单臂上举，出示食指，腕部下屈。

（2）2 分：单臂上举，出示食、中指，腕部下屈。

（3）3 分试投：单臂上举，出示拇、食、中指。

（4）3 分投篮成功：双臂上举，出示拇、食、中指。

（5）取消得分或取消比赛：双臂胸前交叉一次。

2　有关计时钟

（1）停止计时钟或不开动计时钟：单臂上举，五指并拢，掌心向前。

（2）犯规停止计时钟：一手臂握拳直上举，另一手臂掌心向下，直臂指向犯规队员腰部。

（3）计时开始：单臂侧上举，五指并拢，向下做“砍劈”动作。

（4）秒计时钟复位：单臂直上举，出示食指，转动腕关节。

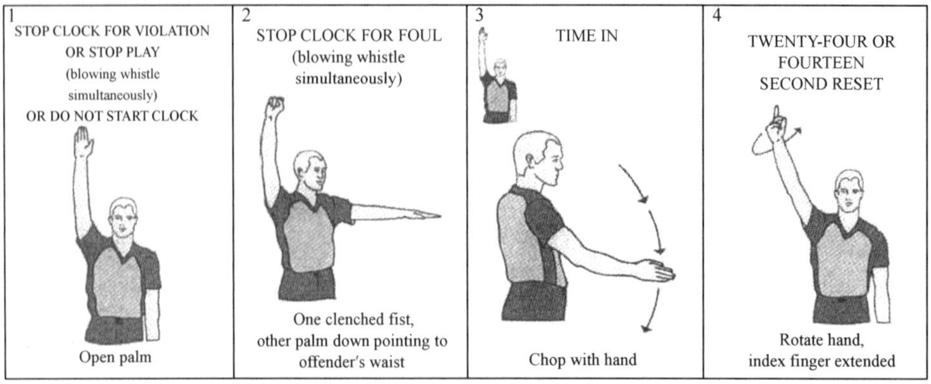

3 管理

（1）替换：两前臂胸前交叉。

（2）招呼入场：单臂前平举，手掌向身体摆动。

（3）要登记的暂停：一手五指并拢置于头上方，掌心斜向下，与另一手的食指交于掌心，双手成“T” 形。

（4）裁判员和记录台人员之间的联系：一臂平举握拳向上伸出拇指。

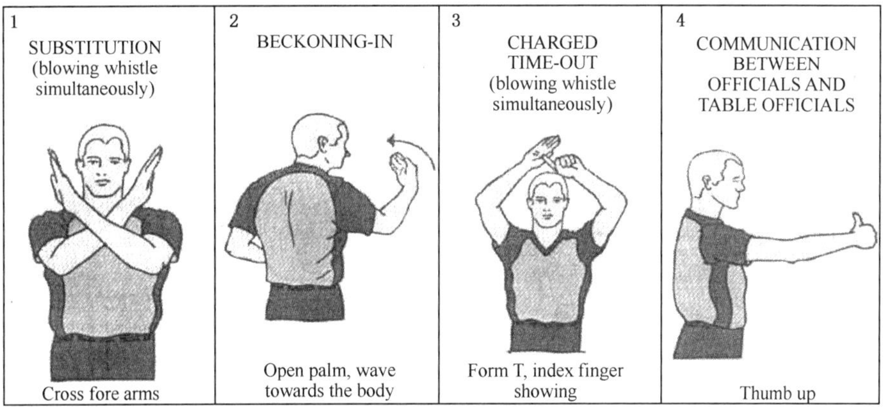

4 违例

（1）带球走：转动双拳。

（2）非法运球或两次运球：双手交替做轻拍动作。

（3）携带球：单臂体侧模仿“翻腕”动作。

（4）3 秒违例：单臂前平举，出示拇、食、中指。

（5）5 秒违例：单臂体前屈，掌心向前，出示五指。

（6）8 秒违例：双臂体前屈，掌心向前，出示八指。

（7）24 秒违例：单臂侧屈于肩上方，手指触肩。

（8）球回后场：单臂平举，用食指先指向前场再指向后场。

（9）故意脚球：一手食指指向脚面。

（10）球出界和/或进攻方向：单臂平行于边线，食指指向下一个进攻方向。

（11）跳球：双臂上举出示拇指。

5 向记录台报告犯规(三个步骤)

5.1 队员的号码

要求：手的高度与眼睛平齐，掌心、拳心向前并离开身体。

(1) 4 号：单臂体前屈，出示食、中、无名和小指。

(2) 5 号：单臂体前屈，出示五指。

(3) 6 号：双臂体前屈，一手出示五指，另一手出示食指。

(4) 7 号：双臂体前屈，一手出示五指，另一手出示食、中指。

(5) 8 号：双臂体前屈，一手出示五指，另一手出示拇、食、中指。

(6) 9 号：双臂体前屈，一手出示五指，另一手出示食、中、无名和小指。

(7) 10 号：双臂体前屈，出示十指。

(8) 11 号：双臂体前屈，一手握拳，另一手出示食指。

(9) 12 号：双臂体前屈，一手握拳，另一手出示食、中指。

(10) 13 号：双臂体前屈，一手握拳，另一手出示拇、食、中指。

(11) 14 号：双臂体前屈，一手握拳，另一手出示食、中、无名和小指。

(12) 15 号：双臂体前屈，一手握拳，另一手出示五指。

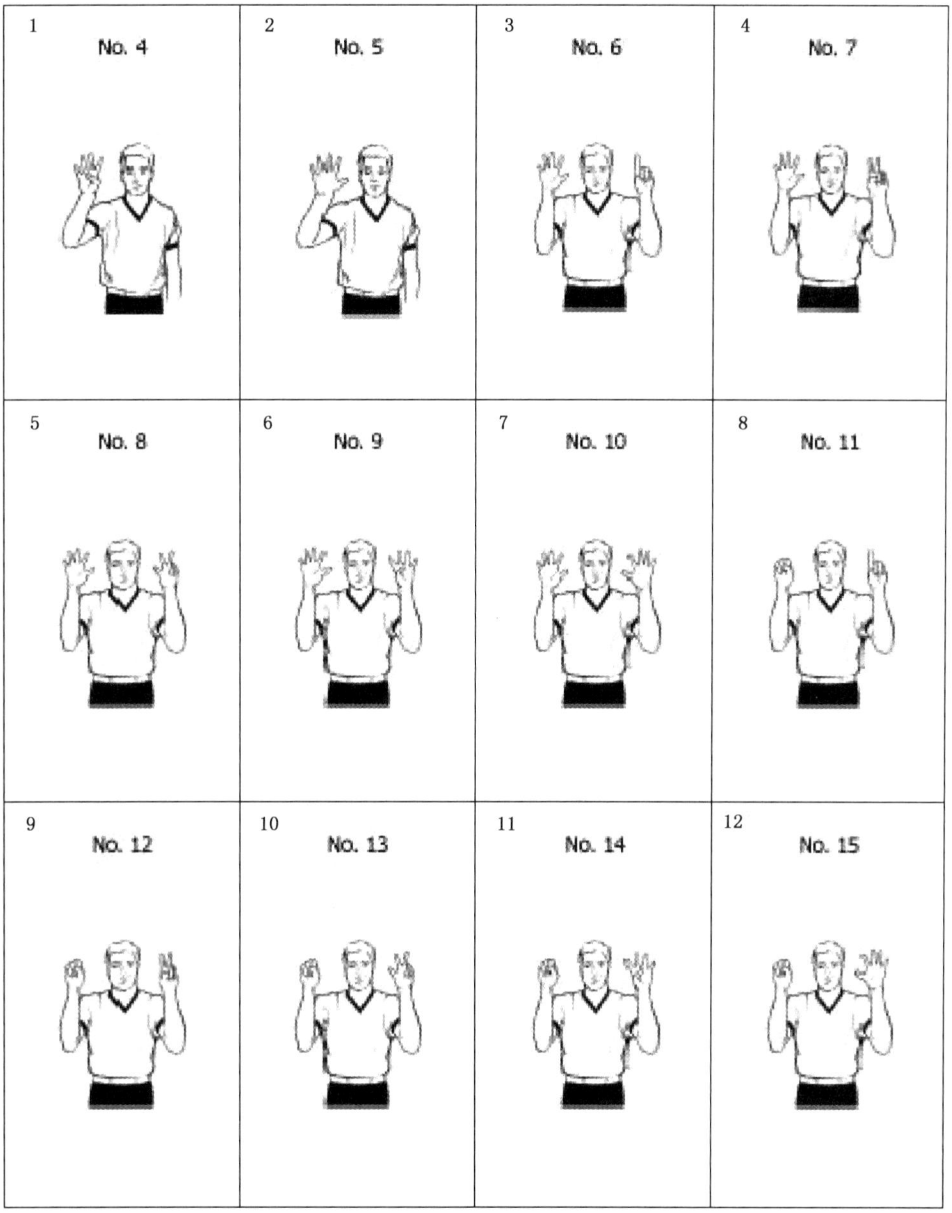

5.2 犯规的类型

(1) 非法用手：一手击另一臂腕部。

(2) 阻挡(进攻或防守)：双手置于髋部。

(3) 过分挥肘：单臂屈肘，水平后摆。

(4) 拉人：一手抓住另一臂腕部。

(5) 推人或徒手撞人：双手模仿“推”的动作。

(6) 带球撞人：一手握拳撞击另一手掌。

(7) 控制球队犯规：单手臂握拳平举，指向犯规队球篮。

(8) 双方犯规：双手臂握拳交叉摆动后，交于头上方。

(9) 技术犯规：一手五指并拢置于头上方，掌心斜向下，与另一五指并拢掌心向前的手交于掌心，双手成“T”形。

（10）违反体育道德的犯规：一手抓住另一握拳手臂的腕部置于头上方。

（11）取消比赛资格的犯规：双手臂握拳直上举。

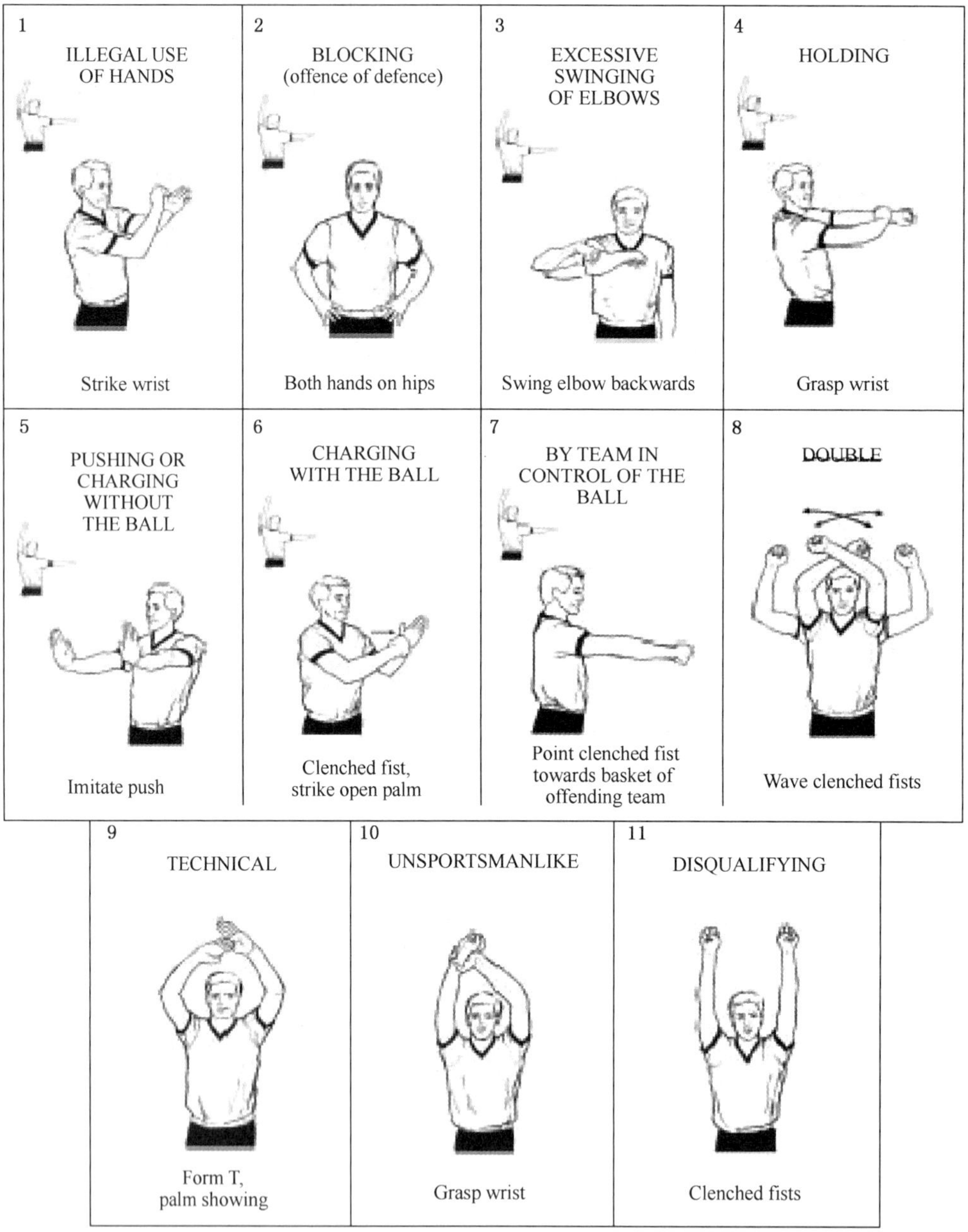

5.3 判给罚球的次数

（1）一次罚球：单臂屈肘上举，出示食指。

（2）两次罚球：单臂屈肘上举，出示食、中指。

（3）三次罚球：单臂屈肘上举，出示拇、食、中指。

（4）或进攻方向（进攻方向）：单臂平行于边线，食指指向下一个进攻方向。

（5）控制球队犯规后：单手臂握拳平行于边线，指向犯规队球篮。

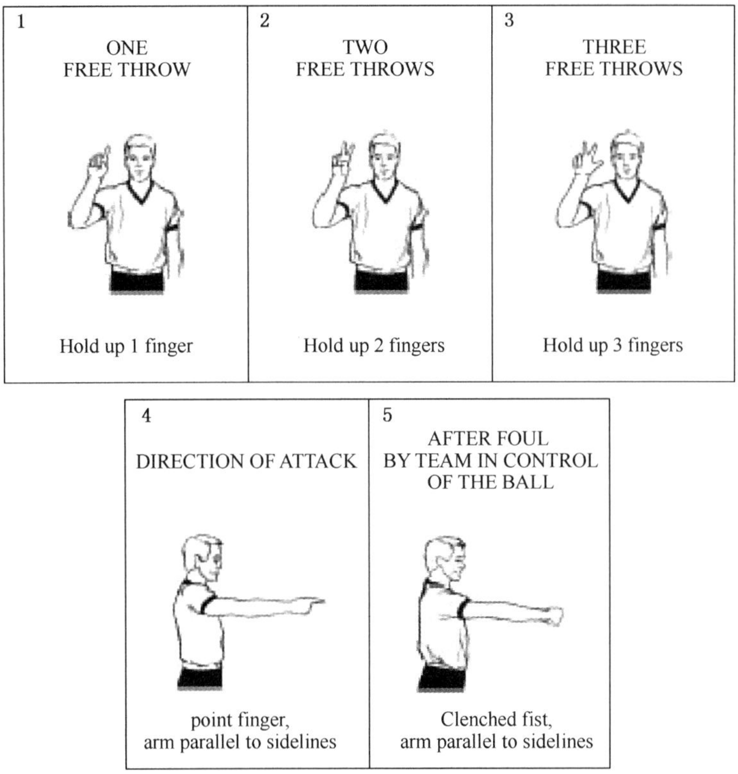

6　执行罚球(两个步骤)

6.1　在限制区内

（1）一次罚球：单臂前平举，出示食指。

（2）两次罚球：单臂前平举，出示食、中指。

（3）三次罚球：单臂前平举，出示拇、食、中指。

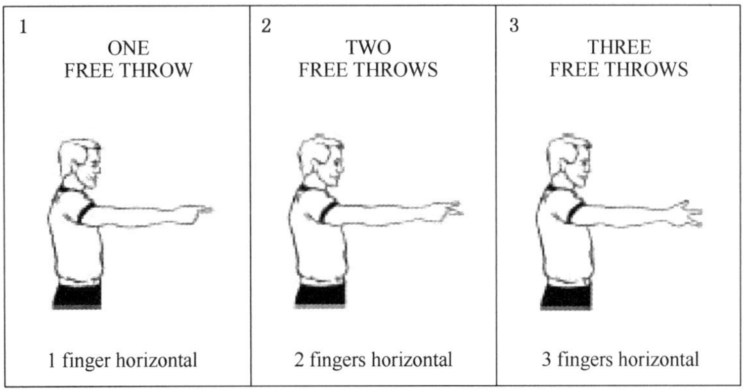

6.2　在限制区外

（1）一次罚球：单臂屈肘侧上举，使大臂与小臂、躯干保持垂直，出示食指。

（2）两次罚球：双臂屈肘侧上举，使大臂与小臂、躯干保持垂直，五指并拢，掌心向前。

（3）三次罚球：双臂屈肘侧上举，使大臂与小臂、躯干保持垂直，出示拇、中、食指。

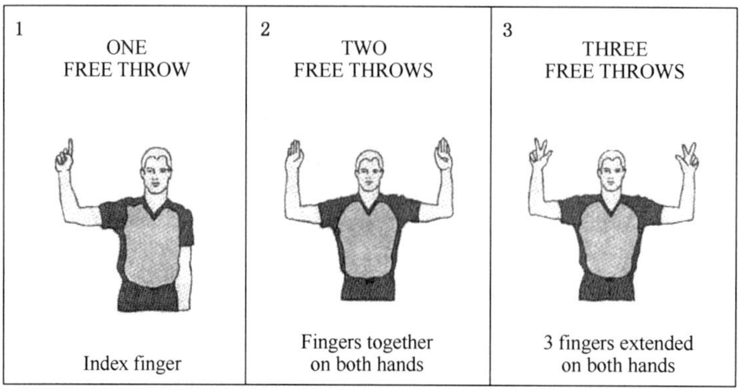

第三章 篮球英文规则

THE LAWS OF BASKETBALL

Art. 1 Definitions

1.1 Basketball game

Basketball is played by two (2) teams of five (5) players each. The aim of each team is to score in the opponents' basket and to prevent the other team from scoring.

The game is controlled by officials, table officials and a commissioner, if present.

1.2 Basket: opponents'/own

The basket that is attacked by a team is the opponents' basket and the basket which is defended by a team is the team's own basket.

1.3 Winner of a game

The team that has scored the greater number of points at the end of playing time shall be the winner.

Art. 2 Court

2.1 Playing court

The playing court shall have a flat, hard surface free from obstructions (Diagram 1) with dimensions of twenty-eight (28) m in length by fifteen (15) m in width measured from the inner edge of the boundary line.

2.2 Backcourt

A team's backcourt consists of its team's own basket, the inbounds part of the backboard and that part of the playing court limited by the endline behind the team's own basket, the sidelines and the centre line.

2.3 Frontcourt

A team's frontcourt consists of the opponents' basket, the inbounds part of the backboard and that part of the playing court limited by the endline behind the opponents' basket, the sidelines and the inner edge of the centre line nearest to the opponents' basket.

2.4 Lines

All lines shall be drawn in white colour, five (5) cm in width and clearly visible.

2.4.1 Boundary line

The playing court shall be limited by the boundary line, consisting of the endlines and the sidelines. These lines are not part of the playing court.

Any obstruction including seated team bench personnel shall be at least two (2) m from the playing court.

2.4.2 Centre line, centre circle and free-throw semi-circles

The centre line shall be marked parallel to the endlines from the mid-points of the sidelines. It shall extend 0.15 m beyond each sideline. The centre line is part of the backcourt.

The centre circle shall be marked in the centre of the playing court and have a radius of 1.80 m measured to the outer edge of the circumference. If the inside of the centre circle is painted, it must be the same colour as the restricted areas.

The free-throw semi-circles shall be marked on the playing court with a radius of 1.80 m measured to the outer edge of the circumference and with their centres at the mid-points of the free-throw lines (Diagram 2).

2.4.3 Free-throw lines, restricted areas and free-throw rebound places

The free-throw line shall be drawn parallel to each endline. It shall have its furthest edge 5.80 m from the inner edge of the endlineand shall be 3.60 m long. Its mid-point shall lie on the imaginary line joining the mid-points of the two (2) endlines.

The restricted areas shall be the rectangular areas marked on the playing court limited by the endlines, the extended free-throw lines and the lines which originate at the endlines, their outer edges being 2.45 m from the mid-points of the endlines and terminating at the outer edge of the extended free-throw lines. These lines, excluding the endlines, are part of the restricted area. The inside of the restricted areas must be painted.

Free-throw rebound places along the restricted areas, reserved for players during free throws, shall be marked as in Diagram 2.

2.4.4 Three-point field goal area

The team's three-point field goal area (Diagram 1 and Diagram 3) shall be the entire floor area of the playing court, except for the area near the opponents' basket, limited by and including:

- Two (2) parallel lines extending from and perpendicular to the endline, with the outer edge 0.90 m from the inner edge of the sidelines.
- An arc of radius 6.75 m measured from the point on the floor beneath the exact centre of the opponents' basket to the outer edge of the arc. The distance of the point on the floor from the inner edge of the mid-point of the endline is 1.575 m. The arc is joined to the parallel lines.

The three-point line is not part of the three-point field goal area.

2.4.5 Team bench areas

The team bench areas shall be marked outside the playing court limited by two (2) lines as shown in Diagram 1.

There must be fourteen (14) seats available in the team bench area for the coaches, the assistant coaches, the substitutes and the team followers. Any other persons shall be at least two (2) m behind the team bench.

2.4.6 Throw-in lines

The two (2) lines of 0.15 m in length shall be marked outside the playing court at the sideline opposite the scorer's table, with the outer edge of the lines 8.325 m from the inner edge of the nearest endline.

2.4.7 No-charge semi-circle areas

The no-charge semi-circle lines shall be marked on the playing court, limited by:

- A semi-circle with the radius of 1.25 m measured from the point on the floor beneath the exact centre of the basket to the inner edge of the semi-circle.

The semi-circle is joined to:

- Two (2) parallel lines perpendicular to the endline, the inner edge 1.25 m from the point on the floor beneath the exact centre of the basket, 0.375 m in length and ending 1.20 m from the inner edge of the endline.

The no-charge semi-circle areas are completed by imaginary lines joining the ends of the parallel lines directly below the front edges of the backboards.

The no-charge semi-circle lines are not part of the no-charge semi-circle areas.

2.5 Position of the scorer's table and substitution chairs (Diagram 4)

Art. 3 Equipment

The following equipment will be required:

- Backstop units, consisting of:

—Backboards

—Baskets comprising (pressure release) rings and nets

—Backboard support structures including padding

- Basketballs
- Game clock
- Scoreboard
- Twenty-four (24) second clock
- Stopwatch or suitable (visible) device (not the game clock) for timing time-outs
- Two (2) separate, distinctly different and loud sound signals
- Scoresheet
- Player foul markers
- Team foul markers
- Alternating possession arrow
- Playing floor
- Playing court
- Adequate lighting

For a more detailed description of basketball equipment, see Appendix on Basketball Equipment.

Art. 4 Teams

4.1 Definition

4.1.1 A team member is eligible to play when he has been authorised to play for a team according to the regulations, including regulations governing age limits, of the organising body of the competition.

4.1.2 A team member is entitled to play when his name has been entered on the scoresheet before the start of the game and as long as he has neither been disqualified nor committed five (5) fouls.

4.1.3 During playing time, a team member is:

- A player when he is on the playing court and is entitled to play.
- A substitute when he is not on the playing court but he is entitled to play.
- An excluded player when he has committed five (5) fouls and is no longer entitled to play.

4.1.4 During an interval of play, all team members entitled to play are considered as players.

4.2 Rule

4.2.1 Each team shall consist of:

- No more than twelve (12) team members entitled to play, including a captain.
- A coach and, if a team wishes, an assistant coach.
- A maximum of five (5) team followers who may sit on the team bench and have special responsibilities, e.g. manager, doctor, physiotherapist, statistician, interpreter, etc.

4.2.2 Five (5) players from each team shall be on the playing court during playing time and may be substituted.

4.2.3 A substitute becomes a player and a player becomes a substitute when:

- The official beckons the substitute to enter the playing court.
- During a time-out or an interval of play, a substitute requests the substitution to the scorer.

4.3 Uniforms

4.3.1 The uniform of the team members shall consist of:

- Shirts of the same dominant colour front and back.

All players must tuck their shirts into their playing shorts. "All-in-ones" are permitted.

- Shorts of the same dominant colour front and back, but not necessarily of the same colour as the shirts.
- Socks of the same dominant colour for all players of the team.

4.3.2 Each team member shall wear a shirt numbered on the front and back with plain numbers, of a solid colour contrasting with the colour of the shirt.

The numbers shall be clearly visible and:

- Those on the back shall be at least twenty (20) cm high.
- Those on the front shall be at least ten (10) cm high.
- The numbers shall be at least two (2) cm wide.
- Teams shall use numbers from four (4) to fifteen (15). National federations have the authority to approve, for their competitions, any other numbers with a maximum of two (2) digits.
- Players on the same team shall not wear the same number.
- Any advertising or logo shall be at least five (5) cm away from the numbers.

4.3.3 Teams must have a minimum of two (2) sets of shirts and:

- The first team named in the programme (home team) shall wear light-coloured shirts (preferably white).
- The second team named in the programme (visiting team) shall wear darkcoloured shirts.

• However, if the two (2) teams agree, they may interchange the colours of the shirts.

4.4 Other equipment

4.4.1 All equipment used by players must be appropriate for the game. Any equipment that is designed to increase a player's height or reach or in any other way give an unfair advantage is not permitted.

4.4.2 Players shall not wear equipment (objects) that may cause injury to other players.

• The following are not permitted:

—Finger, hand, wrist, elbow or forearm guards, casts or braces made of leather, plastic, pliable (soft) plastic, metal or any other hard substance, even if covered with soft padding.

—Objects that could cut or cause abrasions (fingernails must be closely cut).

—Headgear, hair accessories and jewellery.

• The following are permitted:

—Shoulder, upper arm, thigh or lower leg protective equipment if the material is sufficiently padded.

—Undergarments that extend below the shorts of the same dominant colour as the shorts.

—Compression sleeves of the same dominant colour as the shirts.

—Compression stockings of the same dominant colour as the shorts. If for the upper leg it must end above the knee; if for the lower leg it must end below the knee.

—Knee braces if they are properly covered.

—Protector for an injured nose, even if made of a hard material.

—Non-coloured transparent mouth guard.

—Spectacles, if they do not pose a danger to other players.

—Headbands, maximum five (5) cm in width, made of non-abrasive, unicolour cloth, pliable plastic or rubber.

—Non-coloured transparent taping of arms, shoulders, legs, etc.

4.4.3 During the game a player may not display any commercial, promotional or charitable name, mark, logo or other identification including, but not limited to, on his body, in his hair or otherwise.

4.4.4 Any other equipment not specifically mentioned in this article must be approved by the FIBA Technical Commission.

Art. 5 Players: Injury

5.1 In the event of injury to a player(s), the officials may stop the game.

5.2 If the ball is live when an injury occurs, the official shall not blow his whistle until the team in control of the ball has shot for a field goal, lost control of the ball, withheld the ball from play or the ball has become dead. If it is necessary to protect an injured player, the officials may stop the game immediately.

5.3 If the injured player cannot continue to play immediately (within approximately 15 seconds) or, if he receives treatment, he must be substituted unless the team is reduced to fewer than five (5) players on the playing court.

5.4 Coaches, assistant coaches, substitutes, excluded players and team followers may enter the playing court, with the permission of an official, to attend to an injured player beforehe is substituted.

5.5 A doctor may enter the playing court, without permission of an official if, in the doctor's judgement, the injured player requires immediate medical treatment.

5.6 During the game, any player who is bleeding or has an open wound must be substituted. He may return to the playing court only after bleeding has stopped and the affected area or open wound has been completely and securely covered.

If the injured player or any player who is bleeding or has an open wound recovers during a time-out taken by either team before the scorer's signal for the substitution, that player may continue to play.

5.7 Players who have been designated by the coach to start the game may be substituted in the event of an injury. In this case, the opponents are also entitled to substitute the same number of players, if they so wish.

Art. 6 Captain: Duties and powers

6.1 The captain (CAP) is a player designated by his coach to represent his team on the playing court. He may communicate in a courteous manner with the officials during the game to obtain information, however, only when the ball becomes dead and the game clock is stopped.

6.2 The captain shall, immediately at the end of the game, inform the referee if his team is protesting against the result of the game and sign the scoresheet in the space marked "Captain's signature in case of protest".

Art. 7 Coaches: Duties and powers

7.1 At least twenty (20) minutes before the game is scheduled to begin, each coach or his representative shall give the scorer a list with the names and corresponding numbers of the team members who are eligible to play in the game, as well as the name of the captain of the team, the coach and the assistant coach. All team members whose names are entered on the scoresheet are entitled to play, even if they arrive after the beginning of the game.

7.2 At least ten (10) minutes before the game is scheduled to begin, each coach shall confirm his agreement with the names and corresponding numbers of his team members and the names of the coaches by signing the scoresheet. At the same time, they shall indicate the five (5) players who are to start the game. The coach of team "A" shall be the first to provide this information.

7.3 The coaches, assistant coaches, team members and team followers are the only persons permitted to sit on the team bench and remain within their team bench area.

7.4 The coach and the assistant coach may go to the scorer's table during the game to obtain statistical information only when the ball becomes dead and the game clock is stopped.

7.5 Only the coach is permitted to remain standing during the game. He may address the players verbally during the game provided he remains within his team bench area.

7.6 If there is an assistant coach his name must be entered on the scoresheet before the beginning of the game (his signature is not necessary). He shall assume all duties and powers of the coach if, for any reason, the coach is unable to continue.

7.7 When the captain leaves the playing court the coach shall inform an official of the number of the player who will act as captain on the playing court.

7.8 The captain shall act as coach if there is no coach, or if the coach is unable to continue and there is no assistant coach entered on the scoresheet (or the latter is unable to continue). If the captain must leave the playing court, he may continue to act as coach. If he must leave following a disqualifying foul, or if he is unable to act as coach because of injury, his substitute as captain may replace him as coach.

7.9 The coach shall designate the free-throw shooter of his team in all cases where the free-throw shooter is not determined by the rules.

Art. 8 Playing time, tied score and extra periods

8.1 The game shall consist of four (4) periods of ten (10) minutes.

8.2 There shall be an interval of play of twenty (20) minutes before the game is scheduled to begin.

8.3 There shall be intervals of play of two (2) minutes between the first and second period (first half), between the third and fourth period (second half) and before each extra period.

8.4 There shall be a half-time interval of play of fifteen (15) minutes.

8.5 An interval of play begins:

- Twenty (20) minutes before the game is scheduled to begin.
- When the game clock signal sounds for the end of a period.

8.6 An interval of play ends:

- At the beginning of the first period when the ball leaves the hand(s) of the referee on the jump ball.
- At the beginning of all other periods when the ball is at the disposal of the player taking the throw-in.

8.7 If the score is tied at the end of playing time for the fourth period, the game shall continue with as many extra periods of five (5) minutes as is necessary to break the tie.

8.8 If a foul is committed when or just before the game clock signal sounds for the end of playing time, any eventual free throw(s) shall be administered after the end of playing time.

8.9 If an extra period is required as a result of this free throw(s) then all fouls that are committed after the end of playing time shall be considered to have occurred during an interval of play and the free throws shall be administered before the beginning of the extra period.

Art. 9 Beginning and end of a period or the game

9.1 The first period begins when the ball leaves the hand(s) of the referee on the jump ball.

9.2 All other periods begin when the ball is at the disposal of the player taking the throw-in.

9.3 The game cannot begin if one of the teams is not on the playing court with five (5) players ready to play.

9.4 For all games, the first team named in the programme (home team) shall have the team bench and its team's own basket on the left side of the scorer's table, facing the playing court.

However, if the two (2) teams agree, they may interchange the team benches and/or baskets.

9.5 Before the first and third period, teams are entitled to warm-up in the half of the playing court in which their opponents' basket is situated.

9.6 Teams shall exchange baskets for the second half.

9.7 In all extra periods the teams shall continue to play towards the same baskets as in the fourth period.

9.8 A period, extra period or game shall end when the game clock signal sounds for the end of the period.

Art. 10 Status of the ball

10.1 The ball can be either live or dead.

10.2 The ball becomes live when:

- During the jump ball, the ball leaves the hand(s) of the referee on the toss.
- During a free throw, the ball is at the disposal of the free-throw shooter.
- During a throw-in, the ball is at the disposal of the player taking the throw-in.

10.3 The ball becomes dead when:

- Any field goal or free throw is made.
- An official blows his whistle while the ball is live.
- It is apparent that the ball will not enter the basket on a free throw which is to be followed by:

—Another free throw(s).

—A further penalty (free throw(s) and/or possession).

- The game clock signal sounds for the end of the period.
- The twenty-four (24) second clock signal sounds while a team is in control of the ball.
- The ball in flight on a shot for a field goal is touched by a player from either team after:

—An official blows his whistle.

—The game clock signal sounds for the end of the period.

—The twenty-four (24) second clock signal sounds.

10.4 The ball does not become dead and the goal counts if made when:

- The ball is in flight on a shot for a field goal and:

—An official blows his whistle.

—The game clock signal sounds for the end of the period.

—The twenty-four (24) second clock signal sounds.

- The ball is in flight on a free throw when an official blows his whistle for any rule infraction other than by the free-throw shooter.

- A player commits a foul on any opponent while the ball is in the control of the opponent in the act of shooting for a field goal and who finishes his shot with a continuous motion which started before the foul occurred.

This provision does not apply and the goal shall not count if

—after an official blows his whistle an entirely new act of shooting is made.

—during the continuous motion of a player in the act of shooting the game clock signal sounds for an end of period or the twenty-four (24) second clock signal sounds.

Art. 11 Location of a player and an official

11.1 The location of a player is determined by where he is touching the floor.

While he is airborne, he retains the same status he had when he last touched the floor. This includes the boundary line, the centre line, the three-point line, the freethrow line, the lines delimiting the restricted area and the lines delimiting the nocharge semi-circle area.

11.2 The location of an official is determined in the same manner as that of a player.

When the ball touches an official, it is the same as touching the floor at the official's location.

Art. 12 Jump ball and alternating possession

12.1 Jump ball definition

12.1.1 A jump ball occurs when an official tosses the ball in the centre circle between any two (2) opponents at the beginning of the first period.

12.1.2 A held ball occurs when one or more players of each opposing team have one or both hands firmly on the ball so that neither player can gain control without undue roughness.

12.2 Jump ball procedure

12.2.1 Each jumper shall stand with both feet inside the half of the centre circle nearest to his team's own basket with one foot close to the centre line.

12.2.2 Team-mates may not occupy adjacent positions around the circle if an opponent wishes to occupy one of those positions.

12.2.3 The official shall then toss the ball vertically upwards between the two (2) opponents, higher than either of them can reach by jumping.

12.2.4 The ball must be tapped with the hand(s) of at least one of the jumpers after it reaches its highest point.

12.2.5 Neither jumper shall leave his position until the ball has been legally tapped.

12.2.6 Neither jumper may catch the ball or tap it more than twice until it has touched one of the non-jumpers or the floor.

12.2.7 If the ball is not tapped by at least one of the jumpers, the jump ball shall be repeated.

12.2.8 No part of a non-jumper's body may be on or over the circle line (cylinder) before the ball has been tapped.

An infraction of Art. 12.2.1, 12.2.4, 12.2.5, 12.2.6, and 12.2.8 is a violation.

12.3 Jump ball situations

A jump ball situation occurs when:

- A held ball is called.
- The ball goes out-of-bounds and the officials are in doubt or disagree about which of the opponents last touched the ball.
- A double free-throw violation occurs during an unsuccessful last or only free throw.
- A live ball lodges between the ring and the backboard (except between free throws).
- The ball becomes dead when neither team had control of the ball nor was entitled to the ball.
- After the cancellation of equal penalties against both teams, there are no other foul penalties remaining for administration and neither team had control of the ball nor was entitled to the ball before the first foul or violation.
- All periods other than the first period are to begin.

12.4 Alternating possession definition

12.4.1 Alternating possession is a method of causing the ball to become live with a throw-in rather than a jump ball.

12.4.2 Alternating possession throw-in:

- Begins when the ball is at the disposal of the player taking the throw-in.
- Ends when:

—The ball touches or is legally touched by a player on the playing court.

—The team taking the throw-in commits a violation.

—A live ball lodges between the ring and the backboard during a throw-in.

12.5 Alternating possession procedure

12.5.1 In all jump ball situations teams will alternate possession of the ball for a throw-in at the place nearest to where the jump ball situation occurs.

12.5.2 The team that does not gain control of the live ball on the playing court after the jump ball will be entitled to the first alternating possession.

12.5.3 The team entitled to the next alternating possession at the end of any period shall start the next period with a throw-in at the centre line extended, opposite the scorer's table, unless there are further free throws and a possession penalty to be administered.

12.5.4 The team entitled to the alternating possession throw-in shall be indicated by the alternating possession arrow in the direction of the opponents' basket. The direction of the alternating possession arrow will be reversed immediately when the alternating possession throw-in ends.

12.5.5 A violation by a team during its alternating possession throw-in causes that team to lose the alternating possession throw-in. The direction of the alternating possession arrow will be reversed immediately, indicating that the opponents of the violating team will be entitled to the alternating possession throw-in at the next jump ball situation. The game shall then be resumed by awarding the ball to the opponents of the violating team for a throw-in at the place of the original throw-in.

12.5.6 A foul by either team:

- Before the beginning of a period other than the first period, or
- During the alternating possession throw-in, does not cause the team entitled to the throw-in to lose that alternating possession.

Art. 13 How the ball is played

13.1 Definition

During the game, the ball is played with the hand(s) only and may be passed, thrown, tapped, rolled or dribbled in any direction, subject to the restrictions of these rules.

13.2 Rule

A player shall not run with the ball, deliberately kick or block it with any part of the leg or strike it with the fist.

However, to accidentally come into contact with or touch the ball with any part of the leg is not a violation.

An infraction of Art. 13.2 is a violation.

Art. 14 Control of the ball

14.1 Definition

14.1.1 Team control starts when a player of that team is in control of a live ball by holding or dribbling it or has a live ball at his disposal.

14.1.2 Team control continues when:

A player of that team is in control of a live ball.

The ball is being passed between team-mates.

14.1.3 Team control ends when:

An opponent gains control.

The ball becomes dead.

The ball has left the player's hand(s) on a shot for a field goal or for a free throw.

Art. 15 Player in the act of shooting

15.1 Definition

15.1.1 A shot for a field goal or a free throw is when the ball is held in a player's hand(s) and is then thrown into the air towards the opponents' basket.

A tap is when the ball is directed with the hand(s) towards the opponents' basket.

A dunk is when the ball is forced downwards into the opponents' basket with one or both hands.

A tap and a dunk are also considered as shots for a field goal.

15.1.2 The act of shooting:

Begins when the player starts the continuous movement normally preceding the release of the ball and, in the judgement of an official, he has started an attempt to score by throwing, tapping or dunking the ball towards the opponents' basket.

Ends when the ball has left the player's hand(s) and, in case of an airborne shooter, both feet have returned to the floor.

The player attempting to score might have his arm(s) held by an opponent, thus preventing him from scoring, even though he is considered to have made an attempt to score. In this case it is not essential that the ball leaves the player's hand(s).

There is no relationship between the number of legal steps taken and the act of shooting.

15.1.3 A continuous movement in the act of shooting:

Begins when the ball has come to rest in the player's hand(s) and the shooting motion, usually upward, has started.

May include the player's arm(s) and/or body movement in his attempt to shoot for a field goal.

Ends when the ball has left the player's hand(s), or if an entirely new act of shooting is made.

Art. 16 Goal: When made and its value

16.1 Definition

16.1.1 A goal is made when a live ball enters the basket from above and remains within or passes through the basket.

16.1.2 The ball is considered to be within the basket when the slightest part of the ball is within and below the level of the ring.

16.2 Rule

16.2.1 A goal is credited to the team attacking the opponents' basket into which the ball has entered as follows:

A goal from a free throw counts one (1) point.

A goal from the two-point field goal area counts two (2) points.

A goal from the three-point field goal area counts three (3) points.

After the ball has touched the ring on a last or only free throw and is legally touched by an offensive or defensive player before it enters the basket, the goal counts two (2) points.

16.2.2 If a player accidentally scores a field goal in his team's own basket, the goal counts two (2) points and shall be recorded as having been scored by the captain of the opposing team on the playing court.

16.2.3 If a player deliberately scores a field goal in his team's own basket, it is a violation and the goal does not count.

16.2.4 If a player causes the entire ball to pass through the basket from below, it is a violation.

16.2.5 The game clock must indicate 0:00.3 (three tenths of a second) or more for a player to gain control of the ball on a throw-in or on a rebound after the last or only free throw in order to attempt a shot for a field goal. If the game clock indicates 0:00.2 or 0:00.1 the only type of a valid field goal made is by tapping or directly dunking the ball.

Art. 17 Throw-in

17.1 Definition

17.1.1 A throw-in occurs when the ball is passed into the playing court by the out-ofbounds player taking the throw-in.

17.2 Procedure

17.2.1 An official must hand or place the ball at the disposal of the player taking the throw-in.

He may also toss or bounce pass the ball provided that:

The official is no more than four (4) m from the player taking the throw-in.

The player taking the throw-in is at the correct place as designated by the official.

17.2.2 The player shall take the throw-in at the place nearest to the infraction or where the game was stopped by the official, except directly behind the backboard.

17.2.3 In the following situations the subsequent throw-in shall be administered at the centre line extended, opposite the scorer's table:

At the beginning of all periods other than the first period.

Following a free throw(s) resulting from a technical, unsportsmanlike or disqualifying foul.

The player taking the throw-in shall have one foot on either side of the centre line extended, opposite the scorer's table, and shall be entitled to pass the ball to a team-mate at any place on the playing court.

17.2.4 During the last two (2) minutes of the fourth period and during the last two (2) minutes of each extra period, following a time-out taken by the team that is entitled to possession of the ball from its backcourt the throw-in shall be administered at the throw-in line opposite the scorer's table in the team's frontcourt.

17.2.5 Following a personal foul committed by a player of the team in control of the live ball, or of the team entitled to the ball, the subsequent throw-in shall be administered at the place nearest to the infraction.

17.2.6 Whenever the ball enters the basket but the field goal or the free throw is not valid, the subsequent throw-in shall be administered at the free-throw line extended.

17.2.7 Following a successful field goal or a successful last or only free throw:

Any player of the non-scoring team shall take the throw-in at any place behind that team's endline. This is also applicable after an official hands or places the ball at the disposal of the player taking the throw-in after a time-out or after any interruption of the game following a successful field goal or a successful last or only free throw.

The player taking the throw-in may move laterally and/or backwards and the ball may be passed between team-mates behind the endline, but the five (5) second count starts when the ball is at the disposal of the first player out-of bounds.

17.3 Rule

17.3.1 The player taking the throw-in shall not:

Take more than five (5) seconds to release the ball.

Step into the playing court while having the ball in his hand(s).

Cause the ball to touch out-of-bounds, after it has been released on the throw-in.

Touch the ball on the playing court before it has touched another player.

Cause the ball to enter the basket directly.

Move from the designated throw-in place behind the boundary line, other than from his team's endline after a successful field goal or a successful last free throw, laterally in one (1) or in both directions, exceeding a total distance of one (1) m before releasing the ball. He is, however, permitted to move directly backwards from the boundary line as far as circumstances allow.

17.3.2 During the throw-in other player(s) shall not:

Have any part of their bodies over the boundary line before the ball has been thrown-in across the boundary line.

Be closer than one (1) m to the player taking the throw-in when the throw-in place has less than two (2) m between the boundary line and any out-of-bounds obstructions.

An infraction of Art. 17.3 is a violation.

17.4 Penalty

The ball is awarded to the opponents for a throw-in at the place of the original throw-in.

Art. 18 Time-out

18.1 Definition

A time-out is an interruption of the game requested by the coach or assistant coach.

18.2 Rule

18.2.1 Each time-out shall last one (1) minute.

18.2.2 A time-out may be granted during a time-out opportunity.

18.2.3 A time-out opportunity begins when:

For both teams, the ball becomes dead, the game clock is stopped and the official has ended his communication with the scorer's table.

For both teams, the ball becomes dead following a successful last or only free throw.

For the non-scoring team, a field goal is scored.

18.2.4 A time-out opportunity ends when the ball is at the disposal of a player for a throw-in or for a first or only free throw.

18.2.5 Two (2) time-outs may be granted to each team at any time during the first half; three (3) at any time during the second half and one (1) during each extra period.

18.2.6 Unused time-outs may not be carried over to the next half or extra period.

18.2.7 A time-out is charged against the team whose coach first made a request unless the time-out is granted following a field goal scored by the opponents and without an infraction having been called.

18.2.8 A time-out shall not be permitted to the scoring team when the game clock is stopped following a successful field goal during the last two (2) minutes of the fourth period or the last two (2) minutes of each extra period unless an official has stopped the game.

18.3 Procedure

18.3.1 Only a coach or assistant coach has the right to request a time-out. He shall establish visual contact with the scorer or he shall go to the scorer's table and ask clearly for a time-out, making the proper conventional sign with his hands.

18.3.2 A time-out request may be cancelled only before the scorer's signal has sounded for such a request.

18.3.3 The time-out period:

Begins when an official blows his whistle and gives the time-out signal.

Ends when the official blows his whistle and beckons the teams back on the playing court.

18.3.4 As soon as a time-out opportunity begins, the scorer shall sound his signal to notify the officials that a request for a time-out has been made.

If a field goal is scored against a team which has requested a time-out, the timer shall immediately stop the game clock and sound his signal.

18.3.5 During the time-out and during an interval of play before the beginning of the second, fourth or each extra period the players may leave the playing court and sit on the team bench and the persons permitted to be in the team bench area may enter the playing court provided the team members remain within the vicinity of their team bench area.

18.3.6 If the request for the time-out is made by either team after the ball is at the disposal of the free-throw shooter for the first or only free throw, the time-out shall be granted if:

The last or only free throw is successful.

The last or only free throw is followed by a throw-in at the centre line extended, opposite the scorer's table.

A foul is called between free throws. In this case the free throw(s) will be completed and the time-out will be permitted before the new foul penalty is administered.

A foul is called before the ball becomes live after the last or only free throw. In this case the time-out will be permitted before the new foul penalty is administered.

A violation is called before the ball becomes live after the last or only free throw. In this case the time-out will be permitted before the throw-in is administered.

In the event of consecutive sets of free throws and/or possession of the ball resulting from more than one (1) foul penalty, each set is to be treated separately.

Art. 19 Substitution

19.1 Definition

A substitution is an interruption of the game requested by the substitute to become a player.

19.2 Rule

19.2.1 A team may substitute a player(s) during a substitution opportunity.

19.2.2 A substitution opportunity begins when:

For both teams, the ball becomes dead, the game clock is stopped and the official has ended his communication with the scorer's table.

For both teams, the ball becomes dead following a successful last or only free throw.

For the non-scoring team, a field goal is scored in the last two (2) minutes of the fourth period or the last two (2) minutes of each extra period.

19.2.3 A substitution opportunity ends when the ball is at the disposal of a player for a throw-in or a first or only free throw.

19.2.4 A player who has become a substitute and a substitute who has become a player cannot respectively re-enter the game or leave the game until the ball becomes dead again, after a clock-running phase of the game, unless:

The team is reduced to fewer than five (5) players on the playing court.

The player entitled to the free-throws as the result of the correction of an error is on the team bench after having been legally substituted.

19.2.5 A substitution shall not be permitted to the scoring team when the game clock is stopped following a successful field goal during the last two (2) minutes of the fourth period or the last two (2) minutes of each extra period unless an official has stopped the game.

19.3 Procedure

19.3.1 Only a substitute has the right to request a substitution. He (not the coach or the assistant coach) shall go to the scorer's table and ask clearly for a substitution or sit on the substitution chair. He must be ready to play immediately.

19.3.2 A substitution request may be cancelled only before the scorer's signal has sounded for such a request.

19.3.3 As soon as a substitution opportunity begins the scorer shall sound his signal to notify the officials that a request for a substitution has been made.

19.3.4 The substitute shall remain outside the boundary line until the official blows his whistle, gives the substitution signal and beckons him to enter the playing court.

19.3.5 The player being substituted is permitted to go directly to his team bench without reporting either to the scorer or the official.

19.3.6 Substitutions shall be completed as quickly as possible. A player who has committed his five (5) fouls or has been disqualified must be substituted immediately (within approximately 30 seconds). If, in the judgement of an official, there is a delay of the game, a time-out shall be charged against the offending team. If the team has no time-out remaining a technical foul for delaying the game may be charged against the coach, recorded as 'B'.

19.3.7 If a substitution is requested during a time-out or during an interval of play other than the half-time interval, the substitute must report to the scorer before entering the game.

19.3.8 If the free-throw shooter must be substituted because he:

Is injured.

Has committed his five (5) fouls.

Has been disqualified.

The free throw(s) must be attempted by his substitute who may not be substituted again until he has played in the next clock-running phase of the game.

19.3.9 If the request for a substitution is made by either team after the ball is at the disposal of the free-throw shooter for the first or only free throw, the substitution shall be granted if:

The last or only free throw is successful.

The last or only free throw is followed by a throw-in at the centre line extended, opposite the scorer's table.

A foul is called between free throws. In this case the free throw(s) will be completed and the substitution will be permitted before the new foul penalty is administered.

A foul is called before the ball becomes live after the last or only free throw. In this case the substitution will be permitted before the new foul penalty is administered.

A violation is called before the ball becomes live after the last or only free throw. In this case the substitution will be permitted before the throw-in is administered.

In the event of consecutive sets of free throws resulting from more than one (1) foul penalty, each set is to be treated separately.

Art. 20 Game lost by forfeit

20.1 Rule

A team shall lose the game by forfeit if:

Fifteen (15) minutes after the scheduled starting time, the team is not present or is unable to field five (5) players ready to play.

Its actions prevent the game from being played.

It refuses to play after being instructed to do so by the referee.

20.2 Penalty

20.2.1 The game is awarded to the opponents and the score shall be twenty to zero (20 to 0). Furthermore, the forfeiting team shall receive zero (0) points in the classification.

20.2.2 For a two-game (home and away) total points series and for Play-Offs (best of three), the team that forfeits in the first, second or third game shall lose the series or Play-Offs by 'forfeit'. This does not apply for Play-Offs (best of five).

20.2.3 If in a tournament the team forfeits for the second time, the team shall be disqualified from the tournament and the results of all games played by this team shall be nullified.

Art. 21 Game lost by default

21.1 Rule

A team shall lose a game by default if, during the game, the team has fewer than two (2) players on the playing court ready to play.

21.2 Penalty

21.2.1 If the team to which the game is awarded is ahead, the score shall stand as at the time when the game was stopped. If the team to which the game is awarded is not ahead, the score shall be recorded as two to zero (2 to 0) in its favour. The defaulting team shall receive one (1) point in the classification.

21.2.2 For a two-game (home and away) total point series, the team that defaults in the first or in the second game shall lose the series by 'default'.

Art. 22 Violations

22.1 Definition

A violation is an infraction of the rules.

22.2 Penalty

The ball shall be awarded to the opponents for a throw-in at the place nearest to the infraction, except directly behind the backboard, unless otherwise stated in the rules.

Art. 23 Player out-of-bounds and ball out-of-bounds

23.1 Definition

23.1.1 A player is out-of-bounds when any part of his body is in contact with the floor or any object other than a player, on, above or outside the boundary line.

23.1.2 The ball is out-of-bounds when it touches:

A player or any other person who is out-of-bounds.

The floor or any object on, above or outside the boundary line.

The backboard supports, the back of the backboards or any object above the playing court.

23.2 Rule

23.2.1 The ball is caused to go out-of-bounds by the last player to touch or be touched by the ball before it goes out-of-bounds, even if the ball then goes out-of-bounds by touching something other than a player.

23.2.2 If the ball is out-of-bounds because of touching or being touched by a player who is on or outside the boundary line, this player causes the ball to go out-of-bounds.

23.2.3 If a player(s) move(s) to out-of-bounds or to his backcourt during a held ball, a jump ball situation occurs.

Art. 24 Dribbling

24.1 Definition

24.1.1 A dribble is the movement of a live ball caused by a player in control of that ball who throws, taps, rolls the ball on the floor or deliberately throws it against the backboard.

24.1.2 A dribble starts when a player, having gained control of a live ball on the playing court, throws, taps, rolls, dribbles it on the floor or deliberately throws it against the backboard and touches it again before it touches another player.

A dribble ends when the player touches the ball with both hands simultaneously or permits the ball to come to rest in one or both hands.

During a dribble the ball may be thrown into the air provided the ball touches the floor or another player before the player who threw it touches it again with his hand.

There is no limit to the number of steps a player may take when the ball is not in contact with his hand.

24.1.3 A player who accidentally loses and then regains control of a live ball on the playing court is considered to be fumbling the ball.

24. 1. 4 The following are not dribbles:

Successive shots for a field goal.

Fumbling the ball at the beginning or at the end of a dribble.

Attempts to gain control of the ball by tapping it from the vicinity of other players.

Tapping the ball from the control of another player.

Deflecting a pass and gaining control of the ball.

Tossing the ball from hand to hand and allowing it to come to rest in one or both hands before touching the floor, provided that no travelling violation is committed.

24. 2 Rule

A player shall not dribble a second time after his first dribble has ended unless between the two (2) dribbles he has lost control of a live ball on the playing court because of:

A shot for a field goal.

A touch of the ball by an opponent.

A pass or fumble that has touched or been touched by another player.

Art. 25 Travelling

25. 1 Definition

25. 1. 1 Travelling is the illegal movement of one foot or both feet beyond the limits outlined in this article, in any direction, while holding a live ball on the playing court.

25. 1. 2 A pivot is the legal movement in which a player who is holding a live ball on the playing court steps once or more than once in any direction with the same foot, while the other foot, called the pivot foot, is kept at its point of contact with the floor.

25. 2 Rule

25. 2. 1 Establishing a pivot foot for a player who catches a live ball on the playing court:

While standing with both feet on the floor:

—The moment one foot is lifted, the other foot becomes the pivot foot.

While moving:

—If one foot is touching the floor, that foot becomes the pivot foot.

—If both feet are off the floor and the player lands on both feet simultaneously, the moment one foot is lifted, the other foot becomes the pivot foot.

—If both feet are off the floor and the player lands on one foot, then that foot becomes the pivot foot. If a player jumps off that foot and comes to a stop landing on both feet simultaneously, then neither foot is a pivot foot.

25. 2. 2 Progressing with the ball for a player who has established a pivot foot while having the control of a live ball on the playing court:

While standing with both feet on the floor:

—To start a dribble, the pivot foot may not be lifted before the ball is released from the hand(s).

—To pass or shoot for a field goal, the player may jump off a pivot foot, but neither foot may be returned to the floor before the ball is released from the hand(s).

While moving:

—To pass or shoot for a field goal, the player may jump off a pivot foot and land on one foot or both feet simultaneously. After that, one foot or both feet may be lifted from the floor but neither foot may be returned to the floor before the ball is released from the hand(s).

—To start a dribble, the pivot foot may not be lifted before the ball is released from the hand(s).

While coming to a stop when neither foot is the pivot foot:

—To start a dribble, neither foot may be lifted before the ball is released from the hand(s).

—To pass or shoot for a field goal, one foot or both feet may be lifted but may not be returned to the floor before the ball is released from the hand(s).

25.2.3 Player falling, lying or sitting on the floor:

It is legal when a player falls and slides on the floor while holding the ball or, while lying or sitting on the floor, gains control of the ball.

It is a violation if the player then rolls or attempts to stand up while holding the ball.

Art. 26 Three seconds

26.1 Rule

26.1.1 A player shall not remain in the opponents' restricted area for more than three (3) consecutive seconds while his team is in control of a live ball in the frontcourt and the game clock is running.

26.1.2 Allowances must be made for a player who:

Makes an attempt to leave the restricted area.

Is in the restricted area when he or his team-mate is in the act of shooting and the ball is leaving or has just left the player's hand(s) on the shot for a field goal.

Dribbles in the restricted area to shoot for a field goal after having been there for less than three (3) consecutive seconds.

26.1.3 To establish himself outside the restricted area, the player must place both feet on the floor outside the restricted area.

Art. 27 Closely guarded player

27.1 Definition

A player who is holding a live ball on the playing court is closely guarded when an opponent is in an active guarding position at a distance of no more than one (1) m.

27.2 Rule

A closely guarded player must pass, shoot or dribble the ball within five (5) seconds.

Art. 28 Eight seconds

28.1 Rule

28.1.1 Whenever:

A player gains control of a live ball in his backcourt,

On a throw-in, the ball touches or is legally touched by any player in the backcourt and the team of that player taking the throw-in remains in control of the ball in its backcourt, that team must cause the ball to go into its frontcourt within eight (8) seconds.

28.1.2 The team has caused the ball to go into its frontcourt whenever:

The ball, not in control of any player, touches the frontcourt,

The ball touches or is legally touched by an offensive player who has both feet in contact with his frontcourt,

The ball touches or is legally touched by a defensive player who has part of his body in contact with his backcourt,

The ball touches an official who has part of his body in contact with the frontcourt of the team in control of the ball.

During a dribble from the backcourt to the frontcourt, both feet of the dribbler and the ball are in contact with the frontcourt.

28.1.3 The eight (8) second period will continue with any time remaining when the same team that previously had control of the ball is awarded a throw-in in the backcourt, as a result of:

A ball having gone out-of-bounds.

A player of the same team having been injured.

A jump ball situation.

A double foul.

A cancellation of equal penalties against both teams.

Art. 29 Twenty-four seconds

29.1 Rule

29.1.1 Whenever:

A player gains control of a live ball on the playing court,

On a throw-in, the ball touches or is legally touched by any player on the playing court and the team of that player taking the throw-in remains in control of the ball, that team must attempt a shot for a field goal within twenty-four (24) seconds.

To constitute a shot for a field goal within twenty-four (24) seconds:

The ball must leave the player's hand(s) before the twenty-four (24) second clock signal sounds, and

After the ball has left the player's hand(s), the ball must touch the ring or enter the basket.

29.1.2 When a shot for a field goal is attempted near the end of the twenty-four (24) second period and the twenty-four (24) second clock signal sounds while the ball is in the air:

If the ball enters the basket, no violation has occurred, the signal shall be disregarded and the goal shall count.

If the ball touches the ring but does not enter the basket, no violation has occurred, the signal shall be disregarded and the game shall continue.

If the ball misses the ring, a violation has occurred. However, if the opponents have gained immediate and clear control of the ball, the signal shall be disregarded and the game shall continue.

All restrictions related to goaltending and interference shall apply.

29.2 Procedure

29.2.1 If the game is stopped by an official:

—For a foul or violation (not for the ball having gone out-of-bounds) by the team not in control of the ball,

For any valid reason by the team not in control of the ball,

For any valid reason not connected with either team, Possession of the ball shall be awarded to the same team that previously had control of the ball.

If the throw-in is administered in the backcourt, the twenty-four (24) second clock shall be reset to twenty-four (24) seconds.

If the throw-in is administered in the frontcourt, the twenty-four (24) second clock shall be reset as follows:

If fourteen (14) seconds or more is displayed on the twenty-four (24) second clock at the time when the game was stopped, the twenty-four (24) second clock shall not be reset, but shall continue from the time it was stopped.

If thirteen (13) seconds or less is displayed on the twenty-four (24) second clock at the time when the game was stopped, the twenty-four (24) second clock shall be reset to fourteen (14) seconds.

However, if in the judgement of an official, the opponents would be placed at a disadvantage, the twenty-four (24) second clock shall continue from the time it was stopped.

29.2.2 If the twenty-four (24) second clock signal sounds in error while a team has control of the ball or neither team has control of the ball, the signal shall be disregarded and the game shall continue.

However, if in the judgement of an official, the team in control of the ball has been placed at a disadvantage, the game shall be stopped, the twenty-four (24) second clock shall be corrected and the ball shall be awarded to that team.

Art. 30 Ball returned to the backcourt

30.1 Definition

30.1.1 The ball goes into a team's backcourt when:

It touches the backcourt.

It touches or is legally touched by an offensive player who has part of his body in contact with the backcourt.

It touches an official who has part of his body in contact with the backcourt.

30.1.2 The ball has been illegally returned to the backcourt when a player of the team in control of the live ball is the last to touch the ball in his frontcourt, after which that player or a team-mate is the first to touch the ball in the backcourt.

This restriction applies to all situations in a team's frontcourt, including throw-ins.

However, it does not apply to a player who jumps from his frontcourt, establishes new team control while still airborne and then lands in his team's backcourt.

30. 2 Rule

A player whose team is in control of a live ball may not cause the ball to be illegally returned to his backcourt.

30. 3 Penalty

The ball shall be awarded to the opponents for a throw-in in their frontcourt at a place nearest to the infraction except directly behind the backboard.

Art. 31 Goaltending and Interference

31. 1 Definition

31. 1. 1 A shot for a field goal or a free throw:

Begins when the ball leaves the hand(s) of a player in the act of shooting.

Ends when the ball:

—Enters the basket directly from above and remains within or passes through the basket.

—No longer has the possibility of entering the basket.

—Touches the ring.

—Touches the floor.

—Becomes dead.

31. 2 Rule

31. 2. 1 Goaltending occurs during a shot for a field goal when a player touches the ball while it is completely above the level of the ring and:

It is on its downward flight to the basket, or

After it has touched the backboard.

31. 2. 2 Goaltending occurs during a shot for a free throw when a player touches the ball while it is in flight to the basket and before it touches the ring.

31. 2. 3 The goaltending restrictions apply until:

The ball no longer has the possibility of entering the basket.

The ball has touched the ring.

31. 2. 4 Interference occurs when:

After a shot for a field goal or the last or only free throw a player touches the basket or the backboard while the ball is in contact with the ring.

After a free throw followed by an additional free throw(s), a player touches the ball, the basket or the backboard while there is still a possibility that the ball will enter the basket.

A player reaches through the basket from below and touches the ball.

A defensive player touches the ball or the basket while the ball is within the basket, thus preventing the ball from passing through the net.

A player causes the basket to vibrate or grasps the basket in such a way that, in the judgement of an official, the ball has been prevented from entering the basket or has been caused to enter the basket.

A player grasps the basket to play the ball.

31.2.5 When

An official blows the whistle while the ball is in the hands of a player in the act of shooting, or the ball is in flight on a shot for a field goal,

The game clock signal sounds for the end of a period while the ball is in flight on a shot for a field goal,

No player shall touch the ball after it has touched the ring while it still has the possibility of entering the basket.

All restrictions related to goaltending and interference shall apply.

31.3 Penalty

31.3.1 If the violation is committed by an offensive player, no points can be awarded. The ball shall be awarded to the opponents for a throw-in at the free-throw line extended, unless otherwise stated in the rules.

31.3.2 If the violation is committed by a defensive player, the offensive team is awarded:

One (1) point when the ball was released for a free throw.

Two (2) points when the ball was released from the two-point field goal area.

Three (3) points when the ball was released from the three-point field goal area.

The awarding of the points is considered as if the ball had entered the basket.

31.3.3 If the goaltending is committed by a defensive player during a last or only free throw, one (1) point shall be awarded to the offensive team, followed by the technical foul penalty charged against the defensive player.

RULE SIX - FOULS

Art. 32 Fouls

32.1 Definition

32.1.1 A foul is an infraction of the rules concerning illegal personal contact with an opponent and/or unsportsmanlike behaviour.

32.1.2 Any number of fouls may be called against a team. Irrespective of the penalty, each foul shall be charged, entered on the scoresheet against the offender and penalized accordingly.

Art. 33 Contact: General principles

33.1 Cylinder principle

The cylinder principle is defined as the space within an imaginary cylinder occupied by a player on the floor. It includes the space above the player and is limited to:

The front by the palms of the hands,

The rear by the buttocks, and

The sides by the outer edge of the arms and legs.

The hands and arms may be extended in front of the torso no further than the position of the feet, with the arms bent at the elbows so that the forearms and hands are raised. The distance between his feet will vary according to his height.

33.2 Principle of verticality

During the game, each player has the right to occupy any position (cylinder) on the playing court not already occupied by an opponent.

This principle protects the space on the floor which he occupies and the space above him when he jumps vertically within that space.

As soon as the player leaves his vertical position (cylinder) and body contact occurs with an opponent who had already established his own vertical position (cylinder), the player who left his vertical position (cylinder) is responsible for the contact.

The defensive player must not be penalised for leaving the floor vertically (within his cylinder) or having his hands and arms extended above him within his own cylinder.

The offensive player, whether on the floor or airborne, shall not cause contact with the defensive player in a legal guarding position by:

Using his arms to create more space for himself (pushing off).

Spreading his legs or arms to cause contact during or immediately after a shot for a field goal.

33.3 Legal guarding position

A defensive player has established an initial legal guarding position when:

He is facing his opponent, and

He has both feet on the floor.

The legal guarding position extends vertically above him (cylinder) from the floor to the ceiling. He may raise his arms and hands above his head or jump vertically but he must maintain them in a vertical position inside the imaginary cylinder.

33.4 Guarding a player who controls the ball

When guarding a player who controls (holding or dribbling) the ball, the elements of time and distance do not apply.

The player with the ball must expect to be guarded and must be prepared to stop or change his direction whenever an opponent takes an initial legal guarding position in front of him, even if this is done within a fraction of a second.

The guarding (defensive) player must establish an initial legal guarding position without causing contact before taking his position.

Once the defensive player has established an initial legal guarding position, he may move to guard his opponent, but he may not extend his arms, shoulders, hips or legs to prevent the dribbler from passing by him.

When judging a charge/block situation involving a player with the ball, an official shall use the following principles:

The defensive player must establish an initial legal guarding position by facing the player with the ball and having both feet on the floor.

The defensive player may remain stationary, jump vertically, move laterally or backwards in order to maintain the initial legal guarding position.

When moving to maintain the initial legal guarding position, one foot or both feet may be off the floor for an instant, as long as the movement is lateral or backwards, but not towards the player with the ball.

Contact must occur on the torso, in which case the defensive player would be considered as having been at the place of contact first.

Having established a legal guarding position the defensive player may turn within his cylinder to avoid injury.

In any of the above situations, the contact shall be considered as having been caused by the player with the ball.

33.5 Guarding a player who does not control the ball

A player who does not control the ball is entitled to move freely on the playing court and take any position not already occupied by another player.

When guarding a player who does not control the ball, the elements of time and distance shall apply. A defensive player cannot take a position so near and/or so quickly in the path of a moving opponent that the latter does not have sufficient time or distance either to stop or change his direction.

The distance is directly proportional to the speed of the opponent, never less than one (1) and never more than two (2) normal steps.

If a defensive player does not respect the elements of time and distance in taking his initial legal guarding position and contact with an opponent occurs, he is responsible for the contact.

Once a defensive player has established an initial legal guarding position, he may move to guard his opponent. He may not prevent him from passing by extending his arms, shoulders, hips or legs in his path. He may turn within his cylinder to avoid injury.

33.6 A player who is in the air

A player who has jumped into the air from a place on the playing court has the right to land again at the same place.

He has the right to land on another place on the playing court provided that the landing place and the direct path between the take-off and landing place is not already occupied by an opponent(s) at the time of take-off.

If a player has taken off and landed but his momentum causes him to contact an opponent who has taken a legal guarding position beyond the landing place, the jumper is responsible for the contact.

An opponent may not move into the path of a player after that player has jumped into the air.

Moving under a player who is in the air and causing contact is usually an unsportsmanlike foul and in certain circumstances may be a disqualifying foul.

33.7 Screening: Legal and Illegal

Screening is an attempt to delay or prevent an opponent without the ball from reaching a desired position on the playing court.

Legal screening is when the player who is screening an opponent:

Was stationary (inside his cylinder) when contact occurs.

Had both feet on the floor when contact occurs.

Illegal screening is when the player who is screening an opponent:

Was moving when contact occurred.

Did not give sufficient distance in setting a screen outside the field of vision of a stationary opponent when contact occurred.

Did not respect the elements of time and distance of an opponent in motion when contact occurred.

If the screen is set within the field of vision of a stationary opponent (front or lateral), the screener may establish the screen as close to him as he desires, provided there is no contact.

If the screen is set outside the field of vision of a stationary opponent, the screener must permit the opponent to take one (1) normal step towards the screen without making contact.

If the opponent is in motion, the elements of time and distance shall apply. The screener must leave enough space so that the player who is being screened is able to avoid the screen by stopping or changing direction.

The distance required is never less than one (1) and never more than two (2) normal steps.

A player who is legally screened is responsible for any contact with the player who has set the screen.

33.8 Charging

Charging is illegal personal contact, with or without the ball, by pushing or moving into an opponent's torso.

33.9 Blocking

Blocking is illegal personal contact which impedes the progress of an opponent with or without the ball.

A player who is attempting to screen is committing a blocking foul if contact occurs when he is moving and his opponent is stationary or retreating from him.

If a player disregards the ball, faces an opponent and shifts his position as the opponent shifts, he is primarily responsible for any contact that occurs, unless other factors are involved.

The expression 'unless other factors are involved' refers to deliberate pushing, charging or holding of the player who is being screened.

It is legal for a player to extend his arm(s) or elbow(s) outside of his cylinder in taking position on the floor but they must be moved inside his cylinder when an opponent attempts to pass by. If the arm(s) or elbow(s) are outside his cylinder and contact occurs, it is blocking or holding.

33.10 No-charge semi-circle areas

The no-charge semi-circle areas are drawn on the playing court for the purpose of designating a specific area for the interpretation of charge/block situations under the basket.

On any penetration play situation into the no-charge semi-circle area a contact caused by an airborne offensive player with a defensive player inside the no-charge semi-circle shall not be called as an offensive foul, unless the offensive player is illegally using his hands, arms, legs or body, when the offensive player is in control of the ball whilst airborne, and he attempts a shot or passes off, and the defensive player has both feet inside the no-charge semi-circle area.

33.11 Contacting an opponent with the hand(s) and/or arm(s)

The touching of an opponent with a hand(s) is, in itself, not necessarily a foul.

The officials shall decide whether the player who caused the contact has gained an advantage. If contact caused by a player in any way restricts the freedom of movement of an opponent, such contact is a foul.

Illegal use of the hand(s) or extended arm(s) occurs when the defensive player is in a guarding position and his hand(s) or arm(s) is placed upon and remains in contact with an opponent with or without the ball, to impede his progress.

To repeatedly touch or 'jab' an opponent with or without the ball is a foul, as it may lead to rough play.

It is a foul by an offensive player with the ball to:

'Hook' or wrap an arm or an elbow around a defensive player in order to obtain an advantage.

'Push off' to prevent the defensive player from playing or attempting to play the ball, or to create more space for himself.

Use an extended forearm or hand, while dribbling, to prevent an opponent from gaining control of the ball.

It is a foul by an offensive player without the ball to 'push off' to:

Get free to receive the ball.

Prevent the defensive player from playing or attempting to play the ball.

Create more space for himself.

33.12 Post play

The principle of verticality (cylinder principle) applies also to post play.

The offensive player in the post position and the defensive player guarding him must respect each other's rights to a vertical position (cylinder).

It is a foul by an offensive or defensive player in the post position to shoulder or hip his opponent out of position or to interfere with his opponent's freedom of movement using extended arms, shoulders, hips, legs or other parts of the body.

33.13 Illegal guarding from the rear

Illegal guarding from the rear is personal contact with an opponent, by a defensive player, from behind. The fact that the defensive player is attempting to play the ball does not justify his contact with an opponent from the rear.

33.14 Holding

Holding is illegal personal contact with an opponent that interferes with his freedom of movement. This contact (holding) can occur with any part of the body.

33.15 Pushing

Pushing is illegal personal contact with any part of the body in which a player forcibly moves or attempts to move an opponent with or without control of the ball.

Art. 34 Personal foul

34.1 Definition

A personal foul is a player's contact foul with an opponent, whether the ball is live or dead.

A player shall not hold, block, push, charge, trip or impede the progress of an opponent by extending his hand, arm, elbow, shoulder, hip, leg, knee or foot, nor by bending his body into an 'abnormal' position (outside his cylinder), nor shall he indulge in any rough or violent play.

34.2 Penalty

A personal foul shall be charged against the offender.

34.2.1 If the foul is committed on a player not in the act of shooting:

The game shall be resumed with a throw-in by the non-offending team at the place nearest to the infraction.

If the offending team is in a team foul penalty situation, then Art. 41 (Team fouls: Penalty) will apply.

34.2.2 If the foul is committed on a player in the act of shooting, that player shall be awarded a number of free throw(s) as follows:

If the shot from the field goal area is successful, the goal shall count and, in addition, one (1) free throw.

If the shot from the two-point field goal area is unsuccessful, two (2) free throws.

If the shot from the three-point field goal area is unsuccessful, three (3) free throws.

If the player is fouled as, or just before, the game clock signal sounds for the end of the period or as, or just before, the twenty-four (24) second clock signal sounds, while the ball is still in the player's hand(s) and the field goal is successful, the goal shall not count and two (2) or three (3) free throws will be awarded.

Art. 35 Double foul

35.1 Definition

A double foul is a situation in which two (2) opponents commit personal fouls against each other at approximately the same time.

35.2 Penalty

A personal foul shall be charged against each offender. No free throws shall be awarded and the game shall be resumed as follows:

If at approximately the same time as the double foul

A valid field goal, or a last or only free throw is scored, the ball shall be awarded to the non-scoring team for a throw-in at any place at the endline.

A team had control of the ball or was entitled to the ball, the ball shall be awarded to this team for a throw-in at the place nearest to the infraction.

Neither team had control of the ball nor was entitled to the ball, a jump ball situation occurs.

Art. 36 Unsportsmanlike foul

36.1 Definition

36.1.1 An unsportsmanlike foul is a player contact foul which, in the judgement of an official, is not a legitimate attempt to directly play the ball within the spirit and intent of the rules.

36.1.2 The official must interpret the unsportsmanlike fouls consistently throughout the game and to judge only the action.

36.1.3 To judge whether a foul is unsportsmanlike, the officials should apply the following principles:

If a player is making no effort to play the ball and contact occurs, it is an unsportsmanlike foul.

If a player, in an effort to play the ball, causes excessive contact (hard foul), it is an unsportsmanlike foul.

If a defensive player causes contact with an opponent from behind or laterally in an attempt to stop a fast break and there is no opponent between the offensive player and the opponents' basket, it is an unsportsmanlike foul.

If a player commits a foul while making a legitimate effort to play the ball (normal play), it is not an unsportsmanlike foul.

36.2 Penalty

36.2.1 An unsportsmanlike foul shall be charged against the offender.

36.2.2 Free throw(s) shall be awarded to the player who was fouled, followed by:

A throw-in at the centre line extended, opposite the scorer's table.

A jump ball in the centre circle to begin the first period.

The number of free throws shall be awarded as follows:

If the foul is committed on a player not in the act of shooting: two (2) free throws.

If the foul is committed on a player in the act of shooting: the goal, if made, shall count and, in addition, one (1) free throw.

If the foul is committed on a player in the act of shooting and the goal is not made: two (2) or three (3) free throws.

36.2.3 A player shall be disqualified when he is charged with two (2) unsportsmanlike fouls.

36.2.4 If a player is disqualified under Art. 36.2.3, that unsportsmanlike foul shall be the only foul to be penalised and no additional penalty for the disqualification shall be administered.

Art. 37 Disqualifying foul

37.1 Definition

37.1.1 A disqualifying foul is any flagrantly unsportsmanlike action of a player, substitute, excluded player, coach, assistant coach or team follower.

37. 1. 2 A coach who has received a disqualifying foul shall be replaced by the assistant coach as entered on the scoresheet. If no assistant coach is entered on the scoresheet, he shall be replaced by the captain (CAP).

37. 2 Penalty

37. 2. 1 A disqualifying foul shall be charged against the offender.

37. 2. 2 Whenever the offender is disqualified according to the respective articles of these rules, he shall go to and remain in his team's dressing room for the duration of the game or, if he so chooses, he shall leave the building.

37. 2. 3 Free throw(s) shall be awarded:

To any opponent, as designated by his coach in the case of a non-contact foul.

To the player who was fouled in the case of a contact foul.

Followed by:

A throw-in at the centre line extended, opposite the scorer's table.

A jump ball in the centre circle to begin the first period.

37. 2. 4 The number of free throws shall be awarded as follows:

If the foul is committed on a player not in the act of shooting: two (2) free throws.

If the foul is committed on a player in the act of shooting: the goal, if made, shall count and in addition one (1) free throw.

If the foul is committed on a player in the act of shooting and the goal is not made: two (2) or three (3) free throws.

Art. 38 Technical foul

38. 1 Rules of conduct

38. 1. 1 The proper conduct of the game demands the full and loyal cooperation of the members of both teams (players, substitutes, coaches, assistant coaches, excluded players and team followers) with the officials, table officials and commissioner, if present.

38. 1. 2 Each team shall do its best to secure victory, but this must be done in the spirit of sportsmanship and fair play.

38. 1. 3 Any deliberate or repeated non-cooperation or non-compliance with the spirit and intent of this rule shall be considered as a technical foul.

38. 1. 4 The official may prevent technical fouls by giving warnings or even overlooking minor infractions which are obviously unintentional and have no direct effect upon the game, unless there is repetition of the same infraction after the warning.

38. 1. 5 If an infraction is recognised after the ball becomes live, the game shall be stopped and a technical foul charged. The penalty shall be administered as if the technical foul had occurred at the time it is charged. Whatever occurred during the interval between the infraction and the game being stopped shall remain valid.

38. 2 Violence

38. 2. 1 Acts of violence may occur during the game, contrary to the spirit of sportsmanship and fair play. These should be stopped immediately by the officials and, if necessary, by public

order enforcement officers.

38.2.2 Whenever acts of violence occur between players, substitutes, excluded players, coaches, assistant coaches or team followers, on the playing court or in its vicinity, the officials shall take the necessary action to stop them.

38.2.3 Any of the above persons who are guilty of flagrant acts of aggression against opponents or officials shall be disqualified. The referee must report the incident to the organising body of the competition.

38.2.4 Public order enforcement officers may enter the playing court only if requested to do so by the officials. However, should spectators enter the playing court with the obvious intention of committing acts of violence, the public order enforcement officers must intervene immediately to protect the teams and officials.

38.2.5 All other areas, including entrances, exits, hallways, dressing rooms, etc., come under the jurisdiction of the organising body of the competition and the public order enforcement officers.

38.2.6 Physical actions by players, substitutes, excluded players, coaches, assistant coaches and team followers which could lead to damaging of game equipment, must not be permitted by the officials.

When behaviour of this nature is observed by the officials, the coach of the offending team shall be given a warning.

Should the action(s) be repeated, a technical foul shall immediately be called on the individual(s) involved.

38.3 Definition

38.3.1 A technical foul is a player non-contact foul of a behavioural nature including, but not limited to:

Disregarding warnings given by officials.

Disrespectfully touching the officials, the commissioner, the table officials or the team bench personnel.

Disrespectfully communicating with the officials, the commissioner, the table officials or the opponents.

Using language or gestures likely to offend or incite the spectators.

Baiting an opponent or obstructing his vision by waving his hands near his eyes.

Excessive swinging of elbows.

Delaying the game by deliberately touching the ball after it passes through the basket or by preventing a throw-in from being taken promptly.

Falling down to fake a foul.

Hanging on the ring in such a way that the weight of the player is supported by the ring, unless a player grasps the ring momentarily following a dunk shot or, in the judgement of an official, is trying to prevent injury to himself or to another player.

Goaltending during a last or only free throw by a defensive player. One (1) point shall be awarded to the offensive team, followed by the technical foul penalty charged against the defensive player.

38. 3. 2 A technical foul by a coach, assistant coach, substitute, excluded player or team follower is a foul for disrespectfully communicating with or touching the officials, the commissioner, the table officials or the opponents, or an infraction of a procedural or an administrative nature.

38. 3. 3 A coach shall be disqualified when:

He is charged with two (2) technical fouls ('C') as a result of his personal unsportsmanlike behaviour.

He is charged with three (3) technical fouls, either all of them ('B') or one of them ('C'), as a result of unsportsmanlike behaviour of the team bench (assistant coach, substitute, excluded player or team follower).

38. 3. 4 If a coach is disqualified under Art. 38. 3. 3, that technical foul shall be the only foul to be penalised and no additional penalty for the disqualification shall be administered.

38. 4 Penalty

38. 4. 1 If a technical foul is committed:

By a player, a technical foul shall be charged against him as a player foul and shall count as one of the team fouls.

By a coach ('C'), assistant coach ('B'), substitute ('B'), excluded player ('B') or team follower ('B'), a technical foul shall be charged against the coach and shall not count as one of the team fouls.

38. 4. 2 Two (2) free throws shall be awarded to the opponents, followed by:

A throw-in at the centre line extended, opposite the scorer's table.

A jump ball in the centre circle to start the first period.

Art. 39 Fighting

39. 1 Definition

Fighting is physical interaction between two (2) or more opponents (players, substitutes, excluded players, coaches, assistant coaches and team followers).

This article only applies to coaches, assistant coaches, substitutes, excluded players and team followers who leave the confines of the team bench area during a fight or during any situation which may lead to a fight.

39. 2 Rule

39. 2. 1 Substitutes, excluded players or team followers who leave the team bench area during a fight, or during any situation which may lead to a fight, shall be disqualified.

39. 2. 2 Only the coach and/or assistant coach is permitted to leave the team bench area during a fight, or during any situation which may lead to a fight, to assist the officials to maintain or to restore order. In this situation, he shall not be disqualified.

39. 2. 3 If a coach and/or assistant coach leaves the team bench area and does not assist or attempt to assist the officials to maintain or to restore order, he shall be disqualified.

39. 3 Penalty

39. 3. 1 Irrespective of the number of coaches, assistant coaches, substitutes, excluded

players or team followers disqualified for leaving the team bench area, a single technical foul ('B') shall be charged against the coach.

39.3.2 If members of both teams are disqualified under this article and there are no other foul penalties remaining for administration, the game shall be resumed as follows.

If at approximately the same time as the game was stopped because of the fighting:

A valid field goal is scored, the ball shall be awarded to the non-scoring team for a throw-in at any place at the endline.

A team had control of the ball or was entitled to the ball, the ball shall be awarded to this team for a throw-in at the centre line extended, opposite the scorer's table.

Neither team has control of the ball nor was entitled to the ball, a jump ball situation occurs.

39.3.3 All disqualifying fouls shall be not count as a team foul.

39.3.4 All possible foul penalties against players on the playing court involved in fighting or any situation which lead to a fight, shall be dealt with in accordance with Art. 42 (Special situations).

Art. 40 Five fouls by a player

40.1 A player who has committed five (5) fouls, personal and/or technical, shall be informed there of by an official and must leave the game immediately. He must be substituted within thirty (30) seconds.

40.2 A foul by a player who has previously committed five (5) fouls is considered as an excluded player's foul and it is charged and entered in the scoresheet against the coach ('B').

Art. 41 Team fouls: Penalty

41.1 Definition

41.1.1 A team is in a team foul penalty situation when it has committed four (4) team fouls in a period.

41.1.2 All team fouls committed in an interval of play shall be considered as being committed in the following period or extra period.

41.1.3 All team fouls committed in an extra period shall be considered as being committed in the fourth period.

41.2 Rule

41.2.1 When a team is in a team foul penalty situation, all subsequent player personal fouls committed on a player not in the act of shooting shall be penalised by two (2) free throws, instead of a throw-in.

41.2.2 If a personal foul is committed by a player of the team in control of the live ball, or of the team entitled to the ball, such a foul shall be penalised by a throw-in for the opponents.

Art. 42 Special situations

42.1 Definition

In the same stopped-clock period which follows an infraction, special situations may arise when additional foul(s) are committed.

42.2 Procedure

42.2.1 All fouls shall be charged and all penalties identified.

42.2.2 The order in which all infractions occurred shall be determined.

42.2.3 All equal penalties against the teams and all double foul penalties shall be cancelled in the order in which they were called. Once the penalties have been cancelled they are considered as never having occurred.

42.2.4 The right to possession of the ball as part of the last penalty shall cancel any prior rights to possession of the ball.

42.2.5 Once the ball has become live on the first or only free throw or on a throw-in penalty, that penalty can no longer be used for cancelling any remaining penalties.

42.2.6 All remaining penalties shall be administered in the order in which they were called.

42.2.7 If, after the cancellation of equal penalties against the teams, there are no other penalties remaining for administration, the game shall be resumed as follows.

If at approximately the same time as the first infraction:

A valid field goal is scored, the ball shall be awarded to the non-scoring team for a throw-in at any place at the endline.

A team had control of the ball or was entitled to the ball, the ball shall be awarded to this team for a throw-in at the place nearest to the first infraction.

Neither team had control of the ball nor was entitled to the ball, a jump ball situation occurs.

Art. 43 Free throws

43.1 Definition

43.1.1 A free throw is an opportunity given to a player to score one (1) point, uncontested, from a position behind the free-throw line and inside the semi-circle.

43.1.2 A set of free throws is defined as all free throws and/or subsequent possession of the ball resulting from a single foul penalty.

43.2 Rule

43.2.1 When a personal foul is called the free throw(s) shall be awarded as follows:

The player against whom the foul was committed shall attempt the free throw(s).

If there is a request for him to be substituted, he must attempt the free throw(s) before leaving the game.

If he must leave the game due to injury, having committed his five (5) fouls or having been disqualified, his substitute shall attempt the free throw(s). If no substitute is available, any team-mate as designated by his coach shall attempt the free throw(s).

43.2.2 When a technical foul is called, any member of the opponent's team as designated by his coach shall attempt the free throws.

43.2.3 The free-throw shooter shall:

Take a position behind the free-throw line and inside the semi-circle.

Use any method to shoot a free throw in such a way that the ball enters the basket from above or the ball touches the ring.

Release the ball within five (5) seconds after it is placed at his disposal by the official.

Not touch the free-throw line or enter the restricted area until the ball has entered the basket or has touched the ring.

Not fake a free throw.

43.2.4 The players in the free-throw rebound places shall be entitled to occupy alternating positions in these spaces, which are considered to be one (1) m in depth (Diagram 6).

During the free throws these players shall not:

Occupy free-throw rebound places to which they are not entitled.

Enter the restricted area, the neutral zone or leave the free-throw rebound place until the ball has left the hand(s) of the free-throw shooter.

Distract the free-throw shooter by their actions.

43.2.5 Players not in the free-throw rebound places shall remain behind the free-throw line extended and behind the three-point field goal line until the free throw ends.

43.2.6 During a free throw(s) to be followed by another set(s) of free throws or by a throw-in, all players shall remain behind the free-throw line extended and behind the three-point field goal line.

An infraction of Art. 43.2.3, 43.2.4, 43.2.5 and 43.2.6 is a violation.

43.3 Penalty

43.3.1 If a free throw is successful and the violation(s) is committed by a free-throw shooter, point, if made, shall not count.

The ball shall be awarded to the opponents for a throw-in at the free-throw line extended unless there is a further free throw(s) or possession penalty to be administered.

43.3.2 If a free throw is successful and the violation(s) is committed by any player(s) other than the free-throw shooter:

Point, if made, shall count.

Violation(s) shall be disregarded.

In case of the last or only free throw, the ball shall be awarded to the opponents for a throw-in at any place at the endline.

43.3.3 If a free throw is not successful and the violation is committed by:

A team-mate of the free-throw shooter on the last or only free throw, the ball shall be awarded to the opponents for a throw-in at the free-throw line extended unless that team is entitled to further possession.

An opponent of the free-throw shooter, a substitute free throw shall be awarded to the free-throw shooter.

Both teams, on the last or only free throw, a jump ball situation occurs.

Art. 44 Correctable errors

44.1 Definition

Officials may correct an error if a rule is inadvertently disregarded in the following situations only:

Awarding an unmerited free throw(s).

Failure to award a merited free throw(s).

Erroneous awarding or cancelling of a point(s).

Permitting the wrong player to attempt a free throw(s).

44.2 General procedure

44.2.1 To be correctable the above-mentioned errors must be recognized by the officials, commissioner, if present, or table officials before the ball becomes live following the first dead ball after the game clock has started following the error.

44.2.2 An official may stop the game immediately upon recognition of a correctable error, as long as neither team is placed at a disadvantage.

44.2.3 Any fouls committed, points scored, time used, additional activity which may have occurred after the error has occurred and before its recognition, shall remain valid.

44.2.4 After the correction of the error the game shall be resumed at the point it was stopped to correct the error, unless otherwise stated in these rules. The ball shall be awarded to the team entitled to the ball at the time the game was stopped for the correction.

44.2.5 Once an error that is still correctable has been recognised, and:

If the player involved in the correction of the error is on the team bench after having been legally substituted (not for having committed five (5) fouls or for having been disqualified), he must re-enter the playing court, unless he is injured, to participate in the correction of the error (at this point he becomes a player).

Upon completion of the correction, he may remain in the game unless a legal substitution has been requested again, in which case the player may leave the playing court.

If the player was substituted due to his injury, having committed five (5) fouls or having been disqualified, his substitute must participate in the correction of the error.

44.2.6 Correctable errors cannot be corrected after the referee has signed the scoresheet.

44.2.7 Any errors in scorekeeping by the scorer or time-keeping by the timer involving the score, number of fouls, number of time-outs or time consumed or omitted, may be corrected by the officials at any time before the referee signs the scoresheet.

44.3 Special procedure

44.3.1 Awarding an unmerited free throw(s).

The free throw(s) attempted as a result of the error shall be cancelled and the game shall be resumed as follows:

If the game clock has not started, the ball shall be awarded for a throw-in to the team whose free throws had been cancelled from the free-throw line extended.

If the game clock has started and:

—The team in control of the ball or entitled to the ball at the time the error is recognised is the same team that was in control of the ball at the time the error occurred, or

—Neither team is in control of the ball at the time the error is recognised, the ball shall be awarded to the team entitled to the ball at the time of the error.

If the game clock has started and, at the time the error is recognised, the team in control of the ball or entitled to the ball is the opponent of the team that was in control of the ball at the time of the error, a jump ball situation occurs.

If the game clock has started and, at the time the error is recognised, a foul penalty involving a free throw(s) has been awarded, the free throw(s) shall be administered and the ball shall be awarded for a throw-in to the team that was in control of the ball at the time the error occurred.

44.3.2 Failure to award a merited free throw(s).

If there has been no change in possession of the ball after the error occurred, the game shall be resumed after correction of the error as after any normal free throw.

If the same team scores after having been erroneously awarded possession of the ball for a throw-in, the error shall be disregarded.

44.3.3 Permitting the wrong player to attempt a free throw(s).

The free throw(s) attempted, and the possession of the ball if part of the penalty, shall be cancelled and the ball shall be awarded to the opponents for a throw-in at the free-throw line extended, unless penalties for further infractions are to be administered.

Art. 45 Officials, Table Officials and Commissioner

45.1 The officials shall be a referee and one (1) or two (2) umpire(s). They shall be assisted by the table officials and by a commissioner, if present.

45.2 The table officials shall be a scorer, an assistant scorer, a timer and a twenty-four (24) second clock operator.

45.3 The commissioner shall sit between the scorer and the timer. His primary duty during the game is to supervise the work of the table officials and to assist the referee and umpire(s) in the smooth functioning of the game.

45.4 The officials of a given game should not be connected in any way with either team on the playing court.

45.5 The officials, the table officials and the commissioner shall conduct the game in accordance with these rules and have no authority to change them.

45.6 The officials' uniform shall consist of an officials' shirt, long black trousers, black socks and black basketball shoes.

45.7 The officials and table officials shall be uniformly dressed.

Art. 46 Referee: Duties and Powers

The referee shall:

46.1 Inspect and approve all equipment to be used during the game.

46.2 Designate the official game clock, twenty-four (24) second clock, stop watch and recognise the table officials.

46.3 Select a game ball from at least two (2) used balls provided by the home team. Should neither of these balls be suitable as the game ball, he may select the best quality ball available.

46.4 Not permit any player to wear objects that may cause injury to other players.

46.5 Administer a jump ball to start the first period and an alternating possession throw-in to start all other periods.

46.6 Have the power to stop a game when conditions warrant it.

46.7 Have the power to determine that a team shall forfeit the game.

46.8 Carefully examine the scoresheet at the end of playing time or at any time he feels is necessary.

46.9 Approve and sign the scoresheet at the end of playing time, terminating the officials' administration and connection with the game. The officials' power shall begin when they arrive on the playing court twenty (20) minutes before the game is scheduled to begin, and end when the game clock signal sounds for the end of the playing time as approved by the officials.

46.10 Record on the reverse side of the scoresheet, before signing it:

—Any forfeit or disqualifying foul,

—Any unsportsmanlike behaviour by players, coaches, assistant coaches or team followers that occurs prior to the twenty (20) minutes before the game is scheduled to begin, or between the end of playing time and the approval and signing of the scoresheet.

In such acase, the referee (commissioner, if present) must send a detailed report to the organising body of the competition.

46.11 Make the final decision whenever necessary or when the officials disagree. To make a final decision he may consult the umpire(s), the commissioner, if present, and/or the table officials.

46.12 Be authorised to approve and use the technical equipment, if available, to decide, before he signs the scoresheet, if a last shot for a field goal at the end of each period or each extra period was released during playing time and/or whether that shot for a field goal counts for two (2) or three (3) points.

46.13 Have the power to make decisions on any point not specifically covered by these rules.

Art. 47 Officials: Duties and powers

47.1 The officials shall have the power to make decisions on infractions of the rules committed either within or outside the boundary line including the scorer's table, the team benches and the areas immediately behind the lines.

47.2 The officials shall blow their whistles when an infraction of the rules occurs, a period ends or the officials find it necessary to stop the game. The officials shall not blow their whistles after a successful field goal, a successful free throw or when the ball becomes live.

47.3 When deciding on a personal contact or violation, the officials shall, in each instance, have regard to and weigh the following fundamental principles:

The spirit and intent of the rules and the need to uphold the integrity of the game.

Consistency in application of the concept of 'advantage/disadvantage'. The officials should not seek to interrupt the flow of the game unnecessarily in order to penalise incidental personal contact which does not give the player responsible an advantage nor place his opponent at a disadvantage.

Consistency in the application of common sense to each game, bearing in mind the abilities of the players concerned and their attitude and conduct during the game.

Consistency in the maintenance of a balance between game control and game flow, having a 'feeling' for what the participants are trying to do and calling what is right for the game.

47.4 Should a protest be filed by one of the teams, the referee (commissioner, if present) shall, within one (1) hour following the end of playing time, report the protest to the organising body of the competition.

47.5 If an official is injured or for any other reason cannot continue to perform his duties within five (5) minutes of the incident, the game shall be resumed. The remaining official(s) will officiate alone until the end of the game, unless there is the possibility of replacing the injured official with a qualified substitute official. After consulting with the commissioner, if present, the other official will decide upon the possible replacement.

47.6 For all international games, if verbal communication is necessary to make a decision clear, it shall be conducted in English language.

47.7 Each official has the power to make decisions within the limits of his duties, but has no authority to disregard or question decisions made by the other official(s).

47.8 Decisions made by the officials are final and cannot be contested or disregarded.

Art. 48 Scorer and Assistant Scorer: Duties

48.1 The scorer shall be provided with a scoresheet and shall keep a record of:

Teams, by entering the names and numbers of the players who are to start the game and of all substitutes who enter the game. When there is an infraction of the rules regarding the five (5) players to start the game, substitutions or numbers of players, he shall notify the nearest official as soon as possible.

Running summary of points scored, by entering the field goals and the free throws made.

Fouls charged against each player. The scorer must notify an official immediately when five (5) fouls are charged against any player. He shall record the fouls charged against each coach and must notify an official immediately when a coach should be disqualified. Similarly, he must notify an official immediately when a player has committed two (2) unsportsmanlike fouls and should be disqualified.

Time-outs. He must notify the officials of the time-out opportunity when a team has requested a time-out and notify the coach through an official when the coach has no more time-out(s) left in a half or extra period.

The next alternating possession, by operating the alternating possession arrow.

The scorer shall reverse the direction of the alternating possession arrow.

immediately after the end of the first half as the teams shall exchange baskets for the second half.

48.2 The scorer shall also:

Indicate the number of fouls committed by each player by raising, in a manner visible to both coaches, the marker with the number of fouls committed by that player.

Position the team foul marker on the scorer's table, at the end nearest to the bench of the team in a team foul penalty situation, when the ball becomes live following the fourth team foul in a period.

Effect substitutions.

Sound his signal only when the ball becomes dead and before the ball becomes live again. The sound of his signal does not stop the game clock or the game nor cause the ball to become dead.

48.3 The assistant scorer shall operate the scoreboard and assist the scorer. In the case of any discrepancy between the scoreboard and the scoresheet which cannot be resolved, the scoresheet shall take precedence and the scoreboard shall be corrected accordingly.

48.4 If a scorekeeping error is recognised:

During the game, the scorer must wait for the first dead ball before sounding his signal.

After the end of the playing time and before the scoresheet has been signed by the referee, the error shall be corrected, even if this correction influences the final result of the game.

After the scoresheet has been signed by the referee, the error may no longer be corrected. The referee or the commissioner, if present, must send a detailed report to the organising body of the competition.

Art. 49 Timer: Duties

49.1 The timer shall be provided with a game clock and a stopwatch and shall:

Measure playing time, time-outs and intervals of play.

Ensure that the game clock signal sounds very loudly and automatically at the end of playing time in a period.

Use any means possible to notify the officials immediately if his signal fails to sound or is not heard.

Notify the teams and the officials at least three (3) minutes before the third period is to start.

49.2 The timer shall measure playing time as follows:

Starting the game clock when:

—During a jump ball, the ball is legally tapped by a jumper.

—After an unsuccessful last or only free throw and the ball continues to be live, the ball touches or is touched by a player on the playing court.

—During a throw-in, the ball touches or is legally touched by a player on the playing court.

Stopping the game clock when:

—Time expires at the end of playing time for a period, if not stopped automatically by the game clock itself.

—An official blows his whistle while the ball is live.

—A field goal is scored against a team which has requested a time-out.

—A field goal is scored in the last two (2) minutes of the fourth period and in the last two (2) minutes of each extra period.

—The twenty-four (24) second clock signal sounds while a team is in control of the ball.

49.3 The timer shall measure a time-out as follows:

Starting the stopwatch immediately when the official blows his whistle and gives the time-out signal.

Sounding his signal when fifty (50) seconds of the time-out have elapsed.

Sounding his signal when the time-out has ended.

49.4 The timer shall measure an interval of play as follows:

Starting the stopwatch immediately when a previous period has ended.

Sounding his signal before the first and third period when three (3) minutes, one (1) minute and thirty (30) seconds remain until the beginning of the period.

Sounding his signal before the second, fourth and each extra period when thirty (30) seconds remain until the beginning of the period.

Sounding his signal and simultaneously stopping the stopwatch immediately when an interval of play has ended.

Art. 50 Twenty-four (24) second operator: Duties

The twenty-four (24) second clock operator shall be provided with a twenty-four (24) second clock which shall be:

50.1 Started or restarted when:

A team gains control of a live ball on the playing court.

On a throw-in, the ball touches or is legally touched by any player on the playing court.

The mere touching of the ball by an opponent does not start a new twenty-four (24) second period if the same team remains in control of the ball.

50.2 Whenever an official blows the whistle as a result of:

A foul or violation (not for the ball having gone out-of-bounds by the team not in control of the ball).

The game being stopped because of an action not connected with the team in control of the ball.

The game being stopped because of an action not connected with either team, unless the opponents would be placed at a disadvantage, the twenty-four (24) second clock shall be:

(1) Stopped and reset to twenty-four (24) seconds, with no display visible, when:

—The ball legally enters the basket.

—The ball touches the ring of the opponents' basket (unless the ball lodges between the ring and the backboard).

—The team is awarded a backcourt throw-in or free throw(s).

—The infraction of the rules is committed by the team in control of the ball.

(2) Stopped but not reset to twenty-four (24) seconds when the same team that previously had control of the ball is awarded a frontcourt throw-in and fourteen (14) seconds or more are displayed on the twenty-four (24) second clock.

(3) Stopped and reset to fourteen (14) seconds when the same team that previously had control of the ball is awarded a frontcourt throw-in and thirteen (13) seconds or less are displayed on the twenty-four (24) second clock.

50.3 Stopped, but not reset, when the same team that previously had control of the ball is awarded a throw-in as a result of:

A ball having gone out-of-bounds.

A player of the same team having been injured.

A jump ball situation.

A double foul.

A cancellation of equal penalties against the teams.

The twenty-four (24) second clock signal does not stop the game clock or the game, nor 50.4 switched off, after the ball became dead and the game clock has been stopped, when there are fewer than twenty-four (24) or fourteen (14) seconds remaining on the game clock in any period.

Cause the ball to become dead, unless a team is in a control of the ball.

第三篇　排　球

第一章 排球竞赛规则及裁判法

1 比赛场地

比赛场地为对称的长方形，包括比赛场区和无障碍区(图3-1)。

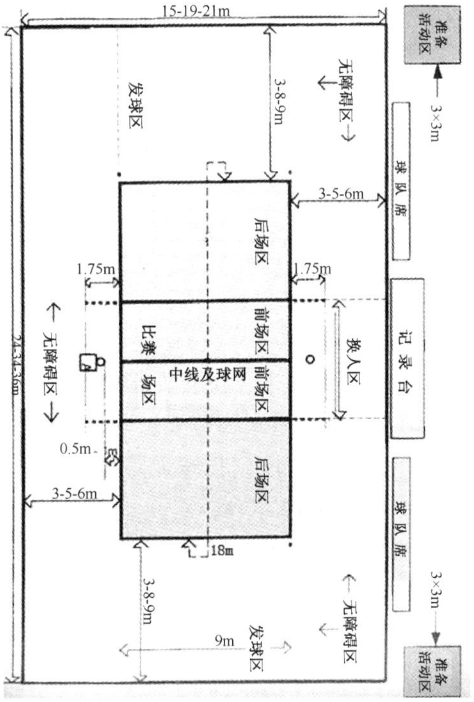

图3-1 比赛场地

1.1 面积

比赛场区为18米×9米的长方形。其四周至少有3米宽的无障碍区，比赛场区上空的无障碍空间从地面量起至少高7米，其间不得有任何障碍物。

国际排联世界性比赛场地边线外的无障碍区至少宽5米，端线外至少宽8米，比赛场地上空的无障碍空间至少高12.5米。

1.2 比赛场地的地面

1.2.1 场地的地面必须平坦、水平、划一。场地的地面不得有任何可能伤害队员的隐患。不得在湿、滑或粗糙的地面上比赛。

国际排联世界性比赛场地的地面只能是木制的或合成物质的。任何地面都必须事先经国际排联验准。

1.2.2 室内比赛场地的地面必须是浅色。

国际排联世界性比赛场地界线为白色。比赛场区和无障碍区分别为另外不同的颜色。

1.2.3 室外场地为了排水，每米可以有5毫米的坡度。不得用任何坚硬的物体作为地界线。

1.3 场地上的画线

1.3.1 所有的画线宽5厘米。其颜色应该是与地面以及其他项目场地画线不同的颜色。

1.3.2 界线

两条边线和两条端线划定了比赛场区。边线和端线都包括在比赛场区的面积之内。

1.3.3 中线

中线在网下连接两条边线的中点。中线的中心线将比赛场区分为长9米、宽9米的两个相等场区。

1.3.4 进攻线

每个场区各画一条距离中线中心线3米的进攻线，标出了前场区。

国际排联世界性比赛时，在每条进攻线两端各画5段长15厘米、宽5厘米、间隔20厘米的虚线，虚线总长1.75米。“教练员限制线”由一组长15厘米、间隔20厘米的虚线组成，虚线自进攻线的延长线至底线延长线，距边线 1.75 米并平行于边线。限制线限制教练员的活动区域。

1.4　区和区间

1.4.1　前场区

中线中心线与进攻线之间为前场区。前场区被认为是向边线外延长的，直至无障碍区的边沿。

1.4.2　发球区(图 3-2)

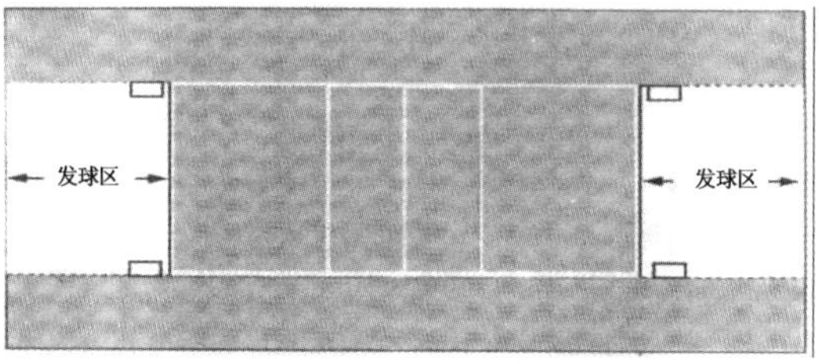

图 3-2　发球区

发球区宽 9 米，位置在端线后。端线后两条边线的延长线各画一条长 15 厘米、垂直并距离端线 20 厘米的短线，两条短线之间的区域为发球区，短线的宽度包括在发球区之内。发球区的深度延长至无障碍区的终端。

1.4.3　换人区

两条进攻线的延长线之间，记录台一侧边线外的范围为换人区。

1.4.4　后排自由防守队员替补区

后排自由防守队员替换区是无障碍区的一部分，在替补席一侧的进攻线延长线和底线延长线之间。

1.4.5　准备活动区域

国际排联世界性比赛的无障碍区外的球队席远端角落，画有 3 米×3 米的准备活动区域。

1.4.6　判罚区域

判罚区域位于控制区域内各端线的延长线后，放有两把椅子。其长宽各为 1 米，线宽 5 厘米，为红色。

1.5　温度

最低温度不得低于 10℃(50°F)。

国际排联世界性比赛的室内温度，最高不得高于 25℃(77°F)，最低不得低于 16℃(61°F)。

1.6　照明

国际排联世界性比赛室内照明度在距比赛场地地面 1 米高处进行测量，应为 1000～1500 勒克斯。

2　球网与网柱

2.1　球网高度

2.1.1　球网架设在中线上空，高度为男子 2.43 米，女子 2.24 米。

2.1.2　球网的高度应从场地中间丈量，球网两端(边线上空)的高度必须相等，并不得超过规定网高 2 厘米。

2.2 构造

球网为黑色，宽 1 米，长 9.50～10 米(每边标志带外 25～50 厘米)，网眼直径 10 厘米。球网上沿的全长缝有 7 厘米宽的双层白帆布带。帆布带的两端留有孔，用绳索系在网柱上使网上沿拉紧。用一根柔韧的钢丝穿过帆布带，拉紧网上沿，固定在网柱上。

2.3 标志带

两条宽 5 厘米、长 1 米的白色带子为标志带，分别系在球网两端，垂直于边线。标志带被认为是球网的一部分。

2.4 标志杆

标志杆是有韧性的两根杆子，长 1.8 米，直径 10 毫米，由玻璃纤维或类似材料制成。两根标志杆分别设置在标志带外沿球网的不同侧面。

标志杆高出球网 80 厘米。高出部分每 10 厘米应涂有明显对比的颜色，最好为红白相间。标志杆被认为是球网的一部分，并视为过球网的边界(图 3-3)。

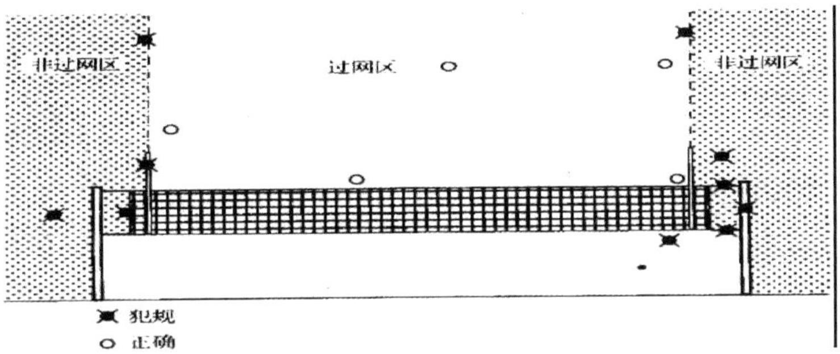

图 3-3 球从过网区或非过网区通过示意

2.5 网柱

2.5.1 两根网柱分别架设在两条边线外 0.5～1 米处，高 2.55 米，最好可以调节高度(图 3-4)。

国际排联世界性比赛中网柱应架设在两条边线外 1 米处。

2.5.2 网柱应为圆柱形，光滑并无拉链。一切危险设施和障碍物都必须清除。

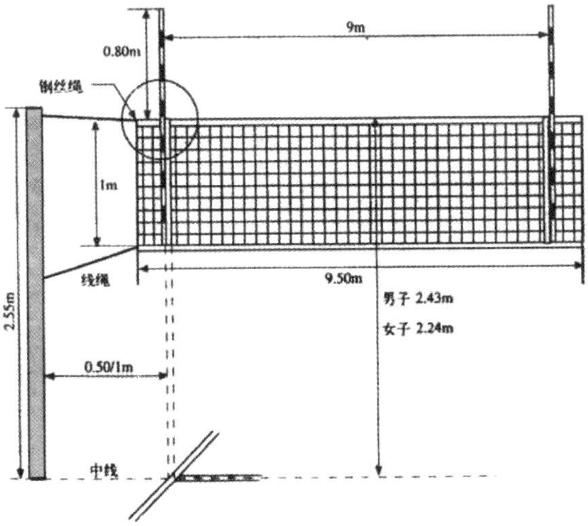

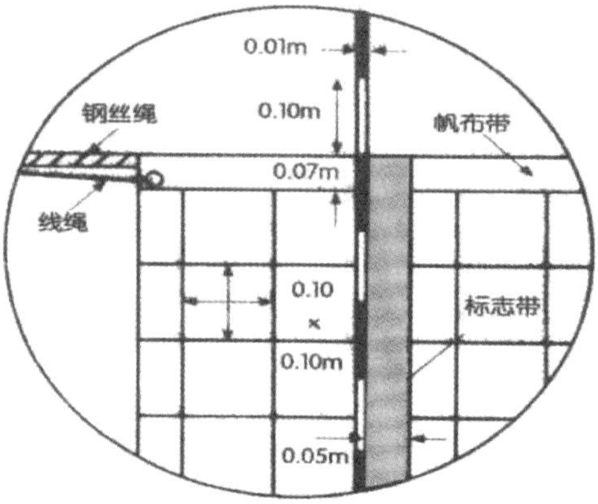

图 3-4　球网的规格

2.6　附加设施

一切附加设备都必须符合国际排联的规定。

3　球

3.1

球是圆形的，由柔软皮革或合成革制成外壳，内装橡皮或类似质料制成的球胆。

国际排联世界性比赛使用的合成革和彩色球须经国际排联同意并符合其标准。圆周：65~67 厘米。重量：260~280 克。气压：0.30~0.325 千克/平方厘米(294.3~318.82 百帕)。

3.2　统一性

在一次比赛中所用的球，其特性，包括圆周、重量、气压、牌号及颜色等都必须是统一标准的。

国际排联世界性比赛、国家联赛和锦标赛所用的球必须是国际排联批准的用球，或经过 FIVB 特许。

3.3　三球制

国际排联世界性比赛应采用三球制。设六名捡球员，无障碍区的四个角落各一人，第一、二裁判后面各一人。

4　比赛队

4.1　队的组成

4.1.1　一个队最多有 12 名队员，1 名教练员、一名助理教练员、1 名训练员和 1 名队医。

国际排联世界性比赛中，医生必须事先得到国际排联的认可。国际排联成年人世界大赛，一个队最多可以有 14 名队员(但非后排自由防守队员不得超过 12 名)。

4.1.2　除后排自由防守队员外的一名队员为队长，队长在记录表上被注明。

4.1.3 只有登记在记录表上的队员才可以进入场地和参加比赛。教练员和队长在记分表上签字以后，已登记在记分表上的队员名单不得更改。

4.2　队的位置

4.2.1　比赛时，替补队员应坐在本队场地一侧的球队席上或在准备活动区域内，教练员和其他成员也应坐在球队席上，但可暂时离开。球队席设在记录台的两侧，无障碍区之外。

4.2.2 在比赛中只有队的成员才允许坐在球队席上并参加赛前的准备活动。

4.2.3 替补队员可以做无球的准备活动如下：

4.2.3.1 比赛中，在准备活动区域内；

4.2.3.2 暂停或技术暂停时在本队场区之后的无障碍区。

4.2.4 两局比赛之间队员可以在无障碍区用球做准备活动。

4.3 服装

队员服装包括上衣、短裤、袜子(必须一致)和运动鞋。

4.3.1 全队上衣、短裤和袜子的颜色、样式必须统一(后排自由防守队员除外)，服装必须整洁。

4.3.2 运动鞋必须是没有后跟的柔软轻便的胶底或皮底鞋。

国际排联世界性比赛不允许穿鞋底可画出黑色痕迹的鞋。上衣和短裤须完全符合国际排联标准。

4.3.3 队员上衣必须有号码，序号为 1~18 号。

国际排联世界性比赛，队员服装的号码序号是 1~20 号。

4.3.3.1 号码必须在身前和身后的中间位置，并与上衣的颜色明显不同。

4.3.3.2 身前号码至少 15 厘米高，身后号码至少 20 厘米高，号码笔画宽度至少 2 厘米。

国际排联世界性比赛，队员短裤右腿处须有 4~6 厘米高的号码，号码笔画至少宽 1 厘米。上衣和短裤要符合 FIVB 标准(图 3-5)。

图 3-5 号码示意图

4.3.4 队长上衣胸前号码下，应有一条与上衣颜色不同的长 8 厘米、宽 2 厘米的条状标志。

4.3.5 禁止穿着不符合规则规定号码的服装和与同队其他队员不同颜色的服装(后排自由防守队员除外)。

4.4 服装的更换

第一裁判员可以允许一名或多名运动员：

4.4.1 国际排联世界性比赛不允许赤脚比赛。

4.4.2 在局间或换人后更换湿的或损坏的服装，但必须是相同的颜色、式样和号码。

4.4.3 天气较冷时穿训练服比赛，但全队服装颜色、样式必须相同(后排自由防守队员除外)，号码符合规定 4.3.3。

4.5 禁止佩戴的物品

4.5.1 禁止佩戴可能对运动员造成伤害及加力的物品。

4.5.2 队员可以戴眼镜比赛，但风险自负。

5 队的领导

队长和教练员应对全队成员的行为和纪律负责。

后排自由防守队员不能担任队长。

5.1 队长

5.1.1 比赛前：队长在记分表上签字，并代表本队抽签。

5.1.2 比赛中：队长担任场上队长。当队长不在场上时，教练员或队长应指定除后排自由防守队员以外的另一名队员担任场上队长代行其职权，直至该队员下场或队长返回场上，或至该局结束。只有场上队长在死球时可以和裁判员讲话：

5.1.2.1 请求对规则和规则的执行进行解释，转达本队队员提出的问题或请求。如果他对解释不满意，可以选择抗议并立即向第一裁判员声明，保留其在比赛结束时将正式的抗议写在记分表的权力。

5.1.2.2 请求允许：

- 更换全部或部分服装；
- 核对双方队员的位置；
- 检查地板、球网和球等。

5.1.2.3 请求暂停或换人

5.1.3 比赛后：

5.1.3.1 感谢裁判员，并在记分表上签字承认比赛结果；

5.1.3.2 如果他曾向第一裁判员作过声明，进一步确认后可将对裁判员的解释或执行规则的正式抗议记录在记分表上。

5.2 教练员

5.2.1 教练员应自始至终在比赛场区之外进行指挥，他与第二裁判员联系填写位置表、请求暂停或换人。

5.2.2 比赛前：在记分表上登记或检查队员姓名、号码并签字。

5.2.3 比赛中：

5.2.3.1 每局开始前填写位置表，签字后交给第二裁判员或记录员；

5.2.3.2 坐在靠近记录员一端的球队席上，但可以暂时离开；

5.2.3.3 请求暂停或换人；

5.2.3.4 与队的其他成员一样，可以对场上队员进行指导。进行指导时可以在球队席前自进攻线延长线至准备活动区域之间的无障碍区内站立或行走，但不得干扰或延误比赛。

国际排联世界性比赛，教练员应在教练员限制线后履行职责。

5.3 助理教练员

5.3.1 助理教练员坐在球队席上，但无任何权力。

5.3.2 如果教练员必须离队时，场上队长请求并经第一裁判员同意，他可以承担教练员职责。

胜一分、胜一局与胜一场

6 胜一分 胜一局 胜一场

6.1 胜一分

6.1.1 得分。某队得一分：

6.1.1.1 球成功地落在对方场区；

6.1.1.2　对方犯规；

6.1.1.3　对方受到判罚。

6.1.2　犯规。当队员的比赛行为违背规则时(或有其他方式的犯规时)，裁判员按以下规则进行判断和作出决定：

6.1.2.1　如果两个或更多队员同时犯规先后发生，只判第一犯规；

6.1.2.2　如果双方队员同时犯规，判为“双方犯规”，该球重新比赛。

6.1.3　比赛过程和完整的比赛过程

比赛过程是指从发球击球起至该球成死球止的比赛行为。完整的比赛过程是造成了得分结果的比赛行为。

6.1.3.1　如果发球队获胜，得一分并继续发球；

6.1.3.2　如果接球队获胜，得一分并获得发球权。

6.2　胜一局

每局(决胜的第五局除外)先得 25 分同时超过对方 2 分的队胜一局。当比分 24∶24 时比赛继续进行至某队领先两分(26∶24、27∶25) 为止。

6.3　胜一场

6.3.1　胜三局的队胜一场。

6.3.2　如果 2∶2 平局时，决胜局(第五局)打至 15 分并领先对方 2 分者获胜。

6.4　弃权与阵容不完整

6.4.1　某队被召唤后拒绝比赛，则宣布该队为弃权。对方以每局 25∶0 的比分和 3∶0 的比局获胜。

6.4.2　某队无正当理由而未准时到达比赛场地，则宣布该队为弃权，处理同规则 6.4.1。

6.4.3　某队被宣布一局或一场比赛阵容不完整时，则输掉该局或该场比赛，判给对方胜局或该场比赛所必要的分数和局数。阵容不完整的队保留其所得分数和局数。

7　比赛的组织

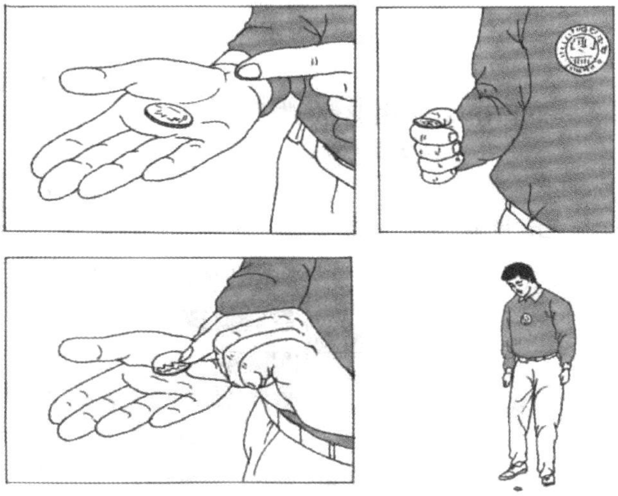

图 3-6　抽签示意图

7.1 抽签

比赛开始前由第一裁判员主持抽签，决定首先发球的队和场区。进行决胜局比赛前，应再次抽签(图 3-6)。

7.1.1 抽签由双方队长参加。

7.1.2 抽签获胜方可以选择：

7.1.2.1 发球或接发球；

7.1.2.2 或场区。另一方挑选余下部分。

7.1.3 如果两队分开进行准备活动，则首先发球的队先使用球网。

7.2 准备活动

7.2.1 在比赛开始前，如另有场地提供比赛队进行活动，则他们可以上网活动 6 分钟，如果没有，则活动 10 分钟。

7.2.2 如果队长要求分开使用球网活动，按照规则 7.2.1 他们可以各自使用 3 或 5 分钟。

7.3 开始阵容

7.3.1 每个队必须始终保持 6 名队员进行比赛。队员的轮转次序应按位置表登记的顺序进行，直至该局结束。

7.3.2 每局比赛开始前，教练员必须及时地将开始阵容登记在位置表上，签字后交给第二裁判员或记录员。

7.3.3 未列入开始阵容的队员，为该局的替补队员(后排自由防守队员除外)。

7.3.4 位置表一经交给第二裁判员或记录员，除正常换人外，阵容不得改变。

7.3.5 当场上队员的位置与位置表不符时：

7.3.5.1 一局开始前，场上队员的位置与位置表不符时，必须按位置表进行纠正，不予判罚。

7.3.5.2 一局开始前，场上有一名或更多队员没有登记在位置表上，必须按位置表进行纠正，不予判罚。

7.3.5.3 如果教练员要保持未登记的队员在场上，他必须请求正常的换人，并登记在记分表上。

7.4 位置

发球队员击球时，双方队员(发球队员除外)必须在本场区内按轮转次序站位。

7.4.1 队员场上位置为(图 3-7)：

7.4.1.1 靠近球网的三名队员为前排队员，其位置为 4 号位(左)、3 号位(中)2 号位(右)。

7.4.1.2 另外三名队员为后排队员，其位置为 5 号位(左)、6 号位(中)和 1 号位(右)。

7.4.2 两名队员之间的位置：

7.4.2.1 每一名后排队员的位置必须比其相应的前排队员距离中线更远；

7.4.2.2 前、后排队员左右之间的位置按规则 7.4.1 的规定站位。

7.4.3 队员的位置应根据其脚的着地部位

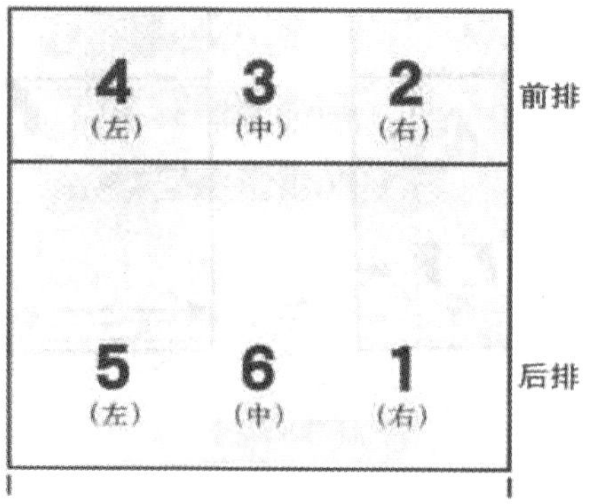

图 3-7 位置

判定：

7.4.3.1　每一名前排队员至少有一只脚的部分，比同列后排队员的双脚距中线更近

7.4.3.2　每一名右(左)边队员至少有一只脚的部分，比同排中间队员的双脚距右(左)边线更近。

7.4.4　发球击球后，队员可以在本场区和无障碍区的任何位置。

7.5　位置错误

7.5.1　当发球队员击球时，如果队员不在其正确位置上，则构成位置错误犯规。

7.5.2　当发球队员击球时的犯规与对方位置错误同时发生，则发球犯规被认为在先。

7.5.3　如果是发球队员在击球后的犯规，则位置错误在先。

7.5.4　位置错误的判罚如下：

7.5.4.1　该队被判失去一球；

7.5.4.2　队员恢复到正确位置。

7.6　轮转

7.6.1　整局比赛中，轮转次序、发球次序以及队员位置均按位置表的顺序进行。

7.6.2　接发球队获得发球权后，该队队员必须按顺时针方向轮转一个位置；2 号为队员转至 1 号位，1 号位队员转至 6 号位等。

7.7　轮转错误

7.7.1　没有按照轮转次序进行发球为轮转错误，应进行如下判罚：

7.7.1.1　该队失一分，由对方发球；

7.7.1.2　纠正队员的轮转次序。

7.7.2　记录员应准确地确定其错误何时发生，从而取消该队自错误发生后的所有得分。对方得分仍然有效。如果不能确定错误发生的时间，则仅判该队失一球。

8　比赛的状态

8.1　进入比赛

经第一裁判员允许，发球队员击球为进入比赛。

8.2　比赛的中止

裁判员鸣哨即为比赛的中止。如果裁判员是因出现犯规而鸣哨，则比赛的中止是由犯规一刻开始的。

8.3　界内球

球触及比赛场区的地面包括界线为界内球。

8.4　界外球

下列为界外球：

8.4.1　球接触地面的部分完全在界线以外；

8.4.2　球触及场外物体、天花板或非场上比赛队员；

8.4.3　球触及标志杆、网绳、网柱或球网标志带以外部分；

8.4.4　球的整体或部分从过网区以外过网，规则 10.1.2 除外；

8.4.5　球的整体从网下空间穿过。

9　击球

比赛队必须在其本方场地及空间进行比赛(规则 10.1.2 除外)，但可以越出无障碍区

救球。

9.1　球队的击球

比赛队员与球的任何触及都视为击球。每队最多击球三次(拦网除外，规则 14.4.1)将球击回对区，如果超过则判为“四次击球犯规”。

9.1.1　连续击球

一名队员不得连续击球两次(规则 9.2.3、14.2 和 14.4.2 除外)。

9.1.2　同时击球

两名或三名队员可以同时触球。

9.1.2.1　同队的两名(或三名)队员同时触到球时，被记为两次(或三次)击球(拦网除外)。如果只有其中一名队员触球，则只记一次。队员之间的碰撞不算犯规。

9.1.2.2　两名不同队的队员在网上同时触球，比赛继续进行，获球一方可再次击三次。如果该球落在某方场区之外，则判对方击球出界。

9.1.2.3　如果两名不同队的队员在网上同时触球并造成“持球”。则判为双方犯规，该球重新比赛。

9.1.3　借助击球

队员不得在比赛场地之内借助同伴或任何物体支持进行击球。但是队员可以挡住或拉住另一名即将犯规(如触网、过中线等)的同队队员。

9.2　击球的性质

9.2.1　球可以触及身体的任何部位。

9.2.2　球不能被接住和/或抛出。它可以向任何方向弹出。

9.2.3　球可以触及身体的不同部位，但必须是同时。下列情况除外：

9.2.3.1　拦网时，一名队员或多名队员可以在一个动作中连续触球；

9.2.3.2　在第一次击球时，允许身体不同部位在一个动作中连续触球。

9.3　击球时的犯规

9.3.1　四次击球：一个队连续击球四次。

9.3.2　借助击球：队员在比赛场地内借助同伴或任何物体的支持进行击球。

9.3.3　持球：球被接住和/或抛出，而不是被弹击出。

9.3.4　连击：一名队员连续击球两次，或球连续触及其身体的不同部位。

10　球网附近的球

10.1　球通过球网

10.1.1　球必须通过球网上空的过网区进入对方场区。过网区是球网垂直平面的一部分，其范围：

10.1.1.1　下至球网上沿；

10.1.1.2　两侧至标志杆及其延长线；

10.1.1.3　上至天花板。

10.1.2　球的整体或部分从延长空间进入对方无障碍区，可以在下列情况将球击回：

10.1.2.1　队员不得触及对方场区；

10.1.2.2　球被击回时，它的整体或部分必须从同侧延长空间通过。对方队员不得阻碍此击球。

10.2 球触球网

球通过球网时可以触及球网。

10.3 球入球网

10.3.1 球入球网后，可以在该队的三次击球内再击。

10.3.2 如果球击破球网或使球网坠落，该球重新进行。

11 球网附近的队员

11.1 越过球网

11.1.1 拦网时允许拦网队员越过球网触球，但不得在对方进攻性击球前或击球时妨碍对方。

11.1.2 进攻性击球后允许手过网，但击球时必须在本方空间。

11.2 网下穿越

11.2.1 在不妨碍对方比赛的情况下，允许队员在网下穿越进入对方空间。

11.2.2 穿越中线进入对方场区；

11.2.2.1 队员的一只(两只)脚或一只(两只)手部分越过中线触及对方场区的同时，其余部分接触中线或置于中线上空是允许的。

11.2.2.2 队员身体的任何其他部位都不允许接触对方场区。

11.2.3 比赛中断后队员可以进入对方场区。

11.2.4 在不妨碍对方比赛的情况下，队员可以穿越进入对方的无障碍区。

11.3 触网

11.3.1 队员触网不是犯规，但击球时或干扰比赛的情况下除外，某些击球可包括实际上没有触及球的击球动作。

11.3.2 队员击球后可以触及网柱、全网长以外的网绳或其他任何物体，但不得影响比赛。

11.3.3 由于球被击入球网而造成的球网触及队员，不算犯规。

11.4 队员在球网附近的犯规

11.4.1 对方进行进攻性击球前或击球时，在对方空间触及球或对方队员。

11.4.2 从网下穿越进入对方空间并妨碍对方比赛。

11.4.3 越过中线进入对方场区。

11.4.4 队员干扰比赛如下列情况(不仅如下)：

击球时触及球网上沿的网带；或球网以上的 80 厘米的标志杆；或击球时借助球网的支持；或造成了对本方有利；或妨碍了对方合法的击球试图。

12 发球

后排右侧队员在发球区将球击出而进入比赛的行动是发球。

12.1 首先发球

12.1.1 第一局和第五局由抽签选定发球权的队首先发球。

12.1.2 其他各局由前一局未首先发球的队首先发球。

12.2 发球次序

12.2.1 队员发球的次序按位置表上的顺序进行。

12.2.2　一局的首先发球后，队员按下列规定进行发球：

12.2.2.1　当发球队胜一球时，原发球队员或其替补队员继续发球；

12.2.2.2　当接发球队胜一球时获得发球权并轮转，由前排右侧队员转至后排右侧，到发球区发球。

12.3　发球的允许

第一裁判员检查发球队员已握球在手，而且双方队员已做好比赛准备时，鸣哨允许发球。

12.4　发球的执行

12.4.1　球被抛起或持球手撤离后，必须在球落地前，用一只手或手臂的任何部分将球击出。

12.4.2　球只能被抛起或撤离一次，但拍球或在手中摆弄球是允许的。

12.4.3　发球队员在击球时或击球起跳时，不得踏及场区（包括端线）和发球区以外地面。击球后可以踏及或落在场区内或发球区以外。

12.4.4　发球队员必须在第一裁判员鸣哨允许发球后8秒钟内将球发出。

12.4.5　裁判员鸣哨允许发球前的发球无效。

12.5　发球掩护（图3-8）

12.5.1　发球队员个人或集体不得利用掩护阻挡对方观察发球队员和球的飞行路线。

12.5.2　在发球时，发球队个人或集体挥臂、跳跃或左右移动，或集体密集站立遮挡了球的飞行路线，构成发球掩护。

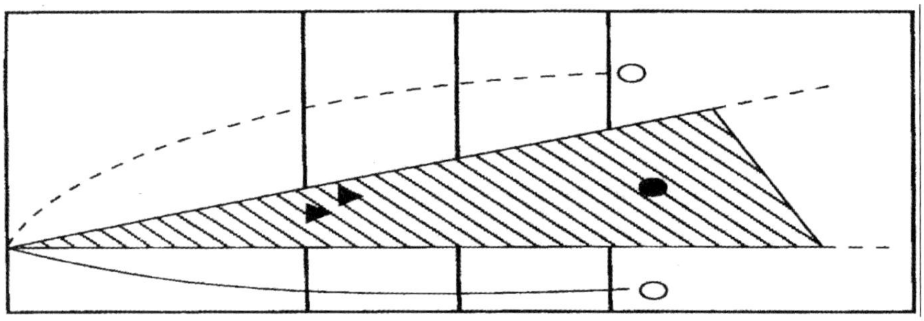

图3-8　发球掩护示意图

12.6　发球时的犯规

12.6.1　发球犯规

下列犯规应判为发球犯规，即使对方位置错误。

12.6.1.1　发球次序错误；

12.6.1.2　没有遵守"发球的执行"的规定。

12.6.2　发球击球后的犯规

球被发出后出现以下情况仍作为发球犯规（除非位置错误）：

12.6.2.1　球触及发球队队员或整体没有从过网区通过球网垂直平面；

12.6.2.2　界外球；

12.6.2.3　球越过发球掩护。

12.7　发球时的犯规与位置错误

12.7.1　如果发球犯规（规则12.6.1）与对方位置错误同时发生，判发球犯规。

12.7.2 如果发球击球后的犯规(规则12.6.2)与对方位置错误同时发生，判位置错误犯规。

13 进攻性击球

13.1 进攻性击球

13.1.1 除发球和拦网外，所有直接向对方的击球都是进攻性击球。

13.1.2 在进攻性击球时，吊球是允许的，但击球必须清晰并不得接住或抛出。

13.1.3 球的整体通过球网垂直平面或触及对方队员，则认为完成进攻性击球。

13.2 进攻性击球的限制

13.2.1 前排队员可以对任何高度的球完成进行性击球。但触球时必须在本方空间(规则13.2.4除外)。

13.2.2 后排队员可以在进攻线后对任何高度的球完成进攻性击球，但是：

13.2.2.1 起跳时脚不得踏及或超过进攻线；

13.2.2.2 击球后可以落在前场区。

13.2.3 后排队员也可以在前场区完成进攻性击球，但触球时球的一部分必须低于球网上沿。

13.2.4 接发球队队员不能对处于前场区内高于球网上沿的对方发球完成进攻性击球。

13.3 进攻性击球的犯规

13.3.1 在对方空间击球。

13.3.2 击球出界。

13.3.3 后排队员在前场区完成进攻性击球，并且击球时球的整体高于球网上沿。

13.3.4 对处于前场区内高于球网上沿的对方发球完成进攻性击球。

13.3.5 后排自由防守队员对高于球网上沿的球完成进攻性击球。

13.3.6 队员在高于球网处，对同队自由防守队员在前场区用上手传的球完成进攻性击球。

14 拦网

14.1 拦网

14.1.1 拦网是队员靠近球网，将手伸向高于球网处阻挡对方来球的动作。只能前排队员可以完成拦网。

14.1.2 拦网试图。没有触及球的拦网行动为拦网试图。

14.1.3 完成拦网。触及球的拦网行动为完成拦网。

14.1.4 集体拦网。两名或三名队员彼此靠近进行拦网为集体拦网，其中一人触球则完成拦网。

14.2 拦网的触球

在一个动作中，球可以连续(迅速而连贯地)触及一名或更多名的拦网队员。

14.3 进入对方空间拦网

拦网时队员可以将手或手臂伸过球网，但不得防碍对方击球。过网拦网的触球必须在对方进攻性击球之后。

14.4 拦网与球队的击球

14.4.1 拦网的触球不算作球队三次击球的一次。

14.4.2 拦网后可以由任何一名队员进行第一次击球，包括拦网时已经触球的队员。

14.5 拦发球

拦对方的发球是被禁止的。

14.6 拦网的犯规

14.6.1 在对方进攻性击球前或击球的同时，在对方空间完成拦网。

14.6.2 后排队员或自由防守队员完成拦网或参加了完成拦网的集体。

14.6.3 拦对方的发球。

14.6.4 拦网出界。

14.6.5 从标志杆以外伸入对方空间拦网。

14.6.6 后排自由防守队员试图进行个人或参加集体拦网。

15 正常的比赛间断

正常的比赛间断有“暂停”和“换人”。

15.1 正常间断的次数

每局比赛中，每队最多请求两次暂停和六人次换人。

15.2 请求正常间断

15.2.1 只有教练员和场上队长可以请求间断。

请求暂停或换人必须在比赛成死球后、裁判员鸣哨允许发球前，并使用相应的手势。

国际排联世界比赛中，必须先使用蜂鸣器然后做出相应的手势。

15.2.2 一局开始前请求换人是允许的，但应计算在正常换人次数之内。

15.3 间断的连续

15.3.1 一次或两次暂停可以与双方的各一次换人相连续，中间无须经过比赛过程。

15.3.2 同一队未经过比赛过程不得连续提出换人请求。但在同一次换人请求中可以替换两名或更多的队员。

15.4 暂停与技术暂停

15.4.1 所有被请求的暂停时间为30秒钟。

国际排联世界性比赛的第1~4局中，每局另外有两次时间为60秒钟的技术暂停，每当领先队达到8分和16分时自动执行。决胜局(第五局)没有技术暂停，只有每队可以请求的、时间为30秒钟的正常暂停。

15.4.2 在所有的暂停时，比赛队员必须离开比赛场区到球队席附近的无障碍区。

15.5 换人

在裁判员的允许下，一名队员离开比赛场地，而由另一名队员经记录员登记后占据其位置的行为称换人(后排自由防守队员的进出除外)。

15.6 换人的限制

15.6.1 每一局每队最多可换六人次。可以同时换一人或多人。

15.6.2 每局开始阵容中的队员，在同一局中可以退出比赛和再上场一次，而且只能回到原阵容的位置。

15.6.3 替补队员只能上场比赛一次，替换开始阵容的队员。而且他只能由被他替换下场的队员来替换。

15.7 特殊换人

某一队员受伤不能继续比赛时(后排自由防守队员除外)，必须进行合法的换人。如果不能进行合法的换人时，可采用超出规则15.6限制的“特殊换人”。

特殊换人时，场外的任何队员除后排自由防守队员或由他/她替换下场的队员外，都可以替换受伤队员，但受伤队员不可在本场比赛中返回场上。

在任何情况下特殊换人都不作为换人的次数计算。

15.8 被判罚出场与取消比赛资格的换人

某队员被“判罚出场”或“取消比赛资格”时，必须进行合法换人。不能进行合法换人时，该队被宣布为“阵容不完整”。

15.9 不合法的换人

15.9.1 超出规则15.6限制的换人是不合法的换人(规则15.7的情况除外)。

15.9.2 某队进行了不合法的换人，而且比赛已重新开始，应按如下步骤进行处理：

15.9.2.1 判该队失一球；

15.9.2.2 对不合法的换人给予纠正；

15.9.2.3 取消该队在此犯规中所得的分数。

15.10 换人的程序

15.10.1 换人必须在换人区内进行。

15.10.2 换人时所持续的时间，仅限记录员登记和队员进出场必需的时间。

15.10.3 在请求换人时，队员必须站在换人区附近并做好进场准备。否则裁判员不接受其请求并判该队延误比赛犯规。

国际排联世界性比赛中，队员换人时须使用换人牌。

15.10.4 如果运动队想替换一名以上的运动员，必须在提出请求换人的同时，用手势表明换人的次数。替换时队员一对对相继进行。

15.11 不符合规定的请求

15.11.1 下列情况为不符合规定的请求：

15.11.1.1 在比赛进行中或裁判员鸣哨允许发球的同时或之后提出请求；

15.11.1.2 无请求权的成员提出请求；

15.11.1.3 同一队没有经过比赛过程再次请求换人。

15.11.1.4 超过规定的正常间断次数的请求。

15.11.2 比赛中第一次没有影响和延误比赛的不符合规定的请求，应给予拒绝而不进行判罚，但同一场比赛中不能再次发生。

15.11.3 比赛中再次提出不符合规定的请求应判延误犯规。

16 延误比赛

16.1 延误比赛的类型

一个队拖延比赛继续进行的不当行为为延误比赛。包括：

16.1.1 延误换人时间；

16.1.2 在裁判员鸣哨恢复比赛后，拖延暂停时间；

16.1.3 请求不合法的换人；

16.1.4 再次提出不符合规定的请求；

16.1.5 球队成员拖延比赛的继续进行。

16.2 对延误比赛的判罚

16.2.1 "延误警告"和"延误判罚"是对全队的延误比赛的判罚。

16.2.1.1 延误比赛的判罚对全场比赛有效。

16.2.1.2 所有延误比赛的判罚都记录在记分表上。

16.2.2 在一场比赛中，对一个队的成员的第一次延误比赛，给予"延误警告"。

16.2.3 在一场比赛中，同一队的任何成员造成不论任何类型的第二次以及其后的延误比赛，都给予"延误判罚"。

16.2.4 局前和局间的延误比赛判罚记在下一局中。

17 例外的比赛间断

17.1 受伤

17.1.1 比赛中出现严重受伤事故，裁判员应该立即中断比赛，允许医务人员进入场地。该球重新比赛。

17.1.2 如果受伤队员已不能进行合法换人和特殊换人，则给予受伤队员 3 分钟的恢复时间。

一场比赛同一名队员只能给予一次供恢复的时间。

如果队员不能恢复，该队被宣布为阵容不完整。

17.2 外因造成的比赛中断

比赛中出现任何外界干扰，都应停止比赛，该球重新比赛。

17.3 被拖延的间断

17.3.1 任何意外情况阻碍比赛继续进行时，第一裁判员、比赛组织者和管委会成员共同研究决定，采取措施恢复比赛。

17.3.2 一次或数次间断时间累计不超过 4 小时：

17.3.2.1 如果比赛仍在原地进行，则间断的一局应保持原比分、原队员和原场上位置。已结束的各局比分保留。

17.3.2.2 如果比赛改为其他场地进行，则间断的一局应取消，但保持该局开始时的阵容和位置重新比赛。已结束的各局比分保留。

17.3.2.3 一次或数次间断时间累计超过 4 小时，全场比赛重新开始。

18 局间休息与交换场区

18.1 局间休息

所有局间休息均为 3 分钟。局间休息用于交换场区和在记分表上登记球队的阵容。应比赛组织者的要求，第 2、3 局之间的休息时间可延长至 10 分钟。

18.2 交换场区

18.2.1 每局结束后比赛队交换场区，决胜局除外。

18.2.2 决胜局中某队获得 8 分时两队交换场区，不休息，队员在原来的位置继续比赛。如果未能及时交换场区，则应在此错误发现时立即交换，保留交换场区时两队已得的比分。

19 后排自由防守队员

19.1 后排自由防守队员的确定

19.1.1 各队可以在确定的12名队员中，确定1名队员为“后排自由防守队员”。

国际排联世界形成年比赛中，队员可以超出12名，但超出的名额必须是“后排自由防守队员”，最多两名。

19.1.2 比赛前，必须将后排自由防守队员登记在记分表的专栏中。

国际排联世界性比赛中，所有后排自由防守队员都必须登记在、只能登记在积分表的专栏中。

19.1.3 如果有两名后排自由防守队员，教练员须在比赛开始前指定其中一名为首发，另一名为替补。

19.1.4 后排自由防守队员不能担任队长和场上队长。

19.2 后排自由防守队员的服装

后排自由防守队员必须穿着有区别其他同队队员颜色的上衣(或后排自由防守队员的专门服装)，样式可以不同，但必须有与全队一样的号码。

国际排联世界性比赛中，新指定的后排自由防守队员上衣的样式和颜色，必须与原后排自由防守队员一致，但保持个人的号码。

19.3 后排自由防守队员的行为

19.3.1 比赛行为

19.3.1.1 他可以替换在后排的任何一名队员。

19.3.1.2 作为特殊的后排队员，他不可在任何的位置上(包括场区和无障碍区)对整个球体高于球网的球完成进攻性击球。

19.3.1.3 他不可以发球、拦网和有拦网试图。

19.3.1.4 如果他在本队的前场区(或延长区)运用了上手传球，则不允许其同伴在高于球网处完成对该球的进攻性击球。但他在其他区的传球无碍。

19.3.2 替换

19.3.2.1 后排自由防守队员的替换不记在该队的换人次数之内，而且没有次数限制。但两次替换之间必须经过比赛过程。替换他的队员必须是由他替换出场的队员。

19.3.2.2 替换必须在比赛成死球后，第一裁判员鸣哨允许发球前进行。比赛开始前，第二裁判员核查完位置后，允许后排自由防守队员进行替换。

19.3.2.3 裁判员鸣哨发球后，发球队员击球前，替换不被拒绝，但死球后必须给予口头告诫。如果再次发生应按延误犯规判处。

19.3.2.4 替换只能在进攻线与端线之间球队席前的边线处进行。

19.3.3 新后排自由防守队员的指定：

19.3.3.1 经第一裁判员的同意，教练员或队长可指定任何一名队员替换受伤的后排自由防守队员。本场比赛中被替换的受伤的后排自由防守队员，不能再次上场比赛。被指定替换他的队员，按照后排自由防守队员的规定完成本场比赛。

19.3.3.2 新指定的后排自由防守队员的号码，必须记在记分表的备注栏内。

20　行为要求

20.1　体育道德

20.1.1　参赛者必须了解并遵守规则。

20.1.2　参赛者必须以良好的体育道德作风服从裁判员的裁定，不允许争辩。如果有疑问，可以并只能通过场上队长提请解释。

20.1.3　参赛者不得有任何目的在于影响裁判员判断，或掩盖本队犯规的动作和行为的表现。

20.2　公正竞赛

20.2.1　参赛者的行为必须符合“公正竞赛”的精神，不仅对裁判员，而且对其他工作人员、对方、本方以及观众都要尊重、有礼貌。

20.2.2　比赛中队的成员之间的交流是允许的。

21　不良行为以及判罚

21.1　轻微的不良行为

对轻微的不良行为不进行判罚，但裁判员有责任用手势或口头通过场上队长给予警告。这个警告无需记在记分表上。

21.2　给予判罚的不良行为

球队成员对裁判员、对方、同伴或观众的不良行为，根据其程度分为三类。

21.2.1　粗鲁行为：违背道德准则和文明举止，或有侮辱性表示。

21.2.2　冒犯行为：诽谤或侮辱的言语或形态。

21.2.3　侵犯行为：人身侵犯或企图侵犯。

21.3　判罚等级

第一裁判员根据不良行为的程度，分别给予如下判罚，判罚出场或取消比赛资格的判罚，并记在记分表上：

21.3.1　判罚

用于全场比赛中任一成员的粗鲁行为，判对方的分并发球。

21.3.2　判罚出场

21.3.2.1　任何成员被判罚出场，都必须坐在判罚区域内，不得继续参加该局的比赛，没有另外的判处。教练员被判罚出场，坐在判罚区域内，失去该局的指挥权力。

21.3.2.2　某成员第一次出现冒犯行为，判罚出场，无其他判罚。

21.3.2.3　同一成员在一场比赛中的第二次粗鲁行为，判罚出场，无其他判罚。

21.3.3　取消比赛资格

21.3.3.1　任何成员被取消比赛资格，必须离开比赛控制区域，不得继续参加该场的比赛，没有另外的判处。

21.3.3.2　某成员第一次出现侵犯行为，取消比赛资格，无其他判罚。

21.3.3.3　同一成员一场比赛中的第二次冒犯行为，取消比赛资格，无其他判罚。

21.3.3.4　同一成员一场比赛中的第三次粗鲁行为，取消比赛资格，无其他判罚。

21.4　判罚的实施

21.4.1　不良行为的判罚是针对个人的，对全场比赛有效，记录在记分表上。

21.4.2 同一成员在同一场比赛中重犯不良行为时，按判罚等级加一级判罚(该成员接受的判罚要重于前一次)。

21.4.3 对冒犯行为或侵犯行为的判罚出场或取消比赛资格，无须有先一次的判罚。

21.5 局前与局间的不良行为

任何局前与局间的不良行为，都应按规则21.3进行判罚，并记录在下一局中。

21.6 判罚牌

警告：口头或手势，无牌。

判罚：黄牌。

判罚出场：红牌。

取消比赛资格：红牌+黄牌(同持于一手)。

表3-1 不良行为判罚等级表

种类	发生次数	违反者	判罚	牌	结果
粗鲁行为	第一次	任一成员	判罚	黄	失一球由对方发球
	第二次	同一成员	判罚出场	红	该局比赛离开比赛场地坐在判罚区域内
	第三次	同一成员	取消比赛资格	红+黄	该场比赛离开比赛控制区域
冒犯行为	第一次	任一成员	判罚出场	红	该局比赛离开比赛场地坐在判罚区域内
	第二次	同一成员	取消比赛资格	红+黄	该场比赛离开比赛控制区域
侵犯行为	第一次	任一成员	取消比赛资格	红+黄	该场比赛离开比赛控制区域
延误判罚等级表					
延误	第一次	同队的任一成员	延误警告	手势25无牌	不予判罚防止重犯
	第二次(及其后的)	同队的任一成员	延误判罚	手势25黄	对方的一分并发球

22 裁判成员和工作程序

22.1 裁判成员

一场比赛的裁判员由以下成员组成：

第一裁判员

第二裁判员

记录员

四名(或两名)司线员

国际排联世界性比赛另设1名助理记录员

22.2 工作程度

22.2.1 在比赛进行中只有第一裁判员和第二裁判员可以鸣哨：

22.2.1.1 第一裁判员鸣哨发球开始比赛。

22.2.1.2 第一裁判员和第二裁判员确认犯规发生并判明其性质，鸣哨中止比赛。

22.2.2 在比赛中断期间，他们可以鸣哨表示同意或拒绝某队的请求。

22.2.3 裁判员鸣哨中止比赛后，应立即以法定手势表明。

22.2.3.1 如果第一裁判员鸣哨终止比赛，它应指出：

- 应发球的队。
- 犯规的性质。
- 犯规的队员（必要时）。

第二裁判员跟随并重复其手势。

22.2.3.2　如果第二裁判员鸣哨终止比赛，它应指出：

- 犯规的性质。
- 犯规的队员（必要时）。
- 跟随第一裁判员指出发球队。

第一裁判员不用指出犯规性质和指出犯规队员，只指出发球队。

22.2.3.3　如果后排队员或后排自由防守队员进攻性击球犯规，两名裁判员都有职责按上述程序做出手势。

22.2.3.4　如果双方犯规，他们都要按顺序指出：

- 犯规的性质。
- 犯规的队员（必要时）。
- 应发球的队（跟随第一裁判员）。

23　第一裁判员

23.1　位置

第一裁判员坐或站在球网一端的裁判台上执行其职责。他的视线水平必须在高出球网上沿约 50 厘米的高度上。

23.2　权力

23.2.1　他自始至终领导该场比赛。他对所有裁判员和比赛队成员行使权力。在比赛中他的判定是最终判定。如果发现其他裁判员的错误，他有权改判，甚至他可以撤换一名不称职的裁判人员。

23.2.2　他同样掌管捡球员和擦地员的工作。

23.2.3　他有权决定涉及比赛的一切问题，包括规则中没有规定的问题。

23.2.4　他不允许对其判定进行任何争辩，但当场上队长提出请求时，他应对其判定所依据的规则和规则的执行给予解释，如果队长立即表示不同意他的解释，并提出保留在比赛后对此提出正式抗议权利的声明，第一裁判员必须给予允准。

23.2.5　在比赛前和比赛中，他负责决定赛场条件是否符合比赛要求。

23.3　责任

23.3.1　比赛前，第一裁判员：

23.3.1.1　检查场地、器材和比赛用球。

23.3.1.2　主持双方队长抽签。

23.3.1.3　掌握两队的准备活动。

23.3.2　比赛中，只有第一裁判员有权：

23.3.2.1　向球队提出警告

23.3.2.2　对不良行为和延误比赛进行判罚。

23.3.2.3　判定：

- 发球犯规和发球位置错误，包括发球掩护；

• 比赛击球的犯规；

• 高于球网和球网上部的犯规；

• 后排队员或后排自由防守队员的进攻性击球犯规；

• 后排自由防守队员在其前场及延长区进行上手传球后同伴在球高于球网处完成进攻性击球犯规；

• 球的整体从网下空间穿越；

• 后排队员完成拦网，或后排自由防守队员试图拦网。

23.3.3 比赛后，检查记分表并签字。

24 第二裁判员

24.1 位置

第二裁判员站在第一裁判员对面、比赛场地外的网柱附近，面对第一裁判员执行其职责。

24.2 权力

24.2.1 第二裁判员是第一裁判员的助手，但是他还有自己的职责。当第一裁判员不能继续工作时，他可以代替第一裁判员执行工作。

24.2.2 他可以用手势指出他职权以外的犯规，但不得鸣哨，也不得向第一裁判员坚持自己的判断。

24.2.3 他掌管记录员的工作。

24.2.4 他监督坐在球队席上的球队成员并将他们的不良行为报告给第一裁判员。

24.2.5 他掌管准备活动区中的队员。

24.2.6 他允许比赛间断的请求，掌握间断的时间和拒绝不合规定的请求。

24.2.7 他掌握各队暂停和换人的次数，并将第二次暂停和第五、第六次换人告之给第一裁判员和有关教练员。

24.2.8 发现队员受伤，他可以允许特殊替换或给予3分钟的恢复时间。

24.2.9 他检查比赛场地地面的条件，主要是前场区。比赛中他还要检查球是否符合比赛要求。

24.2.10 监督判罚区域中受罚的队的成员，并将其不良行为报告给第一裁判员。

24.3 责任

24.3.1 在每局开始、决胜局交换场地、以及任何必要的时候，检查场上队员的实际位置是否与位置表相符。

24.3.2 在比赛中，第二裁判员对以下犯规做出判断，同时鸣哨并做出手势：

24.3.2.1 网下穿越进入对方场区和空间；

24.3.2.2 接发球队位置错误；

24.3.2.3 队员触及球网和第二裁判员一侧的标志杆；

24.3.2.4 后排队员完成拦网和后排自由防守队员试图拦网犯规；后排队员或后排自由防守队员进攻性击球犯规；

24.3.2.5 球触及场外物体；

24.3.2.6 第一裁判员处于难以观察时，球触及地面；

24.3.2.7 球的整体或部分从过网区以外过网，飞入对方场区，或触及他队一侧的标志杆。

24.3.3 比赛结束后在记分表上签字。

25 记录员

25.1 位置

记录员坐在第一裁判员对面的记录台处，面对第一裁判员执行职责。

25.2 职责

根据规则填写记录表并与第二裁判员进行合作。

在必要时，用蜂鸣器通知裁判员场上出现的犯规。

25.2.1 记录员在比赛前和每局前：

25.2.1.1 按照规定程序登记有关比赛和两队的情况，并取得双方队长和教练员的签字。

25.2.2.2 根据位置表登记各队上场阵容。如果没有按时接到位置表，应立即通知第二裁判员。

25.2.2 记录员在比赛中：

25.2.2.1 记录得分，核对计分牌上的比分是否正确。

25.2.2.2 掌握各队的发球次序。发现发球次序错误，应在发球击球后立即通知裁判员。

25.2.2.3 以蜂鸣器认可换人请求，掌握并记录暂停和换人次数，并通知第二裁判员。

25.2.2.4 对违背规则的间断请求，要通知裁判员。

25.2.2.5 每局结束和决胜局8分时，向裁判员宣布。

25.2.2.6 记录各种判罚和不符合规定的请求。

25.2.2.7 在第二裁判员指导下登记其他事件，如特殊换人、恢复时间、被拖延的间断、外因造成的间断等。

25.2.2.8 掌握局间休息。

25.2.3 记录员在比赛结束时：

25.2.3.1 登记最终结果。

25.2.3.2 如果有提出抗议的情况，记录或允许队长将有关抗议的问题写在记录表上。

25.2.3.3 自己在记录表上签字后，取得双方队长然后是裁判员的签字。

26 助理记录员

26.1 位置

助理记录员坐在记录台前记录员的身旁执行职责。

26.2 职责

记录有关后排自由防守队员的替换。协助记录员工作。记录员不能继续工作时，替代他。

26.2.1 比赛和每局开始前，助理记录员：

26.2.1.1 准备好后排自由防守队员替换表；

26.2.1.2　准备好备用记分表。

26.2.2　比赛中，助理记录员：

26.2.2.1　详细记录后排自由防守队员的替换；

26.2.2.2　发现任何有关后排自由防守队员替换的犯规，用蜂鸣器通知裁判员；

26.2.2.3　掌握技术暂停开始和结束的时间；

26.2.2.4　操作记录台上的手动记分；

26.2.2.5　监督记分牌的正确显示；

26.2.2.6　必要时填写好备用记分表的有关内容，交给记录员。

26.2.3　比赛结束后，助理记录员：

26.2.3.1　在后排自由防守队员替换表上签字备查；

26.2.3.2　在记分表上签字。

27　司线员

27.1　位置

如果是两名司线员，其位置应站在每名裁判员右手的场区角端，距场角 1~2 米，他们各自负责一侧的端线和边线。

国际排联世界性比赛必须有四名司线员。他们站在无障碍区距场角 1~3 米的位置上，各负责一条界线。

27.2　职责

27.2.1　司线员用旗(40 厘米×40 厘米)按照规定的旗示执行其职责：

27.2.1.1　当球落在他们所负责线附近时，示以“界内”或“界外”；

27.2.1.2　对触及身体后出界的球，示以“触手出界”；

27.2.1.3　示意球从过网区外过网和触及标志杆；

27.2.1.4　发球时，如有队员脚踏出场外(发球队员除外)，示其犯规；

27.2.1.5　负责端线的司线员示意发球队员脚的犯规；

27.2.1.6　队员击球时或干扰比赛的情况下，触及他一侧的标志杆；

27.2.1.7　球从标志杆外过网并进入对方场区，或触及他一侧的标志杆。

27.2.2　在第一裁判员询问时，司线员必须重复其旗示。

第二章　排球裁判员法定手势

1　法定手势

1.1　裁判员的手势

裁判员必须以法定手势指出鸣哨的原因（犯规的性质或准许的比赛间断目的等）。手势应有短时间的展示。如果是单手做手势，应用与犯规队或请求队同侧的手表示。

（1）允许发球：挥动手臂指明发球方向，如图1。

（2）发球队：平举与发球队同侧的手臂，如图2。

（3）交换场地：两臂屈肘，在身体前后绕旋，如图3。

（4）暂停：一臂屈肘抬起，手指向上；另一手掌放在该手指尖上，然后指明提出请求的队，如图4。

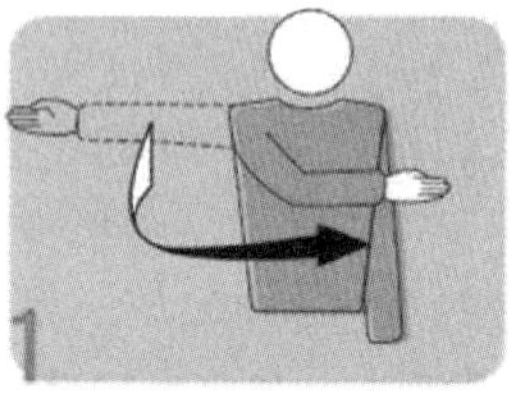

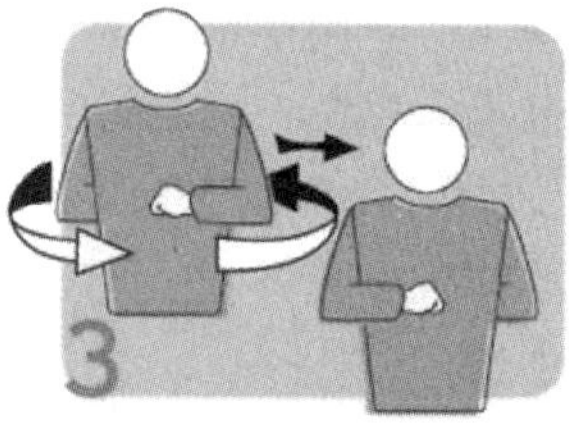

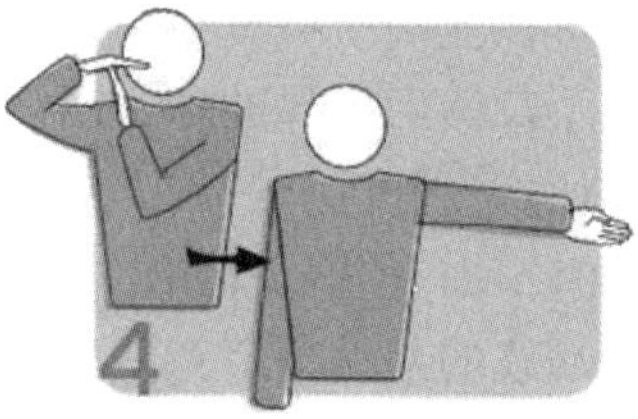

（5）换人：两臂屈肘在胸前绕环，如图5。

（6）不良行为的判罚：一手持黄牌举起，如图6。

（7）判罚出场：一手持红牌举起，如图7。

（8）取消比赛资格：一手持红、黄牌举起，如图8。

(9)示意一局(一场)比赛结束：两臂在胸前交叉，手伸开，掌心向内，如图 9。
(10)发球时球未抛起：一臂慢慢举起，掌心向上，如图 10。
(11)发球延误：举起 8 个手指并分开，掌心向前，如图 11。
(12)发球掩护或拦网犯规：两臂上举，掌心向前，如图 12。

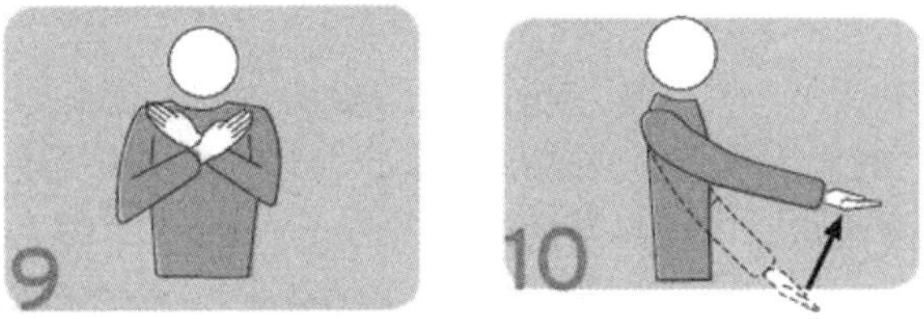

(13)位置或轮转错误：一手食指在体前水平环绕，如图 13。
(14)界内球：手臂和手指向地面，如图 14。
(15)界外球：两臂屈肘上举，掌心向身体，如图 15。
(16)持球：曲肘慢举前臂，掌心向上，如图 16。

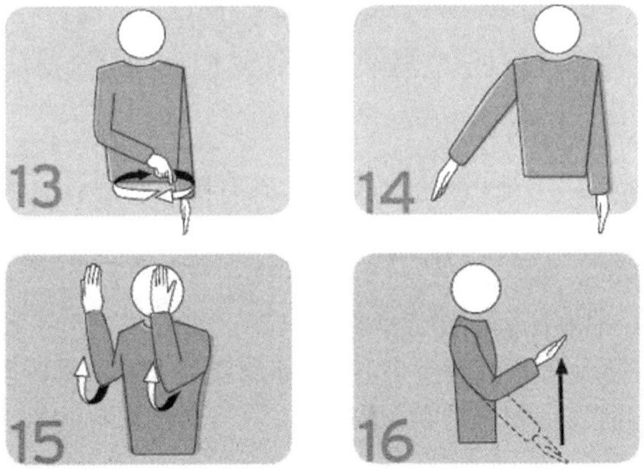

(17)连击：举起两个手指并分开，掌心向前，如图 17。
(18)四次击球：举起 4 个手指并分开，掌心向前，如图 18。
(19)队员触网和发球没有过网：一手触犯规队一侧的球网，如图 19。
(20)过网：前臂置于球网上空，掌心向下，如图 20。

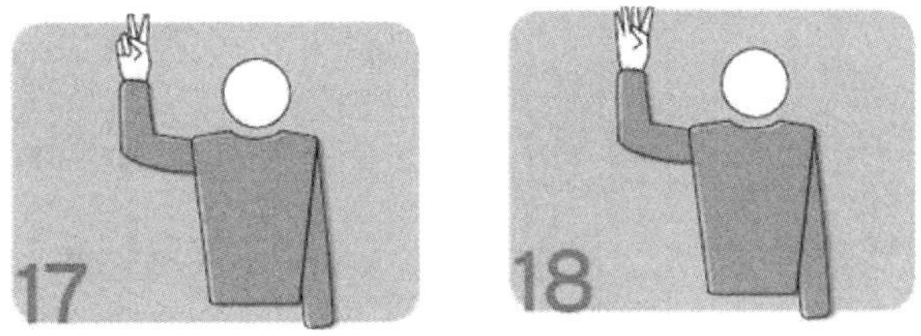

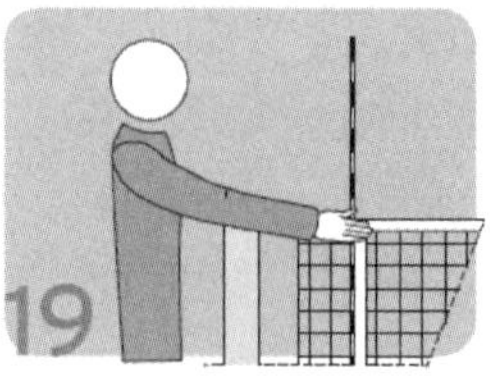 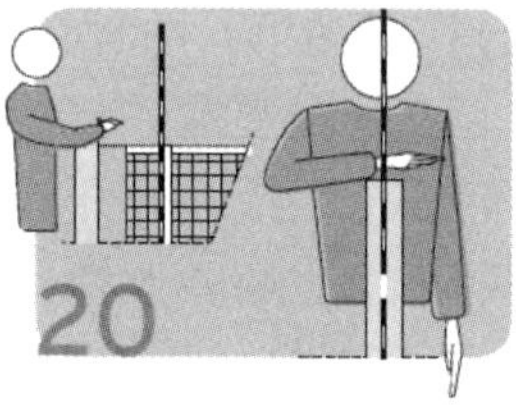

(21)进攻性击球犯规：一臂上举，前臂向下摆动，如图 21。

(22)进入对方场区或球从网下通过或发球时脚的犯规：指向中线或相关的线，如图 22。

(23)双方犯规：两臂屈肘，竖起拇指，如图 23。

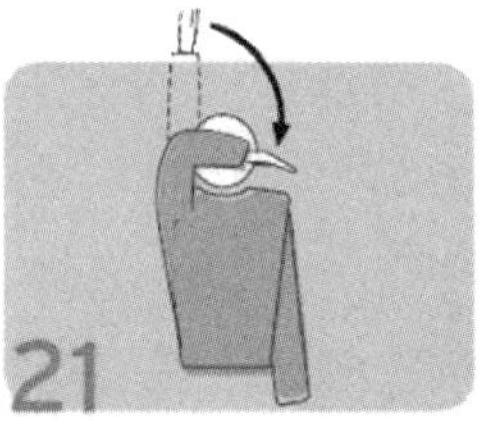 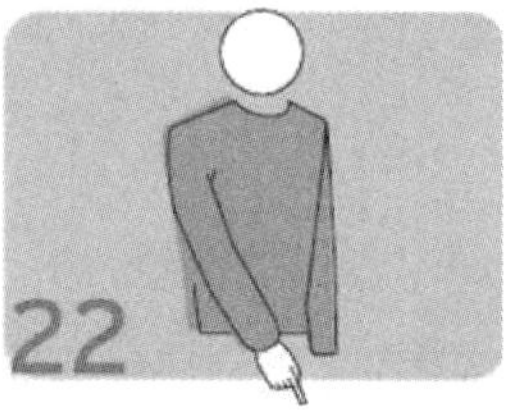 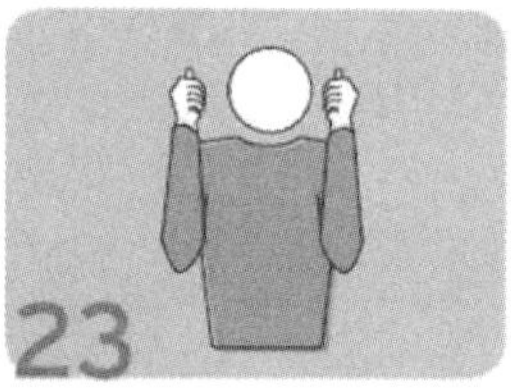

(24)触手出界：用一手掌擦另一曲肘上举的指尖

(25)延误警告和判罚：两臂屈肘举起，用一手掌遮盖另一手腕，掌心向身体(警告)，或用黄牌指手腕(判罚)

1.2　司线员的旗示

司线员必须用法定的旗示指出犯规的性质，并有短时间的展示。

(1)一手拿旗下指表示界内球，如图 1。

(2)上举表示界外球，如图 2。

(3) 放在胸前另一手放在旗上端表示打手出界，如图 3。

(4)一手举旗空中摇晃表示球在空中界外(即球碰到了屋顶或标志杆等)，如图 4。

(5)双手交叉在胸前表示无法判断(是告诉主裁自己没有看清)，如图 5。

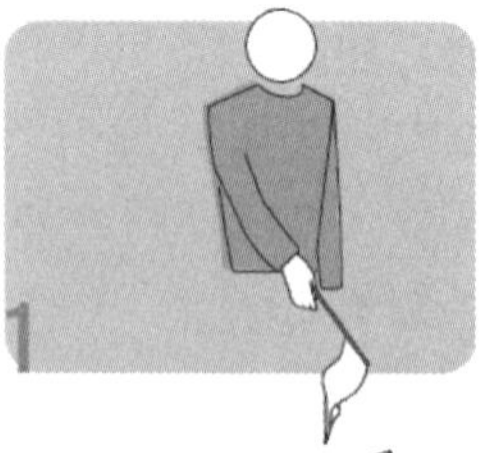 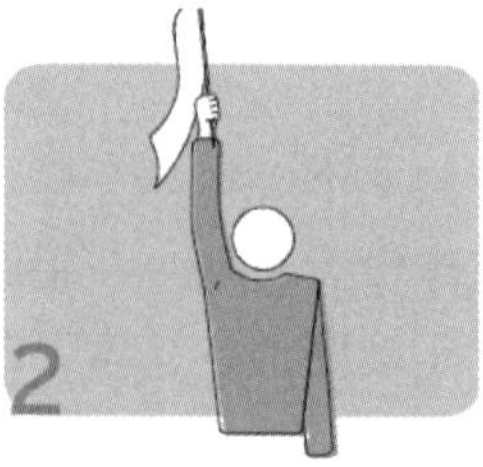

第三章　排球英文规则

1　Playing area

The playing area includes the playing court and the free zone. It shall be rectangular and symmetrical.

1.1　Dimensions

The playing court is a rectangle measuring 18 x 9 m, surrounded by a free zone which is a minimum of 3 m wide on all sides.

The freeplaying space is the space above the playing area which is free from any obstructions. The free playing space shall measure a minimum of 7 m in height from the playing surface.

For FIVB World and Official Competitions, the free zone shall measure a minimum of 5 m from the side lines and 8 m from the end lines. The free playing space shall measure a minimum of 12.5 m in height from the playing surface.

1.2　Playing surface

The surface must be flat, horizontal and uniform. It must not present any danger of injury to the players. It is forbidden to play on rough or slippery surfaces.

For FIVB, World and Official Competitions, only a wooden or synthetic surface is allowed. Any surface must be previously approved by the FIVB.

1.2.1　On indoor courts the surface of the playing court must be of a light colour.

For FIVB, World and Official Competitions, white colours are required for the lines. Other colours, different from each other, are required for the playing court and the free zone.

1.2.2　On outdoor courts a slope of 5 mm per metre is allowed for drainage. Court lines made of solid materials are forbidden.

1.3　Lines on the court

1.3.1　All lines are 5 cm wide. They must be of a light colour which is different from the colour of the floor and from any other lines.

1.3.2　Boundary lines: Two side lines and two end lines mark the playing court. Both side lines and end lines are drawn inside the dimensions of the playing court.

1.3.3　Centre line: The axis of the centre line divides the playing court into two equal courts measuring 9 x 9 m each; however the entire width of the line is considered to belong to both courts equally. This line extends beneath the net from side line to side line.

1.3.4　Attack line: On each court, an attack line, whose rear edge is drawn 3 m back from the axis of the centre line, marks the front zone.

For FIVB, World and Official Competitions, the attack line is extended by the addition of broken lines from the side lines, with five 15 cm short lines 5 cm wide, drawn 20 cm from each other to a totallength of 1.75 m. The "coach's restriction line" (a broken line which extends from the attack line to the end line of the court, parallel to the side line and 1.75 metres from it) is composed of 15 cm short lines drawn 20 cm apart to mark the limit of the coach's area of operation.

1.4 Zones and areas

1.4.1 Front zone

On each court the front zone is limited by the axis of the centre line and the rear edge of the attack line.

The front zone is considered to extend beyond the sidelines to the end of the free zone.

1.4.2 Service zone

The service zone is a 9 m wide area behind each end line.

It is laterally limited by two short lines, each 15 cm long, drawn 20 cm behind the end line as an extension of the side lines. Both short lines are included in the width of the service zone.

In depth, the service zone extends to the end of the free zone.

1.4.3 Substitution zone

The substitution zone is limited by the extension of both attack lines up to the scorer's table.

1.4.4 Libero Replacement Zone

The Libero Replacement Zone is part of the free zone on the side of the team benches, limited by the extension of the attack line up to the end line.

1.4.5 Warm-up area

For FIVB, World and Official Competitions, the warm-up areas, sized approximately 3 x 3 m, are located in both of the bench-side corners, outside the free zone.

1.4.6 Penalty area

A penalty area, sized approximately 1 x 1 m and equipped with two chairs, is located in the control area, outside the prolongation of each end line. They may be limited by a 5 cm wide red line.

1.5 Temperature

The minimum temperature shall not be below 10° C (50° F).

For FIVB, World and Official Competitions, the maximum temperature shall not be higher than 25° C (77° F) and the minimum not lower than 16° C (61° F).

1.6 Lighting

For FIVB, World and Official Competitions, the lighting on the playing area should be 1000 to 1500 lux measured at 1 m above the surface of the playing area.

2 Net and posts

2.1 Height of the net

2.1.1 Placed vertically over the centre line there is a net whose top is set at the height of 2.43 m for men and 2.24 m for women.

2.1.2 Its height is measured from the centre of the playing court. The net height (over the two side lines) must be exactly the same and must not exceed the official height by more than 2 cm.

2. 2 Structure

The net is 1 m wide and 9. 50 to 10 metres long (with 25 to 50 cm on each side of the side bands), made of 10 cm square black mesh.

At its top a horizontal band, 7 cm wide, made of two-fold white canvas, is sewn along its full length. Each extreme end of the band has a hole, through which passes a cord, fastening the band to the posts for keeping its top taut.

Within the band, a flexible cable fastens the net to the posts and keeps its top taut.

At the bottom of the net there is another horizontal band, 5cm wide, similar to the top band, through which is threaded a rope. This rope fastens the net to the posts and keeps its lower part taut.

2. 3 Side bands

Two white bands are fastened vertically to the net and placed directly above each sideline.

They are 5 cm wide and 1 m long, and are considered as part of the net.

2. 4 Antennae

An antenna is a flexible rod, 1. 80 m long and 10 mm in diameter, made of fibreglass or similar material.

An antenna is fastened at the outer edge of each side band. The antennae are placed on opposite sides of the net.

The top 80 cm of each antenna extends above the net and is marked with 10 cm stripes of contrasting colour, preferably red and white.

The antennae are considered as part of the net and laterally delimit the crossing space.

2. 5 Posts

2. 5. 1 The posts supporting the net are placed at a distance of 0. 50 -1. 00 m outside the side lines. They are 2. 55 m high and preferably adjustable.

For all FIVB, World and Official Competitions, the posts supporting the net are placed at a distance of 1 m outside the side lines.

2. 5. 2 The posts are rounded and smooth, fixed to the ground without wires. There shall be no dangerous or obstructing devices.

2. 6 Additional equipment

All additional equipment is determined by FIVB regulations.

3 Balls

3. 1 Standards

The ball shall be spherical, made of a flexible leather or synthetic leather case with a bladder inside made of rubber or a similar material.

Its colour may be a uniform light colour, or a combination of colours.

Synthetic leather material and colour combinations of balls used in International Official competitions should comply with FIVB standards.

Its circumference is 65~67 cm and its weight is 260~280 g.

Its inside pressure shall be 0. 30 to 0. 325 kg/cm2 (4. 26 to 4. 61 psi) (294. 3 to 318. 82

mbar or hPa)

3. 2 Uuniformity of balls

All balls used in a match must have the same standards regarding circumference, weight, pressure, type, colour, etc.

FIVB, World and Official Competitions, as well as National or League Championships must be played with FIVB approved balls, unless by agreement of FIVB.

3. 3 Three-ball system

For FIVB, World and Official Competitions, three balls shall be used. In this case, six ball retrievers are stationed, one at each corner of the free zone and one behind each referee.

4 Teams

4. 1 Team composition

4. 1. 1 A team may consist of up to 12 players, one coach, one assistant coach, one trainer and one medical doctor (unless modified by the Specific Competition Regulations).

For FIVB, Worldand Official Competitions, the medical doctor and trainer must be accredited beforehand by the FIVB.

4. 1. 2 One of the players, other than the Libero, is the team captain, who shall be indicated on the score sheet.

4. 1. 3 Only the players recorded on the score sheet may enter the court and play in the match. Once the coach and the team captain have signed the score sheet, the recorded players can not be changed.

4. 2 Location of the team

4. 2. 1 The players not in play should either sit on their team bench or bein their warm-up area. The coach and other team members sit on the bench, but may temporarily leave it.

The benches for the teams are located beside the scorer's table, outside the free zone.

4. 2. 2 Only the team members are permitted to sit on the bench during the match and to participate in the warm-up session.

4. 2. 3 Players not in play may warm-up without balls as follows:

4. 2. 3. 1 during play: in the warm-up areas;

4. 2. 3. 2 during time-outs and technical time-outs: in the free zone behind their court.

4. 2. 4 During set intervals, players may warm-up using balls in the free zone.

4. 3 Equipment

A player's equipment consists of a jersey, shorts, socks (the uniform) and sport shoes.

4. 3. 1 The colour and the design for the jerseys, shorts and socks must be uniform for the team (*except for the Libero*). The uniforms must be clean.

4. 3. 2 The shoes must be light and pliable with non-marking rubber or composite soles without heels.

For FIVB, World and Official Competitions, it is forbidden to wear shoes which are predominantly black.

4. 3. 3 Players' jerseys must be numbered from 1 to 18.

For FIVB, World and Official Competitions, players' jerseys must be numbered from 1 to 20.

4.3.3.1 The number must be placed on the jersey at the centre of the front and of the back. The colour and brightness of the numbers must contrast with the colour and brightness of the jerseys.

4.3.3.2 The number must be a minimum of 15 cm in height on the chest, and a minimum of 20 cm in height on the back. The stripe forming the numbers shall be a minimum of 2 cm in width.

For FIVB, World and Official Competitions, the player's number shall be repeated on the right leg of the shorts. The number must be of 4 to 6 cm in height and the stripe forming the numbers shall be a minimum of 1 cm in width. Jerseys and shorts should comply with FIVB standards.

4.3.4 The team captain must have on his/her jersey a stripe of 8 x 2 cm underlining the number on the chest.

4.3.5 It is forbidden to wear uniforms of a colour different from that of the other players (*except for the Liberos*), and/or without official numbers.

4.4 Change of equipment

The first referee may authorize one or more players:

4.4.1 to play barefoot, For FIVB, World and Official Competitions it is forbidden to play barefoot.

4.4.2 to change wet or damaged uniforms between sets or after substitution, provided that the colour, design and number of the new uniform(s) are the same.

4.4.3 to play in training suits in cold weather, provided that they are of the same colour and design for the whole team (except for the Liberos) and numbered according to Rule 4.3.3.

4.5 Forbidden objects

4.5.1 It is forbidden to wear objects which may cause injury, or give an artificial advantage to the player.

4.5.2 Players may wear glasses or lenses at their own risk.

5 Team leaders

Both the team captain and the coach are responsible for the conduct and discipline of their team members. The Liberos cannot be the team captain or game captain.

5.1 Captain

5.1.1 Prior to the match, the team captain signs the score sheet and represents his/her team in the toss.

5.1.2 During the match and while on the court, the team captain is the game captain. When the team captain is not on the court, the coach or the team captain must assign another player on the court, but not the Libero, to assume the role of game captain. This game captain maintains his/her responsibilities until he/she is substituted, or the team captain returns to play, or the set ends.

When the ball is out of play, only the game captain is authorized to speak to the referees:

5. 1. 2. 1 to ask for an explanation on the application or interpretation of the rules, and also to submit the requests or questions of his/her team-mates. If the game captain does not agree with the explanation of the first referee, he/she may choose to protest against such decision and immediately indicates to the first referee that he/she reserves the right to record an official protest on the score sheet at the end of the match.

5. 1. 2. 2 to ask authorization:

- to change all or part of the equipment;
- to verify the positions of the teams;
- to check the floor, the net, the ball, etc.

5. 1. 2. 3 in the absence of the coach to request time-outs and substitutions.

5. 1. 3 At the end of the match, the team captain:

5. 1. 3. 1 thanks the referees and signs the score sheet to ratify the outcome;

5. 1. 3. 2 when it has been notified in due time to the first referee, may confirm and record on the score sheet an official protest regarding the referee's application or interpretation of the Rules.

5. 2 Coach

5. 2. 1 Throughout the match, the coach conducts the play of his/her team from outside the playing court. He/she selects the starting line-ups, their substitutes, and takes time-outs. In these functions his/her contacting official is the second referee.

5. 2. 2 Prior to the match, the coach records or checks the names and numbers of his/her players on the score sheet, and then signs it.

5. 2. 3 During the match, the coach:

5. 2. 3. 1 prior to each set, gives the second referee or the scorer the line-up sheet(s) duly filled in and signed;

5. 2. 3. 2 sits on the team bench nearest to the scorer, but may leave it;

5. 2. 3. 3 requests time-outs and substitutions;

5. 2. 3. 4 may, as well as other team members, give instructions to the players on the court. The coach may give these instructions while standing or walking within the free zone in front of his/her team's bench from the extension of the attack line up to the warm-up area, without disturbing or delaying the match.

For FIVB, World and Official Competitions, the coach is restricted to performing his/her function behind the coach's restriction line.

5. 3 Assistant coach

5. 3. 1 The assistant coach sits on the team bench, but has no right to intervene in the match.

5. 3. 2 Should the coach have to leave his/her team for any reason including sanction, the assistant coach may, at the request of the game captain and with the authorization of the first referee, assume the coach's functions for the duration of the absence.

6 To score a point, to win a set and the match

6.1 To score a point

6.1.1 Point

A team scores a point:

6.1.1.1 by successfully grounding the ball on the opponent's court;

6.1.1.2 when the opponent team commits a fault;

6.1.1.3 when the opponent team receives a penalty.

6.1.2 Fault

A team commits a fault by making a playing action contrary to the rules (or by violating them in some other way). The referees judge the faults and determine the consequences according to the Rules:

6.1.2.1 If two or more faults are committed successively, only the first one is counted.

6.1.2.2 If two or more faults are committed by opponent simultaneously, a DOUBLE FAULT is called and the rally is replayed.

6.1.3 Rally and completed rally

A rally is the sequence of playing actions from the moment of the service hit by the server until the ball is out of play. A completed rally is the sequence of playing actions which results in the award of a point.

6.1.3.1 if the serving team wins a rally, it scores a point and continues to serve;

6.1.3.2 if the receiving team wins a rally, it scores a point and it must serve next.

6.2 To win a wet

A set (except the deciding, 5th set) is won by the team which first scores 25 points with a minimum lead of two points. In the case of a 24-24 tie, play is continued until a two-point lead is achieved (26-24; 27-25; …).

6.3 To win the match

6.3.1 The match is won by the team that wins three sets.

6.3.2 In the case of a 2-2 tie, the deciding set (the 5th) is played to 15 points with a minimum lead of 2 points.

6.4 Default and incomplete team

6.4.1 If a team refuses to play after being summoned to do so, it is declared in default and forfeits the match with the result 0-3 for the match and 0-25 for each set.

6.4.2 A team that, without justifiable reason, does not appear on the playing court on time is declared in default with the same result as in Rule 6.4.1.

6.4.3 A team that is declared INCOMPLETE for the set or for the match, loses the set or the match. The opponent team is given the points, or the points and the sets, needed to win the set or the match. The incomplete team keeps its points and sets.

7 Structure of play

7.1 The toss

Before the match, the first referee carries out a toss to decide upon the first service and the sides of the court in the first set.

If a deciding set is to be played, a new toss will be carried out.

7.1.1 The toss is taken in the presence of the two team captains.

7.1.2 The winner of the toss chooses:

7.1.2.1 the right to serve or to receive the service;

7.1.2.2 the side of the court.

The loser takes the remaining choice.

7.1.3 In the case of consecutive warm-ups, the team that has the first service takes the first turn at the net.

7.2 Warm-up session

7.2.1 Prior to the match, if the teams have previously had a playing court at their disposal, they are entitled to a 6-minute warm-up period together at the net; if not, they may have 10 minutes.

7.2.2 If either captain requests separate (consecutive) warm-ups at the net, the teams may do so for 3 minutes each or 5 minutes each, according to Rule 7.2.1.

7.3 Team starting line-up

7.3.1 There must always be six players per team in play.

The team's starting line-up indicates the rotational order of the players on the court. This order must be maintained throughout the set.

7.3.2 Before the start of each set, the coach has to present the starting line-up of his/her team on a line-up sheet. The sheet is submitted, duly filled in and signed, to the second referee or the scorer.

7.3.3 The players who are not in the starting line-up of a set are the substitutes for that set (except for the Liberos).

7.3.4 Once the line-up sheet has been delivered to the second referee or scorer, no change in line-up may be authorized without a regular substitution.

7.3.5 Discrepancies between players' position on court and on the line-up sheet are dealt with as follows:

7.3.5.1 when such a discrepancy is discovered before the start of the set, players' positions must be rectified according to that on the line-up sheet - there will be no sanction;

7.3.5.2 when, before the start of the set, a player on court is found not to be registered on the line-up sheet of that set, this player must be changed to conform to the line-up sheet - there will be no sanction;

7.3.5.3 however, if the coach wishes to keep such non-recorded player(s) on the court, he/she has to request regular substitution(s), which will then be recorded on the score sheet.

If a discrepancy between player positions and the line up sheet is discovered later, the team at fault must revert to the correct positions. All points scored by the team from the exact moment of the fault up to the discovery of the fault are cancelled. The opponent's points remain valid and in addition they receive a point and the next service.

7.4 Positions

At the moment the ball is hit by the server, each team must be positioned within its own court in the rotational order (except the server).

7.4.1 The positions of the players are numbered as follows:

7.4.1.1 the three players along the net are front-row players and occupy positions 4 (front-left), 3 (front-centre) and 2 (front-right);

7.4.1.2 the other three are back-row players occupying positions 5 (back-left), 6 (back-centre) and 1 (back-right).

7.4.2 Relative positions between players:

7.4.2.1 each back-row player must be positioned further back from the centre line than the corresponding front-row player;

7.4.2.2 the front-row players and the back-row players, respectively, must be positioned laterally in the order indicated in Rule 7.4.1.

7.4.3 The positions of players are determined and controlled according to the positions of their feet contacting the ground as follows:

7.4.3.1 each front-row player must have at least a part of his/her foot closer to the centre line than the feet of the corresponding back-row player;

7.4.3.2 each right (left) side player must have at least a part of his/her foot closer to the right (left) sideline than the feet of the centre player in that row.

7.4.4 After the service hit, the players may move around and occupy any position on their court, and the free zone.

7.5 Positional fault

7.5.1 The team commits a positional fault, if any player is not in his/her correct position at the moment the ball is hit by the server.

7.5.2 If the server commits a serving fault at the moment of the service hit, the server's fault is counted before a positional fault.

7.5.3 If the service becomes faulty after the service hit, it is the positional fault that will be counted.

7.5.4 A positional fault leads to the following consequences:

7.5.4.1 the team is sanctioned with a point and service to the opponent;

7.5.4.2 players' positions are rectified.

7.6 Rotation

7.6.1 Rotational order is determined by the team's starting line-up, and controlled with the service order, and players' positions, throughout the set.

7.6.2 When the receiving team has gained the right to serve, its players rotate one position clock-wise: the player in position 2 rotates to position 1 to serve, the player in position 1 rotates to position 6, etc.

7.7 Rotational fault

7.7.1 A rotational fault is committed when the SERVICE is not made according to the rotational order. It leads to the following consequences:

7.7.1.1 the team is sanctioned with a point and service to the opponent;

7.7.1.2 the players' rotational order is rectified.

7.7.2 Additionally, the scorer should determine the exact moment when the fault was committed and all points scored subsequently by the team at fault must be cancelled. The opponent's points remain valid.

If that moment cannot be determined, no point(s) cancellation takes place, anda point and service to the opponent is the only sanction.

8 States of play

8.1 Ball in play

The ball is in play from the moment of the hit of the service authorized by the first referee.

8.2 Ball out of play

The ball is out of play at the moment of the fault which is whistled by one of the referees; in the absence of a fault, at the moment of the whistle.

8.3 Ball "in"

The ball is "in" when it touches the floor of the playing court including the boundary lines.

8.4 Ball "out"

The ball is "out" when:

8.4.1 the part of the ball which contacts the floor is completely outside the boundary lines;

8.4.2 it touches an object outside the court, the ceiling or a person out of play;

8.4.3 it touches the antennae, ropes, posts or the net itself outside the side bands;

8.4.4 it crosses the vertical plane of the net either partially or totally outside the crossing space, except in the case of Rule 10.1.2;

8.4.5 it crosses completely the lower space under the net.

9 Playing the ball

Each team must play within its own playing area and space (except Rule 10.1.2). The ball may, however, be retrieved from beyond the free zone.

9.1 Team hits

A hit is any contact with the ball by a player in play.

The team is entitled to a maximum of three hits (in addition to blocking, Rule 14.4.1), for returning the ball. If more are used, the team commits the fault of: "FOUR HITS".

9.1.1 Consecutive contacts

A player may not hit the ball two times consecutively (except Rules 9.2.3, 14.2 and 14.4.2).

9.1.2 Simultaneous contacts

Two or three players may touch the ball at the same moment.

9. 1. 2. 1 When two (three) team-mates touch the ball simultaneously, it is counted as two (three) hits (with the exception of blocking). If they reach for the ball, but only one of them touches it, one hit is counted. A collision of players does not constitute a fault.

9. 1. 2. 2 When two opponents touch the ball simultaneously over the net and the ball remains in play, the team receiving the ball is entitled to another three hits. If such a ball goes "out", it is the fault of the team on the opposite side.

9. 1. 2. 3 If simultaneous hits by two opponents over the net lead to extended contact with the ball, play continues.

9. 1. 3 Assisted hit

Within the playing area, a player is not permitted to take support from a team-mate or any structure/object in order to hit the ball.

However, a player who is about to commit a fault (touch the net or cross the centre line, etc.) may be stopped or held back by a team-mate.

9. 2 Characteristics of the hit

9. 2. 1 The ball may touch any part of the body.

9. 2. 2 The ball must not be caught and/or thrown. It can rebound in any direction.

9. 2. 3 The ball may touch various parts of the body, provided that the contacts take place simultaneously.

Exceptions:

9. 2. 3. 1 at blocking, consecutive contacts may be made by one or more blocker(s) provided that the contacts occur during one action;

9. 2. 3. 2 at the first hit of the team, the ball may contact various parts of the body consecutively provided that the contacts occur during one action.

9. 3 Faultsin playing the ball

9. 3. 1 Four hits: a team hits the ball four times before returning it.

9. 3. 2 Assisted hit: a player takes support from a team-mate or any structure/object in order to hit the ball within the playing area.

9. 3. 3 Catch: the ball is caughtand/or thrown; it does not rebound from the hit.

9. 3. 4 Double contact: a player hits the ball twice in succession or the ball contacts various parts of his/her body in succession.

10 Ball at the net

10. 1 Ball crossing the net

10. 1. 1 The ball sent to the opponent's court must go over the net within the crossing space. The crossing space is the part of the vertical plane of the net limited as follows:

10. 1. 1. 1 below, by the top of the net;

10. 1. 1. 2 at the sides, by the antennae, and their imaginary extension;

10. 1. 1. 3 above, by the ceiling.

10. 1. 2 The ball that has crossed the net plane to the opponent's free zone totally or partly through the external space, may be played back within the team hits, provided that:

10. 1. 2. 1 the opponent's court is not touched by the player;

10. 1. 2. 2 the ball, when played back, crosses the net plane again totally or partly through the external space on the same side of the court.

The opponent team may not prevent such action.

10. 1. 3 The ball that is heading towards the opponent's court through the lower space is in play until the moment it has completely crossed the vertical plane of the net.

10. 2 Ball touching the net

While crossing the net, the ball may touch it.

10. 3 Ball in the net

10. 3. 1 A ball driven into the net may be recovered within the limits of the three team hits.

10. 3. 2 If the ball rips the mesh of the net or tears it down, the rally is cancelled and replayed.

11 Player at the net

11. 1 Reaching beyond the net

11. 1. 1 In blocking, a blocker may touch the ball beyond the net, provided that he/she does not interfere with the opponent's play before or during the latter's attack hit;

11. 1. 2 After an attack hit, a player is permitted to pass his/her hand beyond the net, provided that the contact has been made within his/her own playing space.

11. 2 Penetration under the net

11. 2. 1 It is permitted to penetrate into the opponent's space under the net, provided that this does not interfere with the opponent's play.

11. 2. 2 Penetration into the opponent's court, beyond the centre line:

11. 2. 2. 1 to touch the opponent's court with a foot (feet) is permitted, provided that some part of the penetrating foot(feet) remains either in contact with or directly above the centre line;

11. 2. 2. 2 to touch the opponent's court with any part of the body above the feet is permitted provided that it does not interfere with the opponent's play.

11. 2. 3 A player may enter the opponent's court after the ball goes out of play.

11. 2. 4 Players may penetrate into the opponent's free zone provided that they donot interfere with the opponent's play.

11. 3 Contact with the net

11. 3. 1 Contact with the net by a player is not a fault, unless it interferes with the play.

11. 3. 2 Players may touch the post, ropes, or any other object outside the antennae, including the net itself, provided that it does not interfere with play.

11. 3. 3 When the ball is driven into the net, causing it to touch an opponent, no fault is committed.

11. 4 Player's faults at the net

11. 4. 1 A player touches the ball or an opponent in the opponent's space before or during the opponent's attack hit.

11. 4. 2 A player interferes with the opponent's play while penetrating into the opponent's

space under the net.

11.4.3 A player's foot (feet) penetrates completely into the opponent's court.

11.4.4 A player interferes with the opponent's play by (amongst others):

- touching the top band of the net or the top 80 cm of the antenna during his/her action of playing the ball, or
- taking support from the net simultaneously with playing the ball, or
- creating an advantage over the opponent, or
- making actions which hinder an opponent's legitimate attempt to play the ball

12 Service

The service is the act of putting the ball into play, by the back right player, placed in the service zone.

12.1 First service in a set

12.1.1 The first service of the first set, as well as that of the deciding set (the 5th) is executed by the team determined by the toss.

12.1.2 The other sets will be started with the service of the team that did not serve first in the previous set.

12.2 Service order

12.2.1 The players must follow the service order recorded on the line-up sheet.

12.2.2 After the first service in a set, the player to serve is determined as follows:

12.2.2.1 when the serving team wins the rally, the player (or his/her substitute) who served before, serves again;

12.2.2.2 when the receiving team wins the rally, it gains the right to serve and rotates before actually serving. The player who moves from the front right position to the back-right position will serve.

12.3 Authorization of the service

The first referee authorizes the service, after having checked that the two teams are ready to play and that the server is in possession of the ball.

12.4 Execution of the service

12.4.1 The ball shall be hit with one hand or any part of the arm after being tossed or released from the hand(s).

12.4.2 Only one toss or release of the ball is allowed. Dribbling or moving the ball in the hands is permitted.

12.4.3 At the moment of the service hit or take-off for a jump service, the server must not touch the court (the end line included) or the floor outside the service zone.

After the hit, he/she may step or land outside the service zone, or inside the court.

12.4.4 The server must hit the ball within 8 seconds after the first referee whistles for service.

12.4.5 A service executed before the referee's whistle is cancelled and repeated.

12.5 Screening

12.5.1 The players of the serving team must not prevent their opponent, through individual or collective screening, from seeing the server or the flight path of the ball.

12.5.2 A player, or group of players, of the serving team makes a screen by waving arms, jumping or moving sideways, during the execution of the service, or by standing grouped to hide the flight path of the ball.

12.6 Faults made dufing the service

12.6.1 Serving faults

The following faults lead to a change of service even if the opponent is out of position. The server:

12.6.1.1 violates the service order;

12.6.1.2 does not execute the service properly.

12.6.2 Faults after the service hit

After the ball has been correctly hit, the service becomes a fault (unless a player is out of position) if the ball:

12.6.2.1 touches a player of the serving team or fails to cross the vertical plane of the net completely through the crossing space;

12.6.2.2 goes "out";

12.6.2.3 passes over a screen.

12.7 Serving faults and positional faults

12.7.1 If the server makes a fault at the moment of the service hit (improper execution, wrong rotational order, etc.) and the opponent is out of position, it is the serving fault which is sanctioned.

12.7.2 Instead, if the execution of the service has been correct, but the service subsequently becomes faulty (goes out, goes over a screen, etc.), the positional fault has taken place first and is sanctioned.

13 Attack hit

13.1 Characteristics of the attack hit

13.1.1 All actions which direct the ball towards the opponent, with the exception of service and block, are considered as attack hits.

13.1.2 During an attack hit, tipping is permitted only if the ball is cleanly hit, and not caught or thrown.

13.1.3 An attack hit is completed at the moment the ball completely crosses the vertical plane of the net or is touched by an opponent.

13.2 Restrictions of the attack hit

13.2.1 A front-row player may complete an attack hit at any height, provided that the contact with the ball has been made within the player's own playing space (except Rule 13.2.4).

13.2.2 A back-row player may complete an attack hit at any height from behind the front zone:

13.2.2.1 at his/her take-off, the player's foot (feet) must neither have touched nor crossed over the attack line;

13.2.2.2 after his/her hit, the player may land within the front zone.

13.2.3 A back-row player may also complete an attack hit from the front zone, if at the moment of the contact part of the ball is lower than the top of the net.

13.2.4 No player is permitted to complete an attack hit on the OPPONENT'S service, when the ball is in the front zone and entirely higher than the top of the net.

13.3 Faults of the attack hit

13.3.1 A player hits the ball within the playing space of the opposing team.

13.3.2 A player hits the ball "out".

13.3.3 A back-row player completes an attack hit from the front zone, if at the moment of the hit the ball is entirely higher than the top of the net.

13.3.4 A player completes an attack hit on the opponent's service, when the ball is in the front zone and entirely higher than the top of the net.

13.3.5 A Libero completes an attack hit if at the moment of the hit the ball is entirely higher than the top of the net.

13.3.6 A player completes an attack hit from higher than the top of the net when the ball is coming from an overhand finger pass by a Libero in his/her front zone.

14 Block

14.1 Blocking

14.1.1 Blocking is the action of players close to the net to intercept the ball coming from the opponent by reaching higher than the top of the net, regardless of the height of the ball contact. Only front-row players are permitted to complete a block, but at the moment of contact with the ball, part of the body must be higher than the top of the net.

14.1.2 Block Attempt

A block attempt is the action of blocking without touching the ball.

14.1.3 Completed Block

A block is completed whenever the ball is touched by a blocker.

14.1.4 Collective Block

A collective block is executed by two or three players close to each other and is completed when one of them touches the ball.

14.2 Block contact

Consecutive (quick and continuous) contacts with the ball may occur by one or more blockers provided that the contacts are made during one action.

14.3 Blocking within the opponent's space

In blocking, the player may place his/her hands and arms beyond the net provided that this action does not interfere with the opponent's play. Thus, it is not permitted to touch the ball beyond the net until an opponent has executed an attack hit.

14.4 Block and team hits

14.4.1 A block contact is not counted as a team hit. Consequently, after a block contact, a team is entitled to three hits to return the ball.

14. 4. 2 The first hit after the block may be executed by any player, including the one who has touched the ball during the block.

14. 5 Blocking the service

To block an opponent's service is forbidden.

14. 6 Blocking faults

14. 6. 1 The blocker touches the ball in the OPPONENT'S space either before or simultaneously with the opponent's attack hit.

14. 6. 2 A back-row player or a Libero completes a block or participates in a completed block.

14. 6. 3 Blocking the opponent's service.

14. 6. 4 The ball is sent "out" off the block.

14. 6. 5 Blocking the ball in the opponent's space from outside the antenna.

14. 6. 6 A Libero attempts an individual or collective block.

CHAPTER FIVE
INTERRUPTIONS, INTERVALS AND DELAYS

15 Regular game interruptions

Regulargame interruptions are TIME-OUTS and SUBSTITUTIONS.

An interruption is the time between one completed rally and the 1st referee's whistle for the next service.

15. 1 Number of regular game interruptions

Each team is entitled to request a maximum of two time-outs and six player substitutions per set.

15. 2 Request for regular game interruptions

15. 2. 1 Regular game interruptions may be requested by the coach, or in the absence of the coach by the game captain, and only by them.

The request is made by showing the corresponding hand signal, when the ball is out of play and before the whistle for service.

For FIVB, World and Official Competitions it is obligatory to use the buzzer and then the hand signal to request time-out.

15. 2. 2 Substitution before the start of a set is permitted, and should be recorded as a regular substitution in that set.

15. 3 Sequence of interruptions

15. 3. 1 Request for one or two time-outs, and one request for player substitution by either team may follow one another, with no need to resume the game.

15. 3. 2 However, a team is not authorized to make consecutive requests for player substitution during the same game interruption. Two or more players may be substituted during the same game interruption.

15. 4 Time-outs and technical time-outs

15. 4. 1 All time-outs that are requested last for 30 seconds.

For FIVB, World and Official Competitions, in sets 1 – 4, two additional 60-second "Technical Time-Outs" are applied automatically when the leading team reaches the 8th and 16th points.

In the deciding (5th) set, there are no "Technical Time-Outs"; only two time-outs of 30 seconds duration may be requested by each team.

15. 4. 2 During all time-outs, the players in play must go to the free zone near their bench.

15. 5 Substitution of players

A substitution is the act by which a player, other than the Libero or his/her replacement player, after being recorded by the scorer, enters the game to occupy the position of another player, who must leave the court at that moment. Substitution requires the referee's authorization.

15. 6 Limitation of substitutions

15. 6. 1 Six substitutions is the maximum permitted per team per set. One or more players may be substituted at the same time.

15. 6. 2 A player of the starting line-up, may leave the game, but only once in a set, and re-enter, but only once in a set, and only to his/her previous position in the line-up.

15. 6. 3 A substitute player may enter the game in place of a player of the starting line-up, but only once per set, and he/she can only be substituted by the same starting player.

15. 7 Exceptional substitution

A player (except the Libero) who cannot continue playing due to injury or illness, should be substituted legally. If this is not possible, the team is entitled to make an EXCEPTIONAL substitution, beyond the limits of Rule 15. 6.

An exceptional substitution means that any player who is not on the court at the time of the injury, except the Libero or his/her replacement player, may be substituted into the game for the injured player. The substituted injured player is not allowed to re-enter the match.

An exceptional substitution cannot be counted in any case as a regular substitution.

15. 8 Substitution for expulsion or disqualification

An EXPELLED or DISQUALIFIED player must be substituted immediately through a legal substitution. If this is not possible, the team is declared INCOMPLETE.

15. 9 Illegal substitution

15. 9. 1 A substitution is illegal, if it exceeds the limitations indicated in Rule 15. 6 (except the case of Rule 15. 7).

15. 9. 2 When a team has made an illegal substitution and the play has been resumed the following procedure shall apply:

15. 9. 2. 1 the team is penalized with a point and service to the opponent;

15. 9. 2. 2 the substitution is rectified;

15. 9. 2. 3 the points scored by the team at fault since the fault was committed are cancelled. The opponent's points remain valid.

15. 10 Substitution procedure

15. 10. 1 Substitution must be carried out within the substitution zone.

15. 10. 2 A substitution shall only last the time needed for recording the substitution on the

score sheet, and allowing entry and exit of the players.

15.10.3.1 The actual request for substitution is the entrance of the substitute player(s) into the substitution zone, ready to play, during a regular interruption.

15.10.3.2 If that is not the case, the substitution is not granted and the team is sanctioned for a delay.

15.10.3.3 The request for substitution is acknowledged and announced by the scorer or second referee, by use of the buzzer or whistle respectively.

For FIVB World and Official Competitions, numbered paddles are used to facilitate the substitution.

15.10.4 If a team intends to make simultaneously more than one substitution, all players being substituted must report to the substitution zone at the same time to be considered in the same request. In this case, substitutions must be made in succession, one pair of players after another.

15.11 Improper requests

15.11.1 It is improper to requestany game interruption:

15.11.1.1 during a rally or at the moment of, or after the whistle to serve;

15.11.1.2 by a non-authorized team member;

15.11.1.3 for player substitution before the game has been resumed from a previous substitution by the same team;

15.11.1.4 after havin g exhausted the authorized number of time-outs and player substitutions.

15.11.2 The first improper request by a team in the match that does not affect or delay the game shall be rejected without any other consequences.

15.11.3 Any further improper request in the match by the same team constitutes a delay.

16 Game delays

16.1 Types of delays

An improper action of a team that defers resumption of the game is a delay and includes, among others:

16.1.1 delaying a substitution;

16.1.2 prolonging other game interruptions, after having been instructed to resume the game;

16.1.3 requesting an illegal substitution;

16.1.4 repeating an improper request;

16.1.5 delaying the game by a team member.

16.2 Delay sanctions

16.2.1 "*Delay warning*" and "*delay penalty*" are team sanctions.

16.2.1.1 Delay sanctions remain in force for the entire match;

16.2.1.2 All delay sanctions are recorded on the score sheet.

16.2.2 The first delay in the match by a team member is sanctioned with a "DELAY WARNING".

16.2.3 The second and subsequent delays of any type by any member of the same team in the same match constitute a fault and are sanctioned with a "DELAY PENALTY": a point and service to the opponent.

16.2.4 Delay sanctions imposed before or between sets are applied in the following set.

17 Exceptional game interruptions

17.1 Injury

17.1.1 Should a serious accident occur while the ball is in play, the referee must stop the game immediately and permit medical assistance to enter the court;

The rally is then replayed.

17.1.2 If an injured player cannot be substituted, legally or exceptionally, the player is given a 3-minute recovery time, but not more than once for the same player in the match.

If the player does not recover, his/her team is declared incomplete.

17.2 External interference

If there is any external interference during the game, play has to be stopped and the rally is replayed.

17.3 Prolonged interruptions

17.3.1 If unforeseen circumstances interrupt the match, the first referee, the organizer and the Control Committee, if there is one, shall decide the measures to be taken to re-establish normal conditions.

17.3.2 Should one or several interruptions occur, not exceeding 4 hours in total:

17.3.2.1 if the match is resumed on the same playing court, the interrupted set shall continue normally with the same score, players and positions. The sets already played will keep their scores;

17.3.2.2 if the match is resumed on another playing court, the interrupted set is cancelled and replayed with the same team members and the same starting line-ups. The sets already played will keep their scores.

17.3.3 Should one or several interruptions occur, exceeding 4 hours in total, the whole match shall be replayed.

18 Intervals and change of courts

18.1 Intervals

An interval is the time between sets. All intervals last three minutes.

During this period of time, the change of courts and line-up registrations of the teams on the score sheet are made.

The interval between the second and the third sets can be extended up to 10 minutes by the competent body at the request of the organizer.

18.2 Change of courts

18.2.1 After each set, the teams change courts, with the exception of the deciding set.

18.2.2 In the deciding set, once the leading team reaches 8 points, the teams change courts without delay and the player positions remain the same.

If the change is not made once the leading team reaches 8 points, it will take place as soon as the error is noticed. The score at the time that the change is made remains the same.

19 The libero player

19.1 Designation of the libero

19.1.1 Each team has the right to designate from the list of players on the score sheet up to two (2) specialised defensive players: Liberos.

19.1.2 All Liberos must be recorded on the score sheet before the match in the special lines reserved for this.

For FIVB, World and Official Competitions, all Liberosmust be recorded only in the special lines reserved for this.

19.1.3 One Libero designated by the coach before the start of the match, will be the starting Libero. The Libero on court is the Acting Libero. If there is another Libero, he/she will act as the second Libero.

19.1.4 Only one Libero may be on court at any time.

19.1.5 The Libero cannot be either team captain or game captain at the same time as performing as a Libero.

19.2 Equipment

The Libero players must wear a uniform (or jacket/bib for the re-designated Libero) whose jerseys at least must contrast in colour with that of the other members of the team. The Libero uniform may have a different design, but it must be numbered like the rest of the team members.

For FIVB, World and Official Competitions the re-designated Libero must, if possible, wear the same style and colour of jersey as the original Libero, but keep his/her own number.

19.3 Actions involving the libero

19.3.1 The playing actions

19.3.1.1 The Libero is allowed to replace any player in a back row position.

19.3.1.2 He/she is restricted to perform as a back row player and is not allowed to complete an attack hit from anywhere (including playing court and free zone) if at the moment of the contact, the ball is entirely higher than the top of the net;

19.3.1.3 He/she may not serve, block or attempt to block;

19.3.1.4 A player may not complete an attack hit from higher than the top of the net, if the ball is coming from an overhand finger pass by a Libero in his/her front zone. The ball may be freely attacked if the Libero makes the same action from outside his/her front zone.

19.3.2 Replacements of players

19.3.2.1 Replacements involving the Libero are not counted as substitutions.

They are unlimited, but there must be acompleted rally between two replacements involving a Libero (unless a penalty causes a rotation to position 4, or the Acting Libero becomes unable to play, making the rally incomplete.)

19.3.2.2 The Acting Libero can only be replaced by the regular replacement player for that position, or by the second Libero. The regular replacement player may replace either Libero;

The coach has the right to replace the Acting Libero with the second Libero for any reason after a completed rally at any time during the match;

19.3.2.3 Replacements must only take place while the ball is out of play and before the whistle for service;

19.3.2.4 At the start of each set, the Libero can not enter the court until the second referee has checked the starting line-up;

19.3.2.5 A replacement made after the whistle for service but before the service hit should not be rejected; however, the game captain must be informed after the end of the rally that this is not a permitted procedure and that future instances will be subject to delay sanctions;

19.3.2.6 Subsequent late replacements shall result in the play being interrupted immediately and the imposition of a delay sanction. The team to serve next will be determined by the result of the delay sanction;

19.3.2.7 The Libero and the replacing player may only enter or leave the court through the "Libero Replacement Zone";

19.3.2.8 All replacements involving Liberos must be recorded in the Libero Control sheet (or electronic score sheet, if one is used);

19.3.2.9 An illegal Libero replacement can involve (amongst others). No completed rally between Libero replacements. The Libero being replaced by a player other than the regular replacement player. The consequences of an illegal Libero replacement are the same as those for a rotational fault.

19.4 Re-designation of a new libero

19.4.1 Team with two Liberos:

19.4.1.1 When a team uses two Liberos but one becomes unable to play (expelled, ill, injured, etc.), the team has the right to play with only one Libero and the second Libero becomes the Acting Libero. No re-designation will be allowed, however, unless the Acting Libero is unable to play for the match and the remaining Libero has also been declared unable to continue.

19.4.2 Team with one Libero:

19.4.2.1 Where only one Libero is registered on the score sheet, in case the Libero is declared unable to play, the coach may re-designate as Libero for the remainder of the match any other player (replacement player excepted) not on the court at the moment of the re-designation. The coach (or game captain, if no coach is present) must contact the second referee with the request for "re-designation";

19.4.2.2 Should the re-designated Liberobe declared unable to play, further re-designations are possible but the original Libero(s) may not return to the match;

19.4.2.3 If the coach requests that the team captain be re-designated as the Libero, this will be permitted - but the team captain must in this case relinquish all leadership privileges.

19.4.2.4 In the case of a re-designated Libero, the number of the player re-designated as Libero must be recorded on the score sheet remarks section and on the Libero Control sheet (or electronic score sheet, if one is used). The re-designated player will be allocated a jacket or bib to show that a new Libero is in play.

19.5 Expulsion and disqualification

If the Libero is expelled or disqualified he/ she may be replaced directly by the team's other Libero. Should the team have only one Libero, then it must play without a Libero for the duration of the sanction.

20 Requirements of conduct

20.1 Sportsmanlike conduct

20.1.1 Participants must know the "Official Volleyball Rules" and abide by them.

20.1.2 Participants must accept referees' decisions with sportsmanlike conduct, without disputing them.

In case of doubt, clarification may be requested only through the game captain.

20.1.3 Participants must refrain from actions or attitudes aimed at influencing the decisions of the referees or covering up faults committed by their team.

20.2 Fair play

20.2.1 Participants must behave respectfully and courteously in the spirit of FAIR PLAY, not only towards the referees, but also towards other officials, the opponent, team-mates and spectators.

20.2.2 Communication between team members during the match is permitted.

21 Misconduct and its sanctions

21.1 Minor misconduct

Minor misconduct offences are not subject to sanctions. It is the first referee's duty to prevent the teams from approaching the sanctioning level by issuing a verbal or hand signal warning to a team member or to the team through the game captain.

This warning is not a sanction and has no immediate consequences. It should not be recorded on the score sheet.

21.2 Misconduct leading to sanctions

Incorrect conduct by a team member towards officials, opponent, team-mates or spectators is classified in three categories according to the seriousness of the offence.

21.2.1 Rude conduct: action contrary to good manners or moral principles, or any action expressing contempt.

21.2.2 Offensive conduct: defamatory or insulting words or gestures.

21.2.3 Aggression: actual physical attackor aggressive or threatening behaviour.

21.3 Sanction scale

According to the judgment of the first referee and depending on the seriousness of the offence, the sanctions to beapplied and recorded on the score sheet are: Penalty, Expulsion or Disqualification.

21.3.1 Penalty

The first rude conduct in the match by any team member is penalized with a point and service to the opponent.

21.3.2 Expulsion

21.3.2.1 A team member who is sanctioned by expulsion shall not play for the rest of the set and must remain seated in the penalty area with no other consequences.

An expelled coach loses his/her right to intervene in the set and must remain seated in the penalty area.

21.3.2.2 The first offensive conduct by a team member is sanctioned by expulsion with no other consequences.

21.3.2.3 The second rude conduct in the same match, by the same team member is sanctioned by expulsion with no other consequences.

21.3.3 Disqualification

21.3.3.1 A team member who is sanctioned by disqualification must leave the Competition Control area for the rest of the match with no other consequences.

21.3.3.2 The firstphysical attack or implied or threatened aggression is sanctioned by disqualification with no other consequences.

21.3.3.3 The second offensive conduct in the same match by the same team member is sanctioned by disqualification with no other consequences.

21.3.3.4 The third rude conduct in the same match by the same team member is sanctioned by disqualification with no other consequences.

21.4 Application of misconduct sanctions

21.4.1 All misconduct sanctions are individual sanctions, remain in force for the entire match and are recorded on the score sheet.

21.4.2 The repetition of misconductby the same team member in the same match is sanctioned progressively (the team member receives a heavier sanction for each successive offence).

21.4.3 Expulsion or disqualification due to offensive conduct or aggression does not require a previous sanction.

21.5 Misconduct before and between sets

Any misconduct occurring before or between sets is sanctioned according to Rule 21.3 and sanctions apply in the following set.

21.6 Sanction cards

Warning: verbal or hand signal, no card

Penalty: yellow card

Expulsion: red card

Disqualification: yellow + red card (jointly)

22 Refereeing corps and procedures

22.1 Composition

The refereeing corps for a match is composed of the following officials:

- the first referee
- the second referee
- the scorer
- four (two) line judges

For FIVB World and Official Competitions, an assistant scorer is compulsory.

22.2 Procedures

22.2.1 Only the first and second referees may blow a whistle during the match:

22.2.1.1 the first referee gives the signal for the service that begins the rally;

22.2.1.2 the first and second referees signal the end of the rally, provided that they are sure that a fault has been committed and they have identified its nature.

22.2.2 They may blow the whistle when the ball is out of play to indicate that they authorize or reject a team request.

22.2.3 Immediately after the referee's whistle to signal the completion of the rally, they have to indicate with the official hand signals:

22.2.3.1 If the fault is whistled by the first referee, he/she will indicate in order:

- the team to serve;
- the nature of the fault;
- the player(s) at fault (if necessary).

The second referee will follow the first referee's hand signals by repeating them.

22.2.3.2 If the fault is whistled by the second referee, he/she will indicate:

- the nature of the fault
- the player at fault (if necessary)
- the team to serve following the hand signal of the first referee.

In this case, the first referee does not show either the nature of the fault or the player at fault, but only the team to serve.

22.2.3.3 In the case of an attack hit fault by back row or Libero players, both referees indicate according to 22.2.3.1 and 22.2.3.2 above.

22.2.3.4 In the case of a double fault both referees indicate in order

- the nature of the fault
- the players at fault (if necessary)
- the team to serve as directed by the first referee

23 FIRST REFEREE

23.1 Location

The first referee carries out his/her functions seated or standing on a referee's stand located at one end of the net. His/her view must be approximately 50 cm above the net.

23.2 Authority

23.2.1 The first referee directs the match from the start until the end. He/she has authority over all members of the refereeing corps and the members of the teams.

During the match the first referee's decisions are final. He/she is authorized to overrule the decisions of other members of the refereeing corps, if it is noticed that they are mistaken.

The first referee may even replace a member of the refereeing corps who is not performing his/her functions properly.

23.2.2 The first referee also controls the work of the ball retrievers, floor wipers and moppers.

23.2.3 The first referee has the power to decide any matter involving the game including those not provided for in the Rules.

23.2.4 The first referee shall not permit any discussion about his/her decisions.

However, at the request of the game captain, the first referee will give an explanation on the application or interpretation of the Rules upon which he/she has based the decision.

If the game captain does not agree with the explanation of the first referee and chooses to protest against such decision, he/she must immediately reserve the right to file and record this protest at the conclusion of the match. The first referee must authorize this right of the game captain.

23.2.5 The first referee is responsible for determining before and during the match whether the playing area equipment and the conditions meet playing requirements.

23.3 Responsibilities

23.3.1 Prior to the match, the first referee:

23.3.1.1 inspects the conditions of the playing area, the balls and other equipment;

23.3.1.2 performs the toss with the team captains;

23.3.1.3 controls the teams' warming-up.

23.3.2 During the match, the first referee is authorized:

23.3.2.1 to issue warnings to the teams;

23.3.2.2 to sanction misconduct and delays;

23.3.2.3 to decide upon:

- the faults of the server and of the positions of the serving team, including the screen;
- the faults in playing the ball;
- the faults above the net and at its upper part;
- the attack hit faults of the Liberoand back-row players;
- the completed attack hits made by a player on a ball above net height coming from an overhand pass with fingers by the Libero in his/her front zone;
- the ball crossingcompletely the lower space under the net.
- the completed block by back row players or the attempted block by the Libero

23.3.3 At the end of the match, he/she checks the score sheet and signs it.

24 Second referee

24.1 Location

The second referee performs his/her functions standing outside the playing court near the post, on the opposite side facing the first referee.

24.2 Authority

24.2.1 The second referee is the assistant of the first referee, but has also his/her own range of jurisdiction.

Should the first referee become unable to continue his/her work, the second referee may replace the first referee.

24.2.2 The second referee may, without whistling, also signal faults outside his/her range of jurisdiction, but may not insist on them to the first referee.

24.2.3 The second referee controls the work of the scorer(s).

24.2.4 The second referee supervises the team members on the team bench and reports their misconduct to the first referee.

24.2.5 The second referee controls the players in the warm-up areas.

24.2.6 The second referee authorizes the interruptions, controls their duration and rejects improper requests.

24.2.7 The second referee controls the number of time-outs and substitutions used by each team and reports the 2nd time-out and 5th and 6th substitutions to the first referee and the coach concerned.

24.2.8 In the case of an injury of a player, the second referee authorizes an exceptional substitution or grants a 3 minute recovery time.

24.2.9 The second referee checks the floor condition, mainly in the front zone. He/she also checks, during the match, that the balls still fulfil the regulations.

24.2.10 The second referee supervises the team members in the penalty areas and reports their misconduct to the first referee.

24.3 Responsibilities

24.3.1 At the start of each set, at the change of courts in the deciding set and whenever necessary, he/she checks that the actual positions of the players on the court correspond to those on the line-up sheets.

24.3.2 During the match, the second referee decides, whistles and signals:

24.3.2.1 penetration into the opponent's court, and the space under the net;

24.3.2.2 positional faults of the receiving team;

24.3.2.3 the faulty contact of the player with the net at its lower part or with the antenna on his/her side of the court;

24.3.2.4 he completed block by back row players or the attempted block by the Libero; or the attack hit fault by back row players or by the Libero;

24.3.2.5 the contact of the ball with an outside object;

24.3.2.6 the contact of the ball with the floor when the first referee is not in position to see the contact;

24. 3. 2. 7 the ball that crosses the net totally or partly outside of the crossing space to the opponent court or contacts the antenna on his/her side of the court;

24. 3. 3 At the end of the match, he/ she signs the score sheet.

25 Scorer

25. 1 Location

The scorer performs his/her functions seated at the scorer's table on the opposite side of the court facing the first referee.

25. 2 Responsibilities

He/she keeps the score sheet according to the Rules, co-operating with the second referee.

He/she uses a buzzer or other sound device to notify irregularities or give signals to the referees on the basis of his/her responsibilities.

25. 2. 1 Prior to the match and set, the scorer:

25. 2. 1. 1 registers the data of the match and teams, including the names and numbers of the Libero players, according to the procedures in force, and obtains the signatures of the captains and the coaches;

25. 2. 1. 2 records the starting line-up of each team from the line-up sheet;

If he/she fails to receive the line-up sheets on time, he/she immediately notifies this fact to the second referee.

25. 2. 2 During the match, the scorer:

25. 2. 2. 1 records the points scored;

25. 2. 2. 2 controls the serving order of each team and indicates any error to the referees immediately after the service hit;

25. 2. 2. 3 is empowered to acknowledge and announce requests for player substitutions by use of the buzzer, controlling their number; and records the substitutions and time-outs, informing the second referee;

25. 2. 2. 4 notifies the referees of a request for interruption that is out of order;

25. 2. 2. 5 announces to the referees the ends of the sets, and the scoring of the 8th point in the deciding set;

25. 2. 2. 6 records any sanctions and improper requests;

25. 2. 2. 7 records all other events as instructed by the second referee, i. e. exceptional substitutions, recovery time, prolonged interruptions, external interference, etc.

25. 2. 2. 8 controls the interval between sets.

25. 2. 3 At the end of the match, the scorer:

25. 2. 3. 1 records the final result;

25. 2. 3. 2 in the case of protest, with the previous authorization of the first referee, writes or permits the team/game captain to write on the score sheet a statement on the incident protested;

25. 2. 3. 3 after signing the score sheet him/herself, obtains the signatures of the team

captains and then the referees.

26 Assistant scorera

26.1 Location

The assistant scorer performs his/her functions seated beside the scorer at the scorer's table.

26.2 Responsibilities

He/she records the replacements involving the Libero.

He/she assists with the administrative duties of the scorer's work.

Should the scorer become unable to continue his/her work, the assistant scorer substitutes for the scorer.

26.2.1 Prior to the match and set, the assistant scorer:

26.2.1.1 prepares the Libero control sheet;

26.2.1.2 prepares the reserve scoresheet.

26.2.2 During the match, the assistant scorer:

26.2.2.1 records the details of the Libero replacements;

26.2.2.2 notifies the referees of any fault of the Libero replacement, by using the buzzer;

26.2.2.3 starts and ends the timing of Technical Time-out;

26.2.2.4 operates the manual scoreboard on the scorer's table;

26.2.2.5 checks that the scoreboard agree;

26.2.2.6 if necessary, updates the reserve scoresheet and gives it to the scorer.

26.2.3 At the end of the match, the assistant scorer:

26.2.3.1 signs the Libero control sheet and submits it for checking;

26.2.3.2 signs the scoresheet.

27 Line judges

27.1 Location

If only two line judges are used, they stand at the corners of the court closest to the right hand of each referee, diagonally at 1 to 2 m from the corner.

Each one of them controls both the end line and sideline on his/her side.

For FIVB, World and Official Competitions, it is compulsory to have four line judges.

They stand in the free zone at 1 to 3 m from each corner of the court, on the imaginary extension of the line that they control.

27.2 Responsibilities

27.2.1 The line judges perform their functions by using flags (40 x 40 cm), as shown in *Diagram* 12, to signal:

27.2.1.1 the ball "in" and "out" whenever the ball lands near their line(s);

27.2.1.2 the touches of "out" balls by the team receiving the ball;

27.2.1.3 the ball touching the antenna, the served ball crossing the net outside the crossing space, etc.;

27.2.1.4 any player (except the server) stepping outside of his/her court at the moment of the service hit;

27.2.1.5 the foot faults of the server;

27.2.1.6 any contact with the antenna on their side of the court by any player during his/her action of playing the ball or interfering with the play;

27.2.1.7 ball crossing the net outside the crossing space into the opponent's court or touching the antenna on his/her side of the court.

27.2.2 At the first referee's request, a line judge must repeat his/her signal.

28 Official signals

28.1 Referees' hand signals

The referees must indicate with the official hand signal the reason for their whistle (the nature of the fault whistled or the purpose of the interruption authorized). The signal has to be maintained for a moment and, if it is indicated with one hand, the hand corresponds to the side of the team which has made the fault or the request.

28.2 Line judges' flag signals

The line judges must indicate with the official flag signal the nature of the called fault, and maintain the signal for a moment.

第四篇　乒乓球

第一章　乒乓球竞赛规则及裁判法

《乒乓球比赛规则》内容分为三个部分：

(1)乒乓球的比赛规则

(2)国际竞赛规则

(3)乒乓球竞赛规程

1　乒乓球竞赛规则

1.1　球台

1.1.1　球台(见图4-1)的上层表面叫做比赛台面，应为与水平面平行的长方形，长2.74米，宽1.525米，离地面高76厘米。

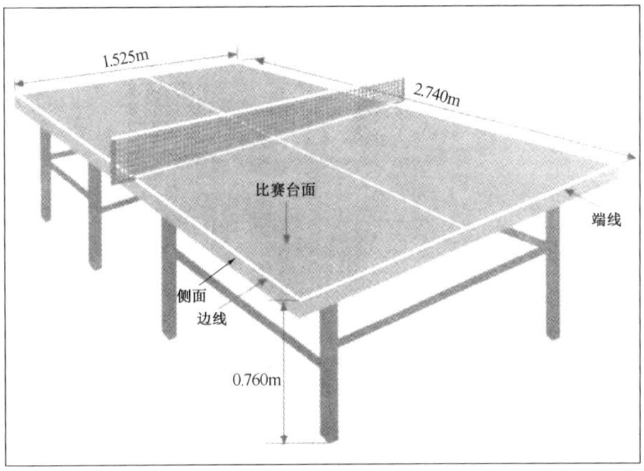

图4-1　乒乓球台

1.1.2　比赛台面不包括与球台台面垂直的侧面。

1.1.3　比赛台面可用任何材料制成，应具有一致的弹性，即当标准球从离台面30厘米高处落至台面时，弹起高度应约为23厘米。

1.1.4　比赛台面应呈均匀的暗色，无光泽，沿每个2.74米的比赛台面边缘各有一条2厘米宽的白色边线，沿每个1.525米的比赛台面边缘各有一条2厘米宽的白色端线。

1.1.5　比赛台面由一个与端线平行的垂直的球网划分为两个相等的台区，各台区的整个面积应是一个整体。

1.1.6　双打时，各台区应由一条3毫米宽的白色中线，划分为两个相等的"半区"。中线与边线平行，并应视为右半区的一部分。

1.2　球网装置

1.2.1　球网装置包括球网、悬网绳、网柱及将它们固定在球台上的夹钳部分。

1.2.2　球网应悬挂在一根绳子上，绳子两端系在高15.25厘米的直立网柱上，网柱外缘离开边线外缘的距离 15. 25 厘米。

1. 2. 3　整个球网的顶端距离比赛台面 15. 25 厘米。

1. 2. 4　整个球网的底边应尽量贴近比赛台面，其两端应尽量贴近网柱。

1. 3　球

1. 3. 1　球应为圆球体，直径为 40 毫米。

1. 3. 2　球重 2. 7 克。

1. 3. 3　球应用赛璐珞或类似的材料制成，呈白色或橙色，且无光泽。

1. 4　球拍

1. 4. 1　球拍的大小，形状和重量不限(见图 4-2)。但底板应平整、坚硬。

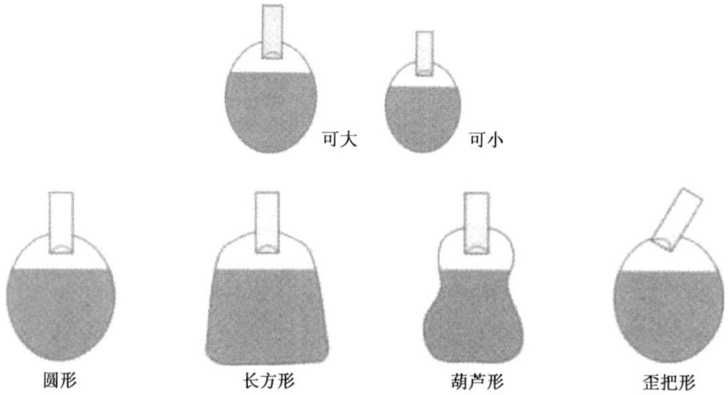

图 4-2　乒乓球拍

1. 4. 2　底板厚度至少应有 85%的天然木料。加强底板的黏合层可用诸如碳纤维，玻璃纤维或压缩纸等纤维材料，每层黏合层不超过底板总厚度的 7. 5%或 0. 35 毫米。

1. 4. 3　用来击球的拍面应用一层颗粒向外的普通颗粒胶覆盖，连同黏合剂，厚度不超过 2 毫米；或用颗粒向内或向外的海绵胶覆盖，连同黏合剂，厚度不超过 4 毫米。

1. 4. 3. 1　“普通颗粒胶”是一层无泡沫的天然橡胶或合成橡胶，其颗粒必须以每平方厘米不少于 10 颗、不多于 50 颗的平均密度分布整个表面。

1. 4. 3. 2　“海绵胶”即在一层泡沫橡胶上覆盖一层普通颗粒胶，普通颗粒胶的厚度不超过 2 毫米。

1. 4. 4　覆盖物应覆盖整个拍面，但不得超过其边缘。靠近拍柄部分以及手指执握部分可不予以覆盖，也可用任何材料覆盖。

1. 4. 5　底板、底板中的任何夹层以及用来击球一面的任何覆盖物及黏合层均应为厚度均匀的一个整体。

1. 4. 6　球拍两面不论是否有覆盖物，必须无光泽，且一面为鲜红色，另一面为黑色。

1. 4. 7　由于意外的损坏、磨损或褪色，造成拍面的整体性和颜色上的一致性出现轻微的差异。只要未明显改变拍面的性能，均可允许使用。

1.4.8 比赛开始时及比赛过程中运动员需要更换球拍时，必须向对方和裁判员展示他将要使用的球拍，并允许他们检查。

1.5 定义

1.5.1 “回合”：球处于比赛状态的一段时间。

1.5.2 “球处比赛状态”：从有意识发球前，球静止在不执拍手掌中的最后瞬间，到该回合被判得分或重发球。

1.5.3 “重发球”：不予判分的回合。

1.5.4 “一分”：判分的回合。

1.5.5 “执拍手”：正握着球拍的手。

1.5.6 “不执拍手”：未握着球拍的手。

1.5.7 “击球”：用握在手中的球拍或执拍手手腕以下部分触球。

1.5.8 “阻挡”：自对方最后一次击球触及本方台区后，如果在台面上方或正向比赛台面方向运动的球，在没有触及本方台区、也未越过端线之前，即触及本方运动员或其穿戴的任何物品。

1.5.9 “发球员”：在一个回合中，首先击球的运动员。

1.5.10 “接发球员”：在一个回合中，第二个击球的运动员。

1.5.11 “裁判员”：被指定管理一场比赛的人。

1.5.12 “副裁判员”：被指定在某些方面协助裁判员工作的人。

1.5.13 “穿或戴”的物品：指运动员在一个回合开始时穿或戴的任何物品，但不包括比赛用球。

1.5.14 “越过或绕过球网装置”：除从球网和比赛台面之间通过以及从球网和网架之间通过的情况外，球均应视做已“越过或绕过”球网装置。

1.5.15 球台的“端线”：包括球台端线以及端线两端的无限延长线。

1.6 合法发球

1.6.1 发球时，球应放在不执拍手的手掌上，手掌张开和伸平。球应是静止的，在发球方的端线之后，比赛台面的水平面之上。

不合法发球

合法发球

1.6.2 发球员须用手把球几乎垂直地向上抛起，不得使球旋转，并使球在离开不执拍手的手掌之后上升不少于16厘米，球下降到被击出前不能碰到任何物体。

1.6.3 当球从抛起的最高点下降时，发球员方可击球，使球首先触及本方台区，然后越过或绕过球网装置，再触及接发球员的台区。在双打中，球应先后触及发球员和接发球员的右半区。

1.6.4 从抛球前球静止的最后一瞬间到击球时，球和球拍应在比赛台面的水平面之上。

1.6.5 击球时，球应在发球方的端线之后，但不能超过发球员身体(手臂、头或腿除外)离端线最远的部分。

1.6.6 运动员发球时，应让裁判员或副裁判员看清他是否按照合法发球的规定发球。

1.6.6.1 如果裁判员怀疑发球员某个发球动作的正确性，并且他或者副裁判员都不能确信该发球动作不合法，一场比赛中此现象第一次出现时，裁判员可以警告发球员而不予判分。

1.6.6.2 在同一场比赛中，如果发球员或其双打同伴发球动作的正确性再次受到怀疑时，不管是否出于同样的原因，均判接发球方得一分。

1.6.6.3 无论是否第一次或任何时候，只要发球员明显没有按照合法发球的规定发球，他将被判失一分，无需警告。

1.6.7 运动员因身体伤病而不能严格遵守合法发球的某些规定时，可由裁判员做出免予执行的决定，但须在赛前向裁判员说明。

1.7 合法还击

对方发球或还击后，本方运动员必须击球，使球直接越过或绕过球网装置，或触及球网装置后，再触及对方台区。

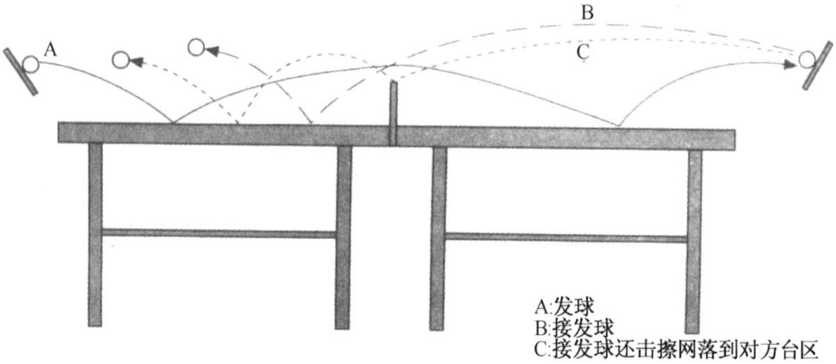

1.8 比赛次序

1.8.1 在单打中，首先由发球员合法发球，再由接发球员合法还击，然后两者交替合法还击。

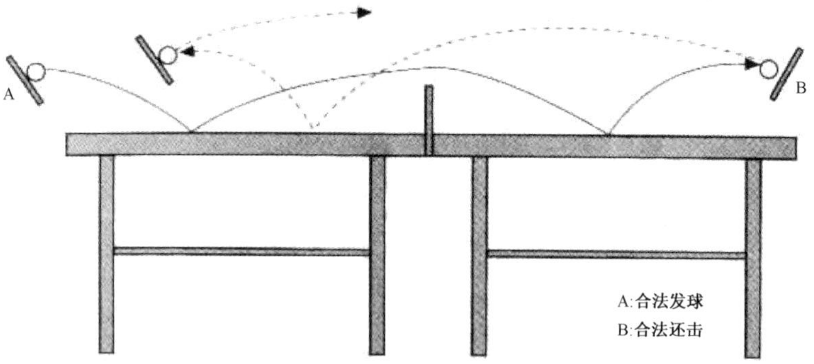

1.8.2 在双打中，首先由发球员合法发球，再由接发球员合法还击，然后由发球员的同伴合法还击，再由接发球员的同伴合法还击，此后，运动员按此次序轮流合法还击。

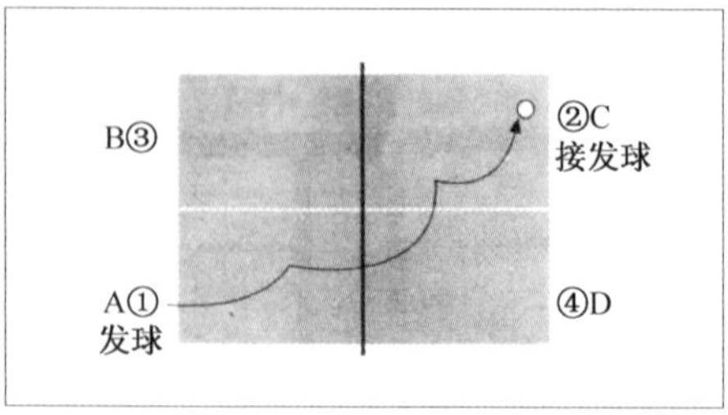

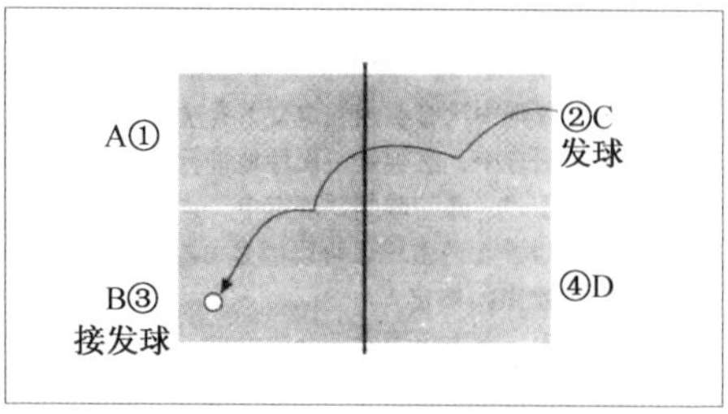

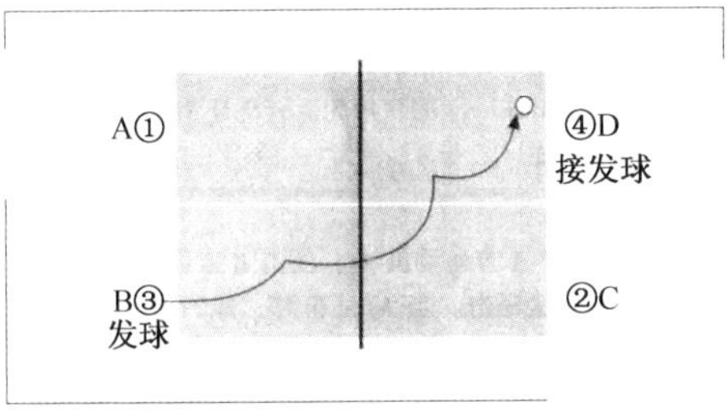

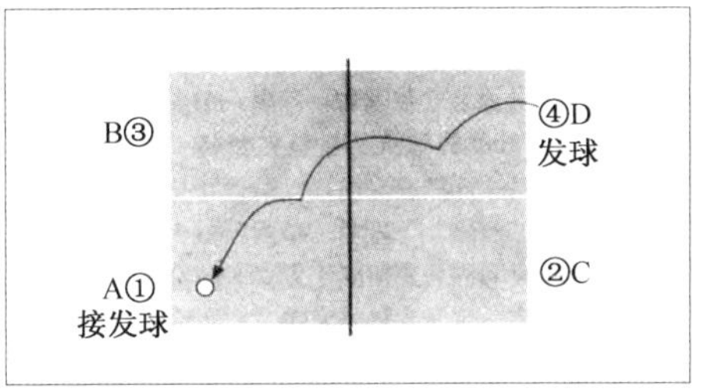

1.9 重发球

1.9.1 回合出现下列情况应判重发球：

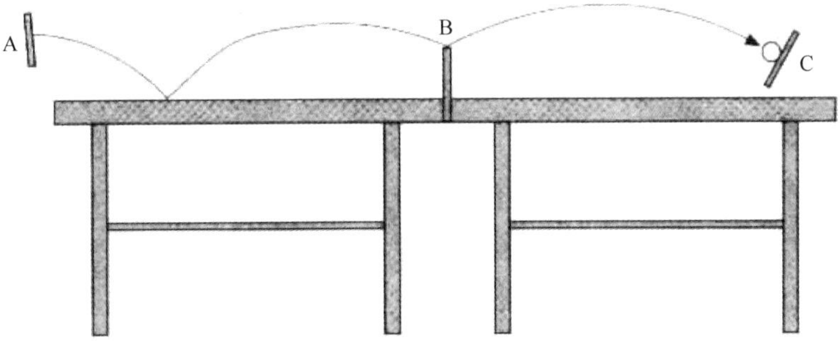

A: 发球 B: 擦网 C: 阻挡

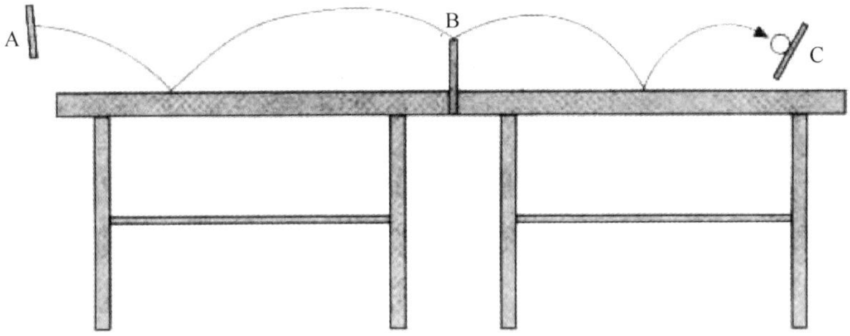

A: 发球 B: 擦网球落到对方台区

1.9.1.1 如果发球员发出的球，在越过或绕过球网装置时，触及球网装置，此后成为合法发球或被接发球员或其同伴阻挡。

1.9.1.2 如果接发球员或接发球方未准备好时，球已发出，而且接发球员或接发球方没有企图击球。

1.9.1.3 由于发生了运动员无法控制的干扰，而使运动员未能合法发球、合法还击或遵守规则。

1.9.1.4 裁判员或副裁判员暂停比赛。

1.9.2 可以在下列情况下暂停比赛：

1.9.2.1 由于要纠正发球、接发球次序或方位错误；

1.9.2.2 由于要实行轮换发球法；

1.9.2.3 由于警告或处罚运动员；

1.9.2.4 由于比赛环境受到干扰，以致该回合结果有可能受到影响。

1.10 一分

除被判重发球的回合，下列情况运动员得一分：

1.10.1　对方运动员未能合法发球；

1.10.2　对方运动员未能合法还击；

1.10.3　运动员在发球或还击后，对方运动员在击球前，球触及了除球网装置以外的任何东西；

1.10.4　对方击球后，该球没有触及本方台区而越过本方端线；

1.10.5　对方阻挡；

1.10.6　对方连击；

1.10.7　对方用不符合 1.4.3、1.4.4 和 1.4.5 条款的拍面击球；

1.10.8　对方运动员或他穿戴的任何东两使球台移动；

1.10.9　对方运动员或他穿戴的任何东西触及球网装置；

1.10.10　对方运动员不执拍手触及比赛台面；

1.10.11　双打时，对方运动员击球次序错误；

1.10.12　执行轮换发球法时，出现 1.15.2 条款情况。

1.11　一局比赛

在一局比赛中，先得 11 分的一方为胜方。10 平后，先多得 2 分的一方为胜方。

1.12　一场比赛

1.12.1　一场比赛由单数局组成。

1.12.2　一场比赛应连续进行，除非是经许可的间歇。

1.13　发球 按发球和方位的选择

1.13.1　选择发球、接发球和这一方、那一方的权力应由抽签来决定。中签者可以选择先发球或先接发球，或选择先在某一方。

1.13.2　当一方运动员选择了先发球或先接发球，或选择先在某一方位后，另一方运动员必须有另一个选择。

1.13.3　在获得每两分之后，接发球方即成为发球方，依此类推，直至该局比赛结束，或者直至双方比分都达到 10 分或实行轮换发球法，这时，发球和接发次序仍然不变，但每人只轮发一分球。

1.13.4　在双打的第一局比赛中，先发球方确定第一发球员，再由先接发球方确定第一接发球员。在以后的各局比赛中，第一发球员确定后，第一接发球员应是前一局发球给他的运动员。

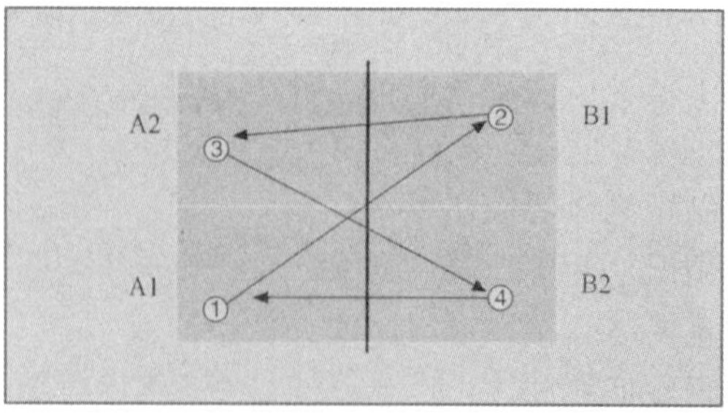

1.13.5　在双打中，每次换发球时，前面的接发球员应成为发球员，前面的发球员的同伴应成为接发球员。

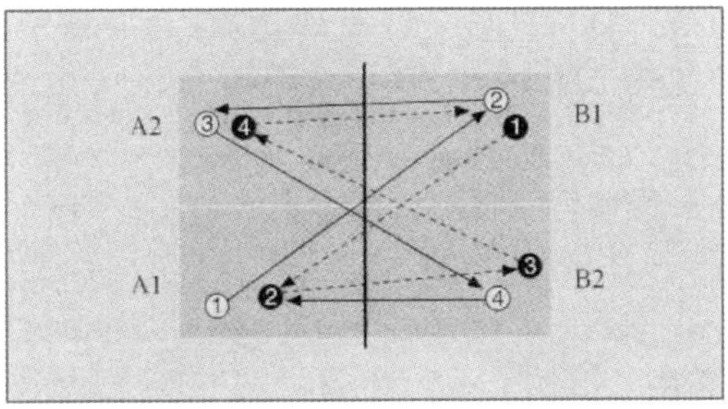

1.13.6 一局中首先发球的一方，在该场下一局应首先接发球。在双打决胜局中，当一方先得 5 分时，接发球方应交换接发球次序。

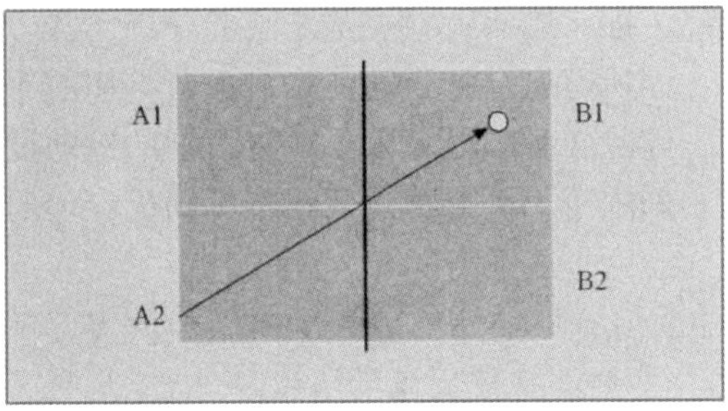

1.13.7 一局中，在某一方位比赛的一方，在该场下一局应换到另一方位。在决胜局中，一方先得 5 分时，双方应交换方位。

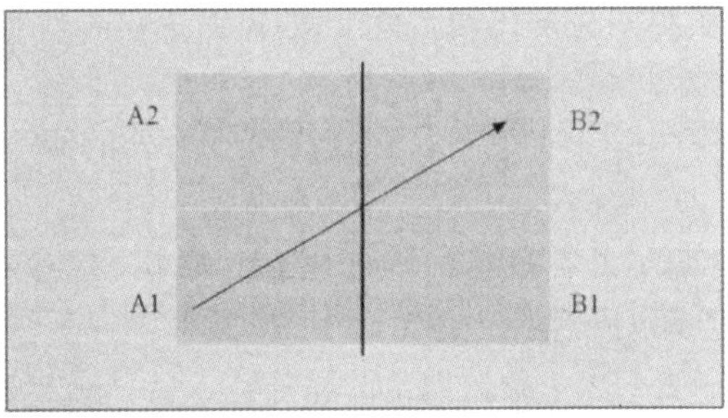

1.14 发球、接发球次序和方位的错误

1.14.1 裁判员一旦发现发球、接发球次序错误，应立即暂停比赛，并按该场比赛开始时确立的次序，按场上比分由应该发球或接发球的运动员发球或接发球；在双打中，则按发现错误时那一局中首先有发球权的一方所确立的次序进行纠正，继续比赛。

1.14.2 裁判员一旦发现运动员应交换方位而未交换时，应立即暂停比赛，并按该场比赛开始时确立的次序，按场上比分运动员应站的正确方位进行纠正，再继续比赛。

1.14.3 在任何情况下，发现错误之前的所有得分均有效。

1.15 轮换发球法

1.15.1 除 1.15.2 条款的情况之外，一局比赛进行到 10 分钟或在任何时间应双方运动员或配对的要求，应实行轮换发球。

1.15.2 如果一局比赛比分已达到至少 18 分，将不实行轮换发球法。

1.15.3 实行轮换发球法的时间到时，球处于比赛状态，裁判员应立即暂停比赛，由被暂停回合的发球员发球，继续比赛；如果实行轮换发球法时，球未处于比赛状态，应由前一回合的接发球员发球，继续比赛。

1.15.4 此后，每个运动员都轮发一分球，直至该局结束。如果接发球方进行了 13

次合法还击，则判发球方失一分。

1.15.5　实行轮换发球法不能更改该场比赛中按1.13.6条款所确定的发球与接发球次序。

1.15.6　轮换发球法一经实行，将一直执行到该场比赛结束。

2　国际竞赛规则

2.1　规则和规程的适用范围

2.1.1　比赛类型

2.1.1.1　“国际竞赛”，即一个以上协会的运动员参加的比赛。

2.1.1.2　“国际比赛”，即不同协会代表队之间的一场比赛。

2.1.1.3　“公开赛”，即所有协会的运动员均可报名参加的比赛。

2.1.1.4　“限制赛”，即除年龄组外只限于特定组别的运动员参加的比赛。

2.1.1.5　“邀请赛”，即限于个别邀请的、指定运动员参加的比赛。

2.1.2　适用范围

2.1.2.1　除了2.1.2.2另有规定外，规则将适用于世界、洲和奥林匹克的比赛，公开赛和国际比赛，除非参加的协会达成另外的协议。

2.1.2.2　理事会可授权公开赛的组织者，采用执委会判发的实验性规则。

2.1.2.3　国际竞赛规程应适用于下列比赛：

2.1.2.3.1　世界和奥林匹克的比赛，除非理事会许可了另外的规程，并事先通知了各参赛协会；

2.1.2.3.2　洲的比赛，除非有关洲联合会许可了另外的规程，并事先通知了各参赛协会；

2.1.2.3.3　公开锦标赛(2.7.1.2)，除非国际乒联执委会许可了另外的规程并由参赛者按3.1.2.4条款规定予以同意；

2.1.2.3.4　公开赛，2.1.2.4条款规定的除外。

2.1.2.4　不符合规程任何条款而举办的公开赛，应在报名表中说明变化的性质和范围；填写并提交报名表应被视为报名者同意包括更改内容在内的比赛条件。

2.1.2.5　建议此竞赛规程应用于所有国际比赛，但在遵守章程的条件下，非会员单位组织的国际限制赛、邀请赛以及经许可的国际比赛，可以按照主办机构制定的规则举行。

2.1.2.6　本规则和国际竞赛规程被认为适用于所有国际比赛，除非各项变化事先得到同意，或明确写入已公布的该比赛规程中。

2.1.2.7　规程的详细说明和理解，包括器材规格的说明，应以理事会许可的《技术文书》《比赛官员手册》和《裁判长手册》的形式公布。

2.2　器材和比赛条件

2.2.1　批准和许可的器材

2.2.1.1　对比赛器材的批准或许可，应由器材委员会代理理事会执行；如果在任何时候发现继续生产或使用某产品对乒乓球运动有害，理事会可以取消对该器材的批准。

2.2.1.2　公开赛的报名表或竞赛指南应详细说明将使用的球台、球网装置以及球的品牌和颜色；器材的选择应由比赛所在地的协会从国际乒联现行批准的品牌和型号中挑选。

2.2.1.3 球拍击球拍面的覆盖物应是国际乒联现行许可的品牌和型号，并在其边缘必须附有清晰可见的商标型号及国际乒联(ITTF)的标记。

2.2.1.4 从秘书处可得到将球拍覆盖物粘合在球拍上的经许可的黏合剂清单。

2.2.2 服装

2.2.2.1 比赛服一般包括短袖运动衫、短裤或短裙、短袜和运动鞋；其他服装，如半套或全套运动服，不得在比赛时穿着，但得到裁判长的允许时除外。

2.2.2.2 短袖运动衫(袖子和领子除外)、短裤或短裙的主要颜色应与比赛用球的颜色明显不同。

2.2.2.3 短袖运动衫的背部可以有号码或字样，用于表明运动员、运动员的协会，或在俱乐部比赛时，表明运动员的俱乐部，以及符合2.2.4.9条款规定的广告。

2.2.2.4 在短袖运动衫背部的中间位置应优先佩带被组织者制定的用于表明运动员身份的号码布，而不是广告。这个号码布应是长方形，面积不大于600平方厘米。

2.2.2.5 在运动服前面或侧面的任何标记或装饰物以及运动员佩戴的任何物品，如珠宝装饰等，均不应过于显眼或反光，以致影响对方的视线。

2.2.2.6 服装上不得带有可能产生不悦或诋毁本项运动声誉的设计和字样。

2.2.2.7 有关比赛服的合法性及可接受性问题，应由裁判长决定。

2.2.2.8 团体赛同队运动员，或同一协会运动员组成的双打，应穿着同样的服装，鞋袜除外。

2.2.2.9 比赛的双方运动员应穿着颜色明显不同的运动服，以使观众能够容易的区分他们。

2.2.2.10 当双方运动员或运动队所穿服装颜色类似，且均不愿更换时，应由抽签决定某一方必须更换。2.2.2.11 运动员参加世界、奥林匹克或国际公开锦标赛时，穿着的短袖运动衫、短裤或短裙等应为其协会批准的种类。

2.2.3 比赛条件：

2.2.3.1 赛区空间应不少于14米长、7米宽、5米高。

2.2.3.2 赛区应由75厘米高的同一深色的挡板围起，以与相邻的赛区及观众隔开。

2.2.3.3 在世界和奥林匹克比赛中，从比赛台面高度测得的照明度不得低于1000勒克斯，且整个比赛台面照度均匀，赛区其他地方的照明度不得低于500勒克斯；其他比赛中，比赛台面的照明度不得低于600勒克斯，且整个比赛照明度均匀，赛区其他地方的照明度不得低于400勒克斯。

2.2.3.4 使用多张球台时的照明水平应是一致的，比赛大厅的背景照明不得高于比赛区域的最低照明度。

2.2.3.5 光源距离地面不得少于5米。

2.2.3.6 场地四周一般应为暗色，不应有明亮光源，或从窗户等透过未加遮盖的日光。

2.2.3.7 地板不能颜色太浅或反光强烈或打滑，而且表面不得为砖、水泥或石头；在世界和奥林匹克比赛中，地板应为木制或国际乒联批准的某品牌和种类的可移动塑胶地板。

2.2.4　广告

2.2.4.1　在赛区内，广告只能在规定设置的器材和装置上展示，而不能单独设置广告。

2.2.4.2　赛区内任何地方不准使用荧光或发光的颜色。

2.2.4.3　挡板内侧的字样和标记禁止使用白色或黄色，亦不得超过两种颜色，其总高度应限制在40厘米以内；建议使用比底色深些或淡些的颜色。

2.2.4.4　地板上和球台端面、侧面上的标记物颜色应深于或浅于底色，或者是黑色。

2.2.4.5　比赛区域地面最多可有4个广告，球台的每个侧面和每个端面可各有1个广告，每个广告的总面积不得超过2.5平方米；广告与挡板的距离不得少于1米，两端的广告语挡板的距离不得超过2米。

2.2.4.6　球台两个侧面各1/2处和端面均可有一个临时性广告，该广告不得是其他乒乓球器材供应商的广告，而且与永久性广告必须有明显区别；每个广告总长度不得超过60厘米。

2.2.4.7　球网上的广告应深于或浅于背景的颜色，与球网顶端的距离不少于3厘米，并且不得遮盖网眼。

2.2.4.8　赛区内裁判桌或其他器材上的广告，其任何一面的总面积不得超过750平方厘米；

2.2.4.9　运动员服装上的广告应受下列限制：

2.2.4.9.1　制造厂家的正常商标、标记或名称，所占总面积不得超过24平方厘米；

2.2.4.9.2　短袖运动衫前面和侧面不得有3条以上的广告，广告总面积不得超过200平方厘米，每条广告必须明显分开；

2.2.4.9.3　短袖运动衫的背部可有一个面积不超过200平方厘米的广告；

2.2.4.9.4　短裤或短裙上可有不超过2个、总面积不超过80平方厘米的广告。

2.2.4.10　运动员号码布上的广告总面积不得超过100平方厘米。

2.2.4.11　裁判员服装上的广告总面积不得超过40平方厘米。

2.2.4.12　比赛服和号码布上不得有烟草制品、含酒精饮料或者有害药品的广告。

2.3　裁判人员的管理权限

2.3.1　裁判长

2.3.1.1　每次竞赛应指派一名裁判长，其身份和工作地点应告知所有参赛者及队长。

2.3.1.2　裁判长应对下列事项负责：

2.3.1.2.1　主持抽签；

2.3.1.2.2　编排比赛日程；

2.3.1.2.3　指派比赛工作人员；

2.3.1.2.4　主持裁判人员的赛前短会；

2.3.1.2.5　审查员动员的参赛资格；

2.3.1.2.6　决定在紧急时刻是否中断比赛；

2.3.1.2.7　决定在一场比赛中运动员是否可以离开赛区；

2.3.1.2.8　决定是否可以延长法定练习时间；

2.3.1.2.9　决定在一场比赛中运动员能否穿长运动服；

2.3.1.2.10　对解释规则和规程的任何问题作出决定，包括服装、比赛器材和比赛条件的可接受性；

2.3.1.2.11　决定在比赛紧急中断时，运动员能否练习以及练习地点；

2.3.1.2.12　对于不良行为或其他违反规程的行为采取纪律行动。

2.3.1.3　经竞赛管理委员会的同意，当裁判长的任何职责托付给一些其他人员时，这些人员中的每人的特殊职责和工作地点应告知参赛者及队长。

2.3.1.4　裁判长或在其缺席是负责代理的副裁判长，在比赛过程中应自始至终亲临比赛场地。

2.3.1.5　如果裁判长认为必要，可在任何时间更换裁判人员，但不得更改被更换者在其职权范围内就事实问题做出的判定。

2.3.2　裁判员

2.3.2.1　每场比赛均应指派1名裁判员和1名副裁判员。

2.3.2.2　裁判员应坐或站在球台一侧，与球网成一直线。副裁判员应面对裁判员坐在球台另一侧。

2.3.2.3　裁判员应对下列事项负责：

2.3.2.3.1　检查比赛器材和比赛条件的可接受性，如有问题向裁判长报告；

2.3.2.3.2　按2.4.2.1.1和2.4.2.1.2条款规定，任意取一只球；

2.3.2.3.3　主持抽签确定发球、接发球和方位；

2.3.2.3.4　决定是否由于运动员身体伤残而放宽合法发球的某些规定；

2.3.2.3.5　控制方位和发球、接发球的次序，纠正上述有关方面出现的错误；

2.3.2.3.6　决定每一个回合得1分或重发球；

2.3.2.3.7　根据规定的程序报分；

2.3.2.3.8　在适当的时间执行轮换发球法；

2.3.2.3.9　保持比赛的连续性；

2.3.2.3.10　对违反场外指导或行为等规定者采取行动。

2.3.2.4　副裁判员决定处于比赛状态中的球是否触及距离他最近的比赛台面的上边缘。

2.3.2.5　裁判员或副裁判员均可判决：

2.3.2.5.1　运动员发球动作不合法；

2.3.2.5.2　合法发球在球越过或绕过球网装置是否触及球网装置；

2.3.2.5.3　运动员阻挡；

2.3.2.5.4　比赛环境受到意外干扰，该回合的结果有可能受到影响；

2.3.2.5.5　掌握练习时间、比赛时间及间歇时间。

2.3.2.6　执行轮换发球法时，副裁判员或另外指派的一名裁判人员均可当计数员，计接发球方运动员的击球板数。

2.3.2.7　裁判员不得否决副裁判员或计数员根据2.3.2.5和2.3.2.6条款所做出的决定。

2.3.3　申诉

2.3.3.1　在单项比赛中的双方运动员或是在团体比赛中的双方队长之间所达成的协议，均不能改变该场比赛的裁判人员就事实问题所作的决定，亦不能改变裁判长就解释规则或规程的问题所作的决定；亦不能改变竞赛管理委员会对竞赛或比赛管理问题所作的决定。

2.3.3.2　对有关裁判人员就事实问题所作的决定，不得向裁判长提出申诉；对裁判长就解释规则或规程的问题所作的决定，不得向管理委员会提出申诉。

2.3.3.3　对裁判人员就解释规则或规程的问题所作的决定不服时，可以向裁判长提出申诉，裁判长的决定为最后决定。

2.3.3.4　对裁判长就未包括在规则或规程中的有关比赛管理问题所作的决定有不同看法时，可向竞赛管理委员会提出申诉，该委员会做出的决定为最后决定。

2.3.3.5　在单项比赛中，只能由参赛的运动员就该场比赛中出现的问题提出申诉；在团体比赛中，则只能由参赛队的队长就比赛中出现的问题提出申诉。

2.3.3.6　对裁判长就解释规则或规程的问题所作的决定，或竞赛管理委员会就比赛管理方面的问题所作的决定仍有异议时，可以由有权申诉的运动员或队长，通过所属协会将问题提交国际乒联规则委员会考虑。

2.3.3.7　规则委员会将就此做出裁决，作为将来决定的指南。所属协会仍可就该裁决向理事会或代表大会提出反对，但不影响裁判长或竞赛管理委员会已做出的任何最后决定。

2.4　比赛的管理

2.4.1　报分

2.4.1.1　当球一结束比赛状态，或在情况允许时，裁判员应立即报分。

2.4.1.1.1　报分时，裁判员应首先报下一回合即将发球一方的得分数，然后报对方的得分数。

2.4.1.1.2　一局比赛开始和交换发球员时，裁判员在报完比分后，应报出下一回合发球员的姓名，并用手势指明发球方。

2.4.1.1.3　一局比赛结束时，裁判员应先报胜方运动员的姓名，然后报胜方得分数，在报负方的得分数。

2.4.1.2　裁判员除报分外，还可以用手势表示他的判决。

2.4.1.2.1　当判得分时，裁判员可将靠近得分方的手举至齐肩高。

2.4.1.2.2　当出于某种原因，回合应被判为重发球时，裁判员可以将手高举过头表示该回合结束。

2.4.1.3　报分，以及在实行轮换发球法时的报数，裁判员应使用英语或双方运动员及裁判员均能接受的任何其他语言。

2.4.1.4　应使用机械或电子设备显示比分，使运动员和观众都能看清楚。

2.4.1.5　当运动员因不良行为受正式警告后，应在记分牌该运动员得分处放置一个黄牌。

2.4.2　器材

2.4.2.1　运动员不得在赛区内挑选比赛用球。

2.4.2.1.1　在进入赛区之前，运动员应有机会挑选一个或几个比赛用球，并由裁判员任意从中取一个球进行比赛。

2.4.2.1.2　如果未能在运动员进入赛区前挑选比赛用球，则由裁判员从一盒大会指定的比赛用球中任意取一个进行比赛。

2.4.2.1.3　如果比赛中球损坏，应由比赛前选定的另外一个球代替；如果没有赛前选定的球，则由裁判员从一盒大会指定的比赛用球中任意取一个球代替。

2.4.2.2 在一场单项比赛中，球拍将不允许更换，除非球拍意外严重损坏到不能使用。如果运动员在比赛中损坏了球拍，应立即替换随身带来的另一块球拍，或场外递进的球拍。

2.4.2.3 运动员在比赛间歇时，应将球拍留在比赛的球台上。得到裁判员的特殊许可除外。

2.4.3 练习

2.4.3.1 在一场比赛开始前2分钟，运动员有权在比赛球台上练习，正常间歇不能练习。只有裁判长有权延长特殊的练习时间。

2.4.3.2 在紧急中断比赛时，裁判长可允许运动员在任何球台上练习，包括比赛用的球台。

2.4.3.3 运动员应有合理的机会检查和熟悉将要使用的器材，在替换破球或损坏的球拍以后，运动员可练习少数几个回合，然后继续比赛。

2.4.4 间歇

2.4.4.1 任何运动员有权要求：

2.4.4.1.1 在局与局之间，不超过1分钟的休息时间；

2.4.4.1.2 每局比赛中，没打完6分球后，或决胜局交换方位时，用短暂的时间擦汗。

2.4.4.2 一名或一队双打运动员可在一场比赛中要求一次暂停，时间不超过1分钟。

2.4.4.2.1 在单项比赛中，暂停应由运动员或指定的场外指导者提出；在团体比赛中，应由运动员或队长提出。

2.4.4.2.2 请求暂停只有在球未处于比赛状态时做出，应用双手做出“T”形表示。

2.4.4.2.3 在一方获得合理的暂停要求后，裁判员应暂停比赛并出示白牌，然后将白牌放在提出要求暂停一方运动员的台区上。

2.4.4.2.4 当提出暂停的一方运动员准备继续比赛或1分钟暂停时间已到时，以时间短的计算，白牌应被拿走并且立即恢复比赛。

2.4.4.3 运动员因意外事件而暂时丧失比赛能力时，裁判长若认为中断比赛不至于给对方带来不利，可允许中断比赛，但时间要尽量短些，在任何情况下都不得超过10分钟。

2.4.4.4 如果失去比赛能力的状态早已存在，或在比赛开始前就有理由可以预见，或由于比赛的正常紧张状态引起，则不能允许中断比赛。如果失去比赛能力的原因在于运动员当时的身体状况或比赛进行的方式，引起抽筋或过度疲劳，这些也不能成为中断比赛的理由。只有因意外事故，如摔倒受伤而丧失比赛能力，才能允许紧急中断。

2.4.4.5 如果赛区内有人受伤流血，应立即中断比赛，直到他接受了医疗救护并将赛区内所有血迹擦干净后再恢复比赛。

2.4.4.6 除非裁判长允许，运动员在一场比赛中应留在赛区内或赛区附近，在局与局之间的法定休息的时间内，运动员应在裁判员的监督下，留在赛区周围3米以内的地方。

2.5 纪律

2.5.1 场外指导

2.5.1.1 团体比赛，运动员可接受任何人的场外指导。

2.5.1.2　单项比赛，运动员只能接受一个人的场外指导，而这个指导者的身份应在该场比赛前向裁判员说明；如果一对双打运动员来自不同协会，则可分别授权一名指导者；如未被授权的人进行指导，裁判员应出示红牌令其远离赛区。

2.5.1.3　在局与局之间的休息时间或经批准的中断时间内，运动员可接受场外指导，但在赛前练习结束后到比赛开始前不能接受场外指导。如被授权的指导者在其他时间内进行指导，裁判员应出示黄牌进行警告；如在警告后再次违犯，将被驱逐出赛区。

2.5.1.4　在一个团体赛或单项比赛中的一场比赛，指导者已被警告过。如任何人再进行非法指导，裁判员将出示红牌，并将其驱逐出赛区，不论其是否曾被警告过。

2.5.1.5　在团体比赛中被驱逐出赛区的人不允许在团体比赛结束前返回，除非需要他上场比赛。在单项比赛中，不允许他在该场单项比赛结束前返回。

2.5.1.6　如被驱逐出赛区的指导者拒离开或在比赛结束前返回，裁判员应中断比赛，并立即向裁判长报告。

2.5.1.7　以上规定只限制对比赛的指导，并不限制运动员或队长就裁判员的决定提出正式申诉，或阻止运动员与所属协会的代表或翻译就某项判决的解释进行商议。

2.5.2　不良行为

2.5.2.1　运动员和教练员应克服那些可能不公平的影响对手、冒犯观众或影响本项运动声誉的不良行为，诸如：辱骂性语言，故意弄坏球或将球打出赛区，踢球台或挡板和不尊重比赛官员等。

2.5.2.2　任何时候，运动员或教练员出现严重冒犯行为，裁判员应中断比赛，立即报告裁判长；如果冒犯行为不太严重，第一次裁判员可出示黄牌，警告冒犯者，如再次冒犯将被判罚。

2.5.2.3　除 2.5.2.2 和 2.5.2.5 条规定外，运动员在受到警告后，在同一场单项比赛获团体比赛中，第二次冒犯，裁判员应判对方得 1 分；再犯，判对方得 2 分，每次判罚，应同时出示黄牌和红牌。

2.5.2.4　在同一场单项比赛或团体比赛中，运动员在被判罚 3 分后继续有不良行为，裁判员应中断比赛，并立即报告裁判长。

2.5.2.5　在一场比赛中，不允许更换球拍，除非球拍意外严重损坏到不能使用。如果运动员没有声明就更换球拍，裁判员应停止比赛，并向裁判长报告。

2.5.2.6　双打配对中的任何一名运动员所受到的警告或判罚均应视做是该对双打运动员的，但未受警告运动员在同一场团体比赛随后的单项比赛中不受影响；双打比赛开始时，配对运动员中任何一名在同一场团体比赛中已经受到的最严重的警告或判罚应视作是该对双打运动员的。

2.5.2.7　除 2.5.2.2 条规定外，教练员在受到警告后，在同一场单项比赛获团体比赛中再次冒犯，裁判员应出示红牌并将其驱逐出赛区，直到该场团体比赛或单项赛中的该场单项比赛结束才可返回。

2.5.2.8　无论是否得到裁判员的报告，裁判长有权取消有严重不公平或冒犯行为运动员的比赛资格，包括取消一场比赛、一项比赛或整个比赛的比赛资格。当他采取行动时应出示红牌。

2.5.2.9　如果一名运动员在团体(或单项)比赛中有两场被取消了比赛资格，就自动取消了其参加团体(或单项)比赛的资格。

2.5.2.10　裁判长有权取消已经两次被驱逐出赛区的任何人在本次竞赛剩余时间里的临场资格。

2.5.2.11　在48个月内累计4次未能通过正式球拍检测的任意一项，该运动员将在12个月内被暂停参加国际乒联的赛事。

2.5.2.12　如果一名运动员因任何原因被取消一场比赛、一个项目或整个赛事的资格，它将自动丧失任何相关的头衔、奖牌、奖金和排名积分。

2.5.2.13　对于十分严重的不良行为，应报告给冒犯者所属协会。

2.5.3　精神面貌

2.5.3.1　运动员、教练员和官员应维护本项运动的良好风貌，运动员尤其应该尽力赢得比赛，除生病、受伤外，不得退出比赛。

2.5.3.2　任何故意不遵守这些规定的运动员，将在有奖金的比赛项目中被处罚扣除全部或部分奖金和/或暂停参加国际乒联的比赛。

2.5.3.3　如果任何指导者或官员被证实共同参与，相关国家协会也应处罚此人。

2.5.3.4　执委会将任命一个由4名成员和1名主席组成的纪律小组，该小组将根据执委会所做的指令，决定是否有违反规定的行为，并且如有必要，做出相应的处罚。

2.5.3.5　受到处罚的运动员、指导者和官员，可在15天之内就纪律小组的决定向国际乒联执委会提出申诉，执委会所做的决定为最后决定。

2.6　淘汰赛的抽签

2.6.1　轮空和预选赛

2.6.1.1　淘汰赛第一轮的位置数应为2的幂。

2.6.1.1.1　如果位置数多于已接纳的报名人数，第一轮应设置足够的轮空位置以补足所需位置数目。

2.6.1.1.2　如果位置数少于已接纳的报名人数，应举行预选赛，使预选赛出线人数和免予参加预选赛的人数的总和等于所需的位置数。

2.6.1.2　轮空位置应按照种子排列先后次序安排，在第一轮中尽可能均匀分布。

2.6.1.3　通过预选赛的选手应视情况尽可能均匀地抽入相应的上下半区、各1/4区、1/8区或1/16区。

2.6.2　按排名排列种子

2.6.2.1　排名在前的选手应被列为种子，以使他们在比赛进行到较后轮次时相遇。

2.6.2.2　种子数不得超过该项比赛第一轮的选手数。

2.6.2.3　第一号种子应安排在上半区的顶部，第二号种子应安排在下半区的底部，其余种子应通过抽签进入规定的位置，具体如下：

2.6.2.3.1　第三、第四号种子应抽入上半区的底部和下半区的顶部；

2.6.2.3.2　第五、八号种子应抽入单数1/4区的底部和双数1/4区的顶部；

2.6.2.3.3　第九、十六号种子应抽入单数1/8区的底部和双数1/8区的顶部；

2.6.2.3.4　第十七、三十二号种子应抽入单数1/16区的底部和双数1/16区的顶部。

2.6.2.4　在团体淘汰赛中，每一协会中排名最高的队才有资格按排名被列为种子。

2.6.2.5　排列种子应按国际乒联最新公布的排名表为准，下列情况除外：

2.6.2.5.1　如果符合种子条件的报名选手(队)均来自同一洲联合会下属的协会，该联合会最新公布的排名表应优先考虑；

2.6.2.5.2 如果符合种子条件的报名选手均来自同一协会，该协会最新公布的排名表应优先考虑。

2.6.3 按协会提名排种子

2.6.3.1 来自同一协会的报名选手应尽可能合理分开，使他们在比赛进行较后轮次时相遇。

2.6.3.2 各协会应按技术水平由强至弱的排列其报名运动员和双打配对的顺序，并应与种子排名表的顺序一致。

2.6.3.3 排列为第一和第二位的选手应被抽入不同的半区，第三和第四号选手应被抽入没有本协会第一、第二号选手所在的另外两个 1/4 区。

2.6.3.4 排名第五～八号的选手，应尽可能均匀地抽入没有前四号选手的 1/8 区。

2.6.3.5 排名第九～十六号的选手应尽可能均匀地抽入没有前八号选手的 1/16 区，以此类推，直到所有报名选手都进入适当位置为止。

2.6.3.6 由不同协会的选手组成的男子双打或女子双打配对，应被视为属于在世界排名表上排名较高选手的协会；如果两名选手在世界排名表无名，则应被视为属于在相应的洲联合会排名表排名较高选手的协会；如果两名选手均不在上述排名表内，则应被视为属于在世界团体赛排名表中排名较高的协会。

2.6.3.7 由不同协会的选手组成的混合双打配对，应被视为属于男选手的协会。

2.6.3.8 在预选赛中，同一协会的不多于预选赛分组数目的选手应抽入不同的小组，并应按 2.6.3.3 和 2.6.3.5 所述的原则使通过预选赛的选手尽可能地合理分开。

2.6.3.9 协会可提名其权限内的运动员参加其有资格参加的任何单项比赛；但有资格代表其他协会的运动员有权接受该协会的提名。

2.6.4 变更抽签

2.6.4.1 只有竞赛管理委员会授权，才能对已经结束的抽签进行更改，情况许可时，还须征得各与之直接有关协会代表的同意。

2.6.4.2 只有在纠正因通知和接受报名方面产生的错误和误解，纠正 2.6.5 所述的严重不平衡或按 2.6.6 所述，加入补报的运动员时才可对抽签进行更改。

2.6.4.3 一个项目比赛开始后，除必要的删减外，抽签结果不可作任何更改，但预选赛可视作一个单独项目，不在此列。

2.6.4.4 未得到有关运动员的许可，不可将其从抽签中除掉，除非其已被取消比赛资格；如果运动员在场，该许可应由运动员本人提出，如果运动员缺席，可由其授权的代表提出。

2.6.4.5 如果两名双打运动员均已到会，健康状况允许比赛，不得变更其配对；变更配对的理由须是其中一名运动员受伤、生病或缺席。

2.6.5 重新抽签

2.6.5.1 除 2.6.4.2、2.6.4.5 和 2.6.5.2 条款情况外，不允许运动员从抽签的一个位置移到另一个位置。如果因任何原因使抽签结果极不平衡，应尽可能全部重新抽签。

2.6.5.2 如果不平衡是由于同一抽签区内若干种子选手缺席造成，只可将剩余种子重新排列顺序，在种子范围内重新抽签，尽可能考虑按协会提名排种子的规定。

2.6.6 增补

2.6.6.1 抽签时未包括在一个项目内的运动员，由竞赛管理委员会许可及经裁判长同意，可以增补。

2.6.6.2　首先应按排名顺序，将实力最强的增补运动员补抽进种子位的空缺；然后，将多出的选手先抽入因缺席或取消资格而出现的空位，而后抽入不与种子位相邻的轮空位。

2.6.6.3　如果运动员或双打配对按照排名可以作为种子进入原抽签，则只能抽入种子位的空缺。

2.7　竞赛的组织工作

2.7.1　许可

2.7.1.1　在遵守章程规定的前提下，任何协会都可以在本土组织或授权组织公开赛、限制赛、邀请赛或安排国际比赛。

2.7.1.2　协会可以在任何赛季提出举办成年和少年公开赛各一次，作为它的成年和少年国际公开赛。只有经其协会允许的运动员，才可以参加此类比赛，但不允许不应是没有理由的限制。

2.7.1.3　运动员未经其协会允许不得参加国际限制赛或国际邀请赛，除非获得国际乒联的允许，或运动员均来自同一洲时，得到洲联合会的允许。

2.7.1.4　被其协会暂停比赛的运动员不得参加国际比赛。

2.7.1.5　未经国际乒联允许，任何比赛不能用“世界”称号；未经洲联合会允许，不能用“洲”称号。

2.7.2　代表资格

2.7.2.1　有选手报名参加国际公开锦标赛的所有协会的代表有权出席抽签，有权参与磋商抽签的更改或可能直接影响其选手的申诉的决定。

2.7.2.2　来访协会应有权提名至少一名代表进入其参加的国际比赛的管理委员会。

2.7.3　报名

2.7.3.1　国际公开锦标赛的报名表，最迟应于比赛开始前两个月和报名截止前一个月寄给所有协会。

2.7.3.2　公开赛的组织者应接受由协会报名参赛的所有选手，但有权将报名选手安排进行预选赛；在决定此安排时，组织者应考虑国际乒联和洲联合会有关的排名表，以及由报名协会提出的报名顺序。

2.7.4　比赛项目

2.7.4.1　国际公开锦标赛可以包括男子单打、女子单打、男子双打、女子双打。也可包括混合双打和代表协会参赛队的团体赛。

2.7.4.2　建议少年和儿童项目的年龄分别17岁和14岁为限，计算年龄的日期应是该比赛赛季开始前的6月30日。

2.7.4.3　建议国际公开锦标赛上的团体赛应按2.7.6条款中的一种比赛方式进行，并在报名表或比赛指南中予以注明所选定的比赛方式。

2.7.4.4　在成年单打比赛中，除预选赛外，比赛应采用五局三胜制，少年单打比赛可以采用三局两胜制或五局三胜制；其他比赛均采用三局两胜制。

2.7.4.5　单项比赛一般应采用淘汰制进行，但团体赛和单项预选赛可以按淘汰制或分组循环制进行。

2.7.5　分组循环

2.7.5.1　在分组循环赛中，小组里每一成员应与组内所有其他成员进行比赛；胜一场得2分，输一场得1分，未出场比赛或未完成比赛输的场次得0分，小组名次应根据所获得的场次分数决定。

2.7.5.2　如果小组的两个或更多的成员得分数相同，他们有关的名词应按他们相互之间比赛的成绩决定。首先计算他们之间获得的场次分数，再根据需要计算个人比赛场次(团体赛时)、局和分的胜负比率，直至算出名次为止。

2.7.5.3　如果在任何阶段已经决定出一个或更多小组成员的名次后，而其他小组成员仍然得分相同，为决定相同分数成员的名次，根据2.7.5.1和2.7.5.2条程序继续计算时，应将已决定出名次的小组成员的比赛成绩删除。

2.7.5.4　如果按照2.7.5.1和2.7.5.3条所规定的程序，仍不能决定某些队(人)的名次时，这些队(人)的名次将由抽签来决定。

2.7.5.5　在世界锦标赛，奥运会和国际公开锦标赛资格赛阶段，参赛运动员根据抽签分组，并尽可能使同一协会的运动员不在同一组，每组中每个运动员都有一个根据实力递减的位置号。

2.7.5.6　除非仲裁委员会有相反的规定，如果有一人获得决赛阶段比赛资格，应排在1号和2号选手之间，如果有2名选手获得决赛阶段比赛资格，则应排在2号和3号选手之间，依此类推。

2.7.6　团体赛形式

2.7.6.1　五场三胜制(五场单打)

2.7.6.1.1　一个队由3名运动员组成。

2.7.6.1.2　比赛顺序是：

(1)A-X；(2)B-Y；(3)C-Z；(4)A-Y；(5)B-X。

2.7.6.2　五场三胜制(四场单打和一场双打)

2.7.6.2.1　一个队由2、3或4名运动员组成。

2.7.6.2.2　比赛顺序是：

(1)A-X；(2)B-Y；(3)双打；(4)A-Y；(5)B-X。

2.7.6.3　七场四胜制(六场单打和一场双打)

2.7.6.3.1　一个队由3、4或5名运动员组成。

2.7.6.3.2　比赛顺序是：

(1)A-Y；(2)B-X；(3)C-Z；(4)双打；(5)A-X；(6)C-Y；(7)B-Z。

2.7.6.4　九场五胜制(九场单打)

2.7.6.4.1　一个队由3名运动员组成。

2.7.6.4.2　比赛顺序是：

(1)A-X；(2)B-Y；(3)C-Z；(4)B-X；(5)A-Z；(6)C-Y；(7)B-Z；(8)C-X；(9)A-Y。

2.7.7　团体比赛程序

2.7.7.1　所有出场运动员应来自团体报名表。

2.7.7.2　团体比赛前由抽签的中签者优先选择A、B、C或X、Y、Z。由队长将该队名单提交给裁判长或其代理人，并对每一名单打运动员确定一个字母所代表的相应位置。

2.7.7.3　双打比赛的配对不必立即提交，直到前一场单打比赛结束。

2.7.7.4 当一个队赢得足够多数场次时，为一次团体比赛结束。

2.7.8 成绩

主办协会在比赛结束后7天之内，应尽快将详细成绩和比分，包括国际比赛、洲和国际公开锦标赛的各轮成绩，以及全国锦标赛的最后几轮的成绩，寄给国际乒联秘书处和有关洲联合会的秘书。

2.7.9 电视转播

2.7.9.1 除世界锦标赛、洲锦标赛和奥运会以外的比赛，只有经主办协会许可，才可对比赛进行电视转播。

2.7.9.2 运动员参加一次国际比赛时，将被认为同意在该比赛中运动员的电视转播事宜由主办协会控制；在参加世界锦标赛、洲锦标赛和奥运会比赛时，运动员将被认为同意在任何地点进行比赛期间的现场直播和赛后一个月之内的录像播出。

2.8 国际比赛资格

2.8.1 以下规定将适用于冠名世界、洲和奥林匹克的比赛以及国际公开锦标赛的团体赛。

2.8.2 一名运动员可以代表一个协会参赛，但他必须是该协会拥有管辖权国家的公民。除非一名运动员在1997年8月31日前，因出生或居住等原因，已有资格代表另一个他不是该国公民的协会。

2.8.2.1 一名运动员同时是一个以上国家的国民时，可以在有关协会中选择一个他将代表的协会。

2.8.2.2 如果一个以上协会的运动员拥有相同的国籍，各有关协会可以决定其关于资格的附加要求。

2.8.3 一名运动员在3年以内不得代表不同的协会。

2.8.4 如果运动员接受了代表一个协会的提名，无论他是否出场比赛，均被视为已经代表了该协会。代表的日期应是提名的日期或比赛的日期中较迟的一个。

2.8.5 如果裁判长需要，运动员或其协会应提供有关比赛资格的文件证明。

2.8.6 一个协会可以提名符合比赛资格，但现在居住在另一个协会所控制的领土上的运动员代表本协会，如果该运动员为被那个协会暂停比赛或开除。

2.8.7 任何有关比赛资格问题的申诉应提交执行局处理，执行局的决定将是最后的决定。

2.8.8 任何有关资格问题的申诉应提交资格委员会，该委员会的决定为最后决定。资格委员会由执行委员会委员、规则和排名委员会主席、运动员委员会主席组成。

3 乒乓球世界级比赛和奥运会比赛规程

3.1 世界锦标赛

3.1.1 组织的权力

3.1.1.1 世界锦标赛，本章简称锦标赛，为国际乒联代表大会指定锦标赛设立项目并委托某协会承办的比赛。

3.1.1.2 申请举办世界锦标赛截止日期由国际乒联执委会确定，并至少提前6个月通告所有的协会。国际乒联只能接受举办下两届世界锦标赛的申请。

3.1.1.3 所有申请应由国际乒联执委会予以审核，并与选择委员会的报告一起送交国际乒联代表大会。

3.1.1.4　如有必要，国际乒联代表大会或执行委员会可以安排一个或几个相关的委员会成员去申办协会考察，以便了解有关比赛各方面的筹备情况，考察的费用由该协会承担。

3.1.1.5　主办协会确定下来后，如果情况发生变化并可能影响到比赛的顺利举办时，赛前一届的国际乒联代表大会可以 2/3 的多数票推翻主办权，在两个代表大会之间理事会有权决定将锦标赛改在异地或采取其他适当行动。

3.1.2　主办协会的职责

3.1.2.1　协会一旦获取举办锦标赛，就称之为“主办协会”。主办协会应该根据《乒乓球规则》《乒乓球国际竞赛规程》和《世界比赛规程》，以及经理事会修改和补充的竞赛指南准备比赛。

3.1.2.2　主办协会应该从锦标赛开始前一个晚上起，到比赛结束的第二天上午止，为下列人员提供食宿：

3.1.2.2.1　一个协会指定的参赛人员，最多不超过 3 名男运动员和 3 名女运动员；

3.1.2.2.2　每协会一名参加国际乒联代表大会的代表，如其姓名不在上述指定的运动员之列；

3.1.2.2.3　国际乒联官员、理事会成员、奥林匹克委员会和其他委员会正式成员；

3.1.2.2.4　由运动科学委员会指定的兴奋剂检测小组人员，最多 4 人；

3.1.2.2.5　赛事工作小组的工作人员，最多 3 人；

3.1.2.2.6　运动员委员会成员，最多 8 人；

3.1.2.2.7　个人名誉委员；

3.1.2.2.8　根据国际乒联颁布的指南所邀请的其他协会的国际裁判和裁判长；

3.1.2.2.9　国际乒联工作人员，最多 3 人。

3.1.2.3　如果国际乒联的业务工作超过锦标赛的时间，主办协会应相应延长对参加该业务的人员的食宿招待。

3.1.2.4　主办者应该对参赛者免费提供医疗和药品，但是每个协会也应确保自己的参赛队员和官员在锦标赛期间的身体健康，避免受伤。

3.1.2.5　主办者从驻地到赛场应免费接送参赛人员，并要求该国家政府免收所有参赛者的签证费。

3.1.2.6　主办协会应确保所有的运动员、官员以及 3.1.2.2 条所列的人员可随意进入赛场以及在相关的比赛区域活动。编外运动员、委员会成员以及国际乒联任命的翻译、医生或医务工作人员也同样享有这种待遇。

3.1.2.7　主办者应提供至少三种语言的、一流的翻译服务，最好有同声传译的设备支持。

3.1.2.8　主办者应在赛场为国际乒联提供办公室，并应其要求提供翻译、文字处理、打印和复印等设备。

3.1.2.9　主办者应该发行一本有关比赛细节的小册子，详细介绍锦标赛的组织情况，内容包括：

3.1.2.9.1　锦标赛的时间和地点；

3.1.2.9.2　锦标赛的项目；

3.1.2.9.3 锦标赛使用的器材；

3.1.2.9.4 锦标赛的报名程序、报名费以及所需的工作；

3.1.2.9.5 抽签的时间和地点；

3.1.2.9.6 仲裁会议和代表大会的时间；

3.1.2.9.7 运动员和官员的接待情况；

3.1.2.9.8 任何由理事会对该锦标赛颁发的指令。

3.1.2.10 在锦标赛期间，主办者应该尽快给国际乒联官员、理事会成员和各队的领队提供比赛成绩，包括具体的比分。全部比赛结束后，应尽快公布包括比分在内的所有比赛成绩，并传发给备参赛协会。

3.1.3 资格

3.1.3.1 只有未拖欠会费的协会才有资格参赛。

3.1.3.2 根据规则 2.8 条的规定，所有由协会指定的参赛选手具有代表该协会的资格。

3.1.4 报名费及征收

3.1.4.1 团体比赛每个队的报名费为 100 美元，每对双打为 50 美元，每名单打为 25 美元。

3.1.4.2 参赛协会在报名时应该向比赛主办协会交纳报名费，报名费由主办协会和国际乒联均分。

3.1.4.3 出于不可控制的原因使得某协会不能参加锦标赛，理事会可免除其报名费，除此之外，每一个报名的协会都应按时交纳报名费。

3.1.5 递交报名

3.1.5.1 有意派队或队员参加锦标赛的协会，应填写秘书处提供的初步报名表，并以此通知组委会和国际乒联。接收初步报名表的截止日期最晚不超过锦标赛开始前四个月。

3.1.5.2 应通过填写由秘书处随同锦标赛指南一同发放的报名表来报名。

3.1.5.3 报名表一式三份，两份返还给主办协会，一份留在秘书处，收到报名表不能晚于锦标赛开始前的两个月。

3.1.5.4 团体比赛每个协会可以最多报 5 名运动员和 1 名教练员，如果没有教练员，可以从 5 名运动员中指定一个。

3.1.5.5 协会应按技术水平为其报名参加单打和双打的运动员排序，排序应符合当时的世界排名。

3.1.5.6 主办协会只接受有参赛资格协会的正式报名，报名表必须由该协会的一名代表签署，在指定的截止日内收到。

3.1.6 报名的更改

3.1.6.1 主办协会可以接受对报名的补充或修改，但必须由该协会一名代表的正式签署，在抽签以前的任何时间上报。

3.1.6.2 报名的协会可以改变团体阵容的组成，但必须在仲裁会议召开前向主办协会提出。比赛一旦开始，就不能更改团体名单。

3.1.6.3 出于错误或缺席原因而需要改变报名的协会，其代表一到比赛地点就应向裁判长、副裁判长报告报名更改的情况，或确认已经通告过的改动，需使用(填写)专为更改报名而准备的表格。

3.1.6.4　如果要求改变报名，必须由该协会的代表一到比赛地就提出，而不能因为后来队员的缺席、双打搭档的生病或受伤临时提出变更。

3.1.6.5　所有经过确定的更改应该立即通知各队教练员或在可能的情况下通知参赛协会代表。

3.1.7　报名须知

3.1.7.1　报名表应包括一个由协会负责人代表指派的运动员、领队签署的声明，表明他们理解和接受锦标赛的意义，准备和自己的对手进行竞争。没有这个声明，报名就不合法。

3.1.7.2　单项比赛中，所有的参赛者都被视为独立的参赛选手，所以，无论他的对手来自与他同一个协会，还是来自不同的协会，他都要尽自己最大的努力赢得所有参加的比赛，除受伤或生病外，不能退出比赛。

3.1.8　仲裁

3.1.8.1　仲裁应该包括技术委员会、排名委员会主席和规则委员会主席、锦标赛竞赛主任(或他的同级)、组委会一名代表和裁判长。裁判长有权发言，但是不能投票。

3.1.8.2　如果排名委员会主席或者规则委员会主席中的一人不能出席仲裁会议，他可以指派他所在委员会的其他成员出席，该成员有发言和投票的权利。

3.1.8.3　仲裁的主席由技术委员会指定。

3.1.8.4　如有协会将受仲裁会议所讨论问题的直接影响，该协会可派人出席仲裁会议，但是无权投票。

3.1.8.5　仲裁有权对在竞赛管理委员会管辖范围内的申诉做出裁决，可批准团队变动。

3.1.8.6　在锦标赛开始以前，仲裁就应召开会议，通报当时所有的抽签变更，对各队成员的变动申请作出决定，抽签更改后出现的相应问题由技术委员会做出决定，当出现对行政决定或裁判长决定提出申诉时，技术委员会将重新召集仲裁开会。

3.1.9　竞赛项目

3.1.9.1　在偶数年份将举行男女团体比赛；而奇数年将举行男女单打、男女双打和混合双打比赛。双打比赛的配对必须来自同一个协会。

3.1.9.2　团体赛包括分组以及分阶段的比赛方式，应该由技术委员会提出方案，由理事会来决定，并在锦标赛开始前六个月通告所有协会。

3.1.9.3　团体赛必须5场3胜，均为单打比赛，参照2.7.6.1条。

3.1.9.4　单打比赛的第一轮，抽签最多不能超过128个位置，双打比赛第一轮不能超过64个位置，除非得到执委会的许可。

3.1.9.5　每个协会均可派一定数量的选手参加单打比赛，主办协会和拥有占据赛前3个月国际乒联排名表前几位选手的协会，可以增加单打的参赛人数；每个协会获准参赛的人数以及以此报名为基础制定的参加预选的人数，应由执行委员会授权，并至少在赛前6个月通告所有协会。

3.1.10　违规

3.1.10.1　进入团体抽签的队，因无正当理由不参加比赛，该协会将受到国际乒联代表大会的纪律处罚。

3.1.10.2　每个队参加该场比赛的阵容，在一场团体赛中应自始至终在现场，除非由于发生意外、生病、受伤或者其他不可控制的因素，包括裁判长取消某名运动员资格时，裁判长可以允许团体赛中的一名队员缺席，或省去一场比赛。

3.1.10.3　如果一个队在团体比赛中，没有打完比赛就中途退出，该协会代表的免费招待可被取消。该协会对此可向仲裁申诉，仲裁的决定将是最终的决定。

3.1.11　兴奋剂检测

兴奋剂检测应该按国际奥委会的规定执行。

3.1.12　奖励和仪式

3.1.12.1　锦标赛永久性的奖杯是：

男子团体斯韦思林杯；女子团体考比伦杯；男子单打圣·勃莱德杯；女子单打吉·盖斯特杯；男子双打伊朗杯；女子双打波普杯；混合双打兹·赫杜塞克杯。

3.1.12.2　获得团体冠军的队，由该协会保存奖杯，获得单项冠军的个人，由本人保存奖杯，直至他们(他)赢得冠军次年的 12 月 31 日；获得双打冠军的选手，可用抽签的方法决定谁先保存奖杯，两人各保存一半时间。

3.1.12.3　对于连续三届获得男子单打或女子单打冠军，或者一共获得 4 次单打冠军的选手，国际乒联将制作一个比真实的奖杯小一半的奖杯复制品，赠送给该运动员，作为永久的纪念。

3.1.12.4　无论团体还是单项，决赛中获胜的冠军将获得金牌，在决赛中失利的选手将获得银牌，在半决赛中失利的选手将获得铜牌。

3.1.12.5　团体和单项的颁奖仪式，应悬挂获得金牌、银牌和铜牌的队或运动员国家的国旗，奏金牌获得者国家的国歌。

3.1.12.6　获得奖杯的协会，应书面确认收到奖杯，在指定期限临近时，应该在秘书处通知的 14 天内，将奖杯在已商定的时间内送到已商定的地点。

3.1.12.7　奖杯应刻有冠军的名字，团体赛中应包括不参赛的教练员的名字；接受奖杯的协会要签收奖杯，并有责任保护好奖杯，包括对奖杯进行保险，保险和刻字的费用由国际乒联承担。

3.1.12.8　如果协会在保管奖杯期间将奖杯丢失了，该协会有责任重新制作与原来相似的奖杯复制品。

3.1.12.9　锦标赛举办城市在比赛期间有权保存埃及杯，埃及杯是锦标赛友谊的象征，在开幕式上交接。

3.1.13　电视

锦标赛的电视转播权归属国际乒联，国际乒联将征收 3.2 万美元，或总费用的 20%，得到执行委员会许可除外。

3.2　世界青年锦标赛

3.2.1　组织职权

3.2.1.1　世界青年锦标赛，本章简称锦标赛，为国际乒联代表大会指定锦标赛设立项目并委托某协会承办的比赛。

3.2.1.2　申请举办世界青年锦标赛截止日期由执行委员会确定，并至少提前六个月通知所有协会。国际乒联只能接收举办下两届世界青年锦标赛的申请。

3.2.1.3　所有申请应由执行委员会审核，并连同比赛场馆详细信息送交理事会，以便答疑。

3.2.1.4 如有必要，理事会或执行委员会可以安排青少年委员会一名成员去申办协会考察，以便了解有关比赛各方面的筹备情况，考察的费用由该协会承担。

3.2.1.5 主办协会确定下来后，如果情况发生变化并可能影响到比赛的顺利举行时，赛前一届国际乒联代表大会可以2/3的多数票推翻主办权，在两个代表大会之间，理事会有权决定将锦标赛改在异地或采取其他适当行动。

3.2.2 主办协会的职责

3.2.2.1 协会一旦获权举办锦标赛，就称之为“主办协会”。主办协会应该根据《乒乓球规则》、《乒乓球国际竞赛规程》和《世界青年锦标赛规程》，以及经过理事会修改和补充的竞赛指南为比赛做准备。

3.2.2.2 主办协会应该从锦标赛开始前一个晚上起，到比赛结束的第二天上午，为下列人员提供食宿：

3.2.2.2.1 一个协会所指定有资格参加青年男子团体比赛的运动员，人数不超过两名；

3.2.2.2.2 一个协会所指定的有资格参加青年女子团体比赛的运动员，人数不超过两名；

3.2.2.2.3 参加1个或2个团体项目的协会不超过1名教练员；

3.2.2.2.4 国际乒联执行委员会和青少年委员会成员；

3.2.2.2.5 由运动科学委员会指定的兴奋剂检测小组人员，最多2名；

3.2.2.2.6 由执行委员会任命的国际乒联委员会主席，最多2名；

3.2.2.2.7 根据国际乒联颁布的指南所邀请的其他协会的国际裁判员和裁判长；

3.2.2.2.8 最多3名国际乒联工作人员。

3.2.2.3 主办协会应对参赛者免费提供医疗和药品，但是每个协会也应确保自己的参赛队员和官员在锦标赛期间的身体健康，避免受伤。

3.2.2.4 主办者应负担接送参赛者往返驻地与比赛场馆间的交通费用。

3.2.2.5 主办者应要求该国政府免收所有参赛者的签证费。

3.2.2.6 主办协会应确保所有运动员、官员和3.2.2.2条所列的人员可随意进入赛场以及在相关比赛区域活动。编外运动员、国际乒联官员，以及国际乒联任命的翻译、医生和医务工作者也同样享有这样的待遇。

3.2.2.7 主办者应在比赛场馆内为国际乒联提供办公室，并应其要求提供翻译、计算机、互联网、电话、传真和复印等设备。

3.2.2.8 主办方应该印制一本小册子，详细介绍锦标赛组织工作的主要情况，内容包括：

3.2.2.8.1 锦标赛的时间和地点；

3.2.2.8.2 锦标赛的项目；

3.2.2.8.3 锦标赛使用的器材；

3.2.2.8.4 锦标赛的报名程序、报名费以及所需的工作；

3.2.2.8.5 抽签的时间和地点；

3.2.2.8.6 仲裁会议的时间；

3.2.2.8.7 运动员和官员的接待情况；

3.2.2.8.8　任何由理事会对该锦标赛颁发的指令。

3.2.2.9　在锦标赛期间，主办方应该尽快给国际乒联执行委员会、理事会成员和各队领队提供比赛成绩，包括具体的比分。全部比赛结束后，应尽快公布包括比分在内的所有比赛成绩，并传发给各参赛协会。

3.2.3　资格

3.2.3.1　只有未拖欠会费的协会(1.16.3.3)才有资格为队或队员报名参加锦标赛。

3.2.3.2　团体和单项的预选方式，将由理事会在锦标赛开赛前18个月作出决定。

3.2.3.3　根据规则2.7.4.2的规定，参赛选手还必须属于青少年。

3.2.3.4　除规则2.8条的规定外，运动员有资格代表的协会与他们打算代表的协会不同时，还应通过新协会向国际乒联注册。

3.2.3.5　如果运动员注册时未满15岁，则该运动员在注册之日起3年内不得代表新的协会。

3.2.4　报名费

3.2.4.1　团体比赛每个队的报名费为50美元，每对双打为30美元，每名单打为15美元。

3.2.4.2　参赛协会在报名时应该向比赛主办协会交纳报名费，报名费由主办协会和国际乒联均分。

3.2.4.3　出于不可控制的原因使得某协会不能参加锦标赛，理事会可免除其报名费，除此之外，每一个报名的协会都应按时交纳报名费。

3.2.5　资格与报名

3.2.5.1　有意派队或运动员参加锦标赛的协会，应填写秘书处提供的初步报名表，并以此通知组委会和国际乒联。接收初步报名表的截止日期最晚不超过锦标赛开始前四个月。

3.2.5.2　应通过填写由秘书处随同锦标赛指南一同发放的报名表来报名。

3.2.5.3　表格一式三份，两份返还主办协会，一份留在秘书处，收到报名表不能晚于锦标赛开始前的两个月。

3.2.5.4　每个协会最多提名符合资格的男、女各4名运动员。

3.2.5.5　协会应根据技术水平为其报名参加单打和双打的运动员排序，排序应符合当时的世界青少年排名表。

3.2.5.6　主办协会只接受由参赛资格协会的正式报名，报名表必须由该协会的一名代表签署，在指定的截止日内收到。

3.2.6　报名的更改

3.2.6.1　报名协会可以改变团体阵容的组成，但必须在仲裁会议召开之前向主办协会提出。比赛一旦开始，就不能更改团体名单。

3.2.6.2　出于错误或缺席原因而需要改变报名的协会，其代表一到比赛地点就应向裁判长或副裁判长报告报名更改情况，或确认已经通告过的改动，需使用(填写)专为更改报名而准备的表格。

3.2.6.3　如果要求改变报名，必须由该协会的代表一到比赛地就提出，而不能因为后来队员的缺席、双打搭档的生病或受伤临时提出变更。

3.2.6.4　所有经过确认的更改应立即通知各队领队或在可能的情况下通知参赛协会

代表。

3.2.7 报名须知

3.2.7.1 报名表应包括一个由协会负责人代表指派的运动员、领队签署的声明，表明他们理解和接受锦标赛的意义，准备和自己的对手竞争，没有这声明，报名就不合法。

3.2.7.2 单项比赛中，所有的参赛者都被视为独立的参赛选手，所以，无论他的对手来自于他同一协会，还是来自不同的协会，他都要尽自己最大努力赢得所有参加的比赛，除受伤或生病外，不能退出比赛。

3.2.8 仲裁委员会

3.2.8.1 仲裁委员会应包括国际乒联青少年委员会主席、国际乒联竞赛部代表1名、国际乒联全球青少年项目的代表1名、锦标赛主任(或他的同级)、组委会代表一名和裁判长。裁判长有发言权，但没有表决权。

3.2.8.2 如果国际乒联青少年委员会主席不能出席仲裁会议，他可以委派1名代表出席，该代表有发言权和投票权。

3.2.8.3 仲裁的主席由国际乒联青少年委员会主席指定。如果他缺席，则由国际乒联青少年项目代表指定。

3.2.8.4 如有协会将受仲裁会议所讨论问题的直接影响，该协会可派代表出席仲裁会议，但无权投票。

3.2.8.5 仲裁有权对在竞赛管理委员会管辖范围内的任何申诉做出裁决。

3.2.8.6 在锦标赛开始之前，仲裁委员会就应召开会议，通报当时所有的抽签变更。抽签变更后出现的相应问题由国际乒联青少年委员会决定，当出现对行政决定或裁判长决定提出申诉时，青少年委员会将重新召集仲裁开会。

3.2.9 竞赛项目

3.2.9.1 锦标赛包括青年男、女团体，青年男子单、双打、青年女子单、双打，混和双打比赛。

3.2.9.1.1 双打比赛的配对必须来自同一个协会，混双项目除外。

3.2.9.2 团体和单项比赛包括分组和分阶段的比赛方式，应由青少年委员会提出方案，由理事会来决定，并在锦标赛开始前六个月通告所有协会。

3.2.10 违规

3.2.10.1 进入团体抽签的队，因无正当理由不参加比赛，该协会将受到国际乒联代表大会的纪律处罚。

3.2.10.2 每个队参加一场团体赛的阵容，在该场比赛中应自始至终在现场，除非由于发生意外、生病、受伤或者其他不可控制的因素，包括裁判长取消某名运动员资格时，裁判长可以允许团体赛中的一名队员缺席，或省去1场比赛。

3.2.10.3 如果一个队在团体比赛中，没有打完比赛就中途退出，该协会代表的在锦标赛中的免费招待可被取消。该协会对此可向仲裁申诉，仲裁的决定将是最终的决定。

3.2.11 兴奋剂检测

3.2.11.1 兴奋剂检测，应该按照国际乒联反兴奋剂条例(第五章)执行。

3.2.12 奖励和仪式

3.2.12.1 无论是团体比赛还是单项比赛，决赛中获胜的冠军将获得金牌，在决赛中失利的选手将获得银牌，在半决赛中失利的选手将获得铜牌。

3.2.12.2 团体和单项的颁奖仪式，应悬挂获得金牌、银牌和铜牌的队或运动员国家的国旗，奏金牌获得者的国歌。

3.2.13 电视

3.2.13.1 锦标赛的电视转播权归属国际乒联。

3.3 世界杯

3.3.1 组成

3.3.1.1 男子世界杯和女子世界杯每年分别举行，只设单打。

3.3.1.2 参赛者将由上届世界杯的冠军、世界锦标赛冠军、6 大洲的冠军或最优秀的运动员、主办协会 1 名运动员、世界排名前 8 的运动员和 2 两名“外卡”选手组成。执行委员会可能会不定期更改运动员的数量。

3.3.1.3 一个协会的参赛选手不能超过两名，除非第三名选手是持“外卡”的运动员。如果世界锦标赛和世界杯的冠军是同一个人，或主办协会的运动员已拥有冠军头衔或根据世界排名入选，则空出的名额将给世界排名下一个最高并符合资格的运动员。

3.3.1.4 参赛选手享受从比赛开始的前一天晚上到比赛结束的第二天上午的免费食宿。代表各洲的运动员免费享受前往比赛场馆所在地的的往返机票。

3.3.2 许可

3.3.2.1 国际乒联独家享有“世界杯”这个名称及比赛的权力。

3.3.2.2 一个协会可获准举办世界杯赛。递交申请就意味着接受以上所有可适用的规则。

3.3.2.3 没有国际乒联的事先批准，主办者不能将权力委托他人，也不能与任何机构，比如地方协会、市政府或赞助商签订合同或协议。

3.3.2.4 主办者和其他机构签订的任何协议，既不能与规则中的条文相抵触，也不能背离规则的原则，如出现争端，国际乒联通过其代表所行使的权力为最终决定。

3.3.2.5 国际乒联可以介入与推广商或赞助商的协议。

3.3.3 委任

3.3.3.1 每次比赛，国际乒联竞赛部将指派 1 名竞赛部主任和 1 名竞赛经理。

3.3.3.2 竞赛主任应向执委会负责，保证比赛条件达到要求，包括主办者对比赛各种仪式的安排，礼仪和各种仪式中席位的安排，赛外活动及比赛本身的展示。

3.3.3.3 竞赛经理应对国际乒联负责，确保确保比赛器材和比赛条件符合要求，监督抽签和编排比赛。

3.3.4 兴奋剂检测

3.2.4.1 兴奋剂检测，应该按照国际乒联反兴奋剂条例执行。

3.3.5 比赛方法

3.3.5.1 比赛方法由执委会根据竞赛部的建议作出决定。在对参赛者发出邀请的同时，应在规程中告知运动员及其协会所采用的比赛方法。

3.3.6 资格

3.3.6.1 除规则 2.8 条款规定外，运动员有资格代表的协会与他们打算代表的协会不同时，还应通过新协会向国际乒联注册。

3.3.6.2 运动员在下列情况下不能代表新协会：

3.3.6.2.1 如果运动员注册时年龄未满 15 岁，自注册之日起未满 3 年；

3.3.6.2.2　如果运动员注册时年满15岁但未到18岁，自注册之日起未满5年；

3.3.6.2.3　如果运动员注册时年满18岁但未到21岁，自注册之日起未满7年。

3.3.6.3　运动员年满或超过21岁，将不能再国际乒联进行转会注册，且在世界杯中没有代表新协会参赛的资格。

3.3.7　仲裁

3.3.7.1　仲裁委员会应包括国际乒联负责世界杯的执行主席、国际乒联竞赛主任、组委会代表一名和裁判长。裁判长有发言权，但没有表决权。

3.3.7.2　如果国际乒联负责世界杯的执行副主席或国际乒联竞赛主任不能出席仲裁会议，他可以委派1名代表出席，该代表有发言权和投票权。

3.3.7.3　仲裁的主席由国际乒联负责世界杯的执行副主席指定。

3.3.7.4　如有协会将受仲裁会议所讨论问题的直接影响，该协会可派代表出席仲裁会议，但无权投票。

3.3.7.5　仲裁委员会有权对在竞赛管理委员会管辖范围内的任何申诉做出裁决。

3.3.7.6　比赛开始之前，仲裁委员会就应召开会议，通报当时所有的抽签变更要求。只有对其行政决定或裁判长决定提出申诉时，仲裁委员会才应再次召开会议。

3.4　团体世界杯

3.4.1　组成

3.4.1.1　团体世界杯每奇数年举行，设男子团体和女子团体。

3.4.1.2　每个项目由12支队伍代表各自协会参赛，包括上一届世界团体锦标赛前7名的队伍，主办协会的1支队伍和另外4支来自各大洲联合会的队伍。

3.4.1.3　如果主办协会的参赛队在上一届世界团体锦标赛中名列前七，那么第八名的队伍将入选。

3.4.1.4　参赛运动员享受从比赛开始前一天晚上到比赛结束第二天上午的免费食宿。

3.4.2　许可

3.4.2.1　国际乒联独家享有“团体世界杯”的名称和比赛的权力。

3.4.2.2　一个协会可以获准举办团体世界杯，递交申请就意味着接受以上所有可使用的规程。

3.4.2.3　没有国际乒联的事先批准，主办者不能将权力委托他人，也不能与任何机构，比如地方协会、市政府或赞助商签订合同或协议。

3.4.2.4　主办者和其他机构签订的任何协议，既不能与规则中的条文相抵触，也不能背离规则的原则，如出现争端，国际乒联通过其代表所行使的权力为最高权力。

3.4.2.5　国际乒联可以介入与推广商或赞助商的协议。

3.4.3　委任

3.4.3.1　每次比赛，国际乒联竞赛部将指派1名竞赛部主任和1名竞赛经理。

3.4.3.2　竞赛主任应对国际乒联竞赛部负责，保证比赛条件达到要求，包括主办者对比赛各种仪式的安排，礼仪和各种仪式中席位的安排，赛外活动及比赛本身的展示。

3.4.3.3　竞赛经理应对国际乒联负责，确保确保比赛器材和比赛条件符合要求，监督抽签和编排比赛。

3.4.4　兴奋剂检测

3.4.4.1　兴奋剂检测，应该按照国际乒联反兴奋剂条例执行。

3.4.5 比赛方法

3.4.5.1　并非通过上一届世界杯团体锦标赛名次入选的另外 4 支来自各大洲联合会的参赛队，将参加“洲际杯”比赛，比赛采用循环赛。

3.4.5.2　“洲际杯”的冠军将与另外 8 支队伍中的排名最低的参赛队(主办协会的参赛队不包括在内)进行一场附加赛。附加赛的胜者将晋级到正赛，即 8 强淘汰赛。

3.4.5.3　根据最新的团体世界排名设定种子。

3.4.5.4　所有团体赛采用奥运会赛制，由 4 场单打和 1 场双打组成(按照 2.7.6.3 条款)。

3.4.5.5　团体赛中的每场比赛采用五局三胜制。

3.4.5.6　比赛方法将由执委会根据竞赛部的建议作出修改。在对参赛队发出邀请的同时，应在规程中告知参赛协会任何有关比赛方法的变动。

3.4.6　资格

3.4.6.1　除规则 2.8 条款规定外，运动员有资格代表的协会与他们打算代表的协会不同时，还应通过新协会向国际乒联注册。

3.4.6.2　运动员在下列情况下不能代表新协会：

3.4.6.2.1　如果运动员注册时年龄未满 15 岁，自注册之日起未满 3 年；

3.4.6.2.2　如果运动员注册时年满 15 岁但未到 18 岁，自注册之日起未满 5 年；

3.4.6.2.3　如果运动员注册时年满 18 岁但未到 21 岁，自注册之日起未满 7 年。

3.4.6.3　运动员年满或超过 21 岁，将不能再国际乒联进行转会注册，且在世界杯中没有代表新协会参赛的资格。

3.4.7　仲裁

3.4.7.1　仲裁委员会应包括国际乒联负责世界杯团体的执行副主席、国际乒联竞赛主任、组委会代表一名和裁判长。裁判长有发言权，但没有表决权。

3.4.7.2　如果国际乒联负责世界杯的执行副主席或国际乒联竞赛主任不能出席仲裁会议，他可以委派 1 名代表出席，该代表有发言权和投票权。

3.4.7.3　仲裁的主席由国际乒联负责世界杯团体的执行副主席指定。

3.4.7.4　如有协会将受仲裁会议所讨论问题的直接影响，该协会可派代表出席仲裁会议，但无权投票。

3.4.7.5　仲裁委员会有权对在竞赛管理委员会管辖范围内的任何申诉做出裁决，并可批准参赛队伍的变动。

3.4.7.6　比赛开始之前，仲裁委员会就应召开会议，通报当时所有的抽签变更要求。只有对其行政决定或裁判长决定提出申诉时，仲裁委员会才应再次召开会议。

3.5　奥运会

3.5.1　资格

3.5.1.1　有资格参加奥运会的运动员、教练员或官员，应该遵守奥林匹克宪章和国际乒联规则。以上人员应该是：

3.5.1.1.1　由其所在国家奥委会报名；

3.5.1.1.2　遵守公平竞争和非暴力的竞赛原则，并在赛场上做出相应的表现；

3.5.1.1.3　遵守世界反兴奋剂准则并在所有方面遵照执行；

3.5.1.1.4　在奥运会期间，不得将他们的身份、姓名、照片或运动行为用于广告目的，除非得到国际奥委会执行局允许。

3.5.1.2　运动员报名或才与奥运会，不得以经济上的考虑为条件。

3.5.1.3　国家奥委会报名的运动员必须是该国国民。

3.5.1.3.1　如果一名运动员同时是两个或两个以上国家的国民，他可以选择代表其中的一个国家。

3.5.1.3.2　一名运动员在奥运会或国际乒联认可的洲际或地区比赛、世界或地区锦标赛中代表了一个国家参赛，该运动员就不能代表另一个国家参赛，除非他符合3.5.1.3.3条款中所列的条件。

3.5.1.3.3　一名运动员在奥运会或国际乒联认可的洲际或地区比赛、世界或地区锦标赛中代表了一个国家，已经改变了他的国籍或取得了新的国籍，那么它可以代表新的国家参加奥运会，条件是他最近代表前一个国家参赛的时间是在3年前。

3.5.1.3.4　如果得到相关的国家奥委会和国际乒联执行委员会的同意，则3.5.1.3.3条款提到的3年期限可以减少甚至取消，这应由国际奥委会执行局根据每个个案的情况进行处理。

3.5.1.3.5　如果一个联合州或海外地区、一个国家或殖民地获得独立，如果一个国家因为边界改变而与另一个国家合并，如果一个新的国家奥委会得到国际奥委会承认，那么运动员可以继续代表它属于或曾属于的国家。但是，如果他愿意，也可以选择代表新的国家，并有新的国家奥委会报名参加奥运会。这样的选择只能有一次。

3.5.1.4　所有关于一名运动员是否能在奥运会代表一个国家参赛的争议，特别是关于运动员的国籍、公民身份证或居住地的具体要求，包括等待期的长短等问题，将由国际奥委会执行局作出决定。

3.5.2　竞赛项目

3.5.2.1　奥运会比赛至少包括男子单打、女子单打、男子团体、女子团体。

3.5.2.2　团体比赛的赛制，以及团体和单项比赛，包括所有预选赛的竞赛方法，应由董事会根据奥运委员会的建议作出决定，并依照国际奥委会指定的日程安排通知所有协会。

3.5.3　兴奋剂检测

3.5.3.1　兴奋剂检测将根据国际奥委会的规定执行。

第二章　乒乓球裁判员法定手势

(1)右手举起，肘部伸直，手掌平伸，表示：停、时间到、擦网、犯规、侧面、台面、移动、连击、两跳、重发球。

(2)右手举起，肘部弯曲，伸出食指、中指，表示：练习两分钟。

(3)举起右手(或左手)，肘部弯曲，握拳，表示：得分(裁判右侧选手得分举右手，左侧选手得分举左手，同时报出比分)。

(4)手臂伸直用食指指向擦边的方向，表示：擦边。

(5)手臂伸直，手掌平伸指向发球选手，表示：发球，同时报出第×局××发球，××(接发球方)准备。

(6)两手掌平伸交叉胸前，表示：交换方位。

(7)当出现“阻挡”时，裁判员的手势是：

第三章 乒乓球英文规则

1 The laws of table tennis

1.1 The table

1.1.1 The upper surface of the table, known as the playing surface, shall be rectangular, 2.74m long and 1.525m wide, and shall lie in a horizontal plane 76cm above the floor.

1.1.2 The playing surface shall not include the vertical sides of the tabletop.

1.1.3 The playing surface may be of any material and shall yield a uniform bounce of about 23cm when a standard ball is dropped on to it from a height of 30cm.

1.1.4 The playing surface shall be uniformly dark coloured and matt, but with a white side line, 2cm wide, along each 2.74m edge and a white end line, 2cm wide, along each 1.525m edge.

1.1.5 The playing surface shall be divided into 2 equal courts by a vertical net running parallel with the end lines, and shall be continuous over the whole area of each court.

1.1.6 For doubles, each court shall be divided into 2 equal half-courts by a white centre line, 3mm wide, running parallel with the side lines; the centre line shall be regarded as part of each right half-court.

1.2 The net assembly

1.2.1 The net assembly shall consist of the net, its suspension and the supporting posts, including the clamps attaching them to the table.

1.2.2 The net shall be suspended by a cord attached at each end to an upright post 15.25cm high, the outside limits of the post being 15.25cm outside the side line.

1.2.3 The top of the net, along its whole length, shall be 15.25cm above the playing surface.

1.2.4 The bottom of the net, along its whole length, shall be as close as possible to the playing surface and the ends of the net shall be as close as possible to the supporting posts.

1.3 The ball

1.3.1 The ball shall be spherical, with a diameter of 40mm.

1.3.2 The ball shall weigh 2.7g.

1.3.3 The ball shall be made of celluloid or similar plastics material and shall be white or orange, and matt.

1.4 The racket

1.4.1 The racket may be of any size, shape or weight but the blade shall be flat and rigid.

1.4.2 At least 85% of the blade by thickness shall be of natural wood; an adhesive layer within the blade may be reinforced with fibrous material such as carbon fibre, glass fibre or compressed paper, but shall not be thicker than 7.5% of the total thickness or 0.35mm, whichever is the smaller.

1.4.3 A side of the blade used for striking the ball shall be covered with either ordinary pimpled rubber, with pimples outwards having a total thickness including adhesive of not more than 2.0mm, or sandwich rubber, with pimples inwards or outwards, having a total thickness including adhesive of not more than 4.0mm.

1.4.3.1 *Ordinary pimpled rubber* is a single layer of non-cellular rubber, natural or synthetic, with pimples evenly distributed over its surface at a density of not less than 10 per cm^2 and not more than 30 per cm^2.

1.4.3.2 *Sandwich rubber* is a single layer of cellular rubber covered with a single outer layer of ordinary pimpled rubber, the thickness of the pimpled rubber not being more than 2.0mm.

1.4.4 The covering material shall extend up to but not beyond the limits of the blade, except that the part nearest the handle and gripped by the fingers may be left uncovered or covered with any material.

1.4.5 The blade, any layer within the blade and any layer of covering material or adhesive on a side used for striking the ball shall be continuous and of even thickness.

1.4.6 The surface of the covering material on a side of the blade, or of a side of the blade if it is left uncovered, shall be matt, bright red on one side and black on the other.

1.4.7 The racket covering shall be used without any physical, chemical or other treatment.

Slight deviations from continuity of surface or uniformity of colour due to accidental damage or wear may be allowed provided that they do not significantly change the characteristics of the surface.

1.4.8 Before the start of a match and whenever he changes his or her racket during a match a player shall show his or her opponent and the umpire the racket he or she is about to use and shall allow them to examine it.

1.5 Definitions

1.5.1 A *rally* is the period during which the ball is in play.

1.5.2 The ball is *in play* from the last moment at which it is stationary on the palm of the free hand before being intentionally projected in service until the rally is decided as a let or a point.

1.5.3 A *let* is a rally of which the result is not scored.

1.5.4 A *point* is a rally of which the result is scored.

1.5.5 The *racket hand* is the hand carrying the racket.

1.5.6 The *free hand* is the hand not carrying the racket; the *free arm* is the arm of the free hand.

1.5.7 A player *strikes* the ball if he or she touches it in play with his or her racket, held in the hand, or with his or her racket hand below the wrist.

1.5.8 A player *obstructs* the ball if he, or anything he or she wears or carries, touches it in play when it is above or travelling towards the playing surface, not having touched his or her court since last being struck by his or her opponent.

1.5.9 The *server* is the player due to strike the ball first in a rally.

1.5.10 The *receiver* is the player due to strike the ball second in a rally.

1.5.11 The *umpire* is the person appointed to control a match.

1.5.12 The *assistant umpire* is the person appointed to assist the umpire with certain decisions.

1.5.13 Anything that a player *wears or carries* includes anything that he or she was wearing or carrying, other than the ball, at the start of the rally.

1.5.14 The ball shall be regarded aspassing *over or around* the net assembly if it passes anywhere other than between the net and the net post or between the net and the playing surface.

1.5.15 The *end line* shall be regarded as extending indefinitely in both directions.

1.6 The service

1.6.1 Service shall start with the ball resting freely on the open palm of the server' s stationary free hand.

1.6.2 The server shall then project the ball near vertically upwards, without imparting spin, so that it rises at least 16cm after leaving the palm of the free hand and then falls without touching anything before being struck.

1.6.3 As the ball is falling the server shall strike it so that it touches first his or her court and then, after passing over or around the net assembly, touches directly the receiver' s court; in doubles, the ball shall touch successively the right half court of server and receiver.

1.6.4 From the start of service until it is struck, the ball shall be above the level of the playing surface and behind the server' s end line, and it shall not be hidden from the receiver by the server or his or her doubles partner or by anything they wear or carry.

1.6.5 As soon as the ball has been projected, the server' s free arm and hand shall be removed from the space between the ball and the net.

The space between the ball and the net is defined by the ball, the net and its indefinite upward extension.

1.6.6 It is the responsibility of the player to serve so that the umpire or the assistant umpire can be satisfied that he or she complies with the requirements of the Laws, and either may decide that a service is incorrect.

If either the umpire or the assistant umpire is not sure about the legality of a service he or she may, on the first occasion in a match, interrupt play and warn the server; but any subsequent service by that player or his or her doubles partner which is not clearly legal shall be considered incorrect.

1.6.7 Exceptionally, the umpire may relax the requirements for a correct service where he or she is satisfied that compliance is prevented by physical disability.

1.7 The return

The ball, having been served or returned, shall be struck so that it passes over or around the net assembly and touches the opponent' s court, either directly or after touching the net assembly.

1.8 The order of play

1.8.1 In singles, the server shall first make a service, the receiver shall then make a return and thereafter server and receiver alternately shall each make a return.

1.8.2 In doubles, the server shall first make a service, the receiver shall then make a return, the partner of the server shall then make a return, the partner of the receiver shall then make a return and thereafter each player in turn in that sequence shall make a return.

1.8.3 When two players who are in wheelchairs due to a physical disability are a pair playing doubles, the server shall first make a service, the receiver shall then make a return but thereafter either player of the disabled pair may make returns. However, no part of a player's wheelchair shall protrude beyond the imaginary extension of the centre line of the table. If it does, the umpire shall award the point to the opposing pair.

1.9 A let

1.9.1 The rally shall be a let:

1.9.1.1 if in service the ball, in passing over or around the net assembly, touches it, provided the service is otherwise correct or the ball is obstructed by the receiver or his or her partner;

1.9.1.2 if the service is delivered when the receiving player or pair is not ready, provided that neither the receiver nor his or her partner attempts to strike the ball;

1.9.1.3 if failure to make a service or a return or otherwise to comply with the Laws is due to a disturbance outside the control of the player;

1.9.1.4 if play is interrupted by the umpire or assistant umpire;

1.9.1.5 if the receiver is in wheelchair owing to a physical disability and in service the ball, provided that the service is otherwise correct;

1.9.1.5.1 after touching the receiver's court returns in the direction of the net;

1.9.1.5.2 comes to rest on the receiver's court;

1.9.1.5.3 in singles leaves the receiver's court after touching it by either of its sidelines.

1.9.2 Play may be interrupted:

1.9.2.1 to correct an error in the order of serving, receiving or ends;

1.9.2.2 to introduce the expedite system;

1.9.2.3 to warn or penalise a player or adviser;

1.9.2.4 because the conditions of play are disturbed in a way which could affect the outcome of the rally.

1.10 A Point

1.10.1 Unless the rally is a let, a player shall score a point

1.10.1.1 if an opponent fails to make a correct service;

1.10.1.2 if an opponent fails to make a correct return;

1.10.1.3 if, after he or she has made a service or a return, the ball touches anything other than the net assembly before being struck by an opponent;

1.10.1.4 if the ball passes over his or her court or beyond his or her end line without touching his or her court, after being struck by an opponent;

1.10.1.5 if an opponent obstructs the ball;

1.10.1.6 if an opponent deliberately strikes the ball twice in succession;

1.10.1.7 if an opponent strikes the ball with a side of the racket blade whose surface does not comply with the requirements of 1.4.3, 1.4.4 and 1.4.5;

1.10.1.8 if an opponent, or anything an opponent wears or carries, moves the playing surface;

1.10.1.9 if an opponent, or anything an opponent wears or carries, touches the net assembly;

1.10.1.10 if an opponent's free hand touches the playing surface;

1.10.1.11 if a doubles opponent strikes the ball out of the sequence established by the first server and first receiver;

1.10.1.12 as provided under the expedite system (1.15.4).

1.10.1.13 if both players or pairs are in a wheelchair due to a physical disability and

1.10.1.13.1 his or her opponent does not maintain a minimum contact with the seat or cushion(s), with the back of the thigh, when the ball is struck;

1.10.1.13.2 his or her opponent touches the table with either hand before striking the ball;

1.10.1.13.3 his or her opponent's footrest or foot touches the floor during play.

1.10.1.14 as provided under the order of play (1.8.3).

1.11 A game

A game shall be won by the player or pair first scoring 11 points unless both players or pairs score 10 points, when the game shall be won by the first player or pair subsequently gaining a lead of 2 points.

1.12 A match

1.12.1 A match shall consist of the best of any odd number of games.

1.13 The order of serving, receiving and ends

1.13.1 The right to choose the initial order of serving, receiving and ends shall be decided by lot and the winner may choose to serve or to receive first or to start at a particular end.

1.13.2 When one player or pair has chosen to serve or to receive first or to start at a particular end, the other player or pair shall have the other choice.

1.13.3 After each 2 points have been scored the receiving player or pair shall become the serving player or pair and so on until the end of the game, unless both players or pairs score 10 points or the expedite system is in operation, when the sequences of serving and receiving shall be the same but each player shall serve for only 1 point in turn.

1.13.4 In each game of a doubles match, the pair having the right to serve first shall choose which of them will do so and in the first game of a match the receiving pair shall decide which of them will receive first; in subsequent games of the match, the first server having been chosen, the first receiver shall be the player who served to him or her in the preceding game.

1.13.5 In doubles, at each change of service the previous receiver shall become the server and the partner of the previous server shall become the receiver.

1. 13. 6 The player or pair serving first in a game shall receive first in the next game of the match and in the last possible game of a doubles match the pair due to receive next shall change their order of receiving when first one pair scores 5 points.

1. 13. 7 The player or pair starting at one end in a game shall start at the other end in the next game of the match and in the last possible game of a match the players or pairs shall change ends when first one player or pair scores 5 points.

1. 14 Out of order of serving, receiving or ends

1. 14. 1 If a player serves or receives out of turn, play shall be interrupted by the umpire as soon as the error is discovered and shall resume with those players serving and receiving who should be server and receiver respectively at the score that has been reached, according to the sequence established at the beginning of the match and, in doubles, to the order of serving chosen by the pair having the right to serve first in the game during which the error is discovered.

1. 14. 2 If the players have not changed ends when they should have done so, play shall be interrupted by the umpire as soon as the error is discovered and shall resume with the players at the ends at which they should be at the score that has been reached, according to the sequence established at the beginning of the match.

1. 14. 3 In any circumstances, all points scored before the discovery of an error shall be reckoned.

1. 15 The expedite system

1. 15. 1 Except as provided in 1. 15. 2, the expedite system shall come into operation after 10 minutes' play in a game or at any time when requested by both players or pairs.

1. 15. 2 The expedite system shall not be introduced in a game if at least 18 points have been scored.

1. 15. 3 If the ball is in play when the time limit is reached and the expedite system is due to come into operation, play shall be interrupted by the umpire and shall resume with service by the player who served in the rally that was interrupted; if the ball is not in play when the expedite system comes into operation, play shall resume with service by the player who received in the immediately preceding rally.

1. 15. 4 Thereafter, each player shall serve for 1 point in turn until the end of the game, and if the receiving player or pair makes 13 correct returns in a rally the receiver shall score a point.

1. 15. 5 Introduction of the expedite system shall not alter the order of serving and receiving in the match, as defined in 1. 13. 6.

1. 15. 6 Once introduced, the expedite system shall remain in operation until the end of the match.

2 Regulatinos for international competitions

2. 1 Scope of laws and regulations

2. 1. 1 Types of Competition

2. 1. 1. 1 An *international competition* is one that may include the players of more than one

Association.

2. 1. 1. 2 An*international match* is a match between teams representing Associations.

2. 1. 1. 3 An *open tournament* is one that is open to the players of all Associations.

2. 1. 1. 4 A*restricted tournament* is one that is restricted to specified groups of players other than age groups.

2. 1. 1. 5 An*invitation tournament* is one that is restricted to specified Associations or players, individually invited.

2. 1. 2 Applicability

2. 1. 2. 1 Except as provided in 2. 1. 2. 2, the Laws shall apply to World, Continental, Olympic and Paralympic title competitions, open tournaments and, unless otherwise agreed by the participating Associations, to international matches.

2. 1. 2. 2 The Board of Directors shall have power to authorise the organiser of an open tournament to adopt experimental law variations specified by the Executive Committee.

2. 1. 2. 3 The Regulations for International Competitions shall apply to

2. 1. 2. 3. 1 World, Olympic and Paralympic title competitions, unless otherwise authorised by the Board of Directors and notified in advance to the participating Associations;

2. 1. 2. 3. 2 Continental title competitions, unless otherwise authorised by the appropriate Continental Federation and notified in advance to the participating Associations;

2. 1. 2. 3. 3 Open International Championships (2. 7. 1. 2), unless otherwise authorised by the Executive Committee and notified in advance to the participants in accordance with 2. 1. 2. 4;

2. 1. 2. 3. 4 open tournaments, except as provided in 2. 1. 2. 4.

2. 1. 2. 4 Where an open tournament does not comply with any of these regulations the nature and extent of the variation shall be specified in the entry form; completion and submission of an entry form shall be regarded as signifying acceptance of the conditions of the competition, including such variations.

2. 1. 2. 5 The Laws and Regulations are recommended for all international competitions but, provided that the Constitution is observed, international restricted and invitation tournaments and recognised international competitions organised by unaffiliated bodies may be held under rules laid down by the organising authority.

2. 1. 2. 6 The Laws and the Regulations for International Competitions shall be presumed to apply unless variations have been agreed in advance or are made clear in the published rules of the competition.

2. 1. 2. 7 Detailed explanations and interpretations of regulations, including equipment specifications, shall be published as Technical Leaflets authorised by the Board of Directors and in Handbooks for Match Officials and Tournament Referees.

2. 2 Equipment and playing conditions

2. 2. 1 Approved and Authorised Equipment

2. 2. 1. 1 The approval and authorisation of playing equipment shall be conducted on behalf of the Board of Directors by the Equipment Committee; approval or authorisation may be withdrawn by the Board of Directors at any time if its continuation is found to be detrimental to the sport.

2. 2. 1. 2 The entry form or prospectus for an open tournament shall specify the brands and colours of table, net assembly and ball to be used; the choice of equipment shall be as laid down by the Association in whose territory the competition is held, selected from brands and types currently approved by the ITTF.

2. 2. 1. 3 The covering material on a side of the blade used for striking the ball shall be currently authorised by the ITTF and shall be identified by the ITTF number (when present), the supplier and brand names and shall be attached to the blade so that this identification is clearly visible nearest the handle.

Lists of all approved and authorised equipment and materials are maintained by the ITTF Office and details are available on the ITTF Website.

2. 2. 1. 4 Table legs shall be at least 40cm from the end line of the table for wheelchair players.

2. 2. 2 Playing Clothing

2. 2. 2. 1 Playing clothing shall normally consist of a short-sleeved or sleeveless shirt and shorts or skirt or one-part sports outfits, socks and playing shoes; other garments, such as part or all of a track suit, shall not be worn during play except with the permission of the referee.

2. 2. 2. 2 The main colour of a shirt, skirt or shorts, other than sleeves and collar of a shirt shall be clearly different from that of the ball in use.

2. 2. 2. 3 Clothing may bear numbers or lettering on the back of the shirt to identify a player, his or her Association or, in club matches, his or her club, and advertisements in accordance with the provisions of 2. 2. 5. 10; if the back of a shirt bears the player's name, this shall be situated just below the collar.

2. 2. 2. 4 Any numbers required by organisers to identify a player shall have priority over advertisements on the centre part of the back of a shirt; such numbers shall be contained within a panel having an area not greater than $600cm^2$.

2. 2. 2. 5 Any markings or trimming on the front or side of a playing garment and any objects such as jewellery worn by a player shall not be so conspicuous or brightly reflecting as to unsight an opponent.

2. 2. 2. 6 Clothing shall not carry designs or lettering which might cause offence or bring the game into disrepute.

2. 2. 2. 7 Any question of the legality or acceptability of playing clothing shall be decided by the referee.

2. 2. 2. 8 The players of a team taking part in a team match, and players of the same Association forming a doubles pair in a World, Olympic or Paralympic Title Competition, shall be dressed uniformly, with the possible exception of socks, shoes and the number, size, colour and design of advertisements on clothing. Players of the same Association forming a doubles pair in other international competitions may wear clothes of different manufacturers, if the basic colours are the same and their National Association authorises this procedure.

2. 2. 2. 9 Opposing players and pairs shall wear shirts that are of sufficiently different colours to enable them to be easily distinguished by spectators.

2.2.2.10 Where opposing players or teams have a similar shirt and cannot agree which of them will change, the decision shall be made by the umpire by lot.

2.2.2.11 Players competing in a World, Olympic or Paralympic title competition or Open International Championships shall wear shirt and shorts or skirt of types authorised by their Association.

2.2.3 Playing Conditions

2.2.3.1 The playing space shall be rectangular and not less than 14m long, 7m wide and 5m high, but the 4 corners may be covered by surrounds of not more than 1.5m length; for wheelchair events, the playing space may be reduced, but shall not be less than 8m long and 6m wide.

2.2.3.2 The following equipment and fittings are to be considered as part of each playing area: The table including the net assembly, umpires tables and chairs, score indicators, towel and ball boxes, printed numbers identifying the table, surrounds, floor mats, boards on the surrounds indicating the names of players or Associations.

2.2.3.3 The playing area shall be enclosed by surrounds about 75cm high, all of the same dark background colour, separating it from adjacent playing areas and from spectators.

2.2.3.4 In World, Olympic and Paralympic title competitions the light intensity, measured at the height of the playing surface, shall be at least 1000 lux uniformly over the whole of the playing surface and at least 500 lux elsewhere in the playing area; in other competitions the intensity shall be at least 600 lux uniformly over the playing surface and at least 400 lux elsewhere in the playing area.

2.2.3.5 Where several tables are in use, the lighting level shall be the same for all of them, and the level of background lighting in the playing hall shall not be greater than the lowest level in the playing area.

2.2.3.6 The light source shall not be less than 5m above the floor.

2.2.3.7 The background shall be generally dark and shall not contain bright light sources or daylight through uncovered windows or other apertures.

2.2.3.8 The flooring shall not be light-coloured, brightly reflecting or slippery and its surface shall not be of brick, ceramics, concrete or stone; but the flooring may be of concrete for wheelchair events.

In World, Olympic and Paralympic title competitions the flooring shall be of wood or of a brand and type of rollable synthetic material authorised by the ITTF.

2.2.4 Racket Control

2.2.4.1 It is the responsibility of each player to ensure that racket coverings are attached to their racket blade with adhesives that do not contain harmful volatile solvents.

2.2.4.2 A racket control centre shall be established at all ITTF World Title, Olympic and Paralympic competitions as well as at a select number of ITTF Pro Tour and Junior Circuit competitions and may be established at Continental and Regional competitions.

2.2.4.2.1 The racket control centre shall test rackets, according to the policy and procedure established by the Executive Committee on recommendation of the Equipment Committee, to ensure that rackets abide by all ITTF regulations including, but not limited to, racket covering thickness, flatness and presence of harmful volatile substances.

2.2.4.2.2 The racket control test should usually be carried out after the match at random, but from the quarter finals on, racket control tests should be carried out before all the matches of individual events and the selected individual matches in all team matches.

2.2.4.2.3 Rackets that do not pass the racket control test before the match cannot be used in the above listed competitions; in the case where rackets do not pass a random racket control test after the match, the offending player will be liable to penalties.

2.2.4.2.4 All players are entitled to have their rackets tested voluntarily without any penalties before the match.

2.2.4.3 Should a player be disqualified for the fourth time in a period of four years due to failing a racket control test, the player may complete the event, but subsequently the Executive Committee will suspend the offending player for 12 months.

2.2.4.3.1 The ITTF shall inform the suspended player in writing of such suspension.

2.2.4.3.2 The suspended player may appeal to the Court of Arbitration for Sport within 21 days of the receiving of the letter of suspension; should such an appeal be submitted, the player's suspension would remain in force.

2.2.4.4 The ITTF shall maintain a register of all racket control failures.

2.2.4.5 A properly ventilated area shall be provided for the attachment of racket coverings to rackets, and liquid adhesives shall not be used anywhere else at the playing venue.

"Playing venue" means the whole establishment in the playing building and the ground where the playing building stands, which contains the doorway, the parking lot and related facilities.

2.2.5 Advertisements

2.2.5.1 Inside the playing area, advertisements shall be displayed only on equipment or fittings listed in 2.2.3.2 and there shall be no special additional displays.

2.2.5.2 At Olympic and Paralympic Games advertisements on playing equipment, on playing clothing and on umpires' clothing shall be according to IOC and IPC regulations respectively.

2.2.5.3 With the exception of LED (light emitting diodes) advertisements on surrounds fluorescent or luminescent colours shall not be used anywhere in the playing area.

2.2.5.3.1 LED advertisements on surrounds shall not move at any other time than before the start and after the end of a match and during authorised intervals (2.4.4).

2.2.5.4 Lettering or symbols on the inside of surrounds shall not include white or orange nor more than two colours and shall be contained within a height of 40cm; it is recommended that they be in a slightly darker or slightly lighter shade of the background colour.

2.2.5.5 Markings on flooring shall not include white or orange; it is recommended that they be in slightly darker or slightly lighter shade of the background colour.

2.2.5.6 There may be up to 4 advertisements on the floor of the playing area, 1 at each end and 1 at each side of the table, each contained within an area of $2.5m^2$; they shall not be less than 1m from the surrounds and those at the ends shall not be more than 2m from the surrounds.

2.2.5.7 There may be 1 temporary advertisement on each half of each side of the tabletop and 1 on each end, clearly separated from any permanent advertisements and each contained within a total length of 60cm; they shallnot be for other table tennis equipment suppliers and there shall be no advertisement or logo of the manufacturer or supplier of the table on the undercarriage.

2.2.5.8 Advertisements on nets shall be in a slightly darker or slightly lighter shade of the background colour, shall not be within 3cm of the tape along the top edge and shall not obscure visibility through the mesh.

2.2.5.9 Advertisements on umpires' tables or other furniture inside the playing area shall be contained within a total area on any face of $750cm^2$.

2.2.5.10 Advertisements on playing clothing shall be limited to

2.2.5.10.1 the maker's normal trademark, symbol or name contained within a total area of $24cm^2$;

2.2.5.10.2 not more than 6 clearly separated advertisements, contained within a combined total area of $600cm^2$, on the front, side or shoulder of a shirt, with not more than 4 advertisements on the front;

2.2.5.10.3 not more than 2 advertisements, contained within a total area of $400cm^2$, on the back of a shirt;

2.2.5.10.4 not more than 2 advertisements, contained within a combined total area of $120cm^2$, only on the front and the sides of shorts or skirt.

2.2.5.11 Advertisements on players' numbers shall be contained within a total area of $100cm^2$.

2.2.5.12 Advertisements on umpires' clothing shall be contained within a total area of $40cm^2$.

2.2.5.13 There shall be no advertisements on players' clothing or numbers for tobacco goods, alcoholic drinks or harmful drugs.

2.2.6 Doping control

2.2.6.1 All players participating in international competitions, including Junior competitions, shall be subject to in-competition testing by the ITTF, the player's National Association and any other Anti-Doping Organisation responsible for testing at a competition in which they participate.

2.3 Match officials

2.3.1 Referee

2.3.1.1 For each competition as a whole a referee shall be appointed and his or her identity and location shall be made known to the participants and, where appropriate, to the team captains.

2.3.1.2 The referee shall be responsible for

2.3.1.2.1 the conduct of the draw;

2.3.1.2.2 the scheduling of the matches by time and table;

2.3.1.2.3 the appointment of match officials;

2. 3. 1. 2. 4 conducting a pre-tournament briefing for match officials;

2. 3. 1. 2. 5 checking the eligibility of players;

2. 3. 1. 2. 6 deciding whether play may be suspended in an emergency;

2. 3. 1. 2. 7 deciding whether players may leave the playing area during a match;

2. 3. 1. 2. 8 deciding whether statutory practice periods may be extended;

2. 3. 1. 2. 9 deciding whether players may wear track suits during a match;

2. 3. 1. 2. 10 deciding any question of interpretation of Laws or Regulations, including the acceptability of clothing, playing equipment and playing conditions;

2. 3. 1. 2. 11 deciding whether, and where, players may practise during an emergency suspension of play;

2. 3. 1. 2. 12 taking disciplinary action for misbehaviour or other breaches of regulations.

2. 3. 1. 3 Where, with the agreement of the competition management committee, any of the duties of the refereeare delegated to other persons, the specific responsibilities and locations of each of these persons shall be made known to the participants and, where appropriate, to the team captains.

2. 3. 1. 4 The referee, or a responsible deputy appointed to exercise authority in his or her absence, shall be present at all times during play.

2. 3. 1. 5 Where the referee is satisfied that it is necessary to do so he or she may replace a match official with another at any time, but he or she may not alter a decision already made by the replaced official on a question of fact within his or her jurisdiction.

2. 3. 1. 6 Players shall be under the jurisdiction of the referee from the time at which they arrive at the playing venue until they leave it.

2. 3. 2 Umpire, Assistant Umpire and Stroke Counter

2. 3. 2. 1 An umpire and an assistant umpire shall be appointed for each match.

2. 3. 2. 2 The umpire shall sit or stand in line with the net and the assistant umpire shall sit directly facing him or her, at the other side of the table.

2. 3. 2. 3 The umpire shall be responsible for:

2. 3. 2. 3. 1 checking the acceptability of equipment and playing conditions and reporting any deficiency to the referee;

2. 3. 2. 3. 2 taking a ball at random as provided in 2. 4. 2. 1. 1 and 2. 4. 2. 1. 2

2. 3. 2. 3. 3 conducting the drawfor the choice of serving, receiving and ends;

2. 3. 2. 3. 4 deciding whether the requirements of the service law may be relaxed for a player with physical disability;

2. 3. 2. 3. 5 controlling the order of serving, receiving and ends and correcting any errors therein;

2. 3. 2. 3. 6 deciding each rally as a point or a let;

2. 3. 2. 3. 7 calling the score, in accordance with specified procedure;

2. 3. 2. 3. 8 introducing the expedite system at the appropriate time;

2. 3. 2. 3. 9 maintaining the continuity of play;

2. 3. 2. 3. 10 taking action for breaches of the advice or behaviour regulations;

2. 3. 2. 3. 11 drawing by lot which player, pair or team shall change their shirt, should opposing players or teams have a similar shirt and cannot agree which of them will change.

2. 3. 2. 3. 12 ensuring that only authorised persons are at the playing area.

2. 3. 2. 4 The assistant umpire shall:

2. 3. 2. 4. 1 decide whether or not the ball in play touches the edge of the playing surface at the side of the table nearest him or her;

2. 3. 2. 4. 2 inform the umpire for breaches of the advice or behaviour regulations.

2. 3. 2. 5 Either the umpire or the assistant umpire may:

2. 3. 2. 5. 1 decide that a player's service action is illegal;

2. 3. 2. 5. 2 decide that, in an otherwise correct service, the ball touches the net assembly while passing over or around it;

2. 3. 2. 5. 3 decide that a player obstructs the ball;

2. 3. 2. 5. 4 decide that the conditions of play are disturbed in a way that may affect the outcome of the rally;

2. 3. 2. 5. 5 time the duration of the practiceperiod, of play and of intervals.

2. 3. 2. 6 Either the assistant umpire or a separate official may act as stroke counter, to count the strokes of the receiving player or pair when the expedite system is in operation.

2. 3. 2. 7 A decision made by the assistant umpire in accordance with the provisions of 2. 3. 2. 5 may not be overruled by the umpire.

2. 3. 2. 8 Players shall be under the jurisdiction of the umpire from the time at which they arrive at the playing area until they leave it.

2. 3. 3 Appeals

2. 3. 3. 1 No agreement between players, in an individual event, or between team captains, in a team event, can alter a decision on a question of fact by the responsible match official, on a question of interpretation of Laws or Regulations by the responsible referee or on any other question of tournament or match conduct by the responsible management committee.

2. 3. 3. 2 No appeal may be made to the referee against a decision on a question of fact by the responsible match official or to the management committee on a question of interpretation of Laws or Regulations by the referee.

2. 3. 3. 3 An appeal may be made to the referee against a decision of a match official on a question of interpretation of Laws or Regulations, and the decision of the referee shall be final.

2. 3. 3. 4 An appeal may be made to the competition management committee against a decision of the referee on a question of tournament or match conduct not covered by the Laws or Regulations, and the decision of the management committee shall be final.

2. 3. 3. 5 In an individual event an appeal may be made only by a player participating in the match in which the question has arisen; in a team event an appeal may be made only by the captain of a team participating in the match in which the question has arisen.

2. 3. 3. 5. 1 The name of the team captain, playing or non-playing, shall be designated beforehand to the umpire.

2. 3. 3. 6 A question of interpretation of Laws or Regulations arising from the decision of a

referee, or a question of tournament or match conduct arising from the decision of a competition management committee, may be submitted by the player or team captain eligible to make an appeal, through his or her parent Association, for consideration by the ITTF Rules Committee.

2. 3. 3. 7 The Rules Committee shall give a ruling as a guide for future decisions, and this ruling may also be made the subject of a protest by an Association to the Board of Directors or a General Meeting, but it shall not affect the finality of any decision already made by the responsible referee or management committee.

2. 4 Match conduct

2. 4. 1 Score Indication

2. 4. 1. 1 The umpire shall call the score as soon as the ball is out of play at the completion of a rally, or as soon as is practicable thereafter.

2. 4. 1. 1. 1 In calling the score during a game the umpire shall call first the number of points scored by the player or pair due to serve in the next rally of the game and then the number of points scored by the opposing player or pair.

2. 4. 1. 1. 2 At the beginning of a game and when a change of server is due, the umpire shall point to the next server, and may also follow the score call with the next server's name.

2. 4. 1. 1. 3 At the end of a game the umpire shall call the number of points scored by the winning player or pair followed by the number of points scored by the losing player or pair and may then name the winning player or pair.

2. 4. 1. 2 In addition to calling the score the umpire may use hand signals to indicate his or her decisions.

2. 4. 1. 2. 1 When a point has been scored, he or she may raise his or her arm nearer to the player or pair who won the point so that the upper arm is horizontal and the forearm is vertical with the closed hand upward.

2. 4. 1. 2. 2 When for any reason the rally is a let, he or she may raise his or her hand above his or her head to show that the rally has ended.

2. 4. 1. 3 The score and, under the expedite system, the number of strokes shall be called in English or in any other language acceptable to both players or pairs and to the umpire.

2. 4. 1. 4 The score shall be displayed on mechanical or electrical indicators so that it is clearly visible to the players and the spectators.

2. 4. 1. 5 When a player is formally warned for bad behaviour, a yellow marker shall be placed on or near the score indicator.

2. 4. 2 Equipment

2. 4. 2. 1 Players shall not choose balls in the playing area.

2. 4. 2. 1. 1 Wherever possible players shall be given the opportunity to choose one or more balls before coming to the playing area and the match shall be played with one of these balls, taken at random by the umpire.

2. 4. 2. 1. 2 If a ball has not been chosen before players come to the playing area, the match shall be played with a ball taken at random by the umpire from a box of those specified for the competition.

2.4.2.1.3 If a ball is damaged during a match, it shall be replaced by another of those chosen before the match or, if such a ball is not available, by one taken at random by the umpire from a box of those specified for the competition.

2.4.2.2 The racket covering shall be used as it has been authorised by the ITTF without any physical, chemical or other treatment, changing or modifying playing properties, friction, outlook, colour, structure, surface, etc.; in particular, no additives shall be used.

2.4.2.3 A racket shall successfully pass all parameters of the racket control tests.

2.4.2.4 A racket shall not be replaced during an individual match unless it is accidentally damaged so badly that it cannot be used; if this happens the damaged racket shall be replaced immediately by another which the player has brought with him or her to the playing area or one which is handed to him or her in the playing area.

2.4.2.5 Unless otherwise authorised by the umpire, players shall leave their rackets on the table during intervals; but if the racket is strapped to the hand, the umpire shall allow the player to retain his or her racket strapped to the hand during intervals.

2.4.3 Practice

2.4.3.1 Players are entitled to practise on the match table for up to 2 minutes immediately before the start of a match but not during normal intervals; the specified practice period may be extended only with the permission of the referee.

2.4.3.2 During an emergency suspension of play the referee may allow players to practise on any table, including the match table.

2.4.3.3 Players shall be given reasonable opportunity to check and to familiarise themselves with any equipment which they are to use, but this shall not automatically entitle them to more than a few practice rallies before resuming play after the replacement of a damaged ball or racket.

2.4.4 Intervals

2.4.4.1 Play shall be continuous throughout an individual match except that any player is entitled to:

2.4.4.1.1 an interval of up to 1 minute between successive games of an individual match;

2.4.4.1.2 brief intervals for towelling after every 6 points from the start of each game and at the change of ends in the last possible game of an individual match.

2.4.4.2 A player or pair may claim one time-out period of up to 1 minute during an individual match.

2.4.4.2.1 In an individual event the request for a time-out may be made by the player or pair or by the designated adviser; in a team event it may be made by the player or pair or by the team captain.

2.4.4.2.2 If a player or pair and an adviser or captain disagree whether a time-out is to be taken, the final decision shall be made by the player or pair in an individual event and by the captain in a team event.

2.4.4.2.3 The request for a time-out, which can be made only between rallies in a game, shall be indicated by making a "T" sign with the hands.

2. 4. 4. 2. 4 On receiving a valid request for a time-out the umpire shall suspend play and shall hold up a white card with the hand on the side of the player or pair who requested it; the white card or another appropriate marker shall be placed on the court of that player or pair.

2. 4. 4. 2. 5 The white card or marker shall be removed and play resumed as soon as the player or pair making the request is ready to continue or at the end of 1 minute, whichever is the sooner.

2. 4. 4. 2. 6 If a valid request for a time-out is made simultaneously by or on behalf of both players or pairs, play will resume when both players or pairs are ready or at the end of 1 minute, whichever is the sooner, and neither player or pair shall be entitled to another time-out during that individual match.

2. 4. 4. 3 There shall be no intervals between successive individual matches of a team match except that a player who is required to play in successive matches may claim an interval of up to 5 minutes between those matches.

2. 4. 4. 4 The referee may allow a suspension of play, of the shortest practical duration, and in no circumstances more than 10 minutes, if a player is temporarily incapacitated by an accident, provided that in the opinion of the referee the suspension is not likely to be unduly disadvantageous to the opposing player or pair.

2. 4. 4. 5 A suspension shall not be allowed for a disability which was present or was reasonably to be expected at the beginning of the match, or where it is due to the normal stress of play; disability such as cramp or exhaustion, caused by the player' s current state of fitness or by the manner in which play has proceeded, does not justify such an emergency suspension, which may be allowed only for incapacity resulting from an accident, such as injury caused by a fall.

2. 4. 4. 6 If anyone in the playing area is bleeding, play shall be suspended immediately and shall not resume until that person has received medical treatment and all traces of blood have been removed from the playing area.

2. 4. 4. 7 Players shall remain in or near the playing area throughout an individual match, except with the permission of the referee; during intervals between games and time-outs they shall remain within 3 metres of the playing area, under the supervision of the umpire.

2. 5 Discipline

2. 5. 1 Advice

2. 5. 1. 1 In a team event, players may receive advice from anyone authorised to be at the playing area.

2. 5. 1. 2 In an individual event, a player or pair may receive advice only from one person, designated beforehand to the umpire, except that where the players of a doubles pair are from different Associations each may designate an adviser, but with regard to 2. 5. 1 and 2. 5. 2 these two advisors shall be treated as a unit; if an unauthorised person gives advice the umpire shall hold up a red card and send him or her away from the playing area.

2. 5. 1. 3 Players may receive advice only during the intervals between games or during other authorised suspension of play, and not between the end of practice and the start of a match; if any authorised person gives advice at other times the umpire shall hold up a yellow card to warn

him or her that any further such offence will result in his or her dismissal from the playing area.

2.5.1.4 After a warning has been given, if in the same team match or the same match of an individual event anyone again gives advice illegally, the umpire shall hold up a red card and send him or her away from the playing area, whether or not he or she was the person warned.

2.5.1.5 In a team match the dismissed adviser shall not be allowed to return, except when required to play, and he or she shall not be replaced by another adviser until the team match has ended; in an individual event he or she shall not be allowed to return until the individual match has ended.

2.5.1.6 If the dismissed adviser refuses to leave, or returns before the end of the match, the umpire shall suspend play and report to the referee.

2.5.1.7 These regulations shall apply only to advice on play and shall not prevent a player or captain, as appropriate, from making a legitimate appeal nor hinder a consultation with an interpreter or Association representative on the explanation of a juridical decision.

2.5.2 Misbehaviour

2.5.2.1 Players and coaches or other advisers shall refrain from behaviour that may unfairly affect an opponent, offend spectators or bring the sport into disrepute, such as abusive language, deliberately breaking the ball or hitting it out of the playing area, kicking the table or surrounds and disrespect of match officials.

2.5.2.2 If at any time a player, a coach or another adviser commits a serious offence the umpire shall suspend play and report immediately to the referee; for less serious offences the umpire may, on the first occasion, hold up a yellow card and warn the offender that any further offence is liable to incur penalties.

2.5.2.3 Except as provided in 2.5.2.2 and 2.5.2.5, if a player who has been warned commits a second offence in the same individual match or team match, the umpire shall award 1 point to the offender's opponent and for a further offence he shall award 2 points, each time holding up a yellow and a red card together.

2.5.2.4 If a player against whom 3 penalty points have been awarded in the same individual match or team match continues to misbehave, the umpire shall suspend play and report immediately to the referee.

2.5.2.5 If a player changes his or her racket during an individual match when it has not been damaged, the umpire shall suspend play and report to the referee.

2.5.2.6 A warning or penalty incurred by either player of a doubles pair shall apply to the pair, but not to the non-offending player in a subsequent individual match of the same team match; at the start of a doubles match the pair shall be regarded as having incurred the higher of any warnings or penalties incurred by either player in the same team match.

2.5.2.7 Except as provided in 2.5.2.2, if a coach or another adviser who has been warned commits a further offence in the same individual match or team match, the umpire shall hold up a red card and send him or her away from the playing area until the end of the team match or, in an individual event, of the individual match.

2.5.2.8 The referee shall have power to disqualify a player from a match, an event or a competition for seriously unfair or offensive behaviour, whether reported by the umpire or not; as he or she does so he or she shall hold up a red card.

2. 5. 2. 9 If a player is disqualified from 2 matches of a team or individual event he or she shall automatically be disqualified from that team event or individual competition.

2. 5. 2. 10 The referee may disqualify for the remainder of a competition anyone who has twice been sent away from the playing area during that competition.

2. 5. 2. 11 Following 4 accumulated failures on any aspect of official racket testing over 48 months, a player shall be suspended for 12 months from participating in ITTF events.

2. 5. 2. 12 If a player is disqualified from a match, event or competition for any reason, he or she shall automatically forfeit any associated title, medal, prize money or ranking points.

2. 5. 2. 13 Cases of very serious misbehaviour shall be reported to the offender's Association.

2. 5. 3 Good Presentation

2. 5. 3. 1 Players, coaches and officials shall uphold the object of good presentation of the sport; in particular players have to do their utmost to win a match and shall not withdraw except for reasons of illness or injury.

2. 5. 3. 2 Any player who deliberately fails tocomply with these principles shall be disciplined by total or partial loss of prize money in prize events and/or by suspension from ITTF events.

2. 5. 3. 3 In the event of complicity proven against any adviser or official the relevant national Association is also expected to discipline this person.

2. 5. 3. 4 A Disciplinary Panel appointed by the Executive Committee, consisting of 4 members and a chair, shall decide on whether an infringement committed and if necessary on appropriate sanctions; this Disciplinary Panel shall decide according to directives given by the Executive Committee.

2. 5. 3. 5 An appeal against the Disciplinary Panel's decision may be made by the disciplined player, adviser or official within 15 days to the ITTF Executive Committee whose decision on the matter shall be final.

2. 6 Draw For Knook-out Competitions

2. 6. 1 Byes and Qualifiers

2. 6. 1. 1 The number of places in the first round proper of a knockout event shall be a power of 2.

2. 6. 1. 1. 1 If there are fewer entries than places, the first round shall include enough byes to make up the required number.

2. 6. 1. 1. 2 If there are more entries than places, a qualifying competition shall be held such that the number of qualifiers and the number of direct entries together make up the required number.

2. 6. 1. 2 Byes shall be distributed as evenly as possible throughout the first round, being placed first against seeded places, in seeding order.

2. 6. 1. 3 Qualifiers shall be drawn as evenly as possible among the halves, quarters, eighths or sixteenths of the draw, as appropriate.

2.6.2 Seeding by Ranking

2.6.2.1 The highest ranked entries in an event shall be seeded so that they cannot meet before the closing rounds.

2.6.2.2 The number of entries to be seeded shall not exceed the number of entries in the 1st round proper of the event.

2.6.2.3 The entry ranked 1 shall be placed at the top of the first half of the draw and the entry ranked 2 at the bottom of the second half, but all other seeded entries shall be drawn among specified places in the draw, as follows:

2.6.2.3.1 the entries ranked 3 and 4 shall be drawn between the bottom of the first half of the draw and the top of the second half;

2.6.2.3.2 the entries ranked 5 ~ 8 shall be drawn among the bottom places of the odd-numbered quarters of the draw and the top places of the even-numbered quarters;

2.6.2.3.3 the entries ranked 9 ~ 16 shall be drawn among the bottom places of the odd-numbered eighths of the draw and the top places of the even-numbered eighths;

2.6.2.3.4 the entries ranked 17 ~ 32 shall be drawn among the bottom places of the odd-numbered sixteenths of the draw and the top places of the even-numbered sixteenths.

2.6.2.4 In a team knockout event only the highest ranked team from an Association shall be eligible for seeding by ranking.

2.6.2.5 Seeding by ranking shall follow the order of the latest ranking list published by the ITTF except that:

2.6.2.5.1 where all the entries eligible for seeding are from Associations belonging to the same Continental Federation the latest list published by that Federation shall take precedence;

2.6.2.5.2 where all the entries eligible for seeding are from the same Association the latest list published by that Association shall take precedence.

2.6.3 Seeding by Association Nomination

2.6.3.1 Nominated players and pairs of the same Association shall, as far as possible, be separated so that they cannot meet before the closing rounds of an event.

2.6.3.2 Associations shall list their nominated players and pairs in descending order of playing strength, starting with any players included in the ranking list used for seeding, in the order of that list.

2.6.3.3 The entries ranked 1 and 2 shall be drawn into different halves and those ranked 3 and 4 into quarters other than those occupied by the first two.

2.6.3.4 The entries ranked 5 ~ 8 shall be drawn as evenly as possible into eighths other than those occupied by the first four.

2.6.3.5 The entries ranked 9 ~ 16 shall be drawn as evenly as possible into sixteenths other than those occupied by higher ranked players or pairs and so on, until all the entries have been allocated.

2.6.3.6 A men's or women's doubles pair consisting of players from different Associations shall be considered a pair of the Association of the player ranked higher in the World Ranking List, or, if neither player is in this list, in the appropriate Continental Ranking List; if neither player is included in a World or Continental Ranking List, the pair shall be considered a member of the Association whose team is ranked higher in the appropriate World Team Ranking List.

2.6.3.7 A mixed doubles pair consisting of players from different Associations shall be considered a pair of the Association to which the man belongs.

2.6.3.8 Alternatively, any doubles pair consisting of players from different Associations may be considered a pair of both of these Associations.

2.6.3.9 In a qualifying competition, entries from the same Association, up to the number of qualifying groups, shall be drawn into separate groups in such a way that qualifiers are, as far as possible, separated in accordance with the principles of 2.6.3.3 ~5.

2.6.4 Alterations

2.6.4.1 A completed draw may be altered only with the permission of the responsible management committee and, where appropriate, the agreement of the representatives of Associations directly concerned.

2.6.4.2 The draw may be altered only to correct errors and genuine misunderstandings in the notification and acceptance of entry, to correct serious imbalance, as provided in 2.6.5, or to include additional players or pairs, as provided in 2.6.6.

2.6.4.3 No alterations other than necessary deletions shall be made to the draw of an event after it has started; for the purpose of this regulation a qualifying competition may be regarded as a separate event.

2.6.4.4 A player shall not be deleted from the draw without his or her permission, unless he or she is disqualified; such permission must be given either by the player if he or she is present or, if he or she is absent, by his or her authorised representative.

2.6.4.5 A doubles pair shall not be altered if both players are present and fit to play, but injury, illness or absence of one player may be accepted as justification for an alteration.

2.6.5 Re-draw

2.6.5.1 Except as provided in 2.6.4.2, 2.6.4.5 and 2.6.5.2, a player shall not be moved from one place in the draw to another and if for any reason the draw becomes seriously unbalanced the event shall, wherever possible, be completely re-drawn.

2.6.5.2 Exceptionally, where the imbalance is due to theabsence of several seeded players or pairs from the same section of the draw, the remaining seeded players or pairs only may be re-numbered in ranking order and re-drawn to the extent possible among the seeded places, taking account as far as is practicable of the requirements for seeding by Association nomination.

2.6.6 Additions

2.6.6.1 Players not included in the original draw may be added later, at the discretion of the responsible management committee and with the agreement of the referee.

2.6.6.2 Any vacancies in seeded places shall first be filled, in ranking order, by drawing into them the strongest new players or pairs; any further players or pairs shall be drawn into vacancies due to absence or disqualification and then into byes other than those against seeded players or pairs.

2.6.6.3 Any players or pairs who would have been seeded by ranking if they had been included in the original draw may be drawn only into vacancies in seeded places.

2.7 Organisation of Competitions

2.7.1 Authority

2.7.1.1 Provided the Constitution is observed, any Association may organise or authorise open, restricted or invitation tournaments within its territory or may arrange international matches.

2.7.1.2 In any season, an Association may nominate one senior, one junior and one veterans' open tournament which it organises as its Senior, Junior or Veterans' Open International Championships.

2.7.1.3 Players from affiliated ITTF member Associations, when competing internationally, can only participate in ITTF events, ITTF approved events and ITTF registered events entered through their national Association, as well as in ITTF recognised events entered through their National Olympic Committee or National Paralympic Committee respectively. Participation in any other type of event can only be allowed with the express written permission of the national Association of the player or the ITTF; permission to players will be considered given unless a specific or general notification is made by the national Association of the player or the ITTF withholding the permission to participate in an event or series of events.

2.7.1.4 A player or team may not take part in an international competition if he or she or it is suspended by his or he or its Association or Continental Federation.

2.7.1.5 No event may use a World title without the permission of the ITTF, or a Continental title without the permission of the appropriate Continental Federation.

2.7.2 Representation

2.7.2.1 Representatives of all Associations whose players are taking part in an Open International Championships event shall be entitled to attend the draw and shall be consulted on any alterations to the draw or any decisions of appeal that may directly affect their players.

2.7.3 Entries

2.7.3.1 Entry forms for Open International Championships shall be sent to all Associations not later than 2 calendar months before the start of the competition and not later than 1 calendar month before the date for the close of entries.

2.7.3.2 All entries nominated by Associations for open tournaments shall be accepted but the organisers shall have power to allocate entries to a qualifying competition; in deciding this allocation they shall take account of the relevant ITTF and Continental ranking lists and of any ranking order of entries specified by the nominating Association.

2.7.4 Events

2.7.4.1 Open International Championships shall include men's singles, women's singles, men's doubles and women's doubles and may include mixed doubles and international team events for teams representing Associations.

2.7.4.2 In world title competitions, players in youth, junior and cadet events must be under 21, under 18 and under 15 respectively on 31st December immediately before the calendar year in which the competition takes place; these age limits are recommended for corresponding events in other competitions.

2. 7. 4. 3 It is recommended that team matches at Open International Championships be played according to one of the systems specified in 2. 7. 6; the entry form or prospectus shall show which system has been chosen.

2. 7. 4. 4 Individual events proper shall be played on a knockout basis, but team events and qualifying rounds of individual events may be played on either a knockout or a group basis.

2. 7. 5 Group Competitions

2. 7. 5. 1 In a group, or "round robin", competition, all members of the group shall compete against each other and shall gain 2 match points for a win, 1 for a loss in a played match and 0 for a loss in an unplayed or unfinished match; the ranking order shall be determined primarily by the number of match points gained. If a player is defaulted after the completion of a match for any reason, he or she shall be deemed to have lost the match, which shall subsequently be recorded as a loss in an unplayed match.

2. 7. 5. 2 If two or more members of the group have gained the same number of match points their relative positions shall be determined only by the results of the matches between them, by considering successively the numbers of matchpoints, the ratios of wins to losses first in individual matches (for a team event), games and points, as far as is necessary to resolve the order.

2. 7. 5. 3 If at any step in the calculations the positions of one or more members of the group have been determined while the others are still equal, the results of matches in which those members took part shall be excluded from any further calculations needed to resolve the equalities in accordance with the procedure of 2. 7. 5. 1 and 2. 7. 5. 2.

2. 7. 5. 4 If it is not possible to resolve equalities by means of the procedure specified in 2. 7. 5. 1 ~3 the relative positions shall be decided by lot.

2. 7. 5. 5 In the qualifying stages of World, Olympic and Open International Championships players shall be drawn into groups and assigned group positions in descendingorder of their current world ranking, taking account as far as possible of separation by Association.

2. 7. 5. 6 Unless otherwise authorised by the Jury, if 1 player or team is to qualify the final match in the group shall be between the players or teams numbered 1 and 2, if 2 are to qualify the final match shall be between the players or teams numbered 2 and 3 and so on.

2. 7. 6 Team Match Systems

2. 7. 6. 1 Best of 5 matches (New Swaythling Cup system, 5 singles)

2. 7. 6. 1. 1 A team shall consist of 3 players.

2. 7. 6. 1. 2 The order of play shall be

(1) A v X

(2) B v Y

(3) C v Z

(4) A v Y

(5) B v X

2. 7. 6. 2 Best of 5 matches (Corbillon Cup system, 4 singles and 1 doubles)

2. 7. 6. 2. 1 A team shall consist of 2, 3 or 4 players.

2.7.6.2.2 The order of play shall be

(1) A v X

(2) B v Y

(3) doubles

(4) A v Y

(5) B v X

2.7.6.2.3 In Para TT events, the order of play may be as in 2.7.6.2.2 except that the doubles match may be played last.

2.7.6.3 Best of 5 matches (Olympic system, 4 singles and 1 doubles).

2.7.6.3.1 A team shall consist of 3 players; each player shall compete in a maximum of 2 individual matches.

2.7.6.3.2 The order of play shall be

(1) A v X

(2) B v Y

(3) doubles C & A or B v Z & X or Y

(4) B or A v Z

(5) C v Y or X

2.7.6.4 Best of 7 matches (6 singlesand 1 doubles)

2.7.6.4.1 A team shall consist of 3, 4 or 5 players.

2.7.6.4.2 The order of play shall be

(1) A v Y

(2) B v X

(3) C v Z

(4) doubles

(5) A v X

(6) C v Y

(7) B v Z

2.7.6.5 Best of 9 matches (9 singles)

2.7.6.5.1 A team shall consist of 3 players.

2.7.6.5.2 The order of play shall be

(1) A v X

(2) B v Y

(3) C v Z

(4) B v X

(5) A v Z

(6) C v Y

(7) B v Z

(8) C v X

(9) A v Y

2.7.7 Team Match Procedure

2.7.7.1 All players shall be selected from those nominated for the event.

2.7.7.2 The nameof the team captain, playing or non-playing, shall be designated beforehand to the umpire.

2.7.7.3 Before a team match the right to choose A, B, C or X, Y, Z shall be decided by lot and the captains shall name their teams to the referee or his or her representative, assigning a letter to each singles player.

2.7.7.4 The pairs for a doubles match need not be nominated until the end of the immediately preceding singles match.

2.7.7.5 A team match shall end when one team has won a majority of the possible individual matches.

2.7.8 Results

As soon as possible after the end of a competition and not later than 7 days thereafter the organising Association shall send to the ITTF Secretariat and to the Secretary of the appropriate Continental Federationdetails of the results, including points scores, of international matches, of all rounds of Continental and Open International Championships and of the closing rounds of national championships.

2.7.9 Television and Streaming

2.7.9.1 An event other than World, Continental, Olympic or Paralympic title competitions may be broadcast by television only with the permission of the Association from whose territory the broadcast is made.

2.7.9.2 Participation in an international event presumes the consent of the Association controlling the visiting players to the televising of that event; in World, Continental, Olympic or Paralympic title competitions such consent is presumed for the showing anywhere of live or recorded television during the period of the event and within 1 calendar month afterwards.

2.7.9.3 All streaming of ITTF events (all categories) shall be subject to compliance with the ITTF streaming certification process and a Streaming Certification Fee (SCF) shall be charged to the rights holder of the event effective 1 June 2011.

2.8 International Eliglbility

2.8.1 Eligibility in Olympic title competitions is regulated separately by 3.5.1 and eligibility in Paralympic title competitions is regulated separately by the IPC and 3.6.1; additional eligibility regulations apply to World title events (3.1.3, 3.2.3, 3.3.6, 3.4.3).

2.8.2 A player shall be regarded as representing an Association if he or she accepted to be nominated by this Association and subsequently participatesin a competition listed in 2.1.2.3 other than individual events at Open International Championships.

2.8.3 A player is eligible to represent an Association only if he or she is a national of the country in which that Association has jurisdiction, except that a player who has already represented an Association of which he or she was not a national in accordance with previous rules may retain that eligibility.

2.8.3.1 Where the players of more than one Association have the same nationality, a player may represent one of these Associations only, if he or she is born in or has his or her main residence in the territory controlled by that Association.

2. 8. 3. 2 A player who is eligible to represent more than 1 Association shall have the right to choose which of the relevant Associations he or she will represent.

2. 8. 4 A player is eligible to represent a Continental Federation (1. 18. 1) in an event of continental teams only if he or she is eligible to represent a member Association of this Continental Federation according to 2. 8. 3.

2. 8. 5 A player shall not represent different Associations within a period of 3 years.

2. 8. 6 An Association may nominate a player under its jurisdiction (1. 21) to enter any individual events of Open International Championships; such nomination may be indicated in results lists and ITTF publications but does not affect the eligibility of this player according to 2. 8. 2.

2. 8. 7 A player or his or her Association shall, if so requested by the referee, provide documentary evidence of his or her eligibility and his or her passport.

2. 8. 8 Any appeal on a question of eligibility shall be referred to an Eligibility Commission, consisting of the Executive Committee, the chair of the Rules Committee and the chair of the Athletes' Commission, whose decision shall be final.

3 Regulations for World, Olympic and Paralympic Title Competitions

(*Additional to Regulations for International Competitions*)

3. 1 World Championships

3. 1. 1 Authority for Organisation

3. 1. 1. 1 The title "World Championships", referred to in this Section as "Championships", shall be bestowed by the AGM on the championship events at a tournament organised by an Association entrusted with the task.

3. 1. 1. 2 The closing date for applications to stage Championships shall be specified by the Executive Committee and notified to all Associations, giving at least 6 months' notice.

3. 1. 1. 3 All applications shall be considered by the Executive Committee and shall be submitted to the AGM, together with the report of the Selection Committee, if applicable, on venues for the occasion in question.

3. 1. 1. 4 Where necessary, the AGM or the Executive Committee may ask one or more members of the appropriate Committee to visit the country of an Association applying for the right to organise the Championships to satisfy themselves as to the adequacy of the proposed playing and other arrangements; the cost of such visits shall be borne by that Association.

3. 1. 1. 5 If, after an option has been granted, circumstances change in such a way as to be likely to prejudice the satisfactory conduct of the Championships, the option may be revoked by a 2/3 majority vote at an AGM prior to the Championships; between AGMs the Board of Directors shall have power to transfer the Championships or to take any other appropriate action.

3. 1. 2 Responsibilities of Organisers

3. 1. 2. 1 An Association granted the right to organise the Championships, hereafter referred to as the "organisers" shall be responsible for conducting them in accordance with the

Laws of Table Tennis, the Regulations for International Competitions and the Regulations for World Title Competitions, as modified or supplemented by any directives authorised by the Board of Directors.

3. 1. 2. 2 Organisers shall provide accommodation and meals from the evening before the Championships begin until the morning after the Championships end for:

3. 1. 2. 2. 1 not more than 3 men and 3 women players nominated by an Association;

3. 1. 2. 2. 2 1 delegate to the AGM from each Association if he is not already included in the nominated players listed above;

3. 1. 2. 2. 3 members of the ITTF Executive Committee, the Board of Directors and the Olympic and Paralympic Commission and full members of committees;

3. 1. 2. 2. 4 up to 4 members of the Doping Control Panel appointed by the Sports Science Committee;

3. 1. 2. 2. 5 up to 8 members of the Athletes' Commission;

3. 1. 2. 2. 6 Personal Honorary Members;

3. 1. 2. 2. 7 International Umpires and Referees from other Associations invited in accordance with directives issued by the ITTF;

3. 1. 2. 2. 8 up to 3 members of the ITTF staff.

3. 1. 2. 3 If the business of the ITTF extends outside the period of the Championships the period of hospitality for those entitled to participate in such business shall be extended correspondingly.

3. 1. 2. 4 Organisers shall provide free medical care and medicine for all participants, but each Association is recommended to insure its players and officials against illness and injury for the duration of the Championships.

3. 1. 2. 5 Organisers shall meet the cost of transport between the place of accommodation and the playing hall.

3. 1. 2. 6 Organisers shall request their national authorities to waive visa charges for all participants.

3. 1. 2. 7 Organisers shall ensure free access to the playing hall and free circulation therein for all the players, officials and members listed in 3. 1. 2. 2, for any additional players and committee members and for any interpreter, doctor or medical adviser appointed by the ITTF.

3. 1. 2. 8 Organisers shall provide first-class interpreting in at least four languages, preferably by simultaneous translation with the appropriate equipment.

3. 1. 2. 9 Organisers shall provide the ITTF with offices at the venue of the Championships and place at its disposal translation, computer, internet, telephone, telefax and duplicating facilities.

3. 1. 2. 10 Organisers shall publish a prospectus giving the main details of the organisation of the Championships, including:

3. 1. 2. 10. 1 the dates and place of the Championships;

3. 1. 2. 10. 2 the events to be held;

3. 1. 2. 10. 3 the equipment to be used;

3. 1. 2. 10. 4 the procedure for entry, the entry fees and the undertakings required;

3. 1. 2. 10. 5 the date and place of the draw;

3. 1. 2. 10. 6 the dates of Jury meetings and of AGM sessions;

3. 1. 2. 10. 7 the extent of hospitality for players and officials;

3. 1. 2. 10. 8 any directives authorised by the Board of Directors for the Championships.

3. 1. 2. 11 During the Championships Organisers shall make available promptly to members of the ITTF Executive Committee, Board of Directors members and team captains details of results, including points scores; as soon as possible after the completion of the Championships Organisers shall publish the complete results, including points scores, and circulate them to all Associations.

3. 1. 3 Eligibility

3. 1. 3. 1 Only an Association which is not in arrears shall be eligible to enter teams or individual players in the Championships.

3. 1. 3. 2 In addition to provisions of 2. 8, players being eligible to represent an association other than the one they intend to represent, shall register withthe ITTF, through this new Association.

3. 1. 3. 3 Such player shall not represent the new Association before:

3. 1. 3. 3. 1 3 years after the date of registration, if the player is under the age of 15 when registered;

3. 1. 3. 3. 2 5 years after the date of registration, if the player is under the age of 18 but at least 15 years of age when registered;

3. 1. 3. 3. 3 7 years after the date of registration, if the player is under the age of 21 but at least 18 years of age when registered.

3. 1. 3. 4 Players being 21 years of age or older will not be registered with the ITTF and will not be eligible to represent a new association at World Championships.

3. 1. 4 Entry Fees and Levy

3. 1. 4. 1 The entry fees shall be US $100 for each entry in a team event, US $ 50 for each pair in a doubles event and US $ 25 for each entry in a singles event.

3. 1. 4. 2 The entry fees shall be paid to the organisers at the time of entry and shall be shared equally between the organisers and the ITTF.

3. 1. 4. 3 Fees for entries from an Association are due from that Association and shall always be payable, except that the Board of Directors may waive the fees where an Association is prevented from participating in the Championships by circumstances outside its control.

3. 1. 5 Submission of Entries

3. 1. 5. 1 The intention to enter teams or players shall be notified to the ITTF in a preliminary notification form provided by the Secretariat; the closing date for the receipt of this form shall be not later than 4 calendar months before the start of the Championships.

3. 1. 5. 2 Information shall be distributed, together with the prospectus, by the Competition Department and entries shall be submitted as required.

3. 1. 5. 3 The closing date for the final entries shall be not later than 2 calendar months

before the start of the Championships.

3. 1. 5. 4 An Association may nominate up to 5 players and a non-playing captain for a team event; if a non-playing captain is not appointed one of the team players shall be designated as captain.

3. 1. 5. 5 An Association shall rank its nominated players and pairs in order of playing strength, which shall be consistent with their current world ranking.

3. 1. 5. 6 The ITTF may accept only formal nominations by an eligible Association, which are received, properly signed by a responsible representative of the nominating Association, on or before the closing date.

3. 1. 6 Modification of Entries

3. 1. 6. 1 Modified entries shall be accepted, if notified by a representative of the nominating Association, at any time up to the day before the first official draw at World Championships (for individual events).

3. 1. 6. 2 Change the composition of a team may be accepted if notified by a representative of the nominating Association up to the time of the Jury meeting preceding the World Team Championships; no further changes will be accepted after this deadline.

3. 1. 6. 3 As soon as he or she arrives at the Championships venue, the representative of an Association requesting a change to the draw in consequence of any error or absence shall notify the referee or his or her deputy, or confirm any change already notified, on a form provided for the purpose.

3. 1. 6. 4 A request for modification of an entry cannot be considered unless it is made or confirmed by the representative of an Association immediately onarrival, other than a request based on the subsequent absence, illness or injury of one player of a doubles pair, which shall be made as soon as the contingency arises.

3. 1. 6. 5 All alterations that are authorised shall be notified immediately to team captains and, where appropriate, to Association representatives.

3. 1. 7 Entry Obligations

3. 1. 7. 1 The entry form shall contain a statement, to be signed by a responsible representative of the nominating Association on behalf of all its nominated players and captains, that they understand and accept the conditions of the Championships and that they are prepared to compete against all other teams and individuals participating; no entry shall be valid unless accompanied by this declaration.

3. 1. 7. 2 In individualevents all entrants are accepted as individual competitors; they shall be bound to do their utmost to win the events for which they are entered, irrespective of whether other entrants from the same Association have been accepted to take part, and they shall not withdraw except for reasons of illness or injury.

3. 1. 8 Jury

3. 1. 8. 1 The Jury shall consist of the Chairs of the Technical, the Rules and the Umpires' and Referees' Committees, a representative of the Competition Department, a representative of the organising committee and the referee; the referee shall have the right to speak but not to vote.

3.1.8.2 If any of the nominated Chairs is unable to attend a meeting of the Jury he or she may nominate to attend in his or her place another member of his or her Committee, who shall have the right to speak and to vote.

3.1.8.3 The Chair of the Jury shall be appointed by the members of the Jury.

3.1.8.4 Any Association directly affected by a matter under consideration at a Jury meeting shall be entitled tobe represented at that meeting but shall not be entitled to vote.

3.1.8.5 The Jury shall have power to decide any question of appeal within the jurisdiction of a tournament management committee and to authorise team changes.

3.1.8.6 The Jury shall meet before the start of the Championships to be informed of all draw alterations requested up to that time and to decide any requests for changes in the composition of teams; any subsequent questions of draw alteration shall be decided by the Chair of the Technical Committee in conjunction with a representative of the Competition Department and the Jury shall meet again only when convened by the Chair to consider appeals against its administrative decisions or decisions of the referee.

3.1.9 Events

3.1.9.1 In even numbered years, the Championships shall include men's team and women's team events; while in odd numbered years the Championships shall include men's singles, women's singles, men's doubles, women's doubles and mixed doubles events.

3.1.9.2 In doubles events, both players shall be from the same Association.

3.1.9.3 The system of play in team and individual events and its implementation date shall be decided by the Board of Directors, on the recommendation of the Technical Committee.

3.1.9.4 Team matches shall be the best of 5 singles, as provided in 2.7.6.1.

3.1.9.5 There shall not be more than 128 places in the first round proper of a singles and mixed doubles event nor more than 64 places in the first round proper of a men's and women's doubles event, unless otherwise authorised by the Executive Committee.

3.1.9.6 Each Association shall be entitled to 5 entries in each singles event, with one additional player in the appropriate event for each player in the first 20 places of the first issue of the ITTF world ranking list in the year of the Championships up to a limit of 2 men and 2 women in singles with 3 men and 3 women pairs in the doubles and 3 pairs in the mixed doubles; all players may be different.

3.1.9.6.1 The host Association may enter up to 7 men and 7 women in the singles events.

3.1.9.7 Players of the same Association shall be separated according to 2.6.3.1, 2.6.3.3, 2.6.3.4 and 2.6.3.5 only in preliminary rounds and groups and in the first round of the draw but not in further rounds.

3.1.10 Default

3.1.10.1 An Association whose team is entered in the draw but which fails to compete in the event without adequate justification may be subject to disciplinary action by the AGM.

3.1.10.2 A team may begin, continue and complete a team match only with the full complement of players specified for the event, except that the referee may, at his or her discretion, allow a team to play with one player absent or an individual match to be omitted from the sequence where he or she is satisfied that the absence is due to accident, illness, injury or other circumstances outside the control of the player or the Association concerned, including disqualification by the referee in accordance with his or her authority.

3. 1. 10. 3 An Association whose teambegins to play in the event but which fails to complete its schedule of matches shall be liable to forfeit its entitlement to hospitality for its representatives at the Championships; an appeal against forfeit may be made to the Jury, whose decision shall be final.

3. 1. 11 Doping Control

Doping control shall be carried out in accordance with ITTF Anti-Doping rules (Chapter 5).

3. 1. 12 Awards and Presentations

3. 1. 12. 1 The permanent Championship trophies shall be:

3. 1. 12. 1. 1 the Swaythling Cup for the men's team event;

3. 1. 12. 1. 2 the Marcel Corbillon Cup for the women's team event;

3. 1. 12. 1. 3 the St Bride Vase for the men's singles event;

3. 1. 12. 1. 4 the G Geist Prize for the women's singles event;

3. 1. 12. 1. 5 the Iran Cup for the men's doubles event;

3. 1. 12. 1. 6 the W J Pope Trophy for the women's doubles event;

3. 1. 12. 1. 7 the Heydusek prize for the mixed doubles event.

3. 1. 12. 2 The Association whose team wins a team event, and the winner of an individual event, shall be entitled to hold the appropriate trophy until 31st December in the year following that in which it is won; the pair winning a doubles event shall agree or decide by lot the order in which each of them shall hold the trophy for half of the specified period.

3. 1. 12. 3 A player who wins the men's or women's singles event 3 times in succession or 4 times in all shall receive from the ITTF a half-size replica of the appropriate trophy as a permanent possession.

3. 1. 12. 4 In both team and individual events the winners shall receive gold medals, the losing finalists silver medals and the losing semi-finalists bronze medals.

3. 1. 12. 5 At presentation ceremonies for both team and individual events the national flags of the gold, silver and bronze medal winners shall be raised and the national anthem of the gold medal winner shall be played.

3. 1. 12. 6 The Association whose team or player wins a trophy shall acknowledge its receipt in writing and at the end of the specified period shall deliver it, within 14 days of a formal notification by the Secretariat, at an agreed time and to an agreed place.

3. 1. 12. 7 The Association acknowledging receipt of a trophy shall be responsible for its safe keeping including the arrangement of insurance, but the cost of insurance and of inscription of winners' names, which in team events should include any non-playing captain, shall be borne by the ITTF.

3. 1. 12. 8 If a trophy is lost while in the possession of an Association, that Association shall be responsible for the provision of a similar replacement.

3. 1. 12. 9 At the closing ceremony the Egypt Cup, the symbol of the friendship of the

Championships, shall be handed over to a representative of the city in which the next Championships will take place; this city shall hold the Egypt Cup until the next Championships.

3.1.13 Television

The right to televise the Championships shall be vested in the ITTF.

3.2 World Junior Championships

3.2.1 Authority for Organisation

3.2.1.1 The title "World Junior Championships", referred to in this Section as "Championships", shall be bestowed by the AGM on the championship events at a tournament organised by an Association entrusted with the task.

3.2.1.2 The closing date for applications to stage Championships shall be specified by the Executive Committee and notified to all Associations, giving at least 6 months' notice; applications shall be accepted only for the next 2 Championships.

3.2.1.3 All applications shall be considered by the Executive Committee and shall be submitted to the Board, together with details on venues for the occasion in question.

3.2.1.4 Where necessary, the Board or the Executive Committee may ask one member of the Junior Commission to visit the country of an Association applying for the right to organise the Championships to satisfy themselves as to the adequacy of the proposed playing and other arrangements; the cost of such visits shall be borne by that Association.

3.2.1.5 If, after an option has been granted, circumstances change in such a way as to be likely to prejudice the satisfactory conduct of the Championships, the option may be revoked by a 2/3 majority vote at the AGM preceding the Championships; between AGMs the Board of Directors shall have power to transfer the Championships or to take any other appropriate action.

3.2.2 Responsibilities of Organisers

3.2.2.1 An Association granted the right to organise the Championships, hereafter referred to as the "organisers" shall be responsible for conducting them in accordance with the Laws of Table Tennis, the Regulations for International Competitions and the Regulations for World Junior Championships, as modified or supplemented by any directives authorised by the Board of Directors.

3.2.2.2 Organisers shall provide accommodation and meals from the evening before the Championships begin until the morning after the Championships end for

3.2.2.2.1 not more than 2 boys players nominated by an Association eligible for the boys team event;

3.2.2.2.2 not more than 2 girls players nominated by an Association eligible for the girls team event;

3.2.2.2.3 not more than 1 coach of an Association participating in 1 or 2 team events;

3.2.2.2.4 members of the ITTF Executive Committee and the Junior Commission;

3.2.2.2.5 up to 2 members of the Doping Control Panel appointed by the Sports Science Committee;

3.2.2.2.6 up to 2 ITTF Committee or Commission Chairs nominated by the Executive Committee;

3. 2. 2. 2. 7 International Umpires and Referees from other Associations invited in accordance with directives issued by the ITTF;

3. 2. 2. 2. 8 up to 3members of the ITTF staff.

3. 2. 2. 3 Organisers shall provide free medical care and medicine for all participants, but each Association is recommended to insure its players and officials against illness and injury for the duration of the Championships.

3. 2. 2. 4 Organisers shall meet the cost of transport between the place of accommodation and the playing hall.

3. 2. 2. 5 Organisers shall request their national authorities to waive visa charges for all participants.

3. 2. 2. 6 Organisers shall ensure free accessto the playing hall and free circulation therein for all the players, officials and members listed in 3. 2. 2. 2, for any additional players and ITTF officials and for any interpreter, doctor or medical adviser appointed by the ITTF.

3. 2. 2. 7 Organisers shall provide the ITTF with offices at the venue of the Championships and place at its disposal translation, computer, internet, telephone, telefax and duplicating facilities.

3. 2. 2. 8 Organisers shall publish a prospectus giving the main details of the organisation of the Championships, including

3. 2. 2. 8. 1 the dates and place of the Championships;

3. 2. 2. 8. 2 the events to be held;

3. 2. 2. 8. 3 the equipment to be used;

3. 2. 2. 8. 4 the procedure for entry, the entry fees and the undertakings required;

3. 2. 2. 8. 5 the date and place of the draw;

3. 2. 2. 8. 6 the dates of Jury meetings;

3. 2. 2. 8. 7 the extent of hospitality for players and officials;

3. 2. 2. 8. 8 any directives authorised by the Board of Directors for the Championships.

3. 2. 2. 9 During the Championships Organisers shall make available promptly to members of the ITTF Executive Committee, Board of Directors members and team captains details of results, including points scores; as soon as possible after the completion of the Championships Organisers shall publish the complete results, including points scores, and circulate them to all Associations.

3. 2. 3 Eligibility

3. 2. 3. 1 Only an Association which is not in arrears shall be eligible to enter teams or individual players in the Championships.

3. 2. 3. 2 The system of qualification for team and individual events shall be determined by the Board not later than 18 months before the start of the Championships.

3. 2. 3. 3 All players shall be juniors according to 2. 7. 4. 2.

3. 2. 3. 4 In addition to provisions of 2. 8, players being eligible to represent an association other than the one they intend to represent, shall register with the ITTF, through this new Association.

3.2.3.5 Such player shall not represent the new Association before 3 years after the date of registration, if the player is under the age of 15 when registered.

3.2.4 Entry Fees

3.2.4.1 The entry fees shall be US $ 50 for each entry in a team event, US $ 30 for each pair in a doubles event and US $ 15 for each entry in a singles event.

3.2.4.2 The entry fees shall be paid to the organisers at the time of entry and shall be shared equally between the organisers and the ITTF.

3.2.4.3 Fees for entries from an Association are due from that Association and shall always be payable, except that the Board of Directors may waive the fees where an Association is prevented from participating in the Championships by circumstances outside its control.

3.2.5 Qualification and Entries

3.2.5.1 The intention of an Association qualified to enter teams or players shall be notified to the organisers and the ITTF in a preliminary notification form provided by the Secretariat; the closing date for the receipt of this form shall be not later than 4 calendar months before the start of the Championships.

3.2.5.2 Information shall be distributed, together with the prospectus, by the Competition Department and entries shall be submitted as required.

3.2.5.3 Two sets of these entry forms shall be returned to the organisers and one set to the Secretariat; the closing date for the receipt of these forms shall be not later than 2 calendar months before the start of the Championships.

3.2.5.4 An Association may nominate up to 4 qualified boys and up to 4 qualified girls players.

3.2.5.5 An Association shall rank its nominated players and pairs in order of playing strength, which shall be consistent with their current ranking in the World Junior Ranking List.

3.2.5.6 Organisers may accept only formal nominations by an eligible Association, which are received, properly signed by a responsible representative of the nominating Association, on or before the closing date.

3.2.6 Modification of Entries

3.2.6.1 The nominating Association may change the composition of a team by notifying the organisers up to the time of the Jury meeting preceding the Championships, but in no circumstances after the start of the event.

3.2.6.2 As soon as he or she arrives at the Championships venue, the representative of an Association requesting a change to the draw in consequence of any error or absenceshall notify the referee or his or her deputy, or confirm any change already notified, on a form provided for the purpose.

3.2.6.3 A request for modification of an entry cannot be considered unless it is made or confirmed by the representative of an Association immediately on arrival, other than a request based on the subsequent absence, illness or injury of one player of a doubles pair, which shall be made as soon as the contingency arises.

3.2.6.4 All alterations that are authorised shall be notified immediately to team captains and, where appropriate, to Association representatives.

3.2.7 Entry Obligations

3.2.7.1 The entry form shall contain a statement, to be signed by a responsible representative of the nominating Association on behalf of all its nominated players and captains, that they understand and accept the conditions of the Championships and that they are prepared to compete against all other teams and individuals participating; no entry shall be valid unless accompanied by this declaration.

3.2.7.2 In individual events all entrants are accepted as individual competitors; they shall be bound to do their utmost to win the events for which they are entered, irrespective of whether other entrants from the same Association have been accepted to take part, and they shall not withdraw except for reasons of illness or injury.

3.2.8 Jury

3.2.8.1 The Jury shall consist of the Chair of the ITTF Junior Commission, a representative of the ITTF Competition Department, a representative of the ITTF GlobalJunior Program, the Championships Director (or his or her equivalent), a representative of the organising committee and the referee; the referee shall have the right to speak but not to vote.

3.2.8.2 If the Chair of the ITTF Junior Commission is unable toattend a meeting of the Jury he or she may nominate an appointee to attend in his or her place who shall have the right to speak and to vote.

3.2.8.3 The Chair of the Jury shall be appointed by the Chair of the ITTF Junior Commission or in his or her absence by the representative of the ITTF Global Junior Program.

3.2.8.4 Any Association directly affected by a matter under consideration at a Jury meeting shall be entitled to be represented at that meeting but shall not be entitled to vote.

3.2.8.5 The Jury shall have power to decide any question of appeal within the jurisdiction of a tournament management committee.

3.2.8.6 The Jury shall meet before the start of the Championships to be informed of all draw alterations requested up to that time; any subsequent questions of draw alteration shall be decided by the ITTF Junior Commission and the Jury shall meet again only when convened by that Commission to consider appeals against its administrative decisions or decisions of the referee.

3.2.9 Events

3.2.9.1 The Championships shall include boys' team and girls' team events as well as boys' singles and doubles, girls' singles and doubles and mixed doubles events.

3.2.9.1.1 With the exception of mixed doubles events, both players of a doubles shall be from the same Association.

3.2.9.2 The system of play in the team and individual events, in groups and stages, shall be decided by the Board of Directors, on the recommendation of the Junior Commission, and shall be notified to all Associations not later than 6 calendar months before the start of the Championships.

3.2.10 Default

3.2.10.1 An Association whose team is entered in the draw but which fails to compete in the event without adequate justification may be subject to disciplinary action by the AGM.

3.2.10.2 A team may begin, continue and complete a team match only with the full complement of players specified for the event, except that the referee may, at his or her discretion, allow a team to play with one player absent or an individual match to be omitted from the sequence where he or she is satisfied that the absence is due to accident, illness, injury or other circumstances outside the control of the player or the Association concerned, including disqualification by the referee in accordance with his or her authority.

3.2.10.3 An Association whose team begins to play in the event but which fails to complete its schedule of matches shall be liable to forfeit its entitlement to hospitality for its representatives at the Championships; an appeal against forfeit may be made to the Jury, whose decision shall be final.

3.2.11 Doping Control

3.2.11.1 Doping control shall be carried out in accordance with ITTF Anti-Doping rules (Chapter 5).

3.2.12 Awards and Presentations

3.2.12.1 In both team and individual events the winners shall receive gold medals, the losing finalists silver medals and the losing semi-finalists bronze medals.

3.2.12.2 At presentation ceremonies for both team and individual events the national flags of the gold, silver and bronze medal winners shall be raised and the national anthem of the gold medal winner shall be played.

3.2.13 Television

3.2.13.1 The right to televise the Championships shall be vested in the ITTF.

3.3 WORLD CUP

3.3.1 Composition

3.3.1.1 Separate World Cup Tournaments for men and women will be held annually and each will be a singles competition.

3.3.1.2 The participants will consist of the current holder of the World Cup, the World Champion, the champion player or the strongest current player from each of the 6 continents, 1 player from the host Association, the top 8 players from the World Ranking List and 2 "wild card" selections. The number of players may be modified by the Executive Committee from time to time.

3.3.1.3 There shall not be more than 2 players from an Association unless a third is invited as a "wild card" selection. If the World Champion and the World Cup title holder is the same player, or the host Association has a player qualified as title holder or from the World Ranking, the available invitation place goes to the next highest eligible player on the World Ranking List.

3.3.1.4 Participants will be provided with free meals and accommodation from dinner on the evening before the start of the competition to breakfast on the morning after it ends; continental representatives will also be provided with free return travel tickets to the venue.

3.3.2 Authority

3.3.2.1 The ITTF shall be the sole owner of the World Cup title and tournaments.

3.3.2.2 An Association may be granted permission to organise the tournament; submission of an application to do so shall be regarded as implying knowledge and acceptance of these and all other applicable regulations.

3.3.2.3 Organisers shall not, without prior consent of the ITTF, delegate any of their authority nor make any contract or agreement with any other body, such as a Regional Association, a municipal authority or a sponsor.

3.3.2.4 Any agreement made between the organisers and any other body shall not conflict with nor derogate from the principle of these regulations; in case of any dispute the authority of the ITTF, as exercised through its representatives, shall be paramount.

3.3.2.5 The ITTF may enter into contracts with promoters or sponsors.

3.3.3 Appointments

3.3.3.1 For each tournament the ITTF Competition Department shall appoint a Tournament Director and a Competition Manager.

3.3.3.2 The Tournament Director shall be responsible to the ITTF Competition Department for ensuring observance of the conditions laid down for the tournament, including approval of the arrangements made by the organisers for ceremonies and presentations, protocol and seating arrangements at ceremonies and social functions and the presentation of play.

3.3.3.3 The Competition Manager shall be responsible to the ITTF for ensuring the adequacy of equipment and playing conditions, supervising the draw and scheduling matches.

3.3.4 Doping control

3.3.4.1 Doping control shall be carried out in accordance with ITTF Anti-Doping rules (Chapter 5).

3.3.5 Playing System

3.3.5.1 The playing system will be determined by the Executive Committee on recommendation by the Competition Department. The selected players and their associations will be informed of the playing system to be used in the prospectus at the same time as the issuance of the invitation to the participants.

3.3.6 Eligibility

3.3.6.1 In addition to provisions of 3.8, players being eligible to represent an association other than the one they intend to represent, shall register with the ITTF, through this new Association.

3.3.6.2 Such player shall not represent the new Association before:

3.3.6.2.1 3 years after the date of registration, if the player is under the age of 15 when registered;

3.3.6.2.2 5 years after the date of registration, if the player is under the age of 18 but at least 15 years of age when registered;

3.3.6.2.3 7 years after the date of registration, if the player is under the age of 21 but at least 18 years of age when registered.

3.3.6.3 Players being 21 years of age or older will not beregistered with the ITTF and will not be eligible to represent a new association at the World Cup.

3.3.7 Jury

3.3.7.1 The Jury shall consist of the ITTF Executive Vice-President responsible for the World Cup, the ITTF Competition Director, a representative of the organising committee and the referee; the referee shall have the right to speak but not to vote.

3.3.7.2 If either the ITTF Executive Vice-President responsible for the World Cup or the ITTF Competition Director is unable to attend a meeting of the Jury he or she may nominate an appointee to attend in his or her place who shall have the right to speak and to vote.

3.3.7.3 The Chair of the Jury shall be appointed by the ITTF Executive Vice-President responsible for the World Cup.

3.3.7.4 Any Association directly affected by a matter under consideration at a Jury meeting shall be entitled to be represented at that meeting but shall not be entitled to vote.

3.3.7.5 The Jury shall have power to decide any question of appeal within the jurisdiction of a tournament management committee.

3.3.7.6 The Jury shall meet before the start of the tournament to be informed of all draw alterations requested up to that time and the Jury shall meet again only when it has to consider appeals against its administrative decisions or decisions of the referee.

3.4 World team cup

3.4.1 Composition

3.4.1.1 The World Team Cup Tournament consisting of a men's and a women's team event will be held each odd numbered year.

3.4.1.2 In each event the 12 participating teams representing national associations will consist of the teams placing 1 to 7 at the preceding World Team Championships, a team of the host Association and 4 teams from Continental Federations not otherwise represented at the event.

3.4.1.3 If the team of the host Association is qualified by its ranking at the preceding World Team Championships then the team placing 8th at these World Team Championships shall participate.

3.4.1.4 Participants will be provided with free meals and accommodation from dinner on the evening before the start of the competition to breakfast on the morning after it ends.

3.4.2 Authority

3.4.2.1 The ITTF shall be the sole owner of the World Team Cup title and tournament.

3.4.2.2 An Association may be granted permission to organise the tournament; submission of an application to do so shall be regarded as implying knowledge and acceptance of these and all other applicable regulations.

3.4.2.3 Organisers shall not, without prior consent of the ITTF, delegate any of their authority nor make any contract or agreement with any other body, such as a Regional Association, a municipal authority or a sponsor.

3.4.2.4 Any agreement made between the organisers and any other body shall not conflict with nor derogate from the principle of theseregulations; in case of any dispute the authority of the ITTF, as exercised through its representatives, shall be paramount.

3.4.2.5 The ITTF may enter into contracts with promoters or sponsors.

3. 4. 3 Appointments

3. 4. 3. 1 For each tournament the ITTF Competition Department shall appoint a Tournament Director and a Competition Manager.

3. 4. 3. 2 The Tournament Director shall be responsible to the ITTF Competition Department for ensuring observance of the conditions laid down for the tournament, including approval of the arrangements made by the organisers for ceremonies and presentations, protocol and seating arrangements at ceremonies and social functions and the presentation of play.

3. 4. 3. 3 The Competition Manager shall be responsible to the ITTF for ensuring the adequacy of equipment and playing conditions, supervising the draw and scheduling matches.

3. 4. 4 Doping control

3. 4. 4. 1 Doping control shall be carried out in accordance with ITTF Anti-Doping rules (Chapter 5).

3. 4. 5 Playing System

3. 4. 5. 1 The 4 teams from Continental Federations not qualified by their ranking at the preceding World Team Championships shall compete in an "Intercontinental Cup" played on round-robin.

3. 4. 5. 2 The winner of the "Intercontinental Cup" shall play a play-off matchagainst the lowest seeded of the other 8 teams, other than the host Association's team. The winner of this play-off match shall promote to the event proper which shall be played on straight knock-out.

3. 4. 5. 3 Seeding shall be done according to the last available Team World Ranking.

3. 4. 5. 4 All team matches shall be played on the Olympic System with a maximum of 4 singles and 1 doubles according to 3. 7. 6. 3.

3. 4. 5. 5 All individual matches of a team match shall be the best of 5 games.

3. 4. 5. 6 The playing system may be modified by the Executive Committee on the recommendation of the Competition Department. Any changes to the playing system will be informed to the participating associations in the prospectus at the time of issuance of the invitation to participate.

3. 4. 6 Eligibility

3. 4. 6. 1 In addition to provisions of 3. 8, players being eligible to represent an association other than the one they intend to represent, shall register with the ITTF, through this new Association.

3. 4. 6. 2 Such player shall notrepresent the new Association before

3. 4. 6. 2. 1 3 years after the date of registration, if the player is under the age of 15 when registered;

3. 4. 6. 2. 2 5 years after the date of registration, if the player is under the age of 18 but at least 15 years of age when registered;

3. 4. 6. 2. 3 7 years after the date of registration, if the player is under the age of 21 but at least 18 years of age when registered.

3. 4. 6. 3 Players being 21 years of age or older will not be registered with the ITTF and will not be eligible to represent a new association at the World Team Cup.

3.4.7 Jury

3.4.7.1 The Jury shall consist of the ITTF Executive Vice-President responsible for the World Team Cup, the ITTF Competition Director, a representative of the organising committee and the referee; the referee shall have the right to speak but not to vote.

3.4.7.2 If either the ITTF Executive Vice-President responsible for the World Team Cup or the ITTF Competition Director is unable to attend a meeting of the Jury he may nominate anappointee to attend in his place who shall have the right to speak and to vote.

3.4.7.3 The Chairman of the Jury shall be appointed by the ITTF Executive Vice-President responsible for the World Team Cup.

3.4.7.4 Any Association directly affected by a matter under consideration at a Jury meeting shall be entitled to be represented at that meeting but shall not be entitled to vote.

3.4.7.5 The Jury shall have power to decide any question of appeal within the jurisdiction of a tournament management committee and to authorise team changes.

3.4.7.6 The Jury shall meet before the start of the tournament to be informed of all draw alterations requested up to that time and the Jury shall meet again only when it has to consider appeals against its administrative decisions or decisions of the referee.

3.5 Olympic Competitions

3.5.1 Eligibility

3.5.1.1 To be eligible for participation in the Olympic Games a player, coach or official shall comply with the Olympic Charter as well as with the ITTF rules. In particular the above mentioned persons shall

3.5.1.1.1 be entered by their National Olympic Committee (NOC);

3.5.1.1.2 respect the spirit of fair play and non violence, and behave accordingly on the field of play;

3.5.1.1.3 respect and comply in all aspects with the World Anti-Doping Code;

3.5.1.1.4 not allow their person, name, picture or sports performances to be used for advertising purposes during the Olympic Games, except as permitted by the IOC Executive Board.

3.5.1.2 The entry or participation of a player in the Olympic Games shall not be conditional on any financial consideration.

3.5.1.3 Any player shall be a national of the country of the NOC which is entering him or her.

3.5.1.3.1 A player who is a national of 2 or more countries at the same timemay represent either one of them, as he or she may elect.

3.5.1.3.2 After having represented one country in the Olympic Games, in continental or regional games or in world or regional championships recognised by the ITTF, a player may not represent another country unless he or she meets the conditions set forth in 3.5.1.3.3.

3.5.1.3.3 A player who has represented one country in the Olympic Games, in continental or regional games or in world or regional championships recognised by the ITTF and who has changed his or her nationality or acquired a new nationality, may participate in the Olympic

Games to represent his or her new country provided that at least 3 years have passed since the player last represented his or her former country.

3. 5. 1. 3. 4 The 3-years-period mentioned in 3. 5. 1. 3. 3 may be reduced or even cancelled, with the agreement of the NOCs concerned and the ITTF Executive Committee, by the IOC Executive Board, which takes into account the circumstances of each case.

3. 5. 1. 3. 5 If an associated state, province or overseas department, a country or colony acquires independence, if a country becomes incorporated within another country by reason of a change of border, or if a new NOC is recognised by the IOC, a player may continue to represent the country to which he or she belongs or belonged. However, he or she may, if he or she prefers, choose to represent his or her country or be entered in the Olympic Games by his or her new NOC if one exists. This particular choice may be made only once.

3. 5. 1. 4 All disputes relating to the determination of the country which a player may represent in the Olympic Games and in particular issue specific requirements relating to nationality, citizenship, domicile or residence of the player, including the duration of any waiting period, shall be resolved by the IOC Executive Board.

3. 5. 2 Events

3. 5. 2. 1 The Olympic competition shall include at least men's singles, women's singles, men's team and women's team events.

3. 5. 2. 2 The Team Match System in team events and the system of play in both team and individual events including any qualifying competitions shall be decided by the Board of Directors, on the recommendation of the Olympic and Paralympic Commission, and all Associations shall be notified in accordance with the schedule set by the IOC.

3. 5. 3 Doping Control

3. 5. 3. 1 Doping control shall be carried out in accordance with IOC rules.

第五篇　羽毛球

第一章　羽毛球竞赛规则及裁判法

1　球场及球场设施

1.1　球场应为一长方形场地，以40毫米宽的线条勾画，如图5－1所示。

1.2　勾画球场的线条应容易识别，最好使用白色或黄色。

1.3　所有线条都是它们所定义的区域的组成部分。

1.4　网柱距球场地面的高度应为1.55米，在球网按第1.10条款的要求拉紧时，网柱应保持垂直。

1.5　无论是单打还是双打比赛，网柱都应位于图5-1所示的双打边线之上。

1.6　球网应由深色、粗细均匀的优质绳索组成，网孔大小应在15毫米至20毫米之间。

1.7　球网应为760毫米高，至少6.1米宽。

1.8　球网的上端应有一条75毫米宽的双层白色带子，内裹一条绳索或绳缆贯穿其中。带子依靠中间的绳索支撑。

1.9　该绳索或绳缆应可以在两根网柱的上端稳固地伸拉平直。

1.10　球网上端距球场地面的高度，在球场中间处应为1.524米，在双打边线处应为1.55米。

1.11　球网左右两边与网柱间不应留有空隙。如有必要，球网的下端应绑定在网柱上。

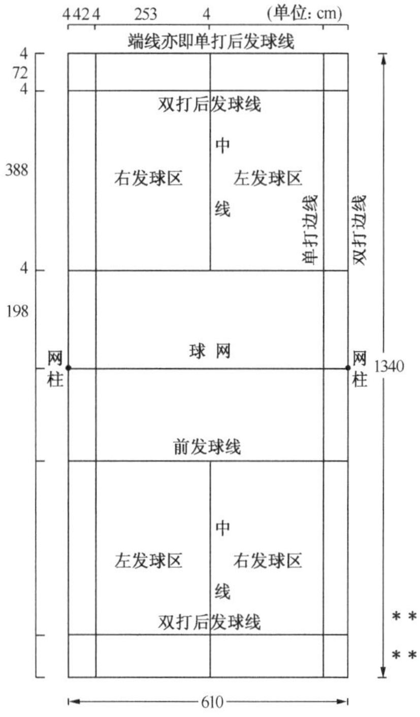

图5－1　羽毛球场地

注：(1) 此场地可用于单、双打比赛；
(2) 整个场地对角线长＝14.723m；
(3) "＊＊"为正常球速区标记。

2　羽毛球

2.1　羽毛球可以用天然或合成的材料制作。

无论使用何种材料制成，羽毛球的飞行特性都应该近似于用天然羽毛和带有皮革薄层的软木所制成的羽毛球。

2.2　用羽毛制作的球：

2.2.1　球上应有16根羽毛固定在软木托上。

2.2.2　羽毛的长度应统一，为62～70毫米之间，长度的测量是从羽毛尖到球托的顶部。

2.2.3　所有羽毛的尖应位于一个直径为58～68毫米的圆上。

2.2.4　羽毛应以细线或其他合适的材料固定好。

2.2.5　球托的直径应为 25～28 毫米，底部为圆球形。

2.2.6　球的重量应为 4.74～5.50 克。

2.3　非羽毛制作的球：

2.3.1　以合成材料制成的裙状物体或羽毛状物体替代天然羽毛。

2.3.2　球托要求同第 2.2.5 款。

2.3.3　尺寸和重量的要求同第 2.2.2、2.2.3 和 2.2.6 款。但是，由于合成材料在重力作用及其他特性方面与天然羽毛的差异，10% 以内的偏差是可接受的。

2.4　为保持羽毛球的设计、速度和飞行特性不变，在有关成员协会同意的前提下，以上规格可以改变，以适应不同地方因大气条件，如海拔或气候，导致标准羽毛球不适用。

3　测试羽毛球的速度

3.1　测试羽毛球时，一位球员应在球场后底线使用全力进行下手击球，球应以上前方角度被击打，并平行于边线。

3.2　正确速度的羽毛球应在比球场另一侧后底线短 530～990 毫米的地方落地，如图 5－2 所示。

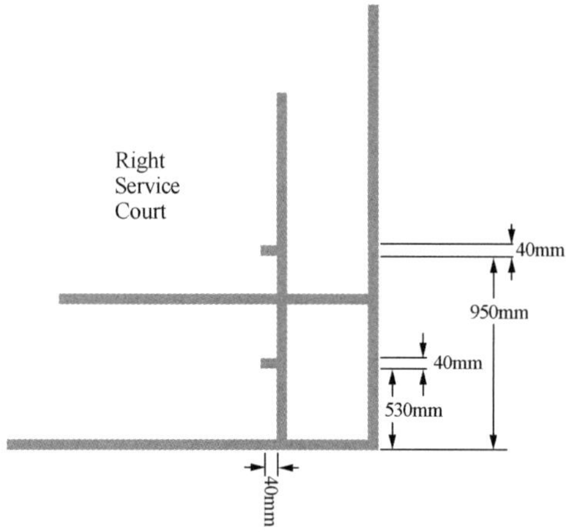

图 5－2　羽毛球正确速度的落点

4　球拍

4.1　球拍的全长不应超过 680 毫米，宽度不应超过 230 毫米，球拍由以下 4.4.1 至 4.4.5 款所述的主要部分组成，如图 5－3。

4.1.1　拍柄是球拍上给球员抓握的部分。

4.1.2　球拍上有弦的区域是用于球员击打羽毛球的部分。

4.1.3　拍头是有弦区域的边界。

4.1.4　拍杆用于连接拍柄和拍头(参见第 4.1.5 款)

4.1.5　连接喉(如有)用于连接拍杆与拍头。

4.2　有弦区域：

4.2.1　应平整，由相互交叉的拍弦构成，拍弦的距离应一致、均匀，不能出现中间

部分比其他部分密的情况；并且

4.2.2　长度不超过 280 毫米，宽度不超过 220 毫米。但是拍弦可以扩展至连接喉的区域，倘若：

4.2.3　扩展部分的弦的宽度不超过 35 毫米，并且

4.2.4　有弦区域的最大长度不超过 330 毫米。

4.3　球拍

4.3.1　不允许有附加物和突出部，除非是为了防止磨损、断裂、震动，或调整重心，或预防球拍脱手而将拍柄系在手上的绳索等单独特定的附加物，但尺寸和位置应合理；并且

4.3.2　不允许改变球拍的规定式样。

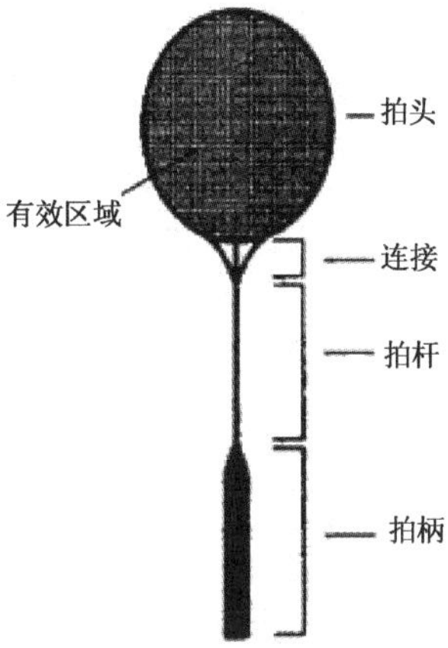

图 5－3　球拍的组成

5　器材的符合性

国际羽毛球联合会有权裁定比赛所用的球拍、羽毛球或其他器材是否符合以上规格。

6　掷币

6.1　比赛开始前，要进行掷币，胜出一方可以选择 6.1.1 或 6.1.2 之一：

6.1.1　先发球或先接发球；

6.1.2　选择某一方球场开始比赛。

6.2　掷币为负的一方进行另一项选择。

7　记分系统

7.1　一场比赛应该为三局两胜制，除非另有安排。

7.2　一局比赛中先得 21 分的一方为胜，第 7.4 和 7.5 款的情况除外。

7.3　赢得一次连续对打的一方加一分。赢得一次连续对打是指，对方违例或羽毛球因接触对方球场的地面而停止飞行。

7.4　如果比分为 20 平，首先赢得 2 分领先的一方为胜。

7.5　如果比分为 29 平，得到 30 分的一方为胜。

7.6　本局胜方将获得下一局的发球权。

8　交换场地

8.1　球员应在以下情况交换场地：

8.1.1　第一局结束时；

8.1.2　第二局结束时且有第三局；

8.1.3　第三局某一方先得 11 分时。

8.2　如果第 8.1 款所要求的换边没有被执行，则应在发现错误后且羽毛球没有在打时，立即交换场地，并保持已有分数不变。

9　发球

9.1　正确的发球：

9.1.1　一旦发球和接发球双方准备好发球，则任何一方都不得故意拖延发球。在发球方的球拍拍头后向移动完成后，任何对发球开始(第9.2款)的拖延，都可以被视为故意拖延；

9.1.2　发球方与接发球方应站在对角的发球区内(见图5-1)，不得接触各自发球区的边界线；

9.1.3　发球方和接发球方的双脚都必须接触球场地面，在发球开始(第9.2款)直至发球结束(第9.3款)，双脚不得移动；

9.1.4　发球方的球拍必须最初击打球的球托部分；

9.1.5　整个羽毛球在被球拍击打时必须低于发球方的腰部，腰部可以假想为围绕身体的一条线，位于发球者最低一根肋骨的最低部分；

9.1.6　发球方球拍的拍杆在击球时必须指向下方；

9.1.7　发球方球拍在发球开始(第9.2款)直至发球结束(第9.3款)，必须保持连续向前运动；

9.1.8　羽毛球的飞行应该从发球方的球拍向前上方越过球网，如果没有被拦截，球应该落入接球方的发球区内(包括边界线上)；

9.1.9　尝试发球时，发球方不得击不中球。

9.2　一旦球员准备好发球，发球方球拍拍头的首次向前移动即为发球开始。

9.3　一旦发球开始(第9.2款)，羽毛球被发球方球拍击中后，或企图发球但没有击中球，都视为发球结束。

9.4　接球方未准备好之前，发球方不得发球。但是如果接球方试图回球，则被视为已准备好。

9.5　双打的发球过程中(第9.2和9.3款)，发球一方不发球的球员可位于本方球场内任意位置，但不得阻挡发球方与接球方的视线。

10　单打

10.1　发球与接发球区

10.1.1　当发球方未得分或得分为偶数分时，双方球员应在本方场地的右发球区发球和接发球。

10.1.2　当发球方得分为奇数分时，双方球员应在本方场地的左发球区发球和接发球。

10.2　打球顺序及场地上的位置

在一次连续对打中，羽毛球应被发球方和接球方交替击打，从球员位于球网的一侧的任意位置，直至羽毛球停止(第15款)。

10.3　记分与发球

10.3.1　如果发球方赢得一次连续对打(第7.3款)，则发球方记一分。发球方从另一个发球区再次发球。

10.3.2　如果接发球方赢得一次连续对打(第7.3款)，则接发球方记一分。接发球方成为新的发球方。

11　双打

11.1　发球与接发球区

11.1.1　当发球一方未得分或得分为偶数分时，发球一方的球员应在本方场地的右发球区发球。

11.1.2　当发球一方得分为奇数分时，发球一方的球员应在本方场地的左发球区发球。

11.1.3　接发球一方中最后发球的球员应在其最后发球时所处的发球区内，另一位球员则在另一个发球区内。

11.1.4　接球一方中位于与发球球员对角线的发球区内的球员为接发球球员。

11.1.5　球员不应交换各自的场区，除非作为发球方赢得一分。

11.1.6　按以上轮转规则进行发球可以保证发球区对应于发球方的得分，除非出现第12款中的情况。

11.2　打球顺序及场地上的位置

在一次连续对打中，羽毛球被接发球方接回后，可以被发球一方和接球一方的任意一位球员交替击打，从球员位于球网的一侧的任意位置，直至羽毛球停止(第15款)。

11.3　记分与发球

11.3.1　如果发球方赢得一次连续对打(第7.3款)，则发球方记一分。发球方从另一个发球区再次发球。

11.3.2　如果接发球方赢得一次连续对打(第7.3款)，则接发球方记一分。接发球方成为新的发球方。

11.4　发球的顺序

在一局中，正确的发球顺序应该是：

11.4.1　首先发球的球员从右发球区开始比赛；

11.4.2　然后轮到首先接发球的球员的同伴；

11.4.3　然后轮到首先发球的球员的同伴；

11.4.4　然后轮到首先接发球的球员；

11.4.5　再回到首先发球的球员，并循环。

11.5　没有球员会不按以上顺序发球和接发球，也不会在同一局内连续接发球两次，除非是第12款的情况。

11.6　上一局的胜方中的任一名球员都可以在下一局首先发球，同样负方的任一名球员都可以首先接发球。

12　发球区错误

12.1　当某球员发生以下情况时，视为发球区错误：

12.1.1　不按顺序发球或接发球，或

12.1.2　从错误的发球区发球或接发球；

12.2　如果发现发球区错误，应立即纠正错误，并保持已有分数。

13 违例

以下情况为“违例”：

13.1 发球不正确(第9.1款)。

13.2 发球时，羽毛球：

13.2.1 触网并停留在网上；

13.2.2 越过网后，卡在网上；或

13.2.3 被接发球球员的同伴击打。

13.3 在对打过程中，羽毛球：

13.3.1 在球场边界以外落地(例如不是在边界上或边界内)；

13.3.2 在球网里或网下越过；

13.3.3 未能过网；

13.3.4 触到天花板或边墙；

13.3.5 触到球员的身体或衣服；

13.3.6 触到球场外的任何物体或人；（由于球场建筑物的需要，各地可修改关于羽毛球触到障碍物的条款细节)；

13.3.7 在一次击球中，球被球拍卡住然后再掷出；

13.3.8 被同一球员连续两次击打，但羽毛球在一次击打中同时击中拍头和有弦区域则不算“违例”；

13.3.9 被一方球员及其同伴连续击打；

13.3.10 触到球员的球拍，但未能回到对方球场。

13.4 在对打过程中，球员：

13.4.1 球拍、身体或衣服触到球网或支撑物；

13.4.2 球拍或身体从球网上方进入对方场地，以下情况除外：击球者在击球动作后球拍跟随球越过球网上方且击球点位于本方场地的；

13.4.3 球拍或身体从球网下方进入对方场地，阻碍或干扰了对方的；

13.4.4 阻挡对方，如当球在飞越球网上方时防止对方进行合法的击球动作；

13.4.5 以任何动作故意干扰对方，如大喊或做手势。

13.5 球员故意重复、持续违反第16款。

14 重发

14.1 “重发”可以由裁判或球员(没有裁判时)提出，以停止击球。

14.2 以下情况可以“重发”：

14.2.1 发球方在接球方准备好前发球(第9.4款)；

14.2.2 发球时，发球方和接球方都有违例；

14.2.3 发球被接回后，羽毛球：

14.2.3.1 触网且停留在网顶，或

14.2.3.2 过网后被网卡住；

14.2.4 击球过程中，羽毛球破裂，球托完全与羽毛分离；

14.2.5 裁判认为比赛混乱，或者一方球员认为被对方教练干扰；

14.2.6　司线裁判未看清且主裁判不能决定；或

14.2.7　任何未预料到的意外情况发生时。

14.3　发生“重发”时，最后一次发球后的比赛不计，由最后发球的球员重新发球。

15　死球

羽毛球在以下情况下为“死球”：

15.1　羽毛球击打到球网或网柱，并在击球者一方开始向地面下落；

15.2　羽毛球触到球场地面；或

15.3　发生“违例”或“重发”。

16　比赛的连续性，不当行为及处罚

16.1　从发球开始，直至比赛结束，比赛应持续进行，第 16.2 和 16.3 款的情况除外。

16.2　暂停：

16.2.1　每一局当一方先得到 11 分时，暂停不超过 60 秒；且

16.2.2　第一局与第二局之间，第二局与第三局之间，暂停不超过 120 秒。

16.2.3　为了电视转播，裁判长有权决定暂停的时长。

16.3　中止比赛：

16.3.1　当出现球员不能控制的情形时，裁判可以中止比赛，由裁判判断其必要性。

16.3.2　特殊情况下，裁判长可以命令裁判中止比赛。

16.3.3　比赛中止后，已有得分将被保持，比赛将从该得分起重新进行。

16.4　拖延比赛：

16.4.1　球员不得拖延比赛以恢复体力，或接受建议。

16.4.2　裁判是判定拖延比赛的唯一标准。

16.5　建议与离开球场：

16.5.1　比赛过程中，只有在羽毛球停止击球时（第 15 款），球员可以允许接受建议。

16.5.2　比赛过程中，没有裁判的许可，球员不得离开球场，除了第 16.2 款所描述的暂停外。

16.6　球员不得：

16.6.1　故意拖延或中止比赛；

16.6.2　故意弄坏羽毛球以改变球的速度和飞行特性；

16.6.3　采取无礼的行为；

16.6.4　采取其他未包含在本规则内的不当行为。

16.7　犯规的管理：

16.7.1　裁判负责对第 16.4，16.5，16.6 款的犯规行为执行：

16.7.1.1　向犯规一方提出警告；

16.7.1.2　对已警告过的犯规方进行罚分。同一方两次以上罚分可被视为连续犯规；

16.7.2　对于严重犯规、连续犯规，或违反第 16.2 款，裁判应对犯规方罚分并立即报告裁判长，裁判长有权判定犯规方丧失比赛资格。

17　各级官员及上诉

17.1　裁判长负责全面掌管整个赛事。

17.2　主裁判仅负责一场比赛、球场及其周边环境。主裁判应向裁判长汇报。

17.3　发球裁判负责指出发球球员的发球违例（第9.1款）。

17.4　司线裁判负责指出羽毛球落地时是在边线的“里”或“外”。

17.5　当主裁判有理由怀疑司线裁判错误时，有权更改司线裁判的判决。

17.6　主裁判应：

17.6.1　支持并执行本规则，在发生“违例”或“重发”时要提出；

17.6.2　在下一次发球之前，对于任何一方的上诉进行判决；

17.6.3　确保球员和观众清晰获知比赛的进展情况；

17.6.4　与裁判长商讨后委任或更换司线裁判或发球裁判；

17.6.5　当某个官员的未指定时，安排人员执行该官员的职责；

17.6.6　当某个指定的官员未看清时，执行该官员的职责，或提出“重发”；

17.6.7　记录下所有第16款相关的事件，并报告裁判长；

17.6.8　向裁判长上报所有未得到满足的上诉（这些上诉应在下一次发球前，或在比赛结束后投诉方未离开球场前处理）。

第二章 羽毛球裁判员法定手势

1 主裁判

（1）停止练习

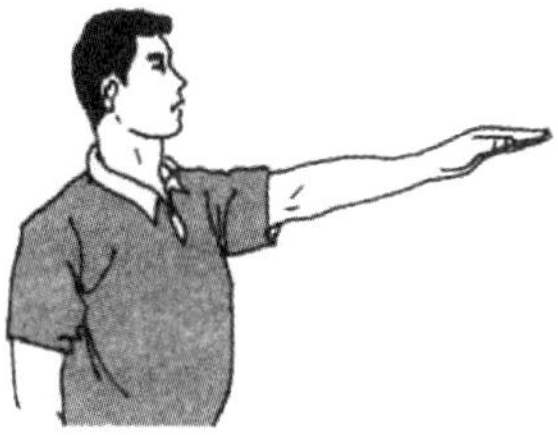

（2）换发球(向轮到发球方的一侧示意)

（3）第二发球、连击

（4）持球、拖带

（5）触网

（6）过网击球

（7）暂停

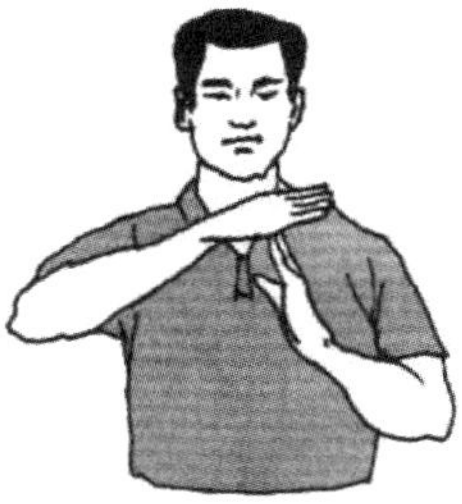

（8）交换场地

（9）方位错误

（10）得分

（11）警告

2　发球时裁判员的手势要求

（1）过手：击球瞬间，球拍杆未指向下方，整个拍头未明显低于发球员的整个握拍手。

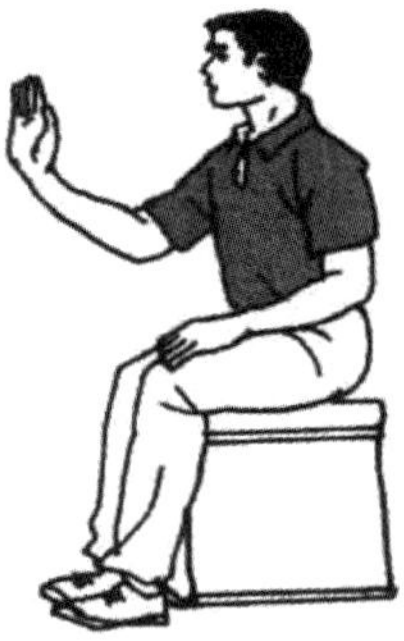

（2）过腰：击球瞬间，球的整体未低于发球员的腰部。

（3）不正当的延误发球的击出。一旦双方站好位置，发球员的球拍头第一次向前挥拍为发球开始，挥拍必须连续向前。

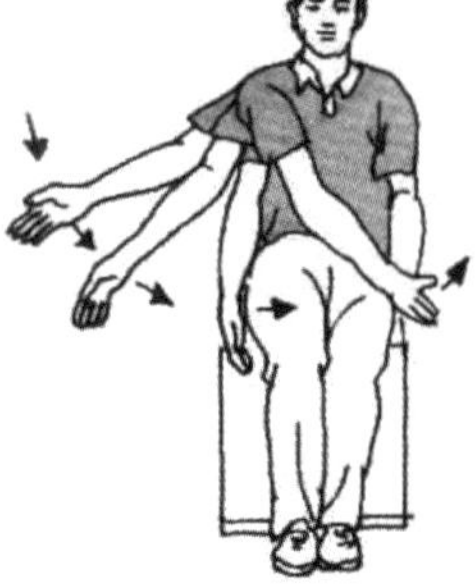

（4）发球击出前，脚在不发球区、触线或移动。

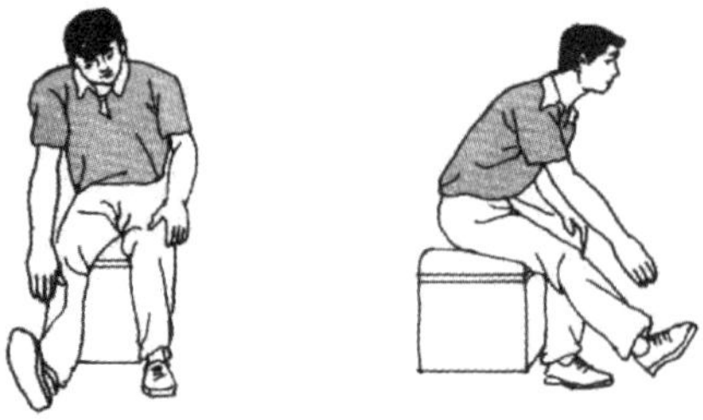

（5）最初的击球点不在球托上。

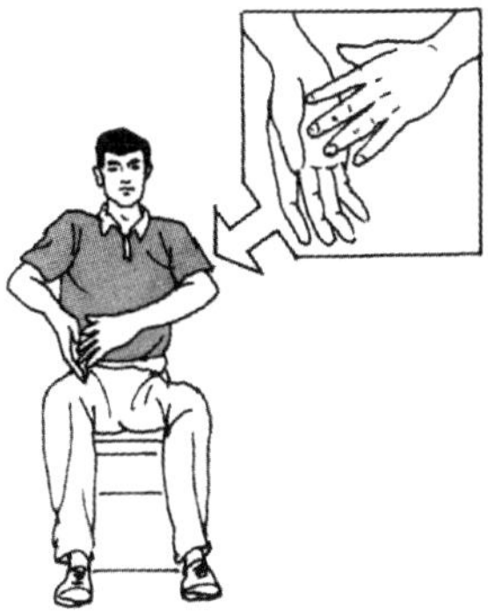

3 司线员的手势

司线员应坐在他所负责的延长线上，最好面向裁判员，在实际安排时，司线员的位置与场地的理想距离约 2. 5 米至 3. 5 米。

（1）界外：如果球落在界外，无论多远，均应立即大声清晰地报“界外”使运动员和观众都能听清，同时两臂侧举，使裁判员能看得清楚。

（2）界内：如果球落在界内，只用右手指向界内。

（3）如果视线被挡，应立即举起双手，盖住眼睛。

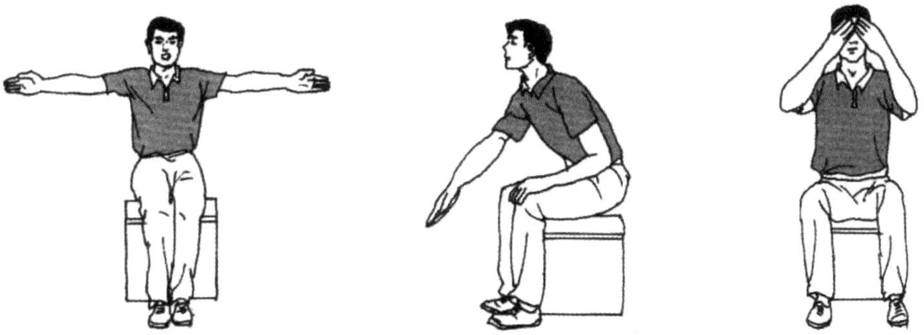

界外　　界内　　视线被挡

第三章 羽毛球英文规则

1 Court and Court Equipment

1.1 The court shall be a rectangle marked out with lines 40 mm wide as shown in Diagram A.

1.2 The lines marking out the court shall be easily distinguishable and preferably be coloured white or yellow.

1.3 All the lines shall form part of the area which they define.

1.4 The posts shall be 1.55 metres in height from the surface of the court and shall remain vertical when the net is strained as provided in Law 1.10. The posts or its supports shall not extend into the court.

1.5 The posts shall be placed on the doubles side lines irrespective of whether singles or doubles is being played.

1.6 The net shall be made of fine cord of dark colour and even thickness with a mesh of not less than 15 mm and not more than 20 mm.

1.7 The net shall be 760 mm in depth and at least 6.1 metres wide.

1.8 The top of the net shall be edged with a 75 mm white tape doubled over a cord or cable running through the tape. This tape shall rest upon the cord or cable.

1.9 The cord or cable shall be stretched firmly, flush with the top of the posts.

1.10 The top of the net from the surface of the court shall be 1.524 metres at the centre of the court and 1.55 metres over the side lines for doubles.

1.11 There shall be no gaps between the ends of the net and the posts. If necessary, the full depth of the net at the ends shall be tied to the posts.

2 Shuttle

2.1 The shuttle shall be made of natural and / or synthetic materials. From whatever material the shuttle is made, the flight characteristics generally shall be similar to those produced by a natural feathered shuttle with a cork base covered by a thin layer of leather.

2.2 Feathered Shuttle:

2.2.1 The shuttle shall have 16 feathers fixed in the base.

2.2.2 The feathers shall have a uniform length between 62 mm to 70 mm when measured from the tip to the top of the base.

2.2.3 The tips of the feathers shall lie on a circle with a diameter from 58 mm to 68 mm.

2.2.4 The feathers shall be fastened firmly with thread or other suitable material.

2.2.5 The base shall be 25 mm to 28 mm in diameter and rounded on the bottom.

2.2.6 The shuttle shall weigh from 4.74 to 5.50 grams.

2.3 Non-Feathered Shuttle:

2.3.1 The skirt, or simulation of feathers in synthetic materials, shall replace natural feathers.

2.3.2 The base shall be as described in Law 2.2.5.

2.3.3 Measurements and weight shall be as in Laws 2.2.2, 2.2.3 and 2.2.6. However, because of the difference in the specific gravity and other properties of synthetic materials in comparison with feathers, a variation of up to 10 per cent shall be acceptable.

2.4 Subject to there being no variation in the general design, speed and flight of the shuttle, modifications in the above specifications may be made with the approval of the Member Association concerned, in places where atmospheric conditions due to either altitude or climate make the standard shuttle unsuitable.

3 Testing a Shuttle for Speed

3.1 To test a shuttle, a player shall use a full underhand stroke which makes contact with the shuttle over the back boundary line. The shuttle shall be hit at an upward angle and in a direction parallel to the side lines.

3.2 A shuttle of correct speed will land not less than 530 mm and not more than 990 mm short of the other back boundary line.

4 Racket

4.1 The racket shall be a frame not exceeding 680 mm in overall length and 230 mm in overall width consisting of the main parts described in Laws 4.1.1 to 4.1.5.

C.

4.1.1 The handle is the part of the racket intended to be gripped by a player.

4.1.2 The stringed area is the part of the racket with which it is intended that a player hits the shuttle.

4.1.3 The head bounds the stringed area.

4.1.4 The shaft connects the handle to the head (subject to Law 4.1.5).

4.1.5 The throat (if present) connects the shaft to the head.

4.2 The stringed area:

4.2.1 shall be flat and consist of a pattern of crossed strings either alternately interlaced or bonded where they cross. The stringing pattern shall be generally uniform and, in particular, not less dense in the centre than in any other area; and

4.2.2 shall not exceed 280 mm in overall length and 220 mm in overall width. However, the strings may extend into an area which otherwise would be the throat, provided that:

4.2.3 the width of the extended stringed area does not exceed 35 mm; and

4.2.4 the overall length of the stringed area does not then exceed 330 mm.

4.3 The racket:

4.3.1 shall be free of attached objects and protrusions, other than those used solely and specifically to limit or prevent wear and tear, or vibration, or to distribute weight, or to secure the handle by cord to the player's hand, and which are reasonable in size and placement for such purposes; and

4.3.2 shall be free of any device that makes it possible for a player to change materially the shape of the racket.

5 Equipment Compliance

The International Badminton Federation shall rule on any question of whether any racket, shuttle or equipment or any prototype used in the playing of Badminton complies with the specifications. Such ruling may be undertaken on the Federation's initiative or on application by any party with a bona fide interest, including any player, technical official, equipment manufacturer or Member Association or member thereof.

6 Toss

6.1 Before play commences, a toss shall be conducted and the side winning the toss shall exercise the choice in either Law 6.1.1 or 6.1.2:

6.1.1 to serve or receive first;

6.1.2 to start play at one end of the court or the other.

6.2 The side losing the toss shall then exercise the remaining choice.

7 Scoring System

7.1 A match shall consist of the best of three games, unless otherwise arranged (Appendix 2 and 3).

7.2 A game shall be won by the side which first scores 21 points, except as provided in Law 7.4 and 7.5.

7.3 The side winning a rally shall add a point to its score. A side shall win a rally, if the opposing side commits a 'fault' or the shuttle ceases to be in play because it touches the surface of the court inside the opponent's court.

7.4 If the score becomes 20-all, the side which gains a two point lead first, shall win that game.

7.5 If the score becomes 29-all, the side scoring the 30th point shall win that game.

7.6 The side winning a game shall serve first in the next game.

8 Change of ends

8.1 Players shall change ends:

8.1.1 at the end of the first game;

8.1.2 at the end of the second game, if there is to be a third game; and

8.1.3 in the third game when a side first scores 11 points.

8.2 If the ends are not changed as indicated in Law 8.1, it shall be done so as soon as the mistake is discovered and when the shuttle is not in play. The existing score shall stand.

9 Service

9.1 In a correct service:

9.1.1 neither side shall cause undue delay to the delivery of the service once the server and the receiver are ready for the service. On completion of the backward movement of server's racket head, any delay in the start of the service (Law 9.2), shall be considered to be an undue delay.

9.1.2 the server and the receiver shall stand within diagonally opposite service courts (Diagram A) without touching the boundary lines of these service courts;

9.1.3 some part of both feet of the server and the receiver shall remain in contact with the surface of the court in a stationary position from the start of the service (Law 9.2) until the service is delivered (Law 9.3);

9.1.4 the server's racket shall initially hit the base of the shuttle;

9.1.5 the whole shuttle shall be below the server's waist at the instant of being hit by the server's racket. The waist shall be considered to be an imaginary line round the body, level with the lowest part of the server's bottom rib;

9.1.6 the shaft of the server's racket at the instant of hitting the shuttle shall be pointing in a downward direction;

9.1.7 the movement of the server's racket shall continue forwards from the start of the service (Law 9.2) until the service is delivered (Law 9.3);

9.1.8 the flight of the shuttle shall be upwards from the server's racket to pass over the net so that, if not intercepted, it shall land in the receiver's service court (i. e. on or within the boundary lines); and

9.1.9 in attempting to serve, the server shall not miss the shuttle.

9.2 Once the players are ready for the service, the first forward movement of the server's racket head shall be the start of the service.

9.3 Once started (Law 9.2), the service is delivered when the shuttle is hit by the server's racket or, in attempting to serve, the server misses the shuttle.

9.4 The server shall not serve before the receiver is ready. However, the receiver shall be considered to have been ready if a return of the service is attempted.

9.5 In doubles, during the delivery of service (Law 9.2, 9.3), the partners may take up any positions within their respective courts, which do not unsight the opposing server or receiver.

10 Singles

10.1 Serving and receiving courts

10.1.1 The players shall serve from, and receive in, their respective right service courts when the server has not scored or has scored an even number of points in that game.

10.1.2 The players shall serve from, and receive in, their respective left service courts when the server has scored an odd number of points in that game.

10.2 Order of play and position on court

In a rally, the shuttle may be hit by the server and the receiver alternately, from any position on that player's side of the net, until the shuttle ceases to be in play (Law 15).

10.3 Scoring and serving

10.3.1 If the server wins a rally (Law 7.3), the server shall score a point. The server shall then serve again from the alternate service court.

10.3.2 If the receiver wins a rally (Law 7.3), the receiver shall score a point. The receiver shall then become the new server.

11 Doubles

11.1 Serving and receiving courts

11.1.1 A player of the serving side shall serve from the right service court when the serving side has not scored or has scored an even number of points in that game.

11.1.2 A player of the serving side shall serve from the left service court when the serving side has scored an odd number of points in that game.

11.1.3 The player of the receiving side who served last shall stay in the same service court from where he served last. The reverse pattern shall apply to the receiver's partner.

11.1.4 The player of the receiving side standing in the diagonally opposite service court to the server shall be the receiver.

11.1.5 The players shall not change their respective service courts until they win a point when their side is serving.

11.1.6 Service in any turn of serving shall be delivered from the service court corresponding to the serving side's score, except as provided in Law 12.

11.2 Order of play and position on court

After the service is returned, in a rally, the shuttle may be hit by either player of the serving side and either player of the receiving side alternately, from any position on that player's side of the net, until the shuttle ceases to be in play (Law 15).

11.3 Scoring and serving

11.3.1 If the serving side wins a rally (Law 7.3), the serving side shall score a point. The server shall then serve again from the alternate service court.

11.3.2 If the receiving side wins a rally (Law 7.3), the receiving side shall score a point. The receiving side shall then become the new serving side.

11.4 Sequence of serving

11.4.1 In any game, the right to serve shall pass consecutively:

11.4.2 from the initial server who started the game from the right service court;

11.4.3 to the partner of the initial receiver;

11.4.4 to the partner of the initial server;

11.4.5 to the initial receiver;

11.4.6 to the initial server and so on.

11.5 No player shall serve or receive out of turn, or receive two consecutive services in the same game, except as provided in Law 12.

11.6 Either player of the winning side may serve first in the next game, and either player of the losing side may receive first in the next game.

12 Service court errors

12.1 A service court error has been made when a player:

12.1.1 has served or received out of turn; or

12.1.2 has served or received from the wrong service court;

12.2 If a service court error is discovered, the error shall be corrected and the existing score shall stand.

13 Faults

It shall be a 'fault':

13.1 if a service is not correct (Law 9.1);

13.2 if, in service, the shuttle:

13.2.1 is caught on the net and remains suspended on its top;

13.2.2 after passing over the net, is caught in the net; or

13.2.3 is hit by the receiver's partner;

13.3 if in play, the shuttle:

13.3.1 lands outside the boundaries of the court (i.e. not on or within the boundary lines);

13.3.2 passes through or under the net;

13.3.3 fails to pass over the net;

13.3.4 touches the ceiling or side walls;

13.3.5 touches the person or dress of a player;

13.3.6 touches any other object or person outside the court;

(Where necessary on account of the structure of the building, the local badminton authority may, subject to the right of veto of its Member Association, make bye-laws dealing with cases in which a shuttle touches an obstruction).

13.3.7 is caught and held on the racket and then slung during the execution of a stroke;

13.3.8 is hit twice in succession by the same player. However, a shuttle hitting the head and the stringed area of the racket in one stroke shall not be a 'fault';

13.3.9 is hit by a player and the player's partner successively; or

13.3.10 touches a player's racket and does not travel towards the opponent's court;

13.4 if, in play, a player:

13.4.1 touches the net or its supports with racket, person or dress;

13.4.2 invades an opponent's court over the net with racket or person except that the striker may follow the shuttle over the net with the racket in the course of a stroke after the initial point of contact with the shuttle is on the striker's side of the net;

13.4.3 invades an opponent's court under the net with racket or person such that an opponent is obstructed or distracted; or

13.4.4 obstructs an opponent, i.e. prevents an opponent from making a legal stroke where the shuttle is followed over the net;

13.4.5 deliberately distracts an opponent by any action such as shouting or making gestures;

13.5 if a player is guilty of flagrant, repeated or persistent offences under Law 16.

14 Lets

14.1 'Let' shall be called by the umpire, or by a player (if there is no umpire), to halt play.

14.2 It shall be a "let", if:

14.2.1 the server serves before the receiver is ready (Law 9.4);

14.2.2 during service, the receiver and the server are both faulted;

14.2.3 after the service is returned, the shuttle is:

14.2.3.1 caught on the net and remains suspended on its top, or

14.2.3.2 after passing over the net is caught in the net;

14.2.4 during play, the shuttle disintegrates and the base completely separates from the rest of the shuttle;

14.2.5 in the opinion of the umpire, play is disrupted or a player of the opposing side is distracted by a coach;

14.2.6 a line judge is unsighted and the umpire is unable to make a decision; or

14.2.7 unforeseen or accidental situation has occurred.

14.3 When a 'let' occurs, play since the last service shall not count and the player who served last shall serve again.

15 Shuttle not in play

A shuttle is not in play when:

15.1 it strikes the net or post and starts to fall towards the surface of the court on the striker's side of the net;

15.2 it hits the surface of the court; or

15.3 a 'fault' or a 'let' has occurred.

16 Continuous play, Misconduct & Penalties

16.1 Play shall be continuous from the first service until the match is concluded, except as allowed in Laws 16.2 and 16.3.

16.2 Intervals:

not exceeding 60 seconds during each game when the leading score reaches 11 points; and

not exceeding 120 seconds between the first and second game, and between the second and third game shall be allowed in all matches.

(For a televised match, the Referee may decide before the match that intervals as in Law 16.2 are mandatory and of fixed duration).

16.3 Suspension of play

16.3.1 When necessitated by circumstances not within the control of the players, the umpire may suspend play for such a period as the umpire may consider necessary.

16.3.2 Under special circumstances the Referee may instruct the umpire to suspend play.

16.3.3 If play is suspended, the existing score shall stand and play shall be resumed from that point.

16.4 Delay in play

16.4.1 Under no circumstances shall play be delayed to enable a player to recover strength or wind or to receive advice.

16.4.2 The umpire shall be the sole judge of any delay in play.

16.5 Advice and leaving the court

16.5.1 Only when the shuttle is not in play (Law 15), shall a player be permitted to receive advice during a match.

16.5.2 No player shall leave the court during a match without the umpire's permission, except during the intervals as described in Law 16.2.

16.6 A player shall not:

16.6.1 deliberately cause delay in, or suspension of, play;

16.6.2 deliberately modify or damage the shuttle in order to change its speed or its flight;

16.6.3 behave in an offensive manner; or

16.6.4 be guilty of misconduct not otherwise covered by the Laws of Badminton.

16.7 Administration of breach

16.7.1 The umpire shall administer any breach of Law 16.4, 16.5 or 16.6 by:

16.7.1.1 issuing a warning to the offending side;

16.7.1.2 faulting the offending side, if previously warned. Two such faults by a side shall be considered to be a persistent offence; or

16.7.2 in cases of flagrant offence, persistent offences or breach of Law 16.2, the umpire shall fault the offending side and report the offending side immediately to the Referee, who shall have the power to disqualify the offending side from the match.

17 Officials and appeals

17.1 The Referee shall be in overall charge of the tournament or event of which a match forms part.

17.2 The umpire, where appointed, shall be in charge of the match, the court and its immediate surrounds. The umpire shall report to the Referee.

17.3 The service judge shall call service faults made by the server should they occur (Law 9.1).

17.4 A line judge shall indicate whether a shuttle landed 'in' or 'out' on the line(s) assigned.

17.5 An official's decision shall be final on all points of fact for which that official is responsible except that if, in the opinion of the umpire, it is beyond reasonable doubt that a line judge has clearly made a wrong call, the umpire shall overrule the decision of the line judge.

17.6 An umpire shall:

17.6.1 uphold and enforce the Laws of Badminton and, especially, call a ‘fault’ or a ‘let’ should either occur;

17.6.2 give a decision on any appeal regarding a point of dispute, if made before the next service is delivered;

17.6.3 ensure players and spectators are kept informed of the progress of the match;

17.6.4 appoint or replace line judges or a service judge in consultation with the Referee;

17.6.5 where another court official is not appointed, arrange for that official's duties to be carried out;

17.6.6 where an appointed official is unsighted, carry out that official's duties or play a ‘let’;

17.6.7 record and report to the Referee all matters relating to Law 16; and

17.6.8 refer to the Referee all unsatisfied appeals on questions of law only. (Such appeals must be made before the next service is delivered or, if at the end of the match, before the side that appeals has left the court).

第六篇　网　球

第一章 网球竞赛规则与裁判法

1 场地

网球场地应该是长方形，长度为23.77米(78英尺)，单打比赛的场地宽度为8. 23米(27英尺)，双打比赛场地的宽度为10.97米(36英尺)。

场地由一条挂在绳索或钢丝绳上的球网，从中间处分隔开，所使用的绳索或钢丝绳附着或挂在1.07米(3.5英尺)高的两根网柱上；球网应充分伸展开，使之能够填满两个网柱之间的空间，其上网孔的大小以确保球不能穿过为宜。球网中心的高度应当为0.914米(3英尺)，并且用中心带向下绷紧固定，网绳或钢丝绳和球网的上端应当用一条网带包裹住，中心带和网带都应完全为白色。

- 网绳或钢丝绳的最大直径为0.8厘米(0.33英寸)。
- 中心带的最大宽度应为5厘米(2英寸)。
- 球网每一边垂直向下的网带宽度应当在5厘米(2英寸)与6. 35厘米(2.5英寸)之间。

双订比赛中，每侧网住的中心应距双打场地的外沿0.9114米(3英尺)。

单打比赛中，如果使用单打球网，每侧网柱的中心应距单打场地的外沿0.914米(3英尺)。如果使用双打球网，那么球网要用两根高1.07米(3.5英尺)的单打支柱支撑起来，每侧单打支柱的中心距单打场地的外沿0.914米(3英尺)。

- 网柱的边长不应超过15厘米(6英寸)或直径不应超过15厘米(6英寸)。
- 单打支柱的边长不应超过7.5厘米(3英寸)或直径不应超过7.5厘米(3英寸)。
- 网柱和单打支柱的上端不能超过网绳顶端以上2.5厘米(1英寸)。

球场两端的界线称为底线，两侧的界线称为边线。

在两条单打边线之间画两条距球网6.40米(21英尺)并且与球网平行的线，这两条线称为发球线。在球网每一边的发球线和球网之间的区域，被一条发球中线分成相同的两个部分称为发球区，发球中线应当和单打边线平行并且与两条边线的距离相等。

每一条底线都被一条长10厘米(4英寸)的中心标志分为相等的两部分，中心标志要被画在场地内并且和单打边线平行。

- 发球中线和中心标志的宽度为5厘米(2英寸)。
- 除底线的最大宽度可以为10厘米(4英寸)外，场上其他所有线的宽度均应介于2.5厘米(1英寸)和5厘米(2英寸)之间。

所有场地的测量都应以线的外沿为标准，所有场地上的线的颜色均必须相同，并且和场地的颜色有明显的区别。

除附录Ⅲ中的规定之外，在球场、球网、中心带、网带、网柱或单打支柱上均不允许有广告。

2　永久固定物

场地上的永久固定物，不仅包括后档网和侧挡网、观众、观众的座位和看台，以及所有场地周围和上方的固定物。而且还应包括处于各自规定位置的主裁判、司线员、司网裁判和球童。

在一个使用双打球网支柱的场地上举行单打比赛时，网柱、单打支柱以外的球网部分属于场地上的永久固定物，而不能视其为网柱或球网的一部分。

3　球

在比赛中根据网球规则被允许使用的球必须符合附录Ⅰ的规定。

国际网联将对任何关于某种球或式样是否符合附录Ⅰ的标准，以及是否可以被批准用于比赛的问题进行裁决。国际网联既可以自行作出此类裁决，也可以根据所有对此真正感兴趣的团体或个人，包括任何的运动员，器材生产厂商或国家网球协会或其会员等所提出的申请进行裁决。这类申请与裁决应当按照国际网联的审查与听证程序来进行（参见附录Ⅶ）。

赛事组织者必须在赛前公布：

（1）比赛中用球的数量（2 个、3 个、4 个或 6 个）；

（2）换球的方案。

如果换球，可采用以下方式的任何一种：

（1）在一个规定换球的单数局结束后。在这种情况下，由于热身活动用球的原因，比赛中第一次换球必须比整场比赛的其他任何时候的换球要提前两局。平局决胜局的换球时也作为一局计算，但如果换球时刚好是平局决胜局开始时，则不应当换球。这种情况下，换球应当推迟到下一盘第二局的开始前；或者按以下方法进行：

（2）在一盘的开始时换球。

如果在比赛期间球破了，这一分应当重赛。

判例 1：如果在赛完一分后发现球软了，这一分球是否应重赛？

答案：如果只是球软了而没有破，这一分不应重赛。

注：在按照网球规则进行的比赛中，任何用球都必须是由国际网联颁布的已被列入官方名字上的批准用球。

4　球拍

在比赛中按照网球规则被允许使用的球拍必须符合附录Ⅱ的特别说明。

国际网联将对任何关于某种球拍或式样是否符合附录Ⅱ的标准，以及是否可以被批准用于比赛的问题进行裁决。国际网联既可以自行作出此类裁决，也可以根据所有对此真正感兴趣的团体或个人，包括任何的运动员，器材生产厂商，或国家网球协会或其会员等所提出的申请来进行裁决。这类申请与裁决应当按照国际网联的审查与听证程序来进行（参见附录Ⅶ）。

判例 1：可否允许球拍击球面有超过一盘的弦线？

答案：不可以，规则中提到交叉的弦线只能是一种式样，而不是几种式样（参见附录Ⅱ）。

判例2：如果弦线是在一个以上的平面上，是否可以认为弦线组成的式样大体是一致的和平坦的？

答案：不可以。

判例3：减振器是否可以安装在球拍的弦线上，如果可以，应当安装在什么位置？

答案：可以，但这种器材只能安装在交叉弦线组成的式样之外。

判例4：在一分的比赛中，一名运动员的弦线突然断了，他可以用这把球拍继续比下一分吗？

答案：可以，但赛事组织者特别规定禁止的除外。

判例5：在比赛中的任何时候，运动员可否使用一把以上的球拍？

答案：不可以。

判例6：可以在球拍内嵌入会影响击球特性的电池吗？

答案：不可以，不能使用电池、太阳能电池或其他类似带有能源动力的设备。

5 一局中的计分

5.1 常规局

在一个常规局的比赛中，报分时应当先报发球运动员的比分，计分如下：

无得分——0

第一分——15

第二分——30

第三分——40

第四分——局比赛结束

若两名运动员/队都获得三分，则比分为“平分”。“平分”后如果一名运动员/队获得了下一分。则比分为“占先”。如果“占先”的这名运动员/队又获得了下一分，他即赢得了这一局；如果“占先”后是另一名运动员/队获得了一分，则比分仍为“平分”。一名运动员/队需要在“平分”后连续获得两分，该运动员/队才能赢得这一局。

5.2 平局决胜局

在平局决胜局中，使用0、1、2、3 分等来计分，首先赢得 7 分并净胜对手两分的运动员/队赢得这一局及这一盘。在需要时决胜局必须继续进行直到一方运动员/队净胜对手两分为止。

轮及应该发球的运动员在平局决胜局中首先发第一分球，随后的两分由他的对手发球(在双打比赛中，对方队中轮及应该发球的运动员进行发球)。此后，每一名运动员/队轮流连续地发两分球直到下局决胜局结束(在双打比赛中，两队应按照与该盘中相同的发球顺序轮流连续发球)。

在平局决胜局中首先发球的运动员/队应当在下一盘的第一局开始时首先接发球。

其他已被批准的可供选择的计分方法参见附录Ⅳ。

6 一盘中的计分

一盘中的计分有不同的方法。主要的计分方法是“长盘制”和“平局决胜局制”两种。比赛中两种计分方法中的任何一种都可以使用，但必须在赛前事先宣布。如果使用的是“平局决胜局制”的计分方法，还必须声明决胜盘将采用的是“平局决胜局制”还是“长盘制”。

6.1 “长盘制”

先赢得 6 局并净胜对手两局的运动员/队才赢得这一盘。如果需要的话，这一盘必须持续到一方运动员/队净胜两局为止。

6.2 “平局决胜制”

先赢得 6 局并净胜对手两局的运动员/队才赢得这一盘。如果局数比分达到 6:6 时，则需进行“平局决胜局”。

其他已被批准的可供选择的计分方法可见附录Ⅳ。

7 一场比赛的计分

一场比赛可以采用三盘两胜制，先赢得两盘的运动员/队赢得这场比赛；或采用五盘三胜制，先赢得三盘的运动员/队赢得这场比赛。

其他已被批准的可供选择的计分方法可参见附录Ⅳ。

8 发球员和接发球员

运动员/队应当分别相对站于球网两侧。发球员是指在开始比赛时发出第一分球的运动员，接发球员是指准备回击发球员所发出球的运动员。

判例 1：接发球员可以站在场地界线以外的地方接球。

答案：可以。接发球员可以随意站在属于他自己球网一侧的场地内或场地外的任何位置接球。

9 场地和发球的选择

在准备活动开始前，通过掷币的方式决定获得挑选场地和比赛的第一局谁作为发球员或接发球员的权利。掷币获胜的运动员/队可以进行以下方式的选择：

（1）在比赛的第一局中选择发球员或接发球员，在这种情况下，对手应选择在比赛的第一局所处哪一边的场地；

（2）选择在比赛的第一局所处哪一边的场地，在这种情况下，对手应选择在比赛的第一局作为发球员或接发球员；

（3）要求对手对以上两种方法作出任何一种的选择。

判例 1：如果准备活动被中断，运动员离开了场地，双方运动员/队是否有重新选择的权利？

答案：是的，原掷币结果仍然有效，但是双方运动员/队都有权利重新选择。

10 交换场地

运动员应在每一盘的第一局、第三局和随后的每一个单数局结束后交换场地。运动员还应在每一盘结束后交换场地，除非在这盘结束后双方所得局数之和为偶数时，在这种情况下运动员则在下一盘第一局结束后交换场地。

在平局决胜局中，运动员应在每 6 分后交换场地。

其他已被批准的可供选择的相关程序参见附录Ⅳ。

11 活球期

除了做出发球失误或重发的呼报之外，球从发球员击出的那一时刻开始直到该分结束都为活球。

12 压线球

如果球接触到线，则这个球被认为是落在由该线作为界线的场地之内。

13 球触永久固定物

如果活球状态下的球落在正确的场地内后弹起触到了永久固定物，则击出该球的运动员赢得该分；如果活球状态下的球在落地前触到了永久固定物，则击出该球的运动员失分。

14 发球次序

在每一个常规局结束后，该局的接发球员在下一局中应该成为发球员，该局的发球员在下一局中应该成为接发球员。

双打比赛中，在每一盘第一局开始前，由先发球的那队选手决定哪一名运动员先在该局发球，同样地，在第二局开始前，他们的对手也应当作出由谁在该局发球的决定。第一局先发球的运动员的同伴在第三局发球。第二局先发球运动员的同伴在第四局发球。这个轮换次序一直延续，直到该盘结束。

15 双打的接发球次序

在每一盘的第一局，首先接发球的那队要决定哪一名运动员在该局接第一分发球。同样，在第二局开始前，他们的对手也应当决定哪一名运动员在该局接第一分发球。先接第一分发球的运动员的同伴应当接本局的第二分发球，这个次序一直延续，直到该局和该盘结束。

接球员接完发球后，该队中的任何一名运动员都可以回击球。

判例 1：可以允许双打搭档中的一名运动员单独和对手进行比赛吗？

答案：不可以。

16 发球

在开始发球动作前，发球员必须立即双脚站在底线后（即远离球网的那一侧），中心标志的假定延长线和边线的假定延长线之内的区域里。

然后，发球员应当用手将球向任何方向抛出并在球触地前用球拍将球击出，在球拍击到球或没有击到球的那一刻，整个发球动作即被认为已经完成。对于只能使用一只手臂的运动员，可以用他的球拍完成抛球。

17 发球的程序

在一个常规发球局中，每一局的发球员都应当从场地的右半区开始，交替站在同侧场地的两个半区后面发球。

在平局决胜局中，第一分发球应当从场地的右半区开始发出，然后交替从场地的两个半区后面发球。

发出的球应当越过球网，在接球员回击发球之前落到对角方向的发球区内。

18 脚误

在发球的整个动作过程中，发球员不可以有以下动作：

（1）通过走动或跑动来改变位置，但脚步轻微地移动是允许的；

（2）或者任何一只脚触及底线或场地内的地面；

（3）或者任何一只脚触及边线假定延长线外的地面；

（4）或者任何一只脚触及中心标志的假定延长线。

如果发球员违反了这些规定就是一次“脚误”。

判例1：在单打比赛中，发球员可否站在底线后的单打边线与双打边线之间的位置发球？

答案：不可以。

判例2：发球过程中是否允许发球员的一只脚或者双脚离开地面？

答案：可以。

19 发球失误

下列情况为一次发球失误：

（1）发球员违反了规则第16、17或18条；

（2）或者发球员试图击球时未能击中；

（3）或者发出的球在触地前碰到了永久固定物、单打支柱或网柱；

（4）或者发出的球触到了发球员或发球员的同伴，或发球员和发球员同伴所穿戴的或携带的任何物品。

判例1：在发球时，发球员将球抛出后决定不击球而接住球，这是一次发球失误吗？

答案：不是。一名运动员将球抛出后决定不击球，而用手或球拍将球接住，或让球落在地上是允许的。

判例2：单打比赛在有网柱和单打支柱场地上进行，发球时球击中了单打支柱后落在了有效的发球区内，这一次发球失误吗？

答案：是的。

20 第二次发球

如果第一次发球失误，发球员应当立即从他该次发球失误的同伴区后面的规定位置再发一次，除非发球失误的这次发球是从错误的半区发出的。

21 何时发球和接发球

发球员应该在接发球员做好准备以后再发球。不管怎样，接发球员应按照发球员合理的发球节奏来比赛，并且在发球员准备发球时，在合理的时间内做好接发球的准备。

接发球员试图回击发球时则被认为他已做好准备。如果能够证实接发球员确未做好准备，那么该次发球也不能被判为失误。

22 发球中的重发

如果出现下列情况应重新发球：

（1）发出的球触到了球网、中心带或网带后落在有效发球区内；或在球触到了球网、中心带或网带后落地前触到了接发球员或其同伴，或他们所穿的或携带的任何物品；

（2）或者球发出后，接发球员还没有做好准备。

在重发球时，引起重发的那次发球不被计算，发球员应重发该发球，但是不能取消重新发球前的发球失误。

其他已被批准的可供选择的相关程序可参见附则Ⅳ。

23 重赛

除了在第二次发球时呼报重赛是指重发该次发球外，在所有其他情况下，当呼报重赛时，这一分必须重赛。

判例 1：在活球期间，另一个球滚入场地内，裁判员呼报重赛，发球员以前有一次发球失误，此时发球员应获得第一次还是第二次发球的权利？

答案：第一次，整个这一分必须重赛。

24 运动员失分

如果出现下列情况，运动员将失分：

（1）发球员连续两次发球失误；

（2）在活球状态下，运动员在连续两次触地前不能将球回击过网；

（3）在活球状态下，运动员回击的球在落地前触到有效击球区外的地面或其他物体；

（4）在活球状态下，运功员回击的球在落地前触到永久固定物；

（5）接球员在球没有落地前回击发球员发出的球；

（6）运动员故意用他的球拍托带或接住处于活球状态中的球，或故意用球拍触球超过一次；

（7）在活球状态下的任何时候，运动员或他的球拍（无沦球拍是否在他手中），或他穿戴的或携带的任何物品触到球网、网柱/单打支柱、网绳或钢丝绳、中心带或网带，或他对手场地的地面；

（8）运动员在球过网前击球；

（9）在活球状态下，除了运动员手中的球拍以外，球触及到运动员身体或他穿戴的或携带的任何物品；

（10）在活球状态下，球触及到了运动员的球拍，但球拍不在他手中；

（11）在活球状态下，运动员故意并实质性地改变了球拍的形状；

（12）双打比赛中，在一次回击球时，同队的两名运动员都触到了球。

判例 1：发球员在发出第一次发球后，球拍从他的手中脱落，在球落地前球拍碰到了球网，这是一次之球失误，还是发球员失分？

答案：发球员失分，因为在活球期间球拍触及了球网。

判例 2：发球在发出第一次发球后，球拍从他的手中脱落，在球落地融及有效发球区以外的地面后球拍碰到球网，这是一次发球失误，还是发球员失分？

答案：这是一次发球失误，因为球拍触及球网时，球已经不在活球期内了。

判例3：双打比赛中，接球方运动员的同伴在对方发出的球触及有效击球区场地外的地面前触及球网，应当如何判定？

答案：接球方失分，因为活球期间接球运动员的同伴触及球网。

判例4：运动员在击球前或击球后越过球网的假定延长线，运动员是否失分？

答案：在这两种情况下，如果运动员没有触及对方的场地，都不失分。

判例5：活球期间运动员可否跳越过球网进入对方的场地内？

答案：不可以，这名运动员失分。

判例6：活球期间运动员抛拍击球，球和球拍均落入对方一侧的场地内，对方未能击到球，哪一名运动员赢得该分？

答案：抛拍击球的运动员失分。

判例7：一个发球在触地前刚好击中接球运动员，或双打接球运动员的同伴，哪一名运动员赢得该分？

答案：发球运动员赢得该分，除非这是一次重发球。

判例8：运动员站在场地外回击或接住还未落地的球，并且宣称赢得该分，因为球明显地飞出有效场地外？

答案：运动员失分，除非这是一次有效的回球，在这种情况下继续此分的比赛。

25　有效回击

如果是下列情况，属于一次有效回击：

（1）球触到了球网、网柱/单打支柱、网绳或钢丝绳、中心带或网带并且越过球网上面后落到有效场地内；规则第2条和24(4)条除外；

（2）在活球状态下球落在有效场地内后由于旋转或被风吹过网，该轮到击球的运动员越过网击球，将球击到有效场地内，并且运动员没有违反规则第24条的现定；

（3）回击的球从网柱外侧，无论该球是高于还是低于球网的上部高度。即使触到网柱，只要落在有效场地内，规则第2条和第24(4)条除外；

（4）球从单打支柱及其附属网柱之间的网绳下面穿过而又没有触及球网、网绳或网柱，并且球落在有效场地内；

（5）运动员的球拍在回击自己球网一侧内的球后随球过网，球落入有效场地内；

（6）在活球状态下，运功员击出的球碰到了停在正确场地内的另一个球。

判例1：运动员的回球击中单打支柱并落入有效场地内，这是否为一次有效击球？

答案：为一次有效击球，但如果发出的球触到单打支柱，则为一次发球失误。

判例2：活球期间，球击中停在有效场地内的另一球，应当如何判定？

答案：继续比赛，然而，如果裁判员此时不能确定回击的球是否为活球状态下的球。则这一分应当重赛。

26　干扰

如果运动员在某一分球的比赛中受到对于故意举动的干扰，那么这名运动员应当赢得该分。

然而，如果运动员在某一分的比赛中受到他对手非故意举动的干扰，或者某些运动员自身无法控制(除场地上的永久固定物外)的妨碍时，这一分应当重赛。

判例1：一次无意的连击是否为一次干扰?

答案：不是，参见规则第24(6)款。

判例2：一名运动员要求停止比赛，因为该运动员认为他的对手受到干扰，这是否为一次干扰?

答案：不是，这名运动员失分。

判例3：比赛中球击中飞过球场上空的鸟，这是否为一次干扰?

答案：是的，这一分应当重赛。

判例4：在一分中，该分开始前已经在运动员这一侧场地内的一个球或其他物体干扰了运动员，这是否为一次干扰?

答案：不是。

判例5：在双打比赛中，允许发球员的同伴或接发球球员的同伴站在何处?

答案：发球员的同伴或接发球员的同伴可以站在球网一侧己方场地内或场地外的任何位置。然而，如果运动员制造干扰妨碍了对方，那么将使用干扰规则。

27 更正错误

作为一项原则，当比赛中发现一例违反网球规则的错误时，先前所有的比分都有效，发现的错误应当按照如下条款更正：

(1) 在一个常规局或一个平局决胜局中，如果一名运功员从错误的半区发球，此错误一经发现就应当立即被纠正，发球员要按照场上的比分从正确的半区发球，错误被发现前发球员已发生的发球失误有效。

(2) 在一个常规局或一个平局决胜局中，如果出现双方的运动员场地站边错误，则此错误一经发现就应当立即被纠正，发球员要按照场上的比分从正确的一边场地发球。

(3) 在常规局中如果运动员的发球次序错误，此错误已经发现，原先轮及发球的该运动员应当立即发球。然而，如果错误被发现前该局已经结束，则发球的次序就按照已改变的次序进行。在这种情况下，此后的所有换球必须比原先规定的局数推后一局进行。

如果发球次序错误被发现前，对手有一次发球失误，则此次发球失误无效。

在双打比赛中，如果是同队的两名运动员出现发球次序错误，则错误发现以前的一次发球失误有效。

(4) 在平局决胜局中，运动员出现发球次序错误，如果此错误是在双数比分结束后被发现的，则错误一经发现就应当立即纠正。如果此错误是在单数比分结束后被发现的，则发球的次序就按照已改变的次序进行。

如果发球次序错误被发现前，对手有一次发球失误则此次发球失误无效。

在双打比赛中，如果是同队的两名运动员出现发球次序错误，则错误被发现前发球员同伴的一次发球失误有效。

(5) 在双打比赛的常规局或平局决胜局中，如果接发球次序出现错误，则按照已发生的错误次序继续进行，直到这一局结束。在这一盘的下一次接发球同时，这对运功员应当重新回到原先的接发球次序。

(6) 赛前规定的是“长盘制”的比赛，但是如果在局数6∶6时错误地进行了“平局决胜局”的比赛，如果此时仅仅进行了第一分的比赛，则此错误应立即被纠正；如果错误被发现时第二分的比赛已经开始，则这盘比赛将按照“长盘制”继续进行，直到双方的局数达到 8∶8 时（或更高的偶数平局时）在进行“平局决胜局”的比赛。

（7）赛前规定的是“平局决胜局制”的比赛，但是如果在局数 6∶6 时错误地开始了常规局的比赛，如果此时仅仅进行了第一分的比赛，则此错误应立即纠正；如果错误被发现时第二分的比赛已经开始，则这盘比赛将按照“长盘制”继续进行，直到双方的局数达到 8∶8（或更高的偶数平局时）在进行“平局决胜局”的比赛。

（8）如果赛前规定决胜盘采用“平盘决胜局制”，但是在决胜盘错误地开始了“平局决胜局制”或“长盘制”的比赛，如果此时仅仅进行了第一分的比赛，则此错误应立即纠正；如果错误被发现时第二分的比赛已经开始，则这一盘比赛继续进行，直到一名运动员/队赢得 3 局由此赢得这一盘，或是到局数 2∶2 平时，再进行“平盘决胜局”的比赛。然而，如果此错误在第五局的第二分比赛开始后才被发现，则这盘将以“平局决胜局制”继续比赛（参考附录Ⅳ）。

（9）如果没有按照正常的顺序换球，那么就要等到下一次再轮到这名运功员/队发球时更换新球。此后的换球顺序仍然应按照原先的规定，在达到既定的换球局数后再进行，在一局比赛进行中不能换球。

28　场上技术官员的作用

在设有指定官员的比赛里，他们的作用和职责参见附录Ⅴ。

29　连续比赛

作为一个原则，比赛从整个比赛的第一分发球开始直到结束应当连续地进行：

（1）分与分之间，最长间隔时间允许有 20 秒。运动员在单数局数结束后交换场地时，最长间隔时间允许有 90 秒。而在每盘的第一局结束后和在平局决胜局进行时，运动员应交换场地而没有休息，比赛应连续进行。

在每一盘结束后，最长盘间间隔时间 120 秒。

最长允许时间是指从上一分球结束时开始，直到下一分第一次发球时球被击出时为止。

赛事组织者可以向国际网联申请批准延长单数局结束时运动员交换场地的 90 秒间隔时间，以及盘与盘之间 120 秒的间隔时间。

（2）如果由于运动员不能控制的原因，如服装、鞋子或必要的装备（不包括球拍）损坏或需要对其进行更换时，可以允许给运动员一个合理的额外时间去解决这些问题。

（3）不能因为一名运动员要恢复他的体力而给其额外的时间。但是，当运动员出现可以治疗的伤病时，可以获得一次 3 分钟的治疗时间来处理此伤病。如果赛前已公布，限定上卫生间/更换衣服的次数也是允许的。

（4）如果赛事组织者赛前已经宣布，整场比赛允许有一次最长为 10 分钟的休息时间，这个时间可以在五盘赛制的第三盘结束之后，或三盘赛制的第二盘结束之后采用。

（5）准备活动时间最长为 5 分钟，除非赛事组织者事先另有规定。

30　指导

以任何可听到的或可看到的方式对运动员进行交流、建议或各种指示被认为是指导。

在团体赛中运动员可以接受坐在场上队长的指导，但是这种指导只能在每盘结束后的间歇和单数局结束运动员交换场地时进行。但是在每一盘的第一局结束后和决胜局中交换场地时不能进行指导。

在其他的任何比赛中，运动员都不能接受指导。

判例 1：如果指导是以一个不易被发觉的暗示做出，运动员可以接受这样的指导吗？

答案：不可以。

判例 2：比赛暂停期间运动员可以接受指导吗？

答案：可以。

附录Ⅰ

球

1. 球的表面是用统一的纺织材料包裹的，颜色应当是白色或黄色。如果有接缝，不应当有缝线。

2. 指定的网球类型不止一种，但球应当符合下表所列出的要求。

	1 型球（快速）	2 型球（中速）①	3 型球（慢速）②	高海拔型球③
重量（质量）	56.0～59.4 克（1.975～2.095 盎司）	56.0～59.4 克（1.975～2.095 盎司）	56.0～59.4 克（1.975～2.095 盎司）	56.0～59.4 克（1.975～2.095 盎司）
尺寸	6.54～6.86 厘米（2.57～2.70 英寸）	6.54～6.86 厘米（2.57～2.70 英寸）	7.00～7.30 厘米（2.76～2.87 英寸）	6.54～6.86 厘米（2.57～2.70 英寸）
弹性	135～147 厘米（53～58 英寸）	135～147 厘米（53～58 英寸）	135～147 厘米（53～58 英寸）	122～135 厘米（48～53 英寸）
向内压缩形变④	0.50～0.60 厘米（0.197～0.236 英寸）	0.56～0.74 厘（0.220～0.291 英寸）	0.56～0.74 厘米（0.220～0.291 英寸）	0.56～0.74 厘米（0.220～0.291 英寸）
反弹形变④	0.67～0.91 厘米（0.264～0.358 英寸）	0.80～1.08 厘米（0.315～0.425 英寸）	0.80～1.08 厘米（0.315～0.425 英寸）	0.80～1.08 厘米（0.315～0.425 英寸）

注：

① 中速球可能是增压的也可能是无压的。无压球的内部压强必须小于 7 千帕，还应在比赛要求的海拔高度为 1219 米（4000 英尺）以上测试 60 天或更多天。

② 慢速球通常用于海拔高速为 1219 米（4000 英尺）以上的各种场地比赛。

③ 高海拔地区用的球是加压的，是作为附加的球专门只为高海拔 1219 米（4000 英尺）以上的比赛用球。

④ 形变的数据应当是从球的 3 个轴方向测试后的平均值，每种情况下任何两个数据之间的差异不能大于 0.08 厘米（0.031 英寸）。

3. 此外，球的耐久性应当与下面表格所要求的一致：

	重量（质量）	弹性	向内压缩形变	反弹形变
最大变化值	0.4 克（0.014 盎司）	4.0 厘米（1.6 英寸）	0.08 厘米（0.031 英寸）	0.10 厘米（0.039 英寸）

注：特殊材质的最大可允许变化来自现版本的国际网联认证的网球和分类球场表面所描述的规定。耐久性检测使用实验室仪器模拟 9 种比赛效果来进行。

4. 有关球反弹、重量、大小、形变和耐久性的所有检测应该按照现版本国际网联认证的网球和分类球场表面所描述的规定进行。

附录Ⅱ

球　拍

1. 球拍的击球面是指拍弦组成的式样的主要部分，无论多少都应当是平坦的，由连接在球拍框上的弦组成一种式样，拍弦在交叉的地方应当是相互交织或相互结合的；拍弦所组成的式样应当大体一致，尤其是中央的拍弦密度不能小于其他区域的密度。

球拍的设计和穿弦应使球拍的两面在击球时的性质保持完全一样。球拍框，包括拍柄上，不应有附属物和装置，除非它仅仅并且非常明确的是用来限制和防止振动、弦线磨损、撕拉或只对于拍框来说有分散球拍重量作用的，而且它的尺寸必须是合理的，且确实被用于上述目的。

2. 球拍的总长度（包括拍柄）不能超过 73.7 厘米（29 英寸）。球拍框的总宽度不能超过 31.7 厘米（12.5 英寸）。击球平面的总长度不能超过 39.4 厘米（15.5 英寸），总宽度不能超过 29.2 厘米（11.5 英寸）。

3. 球拍框，包括拍柄以及弦线上，不能有任何可能从实质上改变球拍形状，或故意改变球拍纵轴方向的重力分布从而使挥拍瞬间的惯性发生变化，或者故意改变任何的物理性质从而在一分球的比赛中影响球拍性能的装置。任何能够改变或影响球拍性能的能源装置都不能装进或附着在球拍上。

4. 在比赛期间，运动员的球拍上不能有任何可听的或可视的，用于提供交流、建议和任何指示的装置。

附录Ⅲ

广　告

1. 在靠近网柱并且距网柱中心内侧 3 英尺（0.914 米）以内的部分球网上可以有广告，但广告的制作不应干扰运动员的视觉和比赛条件。

2. 在场地后面和侧面可以安放广告及其他标志或物体，但不能干扰运动员的视觉或比赛条件。

3. 在场地界线之外的地面上可以安放广告及其他标志或物体，但不能干扰运动员的视觉或比赛条件。

4. 虽然有上述第 1、2、3 条的规定，但安放在球网上，或场地后面和侧面的，或场地界限之外地面上的广告，其颜色都不能是干扰运动员的视觉或比赛条件的白色、黄色或其他的浅颜色。

5. 在球场界线以内的场地表面不能有广告及其他标志或物体。

附录Ⅳ

备选的程序和计分方法

一局中的计分（规则第 5 条）：

“无占先”计分法：

这种备选的计分方法可以被使用。

在一个“无占先”局的比赛中，应先报发球运动员的比分，计分如下：

无得分——0

第一分——15

第二分——30

第三分——40

第四分——局比赛结束

如果双方运动员/队都赢得3分，这时的比分叫“平分”，然后要打一个决胜分。接球方将选择从场地左半区还是从右半区接发球。在双打比赛中，进行决胜分比赛时接球方的两名队员不能改变接球站位。赢得决胜分的运动员/队赢得这一局。

在混双比赛中，与发球员同性别的接球员应当接决胜分的发球。接球方的两名运动员不能改变接球站位去接决胜分的发球。

一盘中的计分(规则第6和第7条)：

1.“短”盘制

谁先赢得四局并净胜对手两句的运动员/队赢得这一盘。如果局数比分达到4∶4时，将进行一个“平局决胜局”的比赛。

2. 七分制平盘决胜局

当比赛的盘数比分达到1∶1，或在五盘三胜制的比赛中盘数比分达到2∶2是，用一个“平局决胜局”来决定比赛的胜负。这个“平局决胜局”代替最后的决胜盘。

谁先赢得对手7分并净胜两分的运动员/队，谁将赢得“平盘决胜局”和整场比赛。

3. 十分制平盘决胜局

当比赛的盘数比分达到1∶1，或在五盘三胜制的比赛中盘数比分达到2∶2是，用一个“平局决胜局”来决定比赛的胜负。这个“平局决胜局”代替最后的决胜盘。

谁先赢得对手10分净胜两分的运动员/队，谁将赢得“平局决胜局”和整场比赛。

注：当采用“平盘决胜局”代替最后的决胜盘时：

- 原先的发球顺序继续不变(规则第5及第14条)。
- 在双打比赛中，就像每盘开始时那样，各队的发球和接发球顺序可以改变。(规则第14及第15条)。
- 在“平盘决胜局”比赛开始前，应有一个120秒的盘间休息。
- 即使在“平盘决胜局”前本应该换球的，此时也不能换球。

交换场地(规则第10条)

下述这个备选的交换场地次序可以在“平局决胜局”中采用。在“平局决胜局”比赛期间，运动员应当在第一分后和随后的每4分之后交换场地。

发球中的重发(规则第22条)

这个备选的发球规则不包括规则第22(1)条中有关重发球的内容。

这就是说发出的球在碰到球网、中心带或网袋后，仍为活球。

这个规则通常被称为“擦网不重赛规则”。

附录V

场上技术官员的作用

裁判长对于所有涉及网球规则的问题有最终裁判权，并且裁判长的决定是最终裁定。

在设有主裁判的比赛中，主裁判对于在整场比赛中所有事实问题有最终裁决权。

运动员对于场上主裁判作出的关于网球规则问题的裁决有疑问时，有权叫裁判长到场。

在设有司线员和司网裁判的比赛中，他们对自己负责的线或球网作出所有呼报(包括脚误的呼报)。如果主裁判确定司线员或司网裁判作出了一个非常明显的误判，主裁判有权改判。如果在没有司线员和司网裁判的比赛中，主裁判负责所有线和球网的呼报(包括脚误的呼报)。

如果司线员没能对场上的情况作出呼报，他应当立即向主裁判示意，主裁判应当立即对场上的情况作出裁决。如果司线员没能对场上的情况做出呼报，或比赛中没有司线员而主裁判也不能对场上的事实问题作出裁决时，这一分应当重赛。

在团体比赛中，当裁判长坐在场上时，裁判长可以对任何事实问题作出最终裁决。

在主裁判认为必要或适当的任何时候，可以中断或暂停比赛。

在光线暗、天气或场地条件不利的情况下，裁判长也可以中断或暂停比赛。当由于光线暗而暂停比赛时，则应当在该盘结束，或在这一盘中的双数局结束后暂停。在比赛暂停后重新开始比赛时，双方的比分和在场地上的位置保持不变。

裁判长和主裁判可以根据被批准并在执行中的行为规范的要求，对于是否继续比赛和指导的问题作出裁决。

判例1：主裁判更正一个错误后判发球员第一次发球，而接球方运动员争辩说发球运动员此前有过一次发球失误，应是第二次发球，裁判长可否被要求到场作出裁决?

答案：可以。对于涉及到的有关网球规则方面的问题，首先由场上的主裁判根据事件具体情况先作出判决。然而，当运动员不同意主裁判的判决时，应有裁判长作出最终裁决。

判例2：一个球被呼报“出界”，但运动员声称是好球，可否要求裁判长到场对此作出判决?

答案：不可以。对于比赛中的“事实问题”，场上主裁判的决定就是最终裁决(因为它涉及到的是在某一个具体事件中实际发生的事情)。

判例3：主裁判可否在比赛中一分结束后改判司线员的判决，因为他认为在刚结束的对打回合中司线员作出的是一个明显的误判?

答案：不可以。主裁判只能在在这个明显的错误发生后立即更改司线员的判决。

判例4：在司线员呼报“出界”之后，一名运动员申辩他的回球是好球，主裁判此时是否可以改判司线员的判决?

答案：不可以。主裁判绝对不能因为运动员的抗议或申诉而作出任何改判。

判例5：一名司线员呼报球“出界”，主裁判虽然认为球是界内的，但是他未能看得非常清楚，那么他是否可以对司线员的判决作出改判?

答案：不可以。主裁判只有在确信司线员作出了明显的误判时才能改判。

判例6：司线员是否可以在主裁判报分之后更改自己的呼报?

答案：可以。如果一名司线员认为他自己犯了错误，只要不是出于袒护的目的或运动员申诉的原因，就应当尽快示意更正。

判例7：在主裁判或司线员呼报"出界"之后更正回球是好球，正确的判罚是怎样的？

答案：主裁判必须作出裁决原先的出界呼报是否干扰了双方运动员。如果是一次干扰，这一分应重赛，如果不是一次干扰，击球的运动员赢得这一分。

判例8：当球从网上被风吹回时，运动员正准备过网击打该球，他的对手妨碍了该运动员的回球动作，正确的判罚是怎样的？

答案：裁判员必须作出判断，如果是对手有意的干扰，该分应判给受到干扰的运动员，如果是无意的干扰则该分要重赛。

附录Ⅵ

10岁及10岁以下年龄组的正式网球比赛

场地

除了标准的比赛场地外，以下尺寸的场地可用于10岁及10岁以下年龄组的正式网球比赛：

- 红色地面的长方形场地，长度为10.97米(36英尺)和12.80米(42英尺)之间，宽度为4.88米(16英尺)和5.79米(19英尺)之间。球网中间的高度为0.8米(31英寸)。
- 橘黄色地面的长方形场地，长度为18.29米(60英尺)，宽度为6.40米(21英尺)和8.23米(27英尺)之间。球网中间的高度为0.914米(36英寸)。

球

推荐以下种类的球用于10岁及10岁以下年龄组的比赛：

- 在红色场地上的比赛建议使用3号(红色)球。
- 在橘黄色场地上的比赛建议使用2号(橘黄色)球。
- 在绿色场地上的比赛建议使用1号(绿色)球。

3号、2号和1号球的特征在《国际网联认可的比赛球和场地面层分类》的国际网联出版物中有详细说明。

计分方法

10岁及10岁以下年龄组运动员在采用3号、2号和1号球比赛时，除了采用时间较短的一个决胜局制、3个决胜局两胜制，或一盘制的计分方法以外，还可以采用标准的网球规则(包括附则)中所阐述的计分方法。

第二章　网球裁判员法定手势

1　网球裁判员法定手势

（1）准备位置站法
（2）放松时站法
（3）准备位置坐法
（4）出界(发球失误)站法

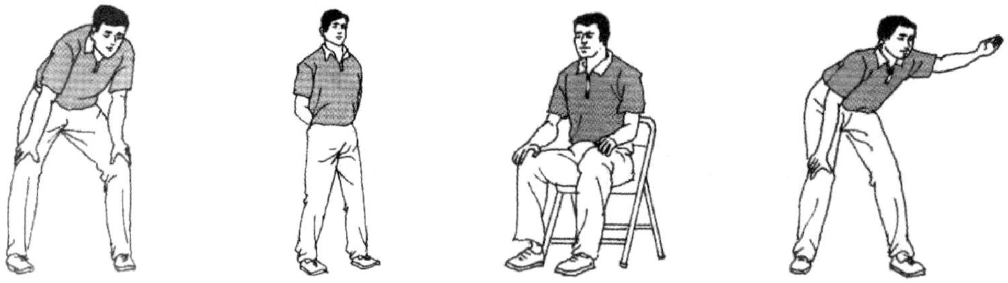

（5）好球站法
（6）出界做法
（7）好球坐法
（8）脚误坐法

（9）纠正(脚误、穿网、擦网等)
（10）没看见动作
（11）擦网动作
（12）司网裁判动作

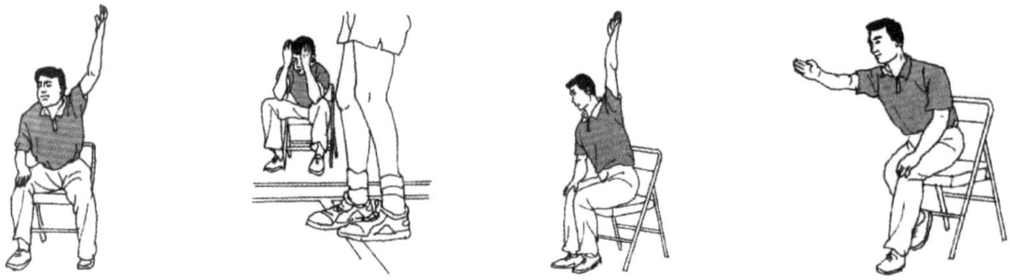

（13）发球线司裁员准备姿势

（14）发球好球动作

（15）发球失误（出界）动作

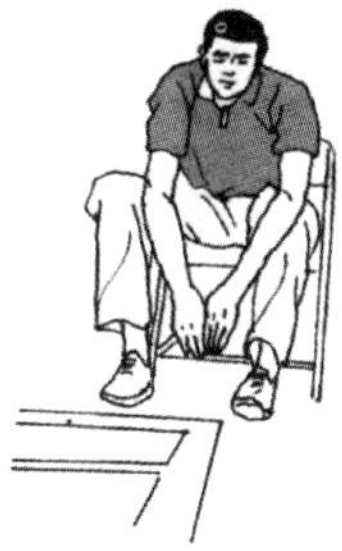

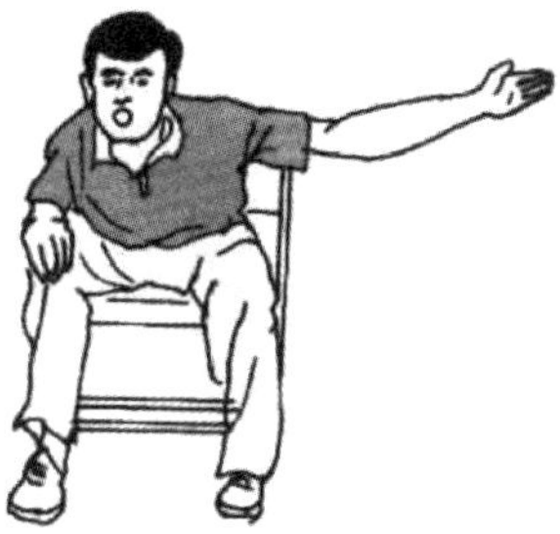

（16）底线司线员的坐角及动作

（17）主裁坐法

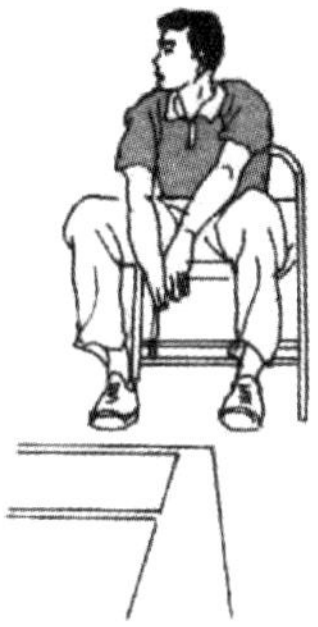

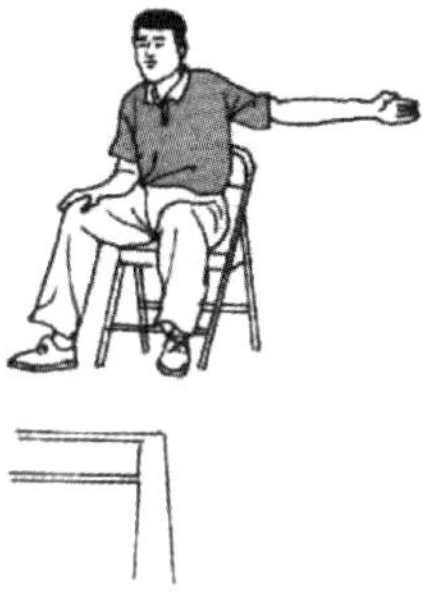

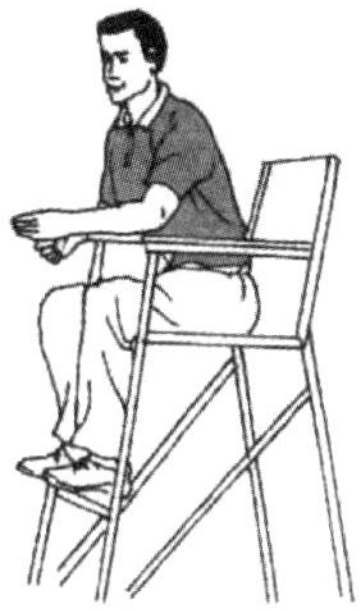

2 裁判员、司线员及拾球员的位置图

2.1 裁判员及司线位置图

（1）1 人裁判（即主裁兼司线、司网）

（2）3 人裁判（主裁及 2 名司线）

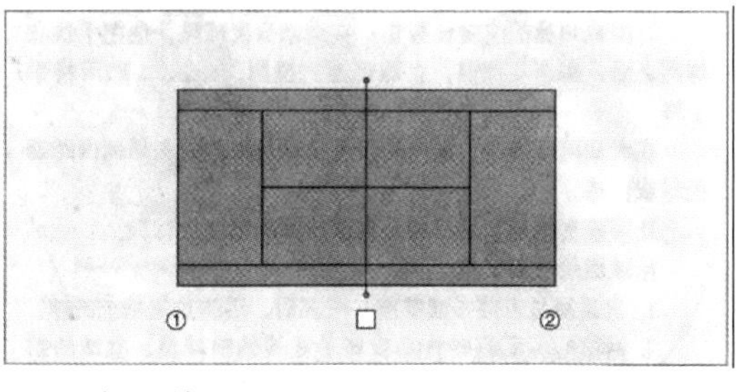

（3）4 个裁判（主裁及 3 名司线）

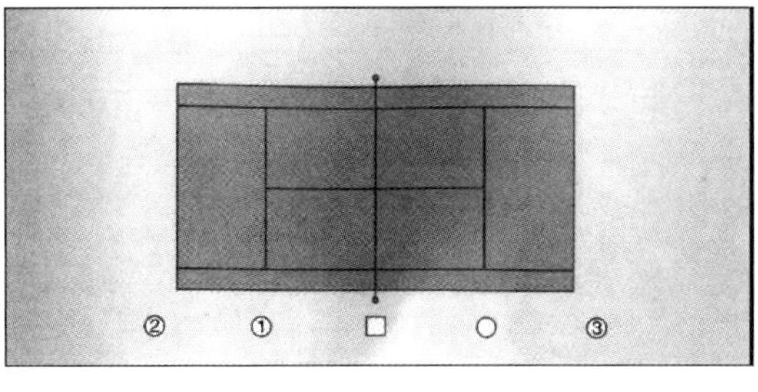

(4) 5 人裁判(主裁及 4 名司线)

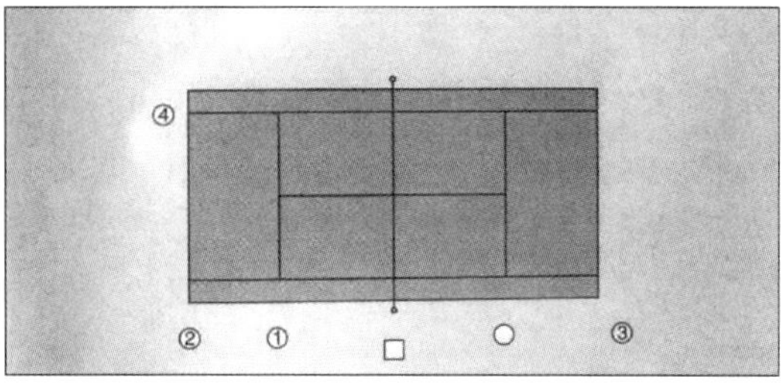

(5) 6 人裁判(主裁及 5 名司线)

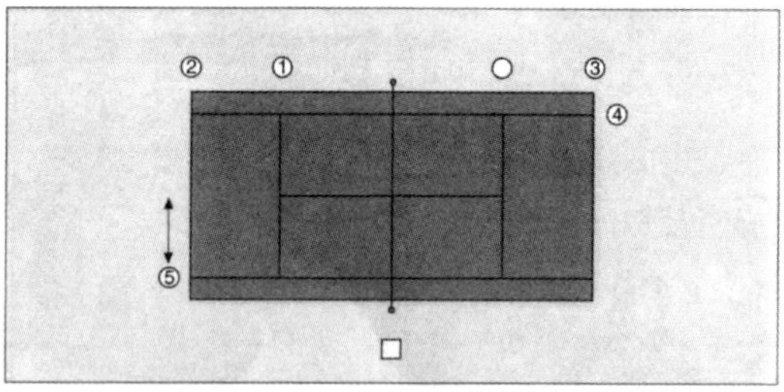

(6) 7 人裁判(主裁及 5 名司线)

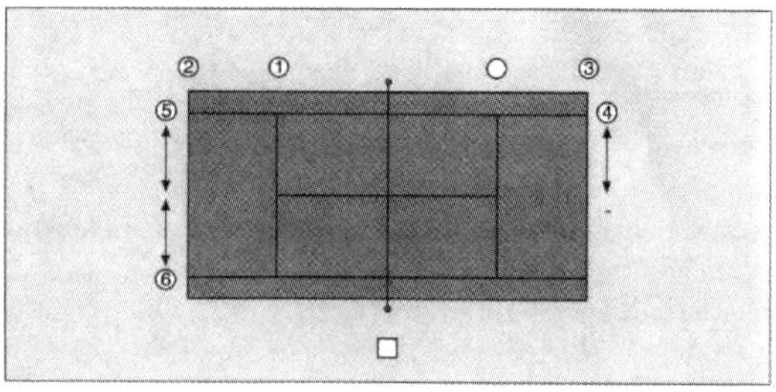

(7) 8 人裁判(主裁及 7 名司线)

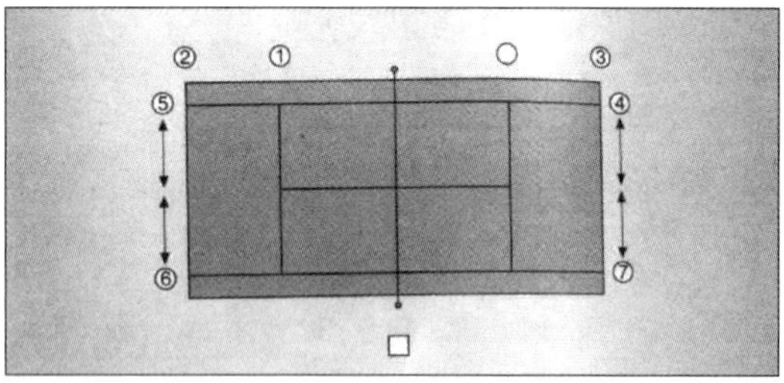

(8) 12 人裁判(主裁及 11 名司线)

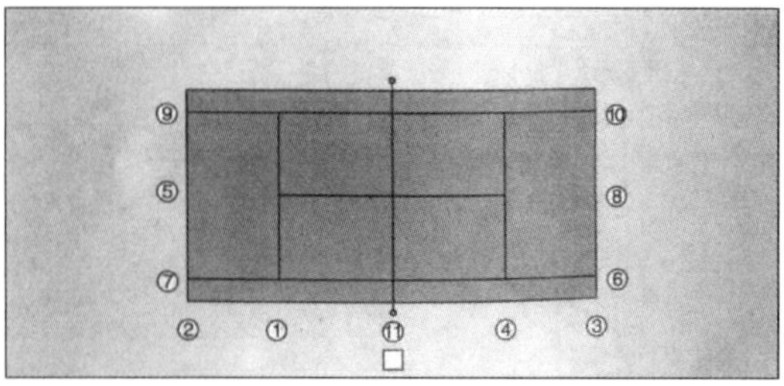

2.2 拾球员位置图

(1) 3 名拾球员位置图

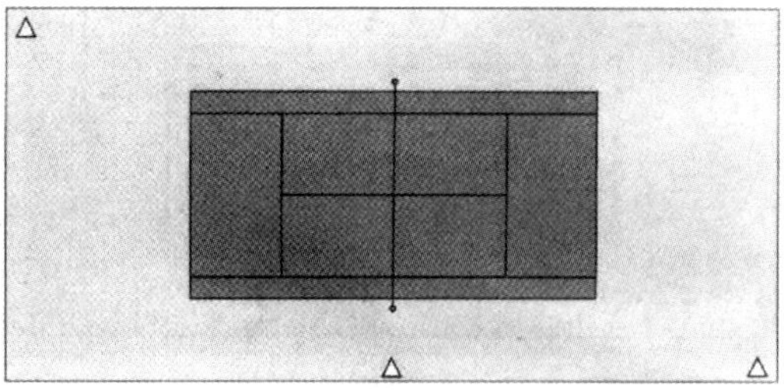

(2) 6 名拾球员位置图

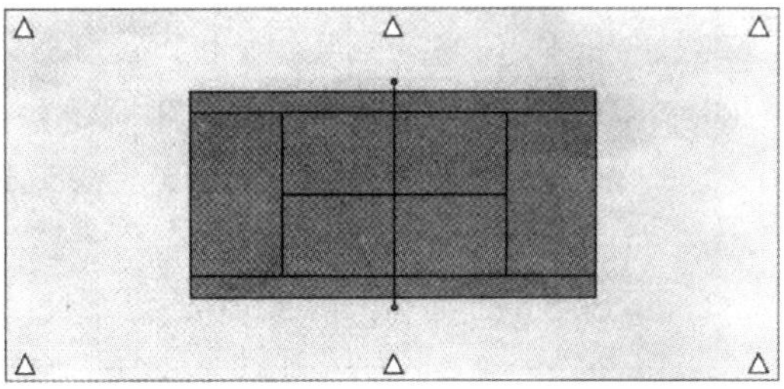

第三章　网球英文规则

1 The court

The court shall be a rectangle, 78 feet (23.77 m) long and, for singles matches, 27 feet (8.23 m) wide. For doubles matches, the court shall be 36 feet (10.97m) wide.

The court shall be divided across the middle by a net suspended by a cord or metal cable which shall pass over or be attached to two net posts at a height of 3½ feet (1.07 m). The net shall be fully extended so that it completely fills the space between the two net posts and it must be of sufficiently small mesh to ensure that a ball cannot pass through it. The height of the net shall be 3 feet (0.914 m) at the centre, where it shall be held down tightly by a strap. A band shall cover the cord or metal cable and the top of the net. The strap and band shall be completely white.

- The maximum diameter of the cord or metal cable shall be 1/3 inch (0.8 cm).
- The maximum width of the strap shall be 2 inches (5 cm).
- The band shall be between 2 inches (5 cm) and 2½ inches (6.35 cm) deep on each side.

For doubles matches, the centers of the net posts shall be 3 feet (0.914 m) outside the doubles court on each side.

For singles matches, if a singles net is used, the centers of the net posts shall be 3 feet (0.914 m) outside the singles court on each side. If a doubles net is used, then the net shall be supported, at a height of 3½ feet (1.07 m), by two singles sticks, the centers of which shall be 3 feet (0.914 m) outside the singles court on each side.

- The net posts shall not be more than 6 inches (15 cm) square or 6 inches (15 cm) in diameter.
- The singles sticks shall not be more than 3 inches (7.5 cm) square or 3 inches (7.5 cm) in diameter.
- The net posts and singles sticks shall not be more than 1 inch (2.5 cm) above the top of the net cord.

The lines at the ends of the court are called baselines and the lines at the sides of the court are called sidelines.

Two lines shall be drawn between the singles sidelines, 21 feet (6.40 m) from each side ofthe net, parallel with the net. These lines are called the service lines. On each side of the net, the area between the service line and the net shall be divided into two equal parts, the service courts, by the centre service line. The centre service line shall be drawn parallel with the singles sidelines and half way between them.

Each baseline shall be divided in half by a centre mark, 4 inches (10 cm) in length, which shall be drawn inside the court and parallel with the single sidelines.

- The centre service line and centre mark shall be 2 inches (5 cm) wide.
- The other lines of the court shall be between 1 inch (2.5 cm) and 2 inches (5 cm) wide, except that the baselines may be up to 4 inches (10 cm) wide.

All court measurements shall be made to the outside of the lines and all lines of the court shall be of the same color clearly contrasting with the color of the surface.

No advertising is allowed on the court, net, strap, band, net posts or singles sticks except as provided in Appendix III.

2 Permanent fixtures

The permanent fixtures of the court include the backstops and side stops, the spectators, the stands and seats for spectators, all other fixtures around and above the court, the chair umpire, line umpires, net umpire and ball persons when in their recognized positions.

In a singles match played with a doubles net and singles sticks, the net posts and the part of the net outside the singles sticks are permanent fixtures and are not considered as net posts or part of the net.

3 The ball

Balls, which are approved for play under the Rules of Tennis, must comply with the specifications in Appendix I.

The International Tennis Federation shall rule on the question of whether any ball or prototype complies with Appendix I or is otherwise approved, or not approved, for play. Such ruling may be taken on its own initiative, or upon application by any party with a bona fide interest therein, including any player, equipment manufacturer or National Association or members thereof. Such rulings and applications shall be made in accordance with the applicable Review and Hearing Procedures of the International Tennis Federation (see Appendix VI).

The event organizers must announce in advance of the event:

(1) The number of balls for play (2, 3, 4 or 6).

(2) The ball change policy, if any.

Ball changes, if any, can be made either:

(1) After an agreed odd number of games, in which case, the first ball change in the match shall take place two games earlier than for the rest of the match, to make allowance for the warm-up. A tie-break game counts as one game for the ball change. A ball change shall not take place at the beginning of a tiebreak game. In this case, the ball change shall be delayed until the beginning of the second game of the next set; or

(2) At the beginning of a set.

If a ball gets broken during play, the point shall be replayed.

Case 1: If a ball is soft at the end of a point, should the point be replayed?

Decision: If the ball is soft, not broken, the point shall not be replayed.

Note: Any ball to be used in a tournament which is played under the Rules of Tennis, must be named on the official ITF list of approved balls issued by the International Tennis Federation.

4 The racket

Rackets, which are approved for play under the Rules of Tennis, must comply with the specifications in Appendix Ⅱ.

The International Tennis Federation shall rule on the question of whether any racket or prototype complies with Appendix II or is otherwise approved, or not approved, for play. Such ruling may be undertaken on its own initiative, or upon application by any party with a bona fide interest therein, including any player, equipment manufacturer or National Association or members thereof. Such rulings and applications shall be made in accordance with the applicable Review and Hearing Procedures of the International Tennis Federation (see Appendix Ⅵ).

Case 1: Is more than one set of strings allowed on the hitting surface of a racket?

Decision: No. The rule mentions a pattern (not patterns) of crossed strings. (See Appendix II)

Case 2: Is the stringing pattern of a racket considered to be generally uniform and flat if the strings are on more than one plane?

Decision: No.

Case 3: Can vibration damping devices be placed on the strings of a racket? If so, where can they be placed?

Decision: Yes, but these devices may only be placed outside the pattern of the crossed strings.

Case 4: During a point, a player accidentally breaks the strings. Can the player continue to play another point with this racket?

Decision: Yes, except where specifically prohibited by event organizers.

Case 5: Is a player allowed to use more than one racket at any time during play?

Decision: No.

Case 6: Can a battery that affects playing characteristics be incorporated into a racket?

Decision: No. A battery is prohibited because it is an energy source, as are solar cells and other similar devices.

5 Score in a game

5.1 Standard game

A standard game is scored as follows with the server's score being called first:

No point——"Love"

First point——"15"

Second point——"30"

Third point——"40"

Fourth point——"Game"

Except that if each player/team has won three points, the score is "Deuce". After "Deuce", the score is "Advantage" for the player/team who wins the next point. If that same player/team also wins the next point, that player/team wins the "Game"; if the opposing player/team wins the next point, the score is again "Deuce". A player/team needs to win two consecutive points immediately after "Deuce" to win the "Game".

5.2 Tie-break game

During a tie-break game, points are scored "Zero", "1", "2", "3", etc. The first player/team to win seven points wins the "Game" and "Set", provided there is a margin of two points over the opponent(s). If necessary, the tie-break game shall continue until this margin is achieved.

The player whose turn it is to serve shall serve the first point of the tie-break game. The following two points shall be served by the opponent(s) (in doubles, the player of the opposing team due to serve next). After this, each player/team shall serve alternately for two consecutive points until the end of the tie-break game (in doubles, the rotation of service within each team shall continue in the same order as during that set).

The player/team whose turn it was to serve first in the tie-break game shall be the receiver in the first game of the following set. Additional approved alternative scoring methods can be found in Appendix IV.

6 Score in a set

There are different methods of scoring in a set. The two main methods are the "Advantage Set" and the "Tie-break Set". Either method may be used provided that the one to be used is announced in advance of the event. If the "Tie-break Set" method is to be used, it must also be announced whether the final set will be played as a "Tie-break Set" or an "Advantage Set".

6.1 "Advantage Set"

The first player/team to win six games wins that "Set", provided there is a margin of two games over the opponent(s). If necessary, the set shall continue until this margin is achieved.

6.2 "Tie-break Set"

The first player/team to win six games wins that "Set", provided there is a margin of two games over the opponent(s). If the score reaches six games all, a tie-break game shall be played. Additional approved alternative scoring methods can be found in Appendix IV.

7 Score in a match

A match can be played to the best of 3 sets (a player/team needs to win 2 sets to win the match) or to the best of 5 sets (a player/team needs to win 3 sets to win the match). Additional approved alternative scoring methods can be found in Appendix IV.

8 Server & Receiver

The players/teams shall stand on opposite sides of the net. The server is the player who puts the ball into play for the first point. The receiver is the player who is ready to return the ball served by the server.

Case 1: Is the receiver allowed to stand outside the lines of the court?

Decision: Yes. The receiver may take any position inside or outside the lines on the receiver's side of the net.

9 Choice of ends & Service

The choice of ends and the choice to be server or receiver in the first game shall be decided by toss before the warm-up starts. The player/team who wins the toss may choose:

(1) To be server or receiver in the first game of the match, in which case the opponent(s) shall choose the end of the court for the first game of the match; or

(2) The end of the court for the first game of the match, in which case the opponent(s) shall choose to be server or receiver for the first game of the match; or

(3) To require the opponent(s) to make one of the above choices.

Case 1: Do both players/teams have the right to new choices if the warm-up is stopped and the players leave the court?

Decision: Yes. The result of the original toss stands, but new choices may be made by both players/teams.

10 Change of ends

The players shall change ends at the end of the first, third and every subsequent odd game of each set. The players shall also change ends at the end of each set unless the total number of games in that set is even, in which case the players change ends at the end of the first game of the next set.

During a tie-break game, players shall change ends after every six points. Additional approved alternative procedures can be found in Appendix IV.

11 Ball in play

Unless a faultor a let is called, the ball is in play from the moment the server hits the ball, and remains in play until the point is decided.

12 Ball touches a line

If a ball touches a line, it is regarded as touching the court bounded by that line.

13 Ball touchesa permanent fixture

If the ball in play touches a permanent fixture after it has hit the correct court, the player who hit the ball wins the point. If the ball in play touches a permanent fixture before it hits the ground, the player who hit the ball loses the point.

14 Order of service

At the end of each standard game, the receiver shall become the server and the server shall become the receiver for the next game.

In doubles, the team due to serve in the first game of each set shall decide which player shall serve for that game. Similarly, before the second game starts, their opponents shall decide which player shall serve for that game. The partner of the player who served in the first game shall serve in the third game and the partner of the player who served in the second game shall serve in the fourth game. This rotation shall continue until the end of the set.

15 Order of receiving in doubles

The team which is due to receive in the first game of a set shall decide which player shall receive the first point in the game. Similarly, before the second game starts, their opponents shall decide which player shall receive the first point of that game. The player who was the receiver's partner for the first point of the game shall receive the second point and this rotation shall continue until the end of the game and the set.

After the receiver has returned the ball, either player in a team can hit the ball.

Case 1: *Is one member of a doubles team allowed to play alone against the opponents?*

Decision: *No.*

16 The service

Immediately before starting the service motion, the server shall stand at rest with both feet behind (i. e. further from the net than) the baseline and within the imaginary extensions of the centre mark and the sideline.

The server shall then release the ball by hand in any direction and hit the ball with the racket before the ball hits the ground. The service motion is completed at the moment that the player's racket hits or misses the ball. A player who is able to use only one arm may use the racket for the release of the ball.

17 Serving

When serving in a standard game, the server shall stand behind alternate halves of the court, starting from the right half of the court in every game.

In a tie-break game, the service shall be served from behind alternate halves of the court, with the first served from the right half of the court.

The service shall pass over the net and hit the service court diagonally opposite, before the receiver returns it.

18 Foot fault

During the service motion, the server shall not:

(1) Change position by walking or running, although slight movements of the feet are permitted; or

(2) Touch the baseline or the court with either foot; or

(3) Touch the area outside the imaginary extension of the sideline with either foot; or

(4) Touch the imaginary extension of the centre mark with either foot.

If the server breaks this rule it is a "Foot Fault".

Case 1: *In a singles match, is the server allowed to serve standing behind the part of the base-*

line between the singles sideline and the doubles sideline?

Decision: No.

Case 2: Is the server allowed to have one or both feet off the ground?

Decision: Yes.

19 Service fault

The service is a fault if:

(1) The server breaks rules 16, 17 or 18; or

(2) The server misses the ball when trying to hit it; or

(3) The ball served touches a permanent fixture, singles stick or net post before it hits the ground; or

(4) The ball served touches the server or server's partner, or anything the server or server's partner is wearing or carrying.

Case 1: After tossing a ball to serve, the server decides not to hit it and catches it instead. Is this a fault?

Decision: No. A player, who tosses the ball and then decides not to hit it, is allowed to catch the ball with the hand or the racket, or to let the ball bounce.

Case 2: During a singles match played on a court with net posts and singles sticks, the ball served hits a singles stick and then hits the correct service court. Is this a fault?

Decision: Yes.

20 Second service

If the first service is a fault, the server shall serve again without delay from behind the same half of the court from which that fault was served, unless the service was from the wrong half.

21 When to serve & receive

The server shall not serve until the receiver is ready. However, the receivershall play to the reasonable pace of the server and shall be ready to receive within a reasonable time of the server being ready.

A receiver who attempts to return the service shall be considered as being ready. If it is demon strated that the receiver is not ready, the service cannot be called a fault.

22 The let during a service

The service is a let if:

(1) The ball served touches the net, strap or band, and is otherwise good; or, after touching the net, strap or band, touches the receiver or the receiver's partner or anything they wear or carry before hitting the ground; or

(2) The ball is served when the receiver is not ready.

In the case of a service let, that particular service shall not count, and the server shall serve again, but a service let does not cancel a previous fault. Additional approved alternative procedures can be found in Appendix IV.

23 The let

In all cases when a let is called, except when a service let is called on a second service, the whole point shall be replayed.

Case 1: When the ball is in play, another ball rolls onto court. A let is called. The server had previously served a fault. Is the server now entitled to a first service or second service?

Decision: First service. The whole point must be replayed.

24 Player loses point

The point is lost if:

(1) The player serves two consecutive faults; or

(2) The player does not return the ball in play before it bounces twice consecutively; or

(3) The player returns the ball in play so that it hits the ground, or before it bounces, an object, outside the correct court; or

(4) The player returns the ball in play so that, before it bounces, it hits a permanent fixture; or

(5) The receiver returns the service before it bounces; or

(6) The player deliberately carries or catches the ball in play onthe racket or deliberately touches it with the racket more than once; or

(7) The player or the racket, whether in the player's hand or not, or anything which the player is wearing or carrying touches the net, net posts/singles sticks, cord or metal cable, strap or band, or the opponent's court at any time while the ball is in play; or

(8) The player hits the ball before it has passed the net; or

(9) The ball in play touches the player or anything that the player is wearing or carrying, except the racket; or

(10) The ball in play touches the racket when the player is not holding it; or

(11) The player deliberately and materially changes the shape of the racket when the ball is in play; or

(12) In doubles, both players touch the ball when returning it.

Case 1: After the server has served a first service, the racket falls out of the server's hand and touches the net before the ball has bounced. Is this a service fault, or does the server lose the point?

Decision: The server loses the point because the racket touches thenet while the ball is in play.

Case 2: After the server has served a first service, the racket falls out of the server's hand and touches the net after the ball has bounced outside the correct service court. Is this a service fault, or does the server lose the point?

Decision: This is a service fault because when the racket touched the net the ball was no longer in play.

Case 3: In a doubles match, the receiver's partner touches the net before the ball that has been served touches the ground outside the correct service court. What is the correct decision?

Decision: The receiving team loses the point because the receiver's partner touched the net while the ball was in play.

Case 4: Does a player lose the point if an imaginary line in the extension of the net is crossed before or after hitting the ball?

Decision: The player does not lose the point in either case provided the player does not touch the opponent's court.

Case 5: Is a player allowed to jump over the net into the opponent's court while the ball is in play?

Decision: No. The player loses the point.

Case 6: A player throws the racket at the ball in play. Both the racket and the ball land in the court on the opponent's side of the net and the opponent(s) is unable to reach the ball. Which player wins the point?

Decision: The player who threw the racket at the ball loses the point.

Case 7: A ball that has just been served hits the receiver or in doubles the receiver's partner before it touches the ground. Which player wins the point?

Decision: The serverwins the point, unless it is a service let.

Case 8: A player standing outside the court hits the ball or catches it before it bounces and claims the point because the ball was definitely going out of the correct court.

Decision: The player loses the point, unless it is a good return, in which case the point continues.

25 A good return

It is a good return if:

(1) The ball touches the net, net posts/singles sticks, cord or metal cable, strap or band, provided that it passes over any of them and hits the ground within the correct court; except as provided in Rule 2 and 24 (4); or

(2) After the ball in play has hit the ground within the correct court and has spun or been blown back over the net, the player reaches over the net and plays the ball into the correct court, provided that the player does not break Rule 24; or

(3) The ball is returned outside the net posts, either above or below the level of the top of the net, even though it touches the net posts, provided that it hits the ground in the correct court; except as provided in Rules 2 and 24 (4); or

(4) The ball passes under the net cord between the singles stick and the adjacent net post without touching either net, net cord or net post and hits the ground in the correct court, or

(5) The player's racket passes over the net after hitting the ball on the player's own side of the net and the ball hits the ground in the correct court; or

(6) The player hits the ball in play, which hits another ball lying in the correct court.

Case 1: A player returns a ball which then hits a singles stick and hits the ground in the correct court. Is this a good return?

Decision: Yes. However, if the ball is served and hits the singles stick, it is a service fault.

Case 2: A ball in play hits another ball which is lying in the correct court. What is the correct decision?

Decision: Play continues. However, if it is not clear that the actual ball in play has been returned, a let should be called.

26 Hindrance

If a player is hindered in playing the point by a deliberate act of the opponent(s), the player shall win the point.

However, the point shall be replayed if a player is hindered in playing the point by either an unintentional act of the opponent(s), or something outside the player's own control (not including a permanent fixture).

Case 1: Is an unintentional double hit a hindrance?

Decision: No. See also Rule 24 (f).

Case 2: A player claims to have stopped play because the player thought that the opponent(s) was being hindered. Is this a hindrance?

Decision: No, the player losesthe point.

Case 3: A ball in play hits a bird flying over the court. Is this a hindrance?

Decision: Yes, the point shall be replayed.

Case 4: During a point, a ball or other object that was lying on the player's side of the net when the point started hinders the player. Is this a hindrance?

Decision: No.

Case 5: In doubles, where are the server's partner and receiver's partner allowed to stand?

Decision: The server's partner and the receiver's partner may take any position on their own side of the net, inside or outside the court. However, if a player is creating a hindrance to the opponent(s), the hindrance rule should be used.

27 Correcting errors

As a principle, when an error in respect of the Rules of Tennis is discovered, all points previously played shall stand. Errors so discovered shall be corrected as follows:

(1) During a standard game or a tie-break game, if a player serves from the wrong half of the court, this should be corrected as soon as the error is discovered and the server shall serve from the correct half of the court according to the score. A fault that was served before the error was discovered shall stand.

(2) During a standard game or a tie-break game, if the players are at the wrong ends of the court, the error should be corrected as soon as it is discovered and the server shall serve from the correct end of the court according to the score.

(3) If a player serves out of turn during a standard game, the player who was originally due to serve shall serve as soon as the error is discovered. However, if a game is completed before the error is discovered the order of service shall remain as altered. In this case, any ball change to be made after an agreed number of games should be made one game later than originally scheduled.

A fault that was served by the opponents(s) before the error was discovered shall not stand. In doubles, if the partners of one team serve out of turn, a fault that was served before the error was discovered shall stand.

(4) If a player serves out of turn during a tie-break game and the error is discovered after an even number of points have been played, the error is corrected immediately. If the error is discovered after an odd number of points have been played, the order of service shall remain as altered. A fault that was served by the opponent(s) before the error was discovered shall not stand. In doubles, if the partners of one team serve out of turn, a fault that was served before the error was discovered shall stand.

(5) During a standard game or a tie-break game in doubles, if there is an error in the order of receiving, this shall remain as altered until the end of the game in which the error is discovered. For the next game in which they are the receivers in that set, the partners shall then resume the original order of receiving.

(6) If in error a tie-break game is started at 6 games all, when it was previously agreed that the set would be an "Advantage set", the error shall be corrected immediately if only one point has been played. If the error is discovered after the second point is in play, the set will continue as a "Tie-break set".

(7) If in error a standard game is started at 6 games all, when it was previously agreed that the set would be a "Tie-break set", the error shall be corrected immediately if only one point has been played. If the error is discovered after the second point is in play, the set will continue as an "Advantage set" until the score reaches 8 games all (or a higher even number), when a tie-break game shall be played.

(8) If in error an "Advantage set" or "Tie-break set" is started, when it was previously agreed that the final set would be a match tie-break, the error shall be corrected immediately if only one point has been played. If the error is discovered after the second point is in play, the set will continue either until a player or team wins three games (and therefore the set) or until the score reaches 2 games all, when a match tie-break shall be played. However, if the error is discovered after the second point of the fifth game has started, the set will continue as a "Tie-break set". (See Appendix Ⅳ)

(9) If the balls are not changed in the correct sequence, the error shall be corrected when the player/team who should have served with new balls is next due to serve a new game. Thereafter the balls shall be changed so that the number of games between ball changes shall be that originally agreed. Balls should not be changed during a game.

28 Role of court officials

For matches where officials are appointed, their roles and responsibilities can be found in Appendix Ⅴ.

29 Continuous play

As a principle, play should be continuous, from the time the match starts (when the first service of the match is put in play) until the match finishes.

(1) Between points, a maximum of twenty (20) seconds is allowed. When the players change ends at the end of a game, a maximum of ninety (90) seconds are allowed. However, after the first game of each set and during a tie-break game, play shall be continuous and the players shall change ends without a rest.

At the end of each set there shall be a set break of a maximum of one hundred and twenty (120) seconds. The maximum time starts from the moment that one point finishes until the first service is struck for the next point.

Event organizers may apply for ITF approval to extend the ninety (90) seconds allowed when the players change ends at the end of a game and the one hundred and twenty (120) seconds allowed at a set break.

(2) If, for reasons outside the player's control, clothing, footwear or necessary equipment (excluding the racket) is broken or needs to be replaced, the player may be allowed reasonable extra time to rectify the problem.

(3) No extra time shall be given to allow a player to recover condition. However, a player suffering from a treatable medical condition may be allowed one medical time-out of three minutes for the treatment of that medical condition.

A limited number of toilet/change of attire breaks may also be allowed, if this is announced in advance of the event.

(4) Event organizers may allow a rest period of a maximum of ten (10) minutes if this is announced in advance of the event. This rest period can be taken after the 3rd set in a best of 5 sets match, or after the 2nd set in a best of 3 sets match.

(5) The warm-up time shall be a maximum of five (5) minutes, unless otherwise decided by the event organizers.

30 Coaching

Coaching is considered to be communication, advice or instruction of any kind, audible or visible, to a player.

In team events where there is a team captain sitting on-court, the team captain may coach the player(s) during a set break and when the players change ends at the end of a game, but not when the players change ends after the first game of each set and not during a tie-break game.

In all other matches, coaching is not allowed.

Case 1: Is a player allowed to be coached, if the coaching is given by signals in a discreet way?

Decision: No.

Case 2: Is a player allowed to receive coaching when play is suspended?

Decision: Yes.

Appendix I the ball

For all measurements in Appendix I, SI units shall take precedence

(1) The ball shall have a uniform outer surface consisting of a fabric cover and shall be white or yellow in color. If there are any seams they shall be stitchless.

(2) More than one type of ball is specified. The ball shall conform to the requirements shown in the table below.

	TYPE 1 (FAST)	TYPE 2 (MEDIUM)1	TYPE3 (SLOW)2	HIGH ALTITUDE3
MASS (WEIGHT)	56.0 ~ 59.4 grams (1.975 ~ 2.095 ounces)	56.0 ~ 59.4 grams (1.975 ~ 2.095 ounces)	56.0 ~ 59.4 grams (1.975 ~ 2.095 ounces)	56.0 ~ 59.4 grams (1.975 ~ 2.095 ounces)
SIZE	6.54 ~ 6.86 cm (2.57 ~ 2.70 inches)	6.54 ~ 6.86 cm (2.57 ~ 2.70 inches)	7.00 ~ 7.30 cm (2.76 ~ 2.87 inches)	6.54 ~ 6.86 cm (2.57 ~ 2.70 inches)
REBOUND	135 ~ 147 cm (53 ~ 58 inches)	135 ~ 147 cm (53 ~ 58 inches)	135 ~ 147 cm (53 ~ 58 inches)	122 ~ 135 cm (48 ~ 53 inches)
FORWARD DEFORMATION4	0.50 ~ 0.60 cm (0.197 ~ 0.236 inches)	0.56 ~ 0.74 cm (0.220 ~ 0.291 inches)	0.56 ~ 0.74 cm (0.220 ~ 0.291 inches)	0.56 ~ 0.74 cm (0.220 ~ 0.291 inches)
RETURN DEFORMATION4	0.67 ~ 0.91 cm (0.264 ~ 0.358 inches)	0.80 ~ 1.08 cm (0.315 ~ 0.425 inches)	0.80 ~ 1.08 cm (0.315 ~ 0.425 inches)	0.80 ~ 1.08 cm (0.315 ~ 0.425 inches)

Notes:

1. This ball may be pressurized or pressureless. The pressureless ball shall have an internal pressure that is no greater than 7 kPa (1 psi) and may be used for high altitude play above 1, 219 m (4, 000 feet) above sea level and shall have been acclimatized for 60 days or more at the altitude of the specific tournament.

2. This ball is also recommended for high altitude play on any court surface type above 1, 219 m (4, 000 feet) above sea level.

3. This ball is pressurized and is an additional ball specified for high altitude play above 1, 219 m (4, 000 feet) above sea level only.

4. The deformation shall be the average of a single reading along each of three perpendicular axes. No two individual readings shall differ by more than 0.08 cm (0.031 inches).

(3) In addition, the ball shall conform to the requirements for durability as shown in the following table:

	MASS (WEIGHT)	REBOUND	FORWARD DEFORMATION	RETURN DEFORMATION
MAXIMUM CHANGE1	0.4 grams (0.014 ounces)	4.0 cm (1.6 inches)	0.08 cm (0.031 inches)	0.10 cm (0.039 inches)

Notes: The largest permissible change in the specified properties resulting from the durability test described in the current edition of *ITF Approved Tennis Balls & Classified Court Surfaces*. The durability test uses laboratory equipment to simulate the effects of nine games of play.

(4) All tests for rebound, mass, size, deformation and durability shall be made in accordance with the Regulations described in the current edition of *ITF Approved Tennis Balls & Classified Court Surfaces*.

Appendix Ⅱ the racket

For all measurements in Appendix II, SI units shall take precedence:

(1) The hitting surface, defined as the main area of the stringing pattern bordered by the points of entry of the strings into the frame or points of contact of the strings with the frame,

whichever is the smaller, shall be flat and consist of a pattern of crossed strings connected to a frame and alternately interlaced or bonded where they cross. The stringing pattern must be generally uniform and, in particular, not less dense in the centre than in any other area.

The racket shall be designed and strung such that the playing characteristics are identical on both faces. The racket shall be free of attached objects, protrusions and devices other than those utilised solely and specifically to limit or prevent wear and tear or vibration or, for the frame only, to distribute weight. These objects, protrusions and devices must be reasonable in size and placement for such purposes.

(2) The frame of the racket shall not exceed 73.7 cm (29.0 inches) in overall length, including the handle. The frame of the racket shall not exceed 31.7 cm (12.5 inches) in overall width. The hitting surface shall not exceed 39.4 cm (15.5 inches) in overall length, and 29.2 cm (11.5 inches) in overall width.

(3) The frame, including the handle, and the strings, shall be free of any device which makes it possible to change materially the shape of the racket, or to change materially the weight distribution in the direction of the longitudinal axis of the racket which would alter the swing moment of inertia, or to change deliberately any physical property which may affect the performance of the racket during the playing of a point. No energy source that in any way changes or affects the playing characteristics of a racket may be built into or attached to a racket.

(4) The racket must be free of any device that may provide communication, advice or instruction of any kind, audible or visible, to a player during a match.

Appendix Ⅲ advertising

1. Advertising is permitted on the net as long as it is placed on the part of the net that is within 3 feet (0.914 m) from the center of the net posts and is produced in such a way that it does not interfere with the vision of the players or the playing conditions.

2. Advertising and other marks or material placed at the back and sides of the court shall be permitted unless it interferes with the vision of the players or the playing conditions.

3. Advertising and other marks or material placed on the court surface outside the lines is permitted unless it interferes with the vision of the players or the playing conditions.

4. Not withstanding paragraphs (1), (2) and (3) above, any advertising, marks or material placed on the net or placed at the back and sides of the court, or on the court surface outside the lines may not contain white or yellow or other light colors that may interfere with the vision of the players or the playing conditions.

5. Advertising and other marks or material are not permitted on the court surface inside the lines of the court.

Appendix Ⅳ alternative procedures and scoring methods

Score in a game (Rule 5):

"No-Ad" Scoring method

This alternative scoring method may be used.

A "No-Ad" game is scored as follows with the server's score being called first:

No point——"Love"

First point——"15"

Second point——"30"

Third point——"40"

Fourth point——"Game"

If both players/teams have won three points each, the score is "Deuce" and a deciding point shall be played. The receiver(s) shall choose whether to receive the service from the right half or the left half of the court. In doubles, the players of the receiving team cannot change positions to receive this deciding point. The player/team who wins the deciding point wins the "Game".

In mixed doubles, the player of the same gender as the server shall receive the deciding point. The players of the receiving team cannot change positions to receive the deciding point.

Score in a set (Rules 6 and 7):

1. "SHORT" SETS

The first player/team who wins four games wins that set, provided there is a margin of two games over the opponent(s). If the score reaches four games all, a tie-break game shall be played.

2. MATCH TIE-BREAK (7 POINTS)

When the score in a match is one set all, or two sets all in best of five sets matches, one tie-break game shall be played to decide the match. This tie-break game replaces the deciding final set.

The player/team who first wins seven points shall win this match tie-break and the match provided there is a margin of two points over the opponent(s).

3. MATCH TIE-BREAK (10 POINTS)

When the score in a match is one set all, or two sets all in best of five sets matches, one tie-break game shall be played to decide the match. This tie-break game replaces the deciding final set.

The player/team who first wins ten points shall win this match tie-break and the match provided there is a margin of two points over the opponent(s).

Note: When using the match tie-break to replace the final set:

- *the original order of service continues. (Rules 5 and 14)*
- *in doubles, the order of serving and receiving within the team may be altered, as in the beginning of each set. (Rules 14 and 15)*
- *before the start of the match tie-break there shall be a 120 seconds set break.*
- *balls should not be changed before the start of the match tie-break even if a ball change is due.*

Change of ends (Rule 10):

This alternative to the change of ends sequence in a tie-break game may be used. During a tie-break game, players shall change ends after the first point and thereafter after every four points.

The let during a service (Rule 22):

This alternative is play without the service let in Rule 22 a. It means that a serve that touches the net, strap or band, is in play. (This alternative is commonly known as the "no let rule")

Appendix V role of court officials

The referee is the final authority on all questions of tennis law and the referee's decision is final.

In matches where a chair umpire is assigned, the chair umpire is the final authority on all questions of fact during the match.

The players have the right to call the referee to court if they disagree with a chair umpire's interpretation of tennis law.

In matches where line umpires and net umpires are assigned, they make all calls (including foot-fault calls) relating to that line or net. The chair umpire has the right to overrule a line umpire or a net umpire if the chair umpire is sure that a clear mistake has been made. The chair umpire is responsible for calling any line (including foot-faults) or net where no line umpire or net umpire is assigned.

A line umpire who can not make a call shall signal this immediately to the chair umpire who shall make a decision. If the line umpire can not make a call, or if there is no line umpire, and the chair umpire can not make a decision on a question of fact, the point shall be replayed.

In team events where the referee is sitting on-court, the referee is also the final authority on questions of fact.

Play may be stopped or suspended at any time the chair umpire decides it is necessary or appropriate.

The referee may also stop or suspend play in the case of darkness, weather or adverse court conditions. When play is suspended for darkness, this should be done at the end of a set, or after an even number of games have been played in the set in progress. After a suspension in play, the score and position of players on-court in the match shall stand when the match resumes.

The chair umpire or referee shall make decisions regarding continuous play and coaching in respect of any Code of Conduct that is approved and in operation.

Case 1: The chair umpire awards the server a first service after an overrule, but the receiver argues that it should be a second service, since the server had already served a fault. Should the referee be called to court to give a decision?

Decision: Yes. The chair umpire makes the first decision about questions of tennis law (issues relating to the application of specific facts). However, if a player appeals the chair umpire's decision, then the referee shall be called to make the final decision.

Case 2: A ball iscalled out, but a player claims that the ball was good. May the referee be called to court to make a decision?

Decision: No. The chair umpire makes the final decision on questions of fact (issues relating to what actually happened during a specific incident).

Case 3: Is a chair umpire allowed to overrule a line umpire at the end of a point if, in the chair umpire's opinion, a clear mistake was made earlier in the point?

Decision: No. A chair umpire may only overrule a line umpire immediately after the clear mistake has been made.

Case 4: A line umpire calls a ball "Out" and then the player argues that the ball was good. Is the chair umpire allowed to overrule the line umpire?

Decision: No. A chair umpire must never overrule as the result of the protest or appeal by a player

Case 5: A line umpire calls a ball "Out". The chair umpire was unable to see clearly, but thought the ball was in. May the chair umpire overrule the line umpire?

Decision: No. The chair umpire may only overrule when sure that the line umpire made a clear mistake.

Case 6: Is a line umpire allowed to change the call after the chair umpire has announced the score?

Decision: Yes. If a line umpire realizes a mistake, a correction should be made as soon as possible provided it is not as the result of a protest or appeal of a player.

Case 7: If a chair umpire or line umpire calls "out" and then corrects the call to good, what is the correct decision?

Decision: The chair umpire must decide if the original "out" call was a hindrance to either player. If it was a hindrance, the point shall be replayed. If it was not a hindrance, the player who hit the ball wins the point.

Case 8: A ball is blown back over the net and the player correctly reaches over the net to try to play the ball. The opponent(s) hinders the player from doing this. What is the correct decision?

Decision: The chair umpire must decide if the hindrance was deliberate or unintentional and either awards the point to the hindered player or order the point to be replayed.

Appendix Ⅵ official 10 and under tennis competition

Courts:

In addition to a full sized court, the following court dimensions may be used for official competitive play involving players aged 10 and under:

- A court, designated "red" for the purposes of 10 and under competition, shall be a rectangle, between 36 feet (10.97 m) and 42 feet (12.80 m) long, and between 16 feet (4.88 m) and 19 feet (5.79 m) wide. The net shall be 31.5 inches (0.80 m) high at the center.
- A court, designated "orange", shall be a rectangle, 60 feet (18.29 m) long, and between 21 feet (6.40 m) and 27 feet (8.23 m) wide. The net shall be between 31.5 inches (0.80 m) and 36.0 inches (0.914 m) high at the center.

Balls:

The following ball types arerecommended for players aged 10 and under:

- A stage 3 (red) ball is recommended for play on a "red" court.
- A stage 2 (orange) ball is recommended for play on an "orange" court.

- A stage 1 (green) ball is recommended for play on a full sized court.

The properties of stage 3, stage 2 and stage 1 balls are described in the ITF publication entitled "ITF approved tennis balls & classified court surfaces".

Scoring methods:

For competition involving players aged 10 and under using stage 3 (red), stage 2 (orange) or stage 1 (green) balls, scoring methods specified in the Rules of Tennis (including the Appendix) can be utilized, in addition to short duration scoring methods involving matches of one match tie-break, best of 3 tie-breaks/match tie breaks or one set.

第七篇　休闲球类常用术语及词汇

第一章　台球(billiards)

台球(总称)billiards
无袋式台球(开仑)carom
有袋式台球(落袋)pocket game
英式三球比利 English billiard
英式 22 球(斯诺克)snooker
美式台球 America pocket billiard, pool
争黑八打法 eight ball
九球打法 nine ball, knapper
台球规则 rules of play
运动员 player
裁判员 referee
记分员 scorer, judge
记分 scoring
记分牌 scoring board
预赛 prelim
半决赛 semifinals
1/4 决赛 quarterfinal
决赛 final
开球 break off, serve
开球区(英式 D 形区)the "D"
开球区(美式)kitchen
开球线 serve line
掷币猜先 coin toss, toss off
抽签猜先 lot
球台 table
球袋 pocket
顶袋 top pocket
中袋 middle pocket
底袋 bottom pocket
台面 playing area
台边 cushion
台面标志 marks
球 ball
球杆 cue
架杆 rest
灯罩 lampshade
巧克 chalk
杆头 tip
滑石粉 powder
球框(用来摆球的那个三角框)tri-angle
球杆连接部 joint
主球 cue-ball
目标球 object-ball
一击(球)stroke
一杆(球)break
手中球 in-hand
局中球 ball in play
活球 ball on
死球 snookered
死角球 angled
障碍球 snooked
自由球 free-ball
指定球 nominated-ball
贴球 touching ball
贴边球 frozen
跳球 jump-ball, jump-shot
角度球 angled
香蕉球(弧线球)sidespin
幸运球 fluke
袋口相挤的球 lawed-ball
争议球 split-hit
罚球 penalty
进球 pot
错击 error
盘 frame
局 game
场 match
暂停 pause
平局 tie score
总分 total points
对方 opponent
失机 loss of chance
失误 miss
犯规 foul
占位 occupied
空杆 miss
置球点 spots
放置彩球 spotting colors(典型的英

式用法)

黄球置点 yellow spot

绿球置点 green spot

棕球置点 brown spot

蓝球置点 blue spot

粉球置点 pink spot

黑球置点 black spot

瞄准 aiming

主球走位练习 position exercise

名次排列 rank

排名第二 starting 2(two)

台球厅 poolroom

自落 drop of the cue-ball

椎杆 push stroke

跟进球 follow-ball

连击 double-hit

扎杆 prick stroke

出界 forced off the table

僵局 stalemate

滑杆 miscue

厚球 thick cut

薄球 thin cut

偏杆 sidespin

定杆 stop shot

缩杆(低杆)sub-side

种子选手 seeded

3 号种子选手 seeded 3(three)

上旋球(推杆，高杆)topspin

下旋球(缩杆)backspin

第二章　壁球(squash/wall ball)

WSF(国际壁球协会)World Squash Federation

PSA(职业壁球协会) Professional Squash Association

WISPA(国际女子壁球协会)Women's International Squash Players Association

保龄球英语词汇 (bowling)

国际保龄球联盟 Federation International Quilleurs(FIQ)

世界十瓶保龄球联合会 World Tenpin Bowling Association(WTBA)

全中 strike

连续两次全中 double

连续三次全中 triple

补中 spare

失误 error

分瓶(技术球) split

死球 dead ball

犯规 foul

慢投球 slow bowling

记分 scoring the game

记分表 score sheet

一局 one game

一格 one frame

一节 one block

最高局分 high game

平均分 average

全中位 impact points

投球 delivery

推球 push away

扬球 follow through

下摆 downswing

后摆 backswing

投球顺序 order of bowling

单人赛 singles

双人赛 doubles

三人赛 trios

五人队际赛 five player teams

全能 all events

精英预赛 master semifinals

精英决赛 master grandfinals

对抗赛 match play

额外队员 extra players

陪打员 pacer

申诉 appeal

抗议 protest

吸烟 smoking

饮酒 drinking

颁奖 medal presentation

竞赛主任 tournament director
技术代表 technical delegate
技术委员会 technical committee
竞赛委员会 tournament committee
仲裁委员会 jury of appeal
保龄球设备 bowling equipment
球道 lane
助走道 approach
犯规线 foul line
犯规探测器 foul detective device
边沟 gutter
边沟侧板 molding
球瓶 pin
放瓶台 pin deck
放瓶点 pin spots
后台板 tail plank
边墙 kick-back
后槽 pit
后部缓冲板 rear cushion
自动摆瓶器 wachanical pinspotting equipment pinsetting
平衡 balance
硬度 hardness
硬度计 durometer

第三章　保龄球 bowling

Essential Terms　常用术语
acceleration 加速摆
address 战立姿势
adjustment 调整
all the way 一路全中
alley bed 球床
alley man 球场工作人员
anchorman 最后投掷者
approach 助跑
arm swing 挥臂
arrow 箭头
automatic pin - setting machine 自动换瓶机
average 平均分
baby split 小技术球
baby the ball 投球太过小心
backup ball 反手球
back swing 向后摆臂
balk 球未投出之前，脚已超越界限
ball deflection 球偏离
ball holes 球孔
ball rack 球架
ball return　回球器
barmaid 暗瓶
bed post 极难球
bench work 用谈话或行动有意干扰对手
big ball 有效的钩球
big fill 大清扫(第二球打倒 8 个以上的全部余瓶)
blind 缺席者加分
blow 未能补中
blow out 击倒 9 瓶
body language 身体语言
bonus　奖励
bowl　投球
bowler 保龄球选手
bowling alley 保龄球场
bowling crease 投球线
bowling equipment 保龄球球场设备
bowling green 草地保龄球场
bowling match 保龄球比赛
bowling shoes 保龄球鞋
broom ball 扫帚球
buzzard 连续 3 局未能击倒全部球瓶
candle pin 蜡状瓶保龄球
center of gravity 球的重心
channel ball 落沟球
cheese cake 芝士蛋糕(出好球的球场)
choke 因紧张未击中目标
clean game　打得好的比赛(不是全中就是补中)
close angle 闭角
cock waist 屈腕
conventional grip 传统式抓球法

count 计分
creeper 慢滚球
crooked arm 曲臂
curtain 最后一个上场的投球失误
curve ball 曲球
cushion 挡球垫
dead ball 死球
dead wood 击倒瓶
deliberate foul 故意犯规
deliver 投球
double 连续 2 次全中
doubles 两人赛
dry lanes 干球道
duckpin 达克球瓶
dump the ball 抛球
error 失误
fair ball 合法投球
fence 瓶墙
finger holes 中指、无名指球孔
fingertip grip 浅握法
five-grip 连续 5 次全中
five men 五人赛
five-step approach 五步步法
flat gutters 平底球槽
follow through 随球动作
footwork 步法
foul 犯规
foul line 犯规线
foul detective device 犯规探测器
foundation 第 9 局全中
foundation frame 第 9 格
four-step approach 四步步法
frame 一轮，计分格
full fingertip grip 完全式抓球法
game 局
grab 急弯球
grandma teeth 球瓶杂乱无章地排列
graveyard 坟场(不出好成绩的球场)
grip 握球法 gutter 球沟
gutter ball 落沟球
gutter shot 投近沟球
hardness scale 硬度表
head pin1 号瓶，顶瓶
high hit 重击
holding lane 很难投出曲球的球场
hook ball 钩球
honey 好球
house 保龄球馆
house ball 公用球
incline 屈身
illegal ball 不合格球
kegler 保龄球手
kick backs 返程槽
kick off 平稳有效的投球
key step 关键步
king-pin 主球瓶(1 号瓶或 5 号瓶)
lane 球道
lane condition 球道情况
lane track 球道上的球滚迹
lead off man 第一个出场的人
leave 残瓶(投球后未被击倒留下的瓶)
light hit 擦瓶球
loft 高投
logs 练习用球瓶
low hit 轻击
match play 一对一比赛
Mister Average 缺席球员
mother-in-law7 号瓶
move in 向内投
move out 向外投
neck 瓶颈
nose hit 打倒 1 号瓶
nothing ball 无效球
off set 排列不正
omni 座席
open angle 开角
open frame 未能击倒全部木瓶的一局
perfect game 得满分的比赛
pie alley 容易得分的球道
pins 球瓶

pin deck 瓶台
pin fall 一次投球击倒瓶数
pin setter 整瓶器
pin spot 球瓶标示点
pin spotter 排列员
pit 球瓶区
platform 助跑区域
play-off 延长赛
playing territory 比赛球道
private ball 个人专用球
puff ball 慢球
punch out 以全中结束比赛
push away 开始助跑
read off 开球者
read the lanes 球道观察
rebowl 重投
release 投球
re-set 重排
rotation 旋球
rubberband duckpin 橡胶圈达克瓶
schleifer 铲刀(轻碰 1 号瓶左面造成的全中)
score sheet 计分表
scratch 平分比赛
semi-fingertip grip 部分式抓球法
shadow bowling 无瓶投球练习
side partition 边隔板
side roll 侧滚
six pack 连续 6 次全中
sleeper 暗瓶
slow alley 慢球道
snow plow 雪犁球(一球全中)
sour apple 酸苹果(打得不好的球)
span 孔间隔
spare 补中
splash 散花投
split 技术球
sportsman like 有体育道德的
stance 站位
starting mark 起投线
stiff alley 硬球场
straight ball 直球
straight wrist 直腕
strike 全中
strike out 以一次全中结束比赛
sweepstakes 保龄球锦标赛
telephone poles 重瓶
targeting dots 瞄准点
thin hit 擦瓶球
three hundred bowler 满分获得者
three-step approach 三步步法
thumb hole 拇指孔
trios 三人赛
triple 三次全中
umbrella ball 雨伞球(打倒 1 号瓶造成的全中)
unusual lane condition 异常球道情况
wooden bottles 木瓶
zero in 观察打全中的最佳位置

第四章 曲棍球(hockey)

backhand stopping 反手停球
back lines 端线
back pass 后传
back stick 棍背
bandy 冰上曲棍球
bandy field 冰上曲棍球场
blade 棍头
body play 用身体冲撞
bully 开球、争球
bullier 争球队员
cage 球门
centre break 中央攻击战术
centre forward 中锋
centre half-back 中前卫
centre line 中线
centre spot 中心点
change ends 交换场地
checking 阻截
chopping 削球

circle 击球圈
clearing 将球击出守区
close dribble 贴紧运球
corner 角球
corner flag 角旗
corner hit 击角球
cutting 切球
deep defence 后卫
defence hit 16 码击球
delayed penalty 暂缓处罚
diagonal pass 对角传
diagonal system 对角线战术
double foul 双方犯规
elbow-pad 护肘
eleven 曲棍球队
face guard 面罩
face off 开球、争球
feed 供球
feint with the stick 用棍虚晃
field hockey 曲棍球运动
five-yard mark 5 码点
first face 棍头正面
flick stroke 转棍推击
forehead hit 正手击球
forward 任意球
free hit 前锋
goal-board 球门板
goal lines 球门线
goal-keepers equipment 守门员装备
goal-post 球门柱
green card 绿牌(警告)
grip 握棍
guard 护身甲
handle 棍柄
hard shot 劲射
head of the stick 棍头
hit 击球
hit and rush 追击球
hit in the air 凌空击球
hockey 曲棍球运动员
hocket ball 曲棍球
hockey glove 曲棍球手套
hockey shoe 曲棍球鞋
hockey stick 曲棍球
hurling 爱尔兰棍球
Indian type of grip 印度握棍法
indoor hockeyfield 室内曲棍球场
interchanging 换位
jab 踢球
knee-pad 护膝
lacrosse 长柄曲棍球
left hand lunge 左手截球
long corner 长角球
long scooping 长铲球
lunge 单手持棍捅球
misconduct 不正当行为
no count 得分不算(射中等)无效
no game 被判为无效的比赛
obstruction 阻碍
off-side 越位
on-side 非越位
parallel pass 横传
pass into space 传球到空中
penalty corner 罚近角球
penalty stroke 罚点球
personaly handle 拉人
pick up 开始盯人
positional play 定位战术
raise the stick 举棍
red card 红牌
reverse stick pass 反棍传球
reverse stick tackle 反棍抢截
reverse stick tap 反棍击球
reverse stopping 反棍截球
roll in 滚球入网
roller hockey 旱冰曲棍球
rolling push 滚推球
run by skipping 垫步跑
shinay 儿童的非正式曲棍球
scoop 铲击球

serve time 受罚
shooting circle 射门圈
short corner 短角球
side-lines 边线
skin guard 护腿
slash at the ball 乱砍击球
spot of seven yards 7 码球点
standard goals 标准球门
stationary push 原地推球
stick checking 干挠球棍(以自己的棍压住对方的棍)
sticks 举棍过肩
stick side 球员右手
stickwork 控制球的技术
stop 停球
stopping with one hand 单手持棍停球
strike 击球
striker 击球队员
swerving dribble 变向运球
tackler 抢球
tacklering back 背后抢球
temporary suspension 暂时罚出场
toe pad 护脚
umpire 裁判员
under cutting 切球
wicket 三柱门
wing forward 边锋
wrist drive 用腕力击球
yellow card 黄牌(罚暂离场至少 5 分钟)

第五章　垒球(softball)

一、垒球定义

异型球棒 altered bat
申诉局面 appeal play
球的压缩系数 ball compression
球的复原系数(ball cor)
垒线(base line)
四坏球上垒 base on balls
垒间跑道 base path
击出的球 batted ball
击球员(batter)
击球区 batter's box
击跑员 batter-runner
击球次序 batting order
球被阻挡 blocked ball
触击球 bunt
合法接球 catch
接手区 catcher's box
暂停作指示(charged conference)
砍击球 chopped ball
教练员 coach
鸦式跳投 crow hop
死球 dead ball
防守队 defensive team
延迟死球 delayed dead ball
指定队员 designated player
移位垒包 dislodged base
双杀 double play
队员席(dugout)
罚离场 ejection from the game
界内球 fair ball
界内地区 fair territory
假触杀 fake tag
守场员 fielder
腾空球 fly ball
自由人(flex player)
封杀出局 force out
弃权 forfeit
界外球 foul ball
界外地区(foul territory)
擦棒球 foul tip
头盔 helmet
主队 home team
不合格球棒 illegal bat
不合法特殊队员 illegal extra player
不合法投手 illegal pitcher
不合法队员 illegal player
不合法再进场 illegal re-entry
不合法替补队员 illegal substitute
不合法击球 illegally batted ball

不合法接球 illegally caught ball

不合格队员 ineligible player

不合格暂替队员 ineligible replacement player

飞行球 in flight

有被杀危险 in jeopardy

内场 infield

内场手(infielder)

内场腾空球 infield fly

局 inning

故意失接腾空球(intentionally dropped fly ball)

妨碍 interference

跳跃投球 leaping

合法触及 legal touch

合法接住的球 legally caught ball

平直球 line drive

上场阵容和上场队员名单 line-up 或(line-up card)

阻挡 obstruction

进攻队 offensive team

准备击球员 on-deck batter

准备击球区(on-deck circle)

1 米线 one meter or three-foot line

选择局面 option play

外场 out field

滑越垒位 over-slide

野传球 over throw

漏接 passed ball

投球 pitch

投手区 pitcher's circle

轴心脚 pivot foot

比赛开始或比赛继续 play ball

赛前碰头会(pre-game meeting)

抗议(protests)

快速连续投球 quick return pitch

再进场 re-entry

罚出场 removal from the game

暂替队员 replacement player

跑垒员 runner

敲击、拖击 slap hit(快投)

抢分战术 squeeze play

开场队员 starting player

偷垒 stealing

好球区 strike zone

替补队员 substitute

腾空球离垒 tagging up

球队成员 team member

传球 throw

暂停 time

一弹球 trapped ball

三杀 triple play

一次轮击 turn at bat

暴投 wild pitch

暴传 wild throw

被暂替队员(withdrawn player)

比赛开始或继续比赛 play ball

棒球运动员 baseball player

垒球运动员 softball player

投手 pitcher

接手 catcher

守场员 fielder

守垒员 baseman

内场手 infielder

一垒手 first baseman

二垒手 second baseman

三垒手 third baseman

游击手 shortstop

外场手 outfielder

候援投手 relief pitcher

指名击球员 designated hitter DH

参 考 文 献

1 刘锡梅，燕呢喃. 体育竞赛裁判学[M]. 北京：高等教育出版社，2011.

2 闫育东. 篮球规则英汉双语教程(第一版)[M]. 北京：北京体育大学出版社，2007.

3 张瑛秋，甄志平. 乒乓球裁判双语教程[M]. 北京：北京体育大学出版社，2006.

4 斯力格. 足球竞赛裁判手册[M]. 北京：人民体育出版社，2004.

5 中国足球协会审定. 足球竞赛规则 2011/2012[M]. 北京：人民体育出版社，2012.

6 中国足球协会审定. 足球竞赛规则(第一版)2009/2011[M]. 北京：人民体育出版社，2009.

7 中国排球协会审定. 排球竞赛规则 2009/2012[M]. 北京：人民体育出版社，2009.

8 中国乒乓球协会审定. 乒乓球竞赛规则 2011[M]. 北京：人民体育出版社，2011.

9 中国篮球协会审定. 篮球规则 2010(第一版)[M]. 光明日报出版社，2010.

10 中国网球协会审定. 网球竞赛规则 2009[M]. 北京：人民体育出版社，2009.

11 闫育东. 篮球裁判晋级必读[M]. 北京：北京体育大学出版社，2011.

12 蔡继玲. 乒乓球[M]. 北京：北京体育大学出版社，2002.

13 陆卫平. 排球竞赛与裁判法[M]. 北京：北京航空航天大学出版社，2009.

14 本书编委会编写. 中英文对照最新体育竞赛规则与裁判法及反兴奋剂条例实用手册[M]. 北京：中国科技文化出版社，2005.